NEGOTIATING THE NEW NORMAL

NEGOTIATING THE NEW NORMAL

How India Must Grow in a Pandemic-Ridden World

SAURAV JHA

hachette INDIA

First published in India in 2022 by Hachette India
(Registered name: Hachette Book Publishing India Pvt. Ltd)
An Hachette UK company
www.hachetteindia.com

1

ISBN: 978-93-5009-577-5

Hachette Book Publishing India Pvt. Ltd
4th & 5th Floors, Corporate Centre,
Plot No. 94, Sector 44, Gurugram – 122003, India

Typeset in Bembo Std
by Jojy Philip, New Delhi – 15

Printed and bound in India
by Manipal Technologies Limited, Manipal

For NKB, SM and CM

INTRODUCTION

GROWTH IS DEAD, LONG LIVE GROWTH

THE WEST HAS LOST; THE WEST HAS WON. AFTER THE FALL OF the Soviet Empire, over 25 years ago, grand proclamations were made about the 'end of history'.[1] I refer here not only to Francis Fukuyama's eponymous book,[2] but an entire body of Western triumphalist literature, which seemed to suggest that the infallibility of the neoliberal order – as typified by the American model – was self-evident. And that this model must, for evermore, be adapted by nations looking to rise to prosperity.

Today, as the Western world is trying to recover from a pandemic-induced recession, just over a decade after the last shock – the Global Financial Crisis (GFC) of 2007–08 – that triumphalism has waned. (Incidentally, in an apparent U-turn, Fukuyama is now espousing socialism.[3]) Every now and then, Western commentators[4] bemoan or celebrate the perceived shift in influence from the West to the East (particularly China), from the new to the old. This perception is in no small measure due to expectations about the global

---

[1] The term 'West' here refers to the United States and Western Europe.

[2] Fukuyama, Francis. *The End of History and the Last Man*. Free Press, 1992.

[3] Fukuyama, Francis. *Identity: Contemporary Identity Politics and the Struggle for Recognition*. Profile Books, 2019.

[4] For example, see: Marquand, David. *The End of the West*. Revised edition, Princeton University Press, 2012.

distribution of future growth and dynamism, which now seem disproportionately skewed against the West, where, after a decade of central bank activism, economic vitality remained a mirage – even before COVID-19 struck.

In fact, even prior to the pandemic, the West seemed to be in the grip of what is called 'secular stagnation', a term first coined by the economist Alvin Hansen in 1938, during the Great Depression, to describe an era of very low or no growth in a market-based economy.[5] Though the expression turned out to be premature at the time, it seems to describe the present state of Western economies rather well. Even though the US economy expanded by 8 per cent in the decade that followed the GFC, this was achieved primarily on the back of extraordinary monetary easing to keep the economy from keeling over, with fiscal stimulus playing a more limited role. Be that as it may, monetary policy (of which the custodian is the central bank of a country) – one of the key themes of this book – was considered the main game in town and the 2010s were considered the 'decade of the central bank'. The pandemic-related lockdowns, however, forced the American treasury to step in with mega stimulus spending – a luxury not available to most other nations, as we shall see – in order to prevent large parts of the economy from being lost forever.

As such, the inevitable and rapid rise in the indebtedness of both the public and private sectors in the West will mean that an extended period of low inflation and low growth – supported by very low interest rates sometimes referred to as 'lowflation' – is the best that these nations can now hope for. Much worse would be a stagflationary course, although Western central banks still hope to avoid that since they expect the supply-side inflation related to pandemic-induced disruption will ultimately wane as economies reopen in full

---

[5] Eggertsson, Gauti B., et al. 'Secular Stagnation in the Open Economy.' *American Economic Review*, Volume 106, Number 5, 2016, pp. 503–07, doi:10.1257/aer.p20161106.

and supply chains normalize. Of course, growth optimists also continue to wish that a new technological wave will boost productivity enough to lift growth rates yet again, as has happened more than once since the industrial age.[6] That, however, remains to be seen. And even optimists would probably acknowledge that there is no guarantee that the incoming tide of new technologies, such as artificial intelligence and 3D printing, to name a few, will lift more boats than it sinks. On account of the disruptions due to COVID-19, automation may well accelerate, but to the detriment of the common worker.

Meanwhile, the 'East',[7] or indeed the larger category of the global 'economic South'[8] (which includes the East), has not managed to fashion an alternative system for global economic stability and growth either. The two main constituents of the emerging world, China and India, have not been able to decouple themselves from the fate of the West. Au contraire, they continue to be vulnerable to the systemic risks emanating from the ways in which Western central banks are 'managing' secular stagnation.

Now, it is not as if the East has not made attempts to craft an alternative paradigm. The BRICS (an association of Brazil, Russia, India, China and South Africa) initiative was arguably a major endeavour in this direction. However, owing to the rivalries and divergent interests among the

---

[6] The first was the age of steam, the second was the age of the assembly line and mass production, and the third was the IT revolution. With AI-machine learning, internet of things, 5G and so on, the world is entering the so-called 'Fourth Industrial Revolution'.

[7] Primarily, India, China, Russia and ASEAN countries. Japan is an advanced economy, which, as we shall see in the course of the book, has already tried and failed to supplant the West.

[8] Basically, everybody apart from the West and Japan. Africa and Latin America are of particular interest, although with the exception of Brazil, and we do go into details of their economic prospects. But the path taken – and to be taken – by India will resonate with its own experiences.

members, especially China and India, it has failed to shine light on a truly different path, at least as of today. China, the foremost economic power in BRICS, has rather chosen to pursue a parallel 'Belt and Road'[9] of its own. But this Sino-centric play, far from being the lodestone for a future based on shared prosperity, is unfortunately in the same mould as the rent-seeking strategies that the incumbent West has adopted in the past, and then some. The world, we argue in this book, must not conflate grand strategies with grand narratives. China's basic idea is to create an enduring stake for itself, such that it can prop up a trading empire, even when its internal strength may be on the wane. As we shall see, the urgency to unfold Pax Sinica is not necessarily a natural outgrowth of strength, but rather an attempt to mitigate, the legacy of an unbalanced growth model while it is still possible. However, China's international belligerence in the wake of the pandemic – that originated on its soil and, by many accounts, was allowed to spread globally by its authorities, whether intentionally or otherwise – has likely dented its prospects irreparably. Especially since the country may have alienated India for good, on account of its border depredations against the latter in the summer of 2020.

Following this sentiment, we will examine the prospects and travails of the global 'economic North'[10] and of China, which is considered the weightiest challenger to the incumbents. While giving a bird's-eye view of these economies, we will also swoop down often to analyse specific trends and practices that warrant attention. After traversing both the macro and the micro, the narrative intends to set the stage for an appraisal of India's place in this new world, and suggest what the country must do to sustain growth for its still rising and overwhelmingly young population.

---

[9] This is a reference to the Belt and Road Initiative (previously known as the One Belt One Road or OBOR Plan).

[10] The West and Japan.

The truth is that in the global North, depressed economic conditions are being mitigated through monetary activism and a kind of creativity on the part of the central banks, which have been assigning ever-greater policy roles to themselves. The roster of national economic objectives, supported by these central banks, has expanded in line with their balance sheets. However, the framing of national policy objectives is ultimately the preserve of governments, and it is not surprising that the issue of central bank independence in the face of rising expenditure by the treasury has once again become a much-debated topic in the West and elsewhere – especially in the post-pandemic scenario.

In China, while fairly intense debates on policy may take place behind closed doors, we find the overarching goal is the creation of alternative pathways for exporting overcapacity-linked deflation,[11] as well as geopolitical influence in the hope of building a more financialized economy. And Beijing hopes that such an economy will exert enough gravity to engage in surplus accumulation, without necessarily remaining wedded to surplus production. The pandemic has, however, created a serious impediment to this plan, with several Belt and Road Initiative (BRI) projects floundering. So much so that China has been quietly dialling back on its BRI outreach. Instead, it is now trying to make a virtue out of necessity by retiring large amounts of capacity in industries such as metallics by seemingly putting in the foreground environmental concerns. At home, the Chinese dictatorship is also playing to the socialist gallery by cutting down to size private tech majors which could be potential threats to the regime's primacy, and promoting revanchism backed by military force as part of its foreign policy.

Overall, secular stagnation has brought with itself a secular rejection of a key pillar of the Western liberal

---

[11] Falling prices due to overproduction leading to a situation where supply is in excess of demand.

order: the salience of the free market theory. Today, many pillars of neoliberalism – that great late twentieth-century 'reimagining' of nineteenth-century liberal capitalist ideas – have either already fallen or are threatening to do so. Governments no longer abide by austerity during a downturn (or even otherwise); rather, they seek to spend their way out of crises. 'Small government' is a misnomer. And as for free trade, subsequent to the COVID-19 shock, the embrace of economic nationalism and protectionism under the broader rubric of populism are fast becoming the new stock ideologies in the West, and there is very little to suggest that the clock can be turned back. Globalization as epitomized by the Washington Consensus framework is in retreat almost everywhere.[12] The surge of new data-driven technologies is also giving rise to new national regulatory frameworks that will in turn add new layers of protection for domestic businesses. The old order is crumbling and a new one is yet to succeed it. 'A new normal' of transactional, even predatory, behaviour has emerged. The West may have lost its liberal order but the militaristic and mercantilist credo

---

[12] The term 'Washington Consensus' was first coined by English economist John Williamson in 1990 to denote a 'lowest common denominator' set of economic reform policies that were typically prescribed by Washington-based global institutions such as the International Monetary Fund (IMF) and World Bank to developing countries in Latin America looking to 'stabilize' their economies. Especially those who were leaving behind socialist practices. According to Williamson, the Washington Consensus set of prescriptions were:

1) Fiscal discipline, 2) Redirection of public expenditure, 3) Tax reform, 4) Financial liberalization, 5) Adoption of a single, competitive exchange rate, 6) Trade liberalization, 7) Elimination of barriers to foreign direct investment, 8) Privatization of public enterprises, 9) Deregulation of market entry and promotion of competition, and 10) Ensuring property rights.

See: Williamson, John. 'What Washington Means by Policy Reform.' *Latin American Adjustment: How Much Has Happened,* Institute for International Economics, April 1990, https://www.piie.com/commentary/speeches-papers/what-washington-means-policy-reform.

that built that framework before it became 'neoliberal' is now back in vogue across the world. The rest have not been able to create a humanist globalism of their own and in that sense the West has won. In fact, incumbent Western economic and military weight, though no longer enough to impose order, continue to afford it more degrees of freedom than the rest. The pre-eminence of the US dollar in particular is likely to remain intact in the near to medium term.

The timing of China's going out strategy was understandable given how America dealt with the last East Asian challenger – Japan (a story that we will encounter in the course of this book) – but it has nonetheless been unable to fashion the right balance between geopolitics and geoeconomics. Moreover, despite American fears, time is against China, with both debt and demographics weighing it down with each passing year. So, in a sense, we now live in a world where both the incumbent leader and the challenger are actually on the decline, regardless of the optics. This simultaneous weakening means that there is scope for a truly multipolar world to emerge, particularly since both parties are now inexorably locked in a twenty-first-century war over industrial standards, emerging technologies and maritime spheres of influence.

Since this is the pandemic-ridden world India must continue to grow in, maybe it is time for the nation to come up with its own strategy of inclusive prosperity in the coming decade, at least for the Indian Ocean region. This book, as is perhaps clear by now, is not focused on India's relationship with the world. Rather, we take a look at what the world looks like at the moment and situate India's options in it only towards the end. This book is ultimately an attempt to navigate the melding of geopolitics and geoeconomics in this era. The characters are mostly central banks, governments and corporations, with individuals featuring only now and then. The idea is to show that irresistible currents may be shaping policy and that they are not contingent upon the idiosyncratic behaviour of any leader in particular.

HOW TO READ THIS BOOK

As such, the book goes into the travails of what are currently the four main economic areas of the world, viz. the US, the European Union (EU), China and Japan, which together account for around two-thirds of global Gross Domestic Product (GDP) in nominal terms.[13] This is not to say that the rest are unimportant, hardly so. But to understand the current direction of the world economy, an investigation into the recent histories of the four largest economic centres is sine qua non. Emerging economies and lower-income countries around the world figure intermittently in the broader narrative, but a detailed treatment of a wider cross-section of their economies is perhaps beyond the scope of this book. To be sure, the construct of BRICS is examined at length. Of course, BRICS has in its ambit China and India, which are currently the largest and third largest national economies of the world in terms of purchasing power parity.[14]

In sum, *Negotiating the New Normal* is a tale that spans the GFC to the COVID-19 crisis with some trips further back in time. After all, origin stories sometimes hold the key to unlocking the causal factors behind emerging trends. The book attempts to show that pandemic-era trends are not really that new at all, but have been in the making since at least the GFC. The pandemic has only served to accelerate these trends which for better or worse will hold sway over the lives of Earth's inhabitants for the foreseeable future.

---

[13] 'World Economic Outlook, April 2021: Managing Divergent Recoveries.' *IMF,* 23 March 2021, https://www.imf.org/en/Publications/WEO/Issues/2021/03/23/world-economic-outlook-april-2021.

[14] Eurostat. 'The 2017 Results of the International Comparison Program: China, US and EU Are the Largest Economies in the World.' European Commission, 19 May 2020,https://ec.europa.eu/eurostat/documents/portlet_file_entry/2995521/2-19052020-BP-EN.pdf/bb14f7f9-fc26-8aa1-60d4-7c2b509dda8e#:~:text=In%202017%2C%20the%20Gross%20Domestic,16.4%25%20and%2016.3%25%20respectively.

ONE

IT IS SOMETIME IN THE WEE HOURS OF THE NIGHT, 15 APRIL 2020. Josiah Charles, a resident of Crown Heights, Brooklyn, is unable to sleep. As a Swedish horror movie plays in the background, Charles logs in and out of her bank account.[1]

Every time she checks it, the credit balance appears the same: 0.73 cents.

'Balloon Saloon', the party store where she worked, recently had to shut shop due to the COVID-19-induced lockdown and Charles has had no income for weeks. The $600 in unemployment benefits, transferred to her a while ago by the US government, dissipated quickly, and for a week now she has been left with only 0.73 cents to her name. She'd read online that the federal government was going to make a cash transfer into bank accounts that night – to the tune of $1,200 – and while she keeps logging in to check her account balance, she knows that she is not alone. Joining her in this online vigil are millions of other Americans, awaiting similar-sized stimulus cheques. 'THE FINAL COUNTDOWN MEGATHREAD' on Reddit begins with the announcement, 'Tonight we shall all join hands and wait for our stimulus checks. This is the moment that we have all waited for.'[2]

---

[1] Aviv, Rachel, et al. 'April 15, 2020: A Coronavirus Chronicle.' *New Yorker*, 27 April 2020, https://www.newyorker.com/magazine/2020/05/04/twenty-four-hours-at-the-epicenter-of-the-coronavirus-pandemic.

[2] U/Austinalexan. 'The Final Countdown Megathread.' *Reddit*, 15 April 2020, https://www.reddit.com/r/stimuluscheck/comments/g1lrot/the_final_countdown_megathread.

People are posting on this thread every minute.

> Zorukia: NOT RECEIVED. didn't get mine yet. everyone else with Bank of America got theirs.
> Eldie1: Ok folks… I just wanted to come let people know that mine came a little bit ago. I've been waiting and watching all day! It's been a long frustrating day!!! Hang in there y'all!!! I was so upset! And then it finally came! Relax a little… It's coming!!! Good luck and Good night!!!

A few minutes later, there were more comments:

> Exceptional Person: I got mine! Finally! After waiting all fuckin day guess we'll just grocery shop tomorrow 🙄
> Zorukia: NOT RECEIVED. i desperately need to grocery shop, but noo. gimme my munni

Rumour has it that those who registered for direct deposits with America's Internal Revenue Service (IRS) – and Charles is one of them – could expect to receive theirs sooner, and she surmises that her rescue package would arrive around 1.30 a.m.: the time when her erstwhile biweekly earnings used to reflect in her account.

A quick check at 1.28 a.m. yields nothing.

She logs in again at 1.36 a.m., but deliverance has not yet arrived.

It comes a minute later, when Charles picks up her phone and refreshes her account for the nth time that day. At 1.37 a.m. exactly. Exhaling in relief, she immediately posts a screenshot – the account balance now shows $1,200.73 – on MEGATHREAD, with only one word:

'Stimulated.'

★

And so, Josiah Charles became the latest recipient of the largest-ever fiscal stimulus package in US history, the Coronavirus Aid, Relief, and Economic Security, or CARES,

Act, which was passed by the US Senate on 25 March 2020.[3] The CARES Act authorized a spending package worth $2.2 trillion, which, taken together with previously budgeted spending and subsequent stimulus measures, pushed the US fiscal deficit to over $3 trillion in financial year 2020.[4] To put the sheer scale of this figure in perspective, one should note that it is basically equivalent to India's nominal GDP at the time of writing.

The US government has an unparalleled ability to borrow from the world over, owing to its status as the sovereign backer of the world's main reserve currency, the dollar. Despite this, financing heightened deficit spending of this magnitude from the market would not have been possible without support from America's central bank, the Federal Reserve (simply called the Fed). Providing extraordinary monetary support to the treasury, in March 2020, the Fed quickly took the short-term policy interest rate down to zero, and began a major purchase of both government debt and private debt in the secondary market.[5]

This move, however, was neither strange nor new.

Implemented in the wake of the GFC of 2007–08, this unconventional approach – involving the expansion of the balance sheet of the Fed – came to be a staple in the toolkit of central banks in advanced economies the world over as they

---

[3] The Act was revised in the Senate, coming to $2 trillion – including $500 billion for loans to larger businesses, such as airlines, $350 billion for small business loans, $250 billion for individuals, $250 billion for unemployment insurance, $150 billion for state and municipal governments, and $130 billion for hospitals.

[4] United States Congress, House. 'Public Law No: 116–36: Coronavirus Aid, Relief, and Economic Security Act or the CARES Act. US Congress.' 27 March 2020, https://www.congress.gov/bill/116th-congress/house-bill/748. https://www.cbo.gov/publication/57339. The US financial year runs from 1 October to 30 September. So, financial year 2020 would run from 1 October 2019, and end on 30 September 2020.

[5] This has been explained in detail under the sub-heading, 'Works in Practice, Doesn't Work in Theory.'

sought to fight recessions.[6] But the standardization of such tools also shows the degree to which the macroeconomic orthodoxy that had come to rule the roost since the 1970s stagflation era has been upended.

US RECOVERY?

In an episode of the popular CBS show *60 Minutes*, recorded in May 2020, the chairman of the Fed, Jerome K. Powell, said:

> The economy was fine. The financial system was fine. We're doing this to protect ourselves from the virus. And that means that when we do that, when the virus outbreak is behind us, the economy should be able to recover substantially. And I expect that it will recover substantially, but that it will take some time.[7]

Ever since the Great Recession spanning December 2007–June 2009 that came in the wake of the GFC, the US economy underwent expansion for 10 straight years (that is, 2010–19, both inclusive) till the pandemic hit. Washington used to tout this fact as reflective of the economy's resilience. However, closer scrutiny reveals (as we shall see in subsequent sections) that despite Powell's claims, America's economy, far from being 'fine', was characterized by deep structural problems even before the pandemic made its impact felt. And as a consequence of this, the rather modest growth seen during this supposed recovery period was all that one could have hoped for. And even this was made possible through the adoption of easy-money policies by the Fed, which are now

---

[6] European Central Bank, Bank of Japan, Royal Bank of Australia, Swiss National Bank, Bank of England and Bank of Canada.

[7] Powell, Jerome. 'Full Transcript: Fed Chair Jerome Powell's *60 Minutes* Interview on Economic Recovery from the Coronavirus Pandemic.' *CBS News*, Interview by Scott Pelley, 17 May 2020, https://www.cbsnews.com/news/full-transcript-fed-chair-jerome-powell-60-minutes-interview-economic-recovery-from-coronavirus-pandemic.

the staple rather than an occasional fix. While there had been some monetary tightening attempted during 2017–18, it was being rolled back even before the virus struck.

In the decade that followed the Great Recession, in America, the rate of growth in the inflation-adjusted, or 'real', annual GDP had been around 2.2 per cent on average. The average yearly growth rate in real GDP posted by the US in the period 2000–07 – that is, from the time of the dot-com crash to right before the GFC – was also just 2.5 per cent. And if the entire 20-year period stretching over 2000–19 is taken into account, the annual average growth rate in real GDP was only 2.08 per cent. These figures make it clear why America was no longer being seen as a primary engine of global growth, despite being the world's single-largest economy in terms of nominal GDP.[8]

For some, the tepid growth since the end of the Great Recession was, nevertheless, enough to constitute what they considered a slow 'cyclical' recovery in the economy. Particularly since it was seemingly accompanied by a major reduction in the headline (that is, 'official') unemployment rate through the creation of new jobs, over and above the 8.7 million that were lost during the Great Recession.[9] The truth, though, is more complex. A keener look at the US labour market conveys a less flattering picture of the jobs' situation even in the pre-COVID-19 period. For starters, the measure of unemployment used by the US Bureau of Labor Standards (BLS) to arrive at the official unemployment rate may itself not be above reproach.

---

[8] Calculated based on data gathered from the World Bank. 'GDP growth (annual %) – United States.' *World Bank*. Based on national accounts data and OECD National Accounts data files from 1961 to 2019, https://data.worldbank.org/indicator/NY.GDP.MKTP.KD.ZG?locations=US.

[9] Puzzhanghera, Jim. 'Economy Has Recovered 8.7 Million Jobs Lost in Great Recession.' *Los Angeles Times*, 6 June 2014, https://www.latimes.com/business/la-fi-jobs-20140607-story.html.

FULL EMPLOYMENT?

Months before COVID-19 struck, it was being reported that the US's official unemployment rate was at a historic low – it was just 3.5 per cent in September 2019,[10] a 50-year low at the time.[11] What journalists were referring to here is basically the BLS's U-3 unemployment measure, which gives:

> The ratio of the number of jobless persons who are available to take a job and have actively sought work in the past four weeks preceding the survey, to that of the total civilian labour force.[12]

The current definition of the U-3 measure was first introduced in 1994 during Bill Clinton's presidency. It was also the first time an official US unemployment survey asked respondents whether they had looked for a job in the four-week period prior to the survey.[13,14] Before 1994, the BLS used to simply ask respondents whether they had looked for employment till the time of the survey. (The U-3 measure does not include so-called 'marginally attached' workers[15]

---

[10] Cox, Jeff. 'September Unemployment Rate Falls to 3.5%, a 50-Year Low, as Payrolls Rise by 136,000.' *CNBC*, 4 October 2019, https://www.cnbc.com/2019/10/04/jobs-report-september-2019.html.

[11] Just as a point of comparison – in April 2020, this was 14.7 per cent, in May 2020 it was 13.3 per cent, and by June 2020 it was 11.1 per cent. We are referring to the U-3 measure here, of course.

[12] United States, Department of Labor, Bureau of Labor Statistics, 'Table A-15: Alternative Measures of Labor Underutilization.' *Data Retrieval: Labor Force Statistics*, last modified 19 February 2020, https://www.bls.gov/webapps/legacy/cpsatab15.htm.

[13] Bregger, John E., and Steven E. Haugen. 'BLS Introduces New Range of Alternative Employment Measures.' Monthly Labor Reports, Bureau of Labour Statistics, October 1995, https://www.bls.gov/opub/mlr/1995/10/art3full.pdf.

[14] Buffie, Nick. 'The Anomaly of U-3: Why the Unemployment Rate Is Overstating the Strength of Today's Labor Market.' CEPR Reports and Issue Briefs, Number 2015–24, December 2015.

[15] According to the BLS, 'marginally attached workers' are people who

and 'part-time' workers[16] in its methodology for calculating the unemployment rate.) Now, the BLS does have a broader measure of unemployment called U-6, which, in addition to U-3-based numbers, takes into account marginally attached and part-time workers as well. When U-6 is considered, the unemployment rate immediately shoots up to 6.9 per cent for both September 2019 and January 2020.[17]

Incidentally, U-6 also includes in its ambit a category the BLS calls 'discouraged workers', a subset of those considered marginally attached. They are the people who have given up looking for work in the 12 months preceding the survey 'specifically because they believed no jobs were available for them or there were none for which they would qualify'. However, according to American unemployment sceptics, such as the authors of *ShadowStats,* even the U-6 measure is not a broad enough marker, despite the inclusion of discouraged workers.[18] For them, U-6 does not take into account those they term as 'long-term discouraged' workers – that is, people who have stopped looking for a job more

---

do want – and are available for – work, and who have looked for a job sometime in the prior 12 months (or since the end of their last job if they held one within the past 12 months), but were not counted as 'unemployed' because they had not searched for work in the four weeks immediately preceding the survey. For this and other related definitions, see also: United States, Department of Labor, Bureau of Labor Statistics, 'Labor Force Statistics from the Current Population Survey: Concepts and Definitions.' *US Bureau of Labor Statistics*, last modified 19 June 2020, https://www.bls.gov/cps/definitions.htm.

[16] Part-time workers are those who have worked between 1 and 34 hours a week in the four weeks preceding the survey, even though they would have preferred full-time employment, which is defined as 35 or more hours of work per week.

[17] Just as a point of comparison – in April 2020, this was 22.8 per cent, in May 2020 it was 21.2 per cent, and in June 2020 it was 18 per cent.

[18] Williams, John. 'Alternate Unemployment Charts.' *ShadowStats Newsletter*, November 2019, http://www.shadowstats.com/alternate_data/unemployment-charts.

than 12 months before the time of the survey and are no longer considered a part of the workforce by any of the BLS's various measures. Such workers used to be counted in the unemployment survey prior to 1994. Unemployment sceptics, who have 'tracked' the numbers since 1994, typically come up with 'alternate' unemployment rates of 20 per cent or more based on their estimates of such 'long-term' discouraged workers.[19]

Former US President Donald Trump used to regularly trot out figures such as these in the course of his first presidential campaign, during which he repeatedly claimed that the real unemployment rate was far greater.[20] That, however, changed the moment he assumed office. Consider this tweet from 31 July 2017:

> Highest Stock Market EVER, best economic numbers in years, unemployment lowest in 17 years, wages raising, border secure, S.C.: No WH chaos![21]

It is hard to miss the irony that the 'unemployment lowest in 17 years' part of the tweet was basically a reference to the same U-3-based headline unemployment rate that he had summarily rejected as false no less than 19 times during his election campaign.[22]

---

[19] Williams. 'Alternate Unemployment Charts.'

[20] Boak, Christopher. "AP Fact Check: Trump Disdained Jobless Rate, Now Loves It." Associated Press, 21 April 2021, https://apnews.com/article/north-america-donald-trump-ap-top-news-barack-obama-unemployment-b237cd77161a4a1aa68d80a735445da9.

[21] @realDonaldTrump. 'Highest Stock Market EVER, best economic numbers in years, unemployment lowest in 17 years, wages raising, border secure, S.C.: No WH chaos!' Twitter, 31 July 2017, 05:58 p.m., https://twitter.com/realdonaldtrump/status/891998881009061888?lang=en.

[22] Ingraham, Christopher. '19 Times Trump Called Jobs Numbers "Fake" before They Made Him Look Good.' *Washington Post*, 10 March 2017, https://www.washingtonpost.com/news/wonk/wp/2017/03/10/19-times-trump-called-the-jobs-numbers-fake-before-they-made-him-look-good.

Regardless of political U-turns, sceptics believe that their assessment of the state of the US labour market explains why real, or inflation-adjusted, wages had barely budged since the GFC, or indeed from even before that. Real annual average hourly wage growth had been less than 0.6 per cent in the period between December 2008 and December 2019, and had shown little sign of tracking the apparent fall in unemployment – seasonal spikes notwithstanding during that period.[23] Now, if one were to disregard the rather high unemployment figures proposed by the sceptics, even the U-6 estimates indicate that a degree of slack existed in the US job market even before the downturn ushered in by COVID-19. Overall, a weaker-than-apparent labour market could partly explain why the real wage rate had remained flat during the pre-lockdown recovery period, despite millions of new jobs being created since 2008.[24]

THE CURVE

This observed weakening of the relationship between unemployment and wages in the US (and indeed in other advanced economies) has led to questions about whether the Phillips Curve – a key macroeconomic tool used by central banks for policymaking – is still viable or not. In its simplest form, the Phillips Curve, first proposed in 1959 by A.W. Phillips, an economist from New Zealand, depicts a negative relationship between unemployment and inflation. The underlying logic being that employers would have to

---

[23] Calculated from available data: United States, Department of Labor, Bureau of Labor Statistics. 'Real Earnings Archived News Releases.' *US Bureau of Labor Statistics*, last modified 15 July 2020, https://www.bls.gov/bls/news-release/realer.htm.

[24] Lindé, Jesper, and Mathias Trabandt. 'Have Economists Solved this Puzzle from the Great Recession?' *World Economic Forum*, 6 December 2019, https://www.weforum.org/agenda/2019/12/resolving-the-missing-deflation-and-inflation-puzzles.

offer better wages at a time of relative labour scarcity, while the opposite would be true when the number of applicants exceeds the number of vacant positions.

Another key reason for the lack of growth in real wages was the fact that net new job creation in the US economy since the GFC, prior to the COVID-19 pandemic, had been mostly in the not particularly well-paying service-providing sectors.[25] It should be noted that services, on an average, pay less than goods-producing sectors, such as manufacturing, construction, mining and logging.[26] In fact, more than two-thirds of those millions of new American jobs that were created during the period 2009–19 were in the service-providing sectors, where the average weekly earnings for non-managerial staff ranged between 39 and 85 per cent of the average weekly pay of a manufacturing worker in June 2019.[27]

This would be consistent with the findings of a growing body of research which reveals that recessions tend to shift net job creation towards low-wage sectors. The standard refrain in the American press in the years since the GFC has been that most of the jobs available in the US today are of the burger-flipping or cash-machine-manning variety – which barely beat the current federal minimum wage rate of $7.25 per hour.[28] And there seemed to be plenty of supply for jobs in these sectors, with automation trends further holding down wage growth.

---

[25] Based on BLS data.

[26] This is BLS terminology.

[27] Calculated by the author from BLS data. See: United States, Department of Labor, Bureau of Labor Statistics. 'Table B-8. Average Hourly and Weekly Earnings of Production and Nonsupervisory Employees on Private Nonfarm Payrolls by Industry Sector, Seasonally Adjusted (1).' *Economic News Release*, last modified 19 February 2020, https://www.bls.gov/news.release/empsit.t24.htm.

[28] Campbell, Alexander F. 'The House Just Passed a $15 Minimum Wage. It Would Be the First Increase in a Decade.' *Vox*, 18 July 2019, https://www.vox.com/2019/7/18/20697509/minimum-wage-bill-raise-the-wage-act.

The US minimum wage rate had peaked in real terms way back in 1968, over 50 years ago, and this has led to plenty of political turmoil with a Democratic Party-dominated US Congress finally passing an Act in July 2019 seeking to gradually double the current minimum wage to $15 per hour by 2025, following which any future hikes would be indexed to median wage growth.[29] The Act also sought to phase out the lower minimum wage paid to tipped workers. Leading advocates of this move, such as the Economic Policy Institute, believe that 'workers in every region of the country will soon need $15 per hour to maintain a modest but adequate standard of living'.[30] Such advocates also believe that this can be achieved via a fairer distribution of national income, since labour productivity exceeds worker compensation for the US economy as a whole. However, a Republican-controlled Senate refused to endorse the Act on the grounds that it would depress what they considered to be a 'hot economy' at the time in mid-2019.[31,32]

Truth be told, given current automation trends, coupled with decades of offshoring and outsourcing, well-paying jobs in the manufacturing and information technology (IT) sectors have not been easy to come by. For instance, the US

---

[29] Ibid. See also: Cooper, David et al. 'Raising the Federal Minimum Wage to $15 by 2025 Would Lift the Pay of 32 Million Workers.' *Economic Policy Institute,* 9 March 2021, https://www.epi.org/publication/raising-the-federal-minimum-wage-to-15-by-2025-would-lift-the-pay-of-32-million-workers.

[30] Zipperer, Ben. 'Gradually Raising the Minimum Wage to $15 Would Be Good for Workers, Good for Businesses, and Good for the Economy.' *Economic Policy Institute*, 7 February 2019, https://www.epi.org/publication/minimum-wage-testimony-feb-2019.

[31] Campbell, 'The House Just Passed a $15 Minimum Wage. It Would Be the First Increase in a Decade.'

[32] The so-called 'Raise the Wage Act' was reintroduced in both houses of the US Congress in January 2021 and had been referred to the relevant Committee of Jurisdiction in August 2021.

manufacturing workforce accounted for only 8 per cent of overall civilian employment in May 2019, as compared to 23 per cent in 1970.[33] And this fact is mirrored in the decline in the absolute number of those employed in manufacturing during the same period. Essentially, as a study by Cornell University's US Private Sector Job Quality Index reveals, 'Lost manufacturing jobs were chiefly replaced by lower-wage/lower-hours service jobs.'[34] Reinforcing the downward pressure being exerted on wages by the lingering effects of recessions and the persistent effects of globalization has been industrial automation. A recent paper by Massachusetts Institute of Technology's (MIT's) Daron Acemoglu and Pascual Restrepo titled 'Robots and Jobs: Evidence from US Labor Markets' estimates that every additional robot per 1,000 workers inducted by industry reduces wages by 0.42 per cent in the US.[35] Given the extant situation it is not difficult to see why the current political milieu in America is increasingly supportive of protectionism, whether it be the inclusion of domestic sourcing provisions in Obama's stimulus programme or Trump's trade wars or Biden's bid to strengthen the 1933 'Buy American' Act.[36]

By January 2020, the absolute level of employment in the manufacturing sector was well below levels recorded on the eve of the GFC in December 2007, and was unlikely to grow – given that US manufacturing had entered a new

---

[33] Denning, Steve. 'Understanding the U.S. Economy: Lots of Rotten Jobs.' *Forbes*, 5 December 2019, https://www.forbes.com/sites/stevedenning/2019/12/05/understanding-the-us-economy-lots-of-rotten-jobs/# 7192ecf82d97.

[34] Ibid.

[35] Acemoglu, Daron, and Pascual Restrepo. 'Robots and Jobs: Evidence from US Labor Markets.' 'Journal of Political Economy', Volume 128, Number 6, April 2020, pp. 2188–2244.

[36] Harwood, John. 'Biden's Buy American Push Is Good Politics but Bad Economics.' CNN, 1 August 2021, https://edition.cnn.com/2021/08/01/politics/biden-buy-american/index.html.

recessionary phase even before COVID-19 struck.[37] This was the case despite *some* 'reshoring' in recent times, which had, in turn, been driven by a mix of factors – including a decline in domestic energy prices due to America's unconventional hydrocarbon (shale) production boom.[38] Indeed, much of the growth in US manufacturing output since the GFC had been concentrated in energy-intensive industries. The phenomenal rise, first in shale gas and then in shale oil production, also stimulated demand for domestic manufacturers of drilling equipment since 2008.[39]

The boom in shale led to overall employment in the mining and logging sectors being at the same level in December 2019 as it had been in December 2007 – despite the fall in coal-working. Of course, the oil and gas (O&G) employment numbers had not grown steadily since 2008; rather, they tracked the fortunes of global crude oil prices. So, while O&G employment rose considerably from 2010 to 2014 – owing to a spike in crude oil prices – it fell just as quickly in consonance with the global decline in these prices from early 2015. This fall lasted till early 2017. By late 2019, O&G drilling-based employment was rising again due to a renewed increase in crude oil prices and was roughly at the same level as it was in December 2007.[40] However, this would prove to be short-lived as the COVID-19-induced

---

[37] United States, Department of Labor, Bureau of Labor Statistics. 'All Employees, Manufacturing [MANEMP] Graph.' Retrieved from the *FRED Blog, Federal Reserve Bank of St. Louis*, last updated on 7 August 2020, https://fred.stlouisfed.org/series/MANEMP.

[38] De Backer, Koen, et al. 'Reshoring: Myth or Reality?' *OECD Science,* Technology and Industry Policy Papers, January 2016, p. 11, doi:https://doi.org/10.1787/5jm56frbm38s-en.

[39] Gopinath, Swetha, and Vaishnavi Bala. 'Analysis: For Oil Explorers, It Pays to Buy, Not Rent.' *Reuters*, 22 September 2011, https://www.reuters.com/article/us-oilexplorers-idINTRE78F3AA20110922.

[40] 'All Employees, Oil and Gas Extraction.' St. Louis FRED, 4 February 2022, https://fred.stlouisfed.org/series/CES1021100001.

lockdowns would lead to a plummeting of oil demand, thereby bringing down oil prices across the globe.[41, 42, 43]

In December 2019, employment in the other great 'blue-collar' sector – construction – was just below what it was before the GFC. After falling precipitously since the crash of 2008, employment in this sector began to rise again in 2011 – but it did not reach the numbers it had attained in December 2007, despite America being in the grip of another housing boom that began sometime in 2014.[44] Overall, the decline in blue-collar employment through a series of recessions, beginning in 1973, has been mirrored by stagnating wages for US workers on the whole. The 'All-American' average hourly wage in 2018 had just about the same purchasing power it did during the 1970s, once adjusted for inflation.[45] The stagnation in average purchasing power has been accompanied by rising inequality. For people in the top 10 percentile of earners, real wages rose by a cumulative 15.7 per cent to $2,112 a week in August 2018, as compared to August 2000, and were almost five times the usual weekly earnings of the bottom tenth percentile.[46]

---

[41] Ibid.

[42] Based on observations from 'Crude Oil Prices: West Texas Intermediate (WTI) – Cushing, Oklahoma.' St. Louis FRED, 4 February 2022, https://fred.stlouisfed.org/series/DCOILWTICO and 'Crude Oil Prices: Brent – Europe.' St. Louis FRED, 24 February 2022, https://fred.stlouisfed.org/series/DCOILBRENTEU.

[43] US O&G employment would show a steady decline till around March 2021 when it would start slowly rising again, tracking a rise in global crude prices.

[44] Bureau of Labor Statistics. 'All Employees, Construction [USCONS].'

[45] Desilver, Drew. 'For Most U.S. Workers, Real Wages Have Barely Budged in Decades.' Pew Research Center, 7 August 2018, https://www.pewresearch.org/fact-tank/2018/08/07/for-most-us-workers-real-wages-have-barely-budged-for-decades.

[46] Ibid.

WHITHER MIDDLE CLASS?

With well-paying jobs hard to come by, the percentage of Americans classified as 'middle class' is either declining or stagnant, depending on the time horizon being considered. According to the Pew Research Center, middle-class households in America stood at 52 per cent in 2016, down from 61 per cent in 1971, although up by 1 per cent from 2011.[47] A 2018 study of the US labour market by a Washington-based think tank further found:

> Nationwide, just 38% of jobs pay enough to afford a middle or upper class life for a dual income-earning family with children; 32% of jobs pay a living-wage; and 30% pay what we call a 'hardship' wage, which is less than what a single adult living on his or her own needs for basic necessities.[48]

A survey from 2017 had also found that 78 per cent of Americans said that they literally lived from 'paycheck to paycheck'.[49] Clearly, with so many Americans living on the financial edge, it is not surprising that credit-card debt had reached an all-time high by the end of 2019.[50] The rise in this form of debt mirrored the trend in overall household debt, which also stood at an all-time high of $13.95 trillion by the third quarter of 2019.[51] US household debt, after

---

[47] Ibid.

[48] Bhandari, Ryan, and David Brown. 'The Opportunity Index: Ranking Opportunity in Metropolitan America.' *Third Way*, 30 October 2018, https://www.thirdway.org/report/the-opportunity-index-ranking-opportunity-in-metropolitan-america.

[49] Martin, Emmie. 'The Government Shutdown Spotlights a Bigger Issue.' *CNBC Make It*, 9 January 2019, https://www.cnbc.com/2019/01/09/shutdown-highlights-that-4-in-5-us-workers-live-paycheck-to-paycheck.html.

[50] Hayashi, Yuka. 'Credit-Card Debt in U.S. Rises to Record $930 Billion.' *Wall Street Journal*, 11 February 2020, https://www.wsj.com/articles/credit-card-debt-in-u-s-rises-to-record-930-billion-11581442140.

[51] Burns, Dan. 'U.S. Household Debt in Four Charts.' *Reuters*, 14 November 2019, https://www.reuters.com/article/us-usa-fed-debt-charts-graphic/u-s-household-debt-in-four-charts-idUSKBN1XN2OH.

dropping continuously from 2008 on account of a wave of bankruptcies and foreclosures, reversed in early 2014, and surpassed the previous high of $12.68 trillion, attained in the summer of 2008, by the first quarter of 2017.[52]

Despite these high numbers, it is true that the household debt position in the US right before the COVID-19 shock had improved in some ways since the days of the GFC. For one, the total household debt, which includes mortgages, home equity lines of credit (HELOCs), auto loans and student loans, apart from credit-card debt, amounted to a lower percentage of disposable personal income by the end of 2019 than it did at the height of the GFC. The debt–service ratio, which measures the amount of interest payments to be made as a percentage of household income, was also at a historic low at the time. Due to stricter lending standards since the GFC, most loan originations in the mortgages category – which accounts for two-thirds of US household debt – came from borrowers with high credit scores. Gone were the days when so-called 'sub-prime' borrowers were being advanced money to chase the quintessential American dream of being homeowners. Gone too were the days of using a house as a cash ATM (that is, drawing loans against the valuation of one's home), as evidenced by the fact that HELOCs were lower in overall size by end-2019 than they were at the time of the GFC.[53]

But while these trends may have seemed reassuring as far as household debt sustainability is concerned, there is another aspect of current household debt in America that

---

[52] 'Household Debt Surpasses Its Peak Reached During the Recession in 2008.' *New York Fed*, 17 May 2017, https://www.newyorkfed.org/newsevents/news/research/2017/rp170517.

[53] Everett, Gwen, and Shahien Nasiripour. 'HELOCs Are So 2007; Americans Aren't Using Homes as Piggy Banks Anymore.' *Los Angeles Times*, 3 November 2019, https://www.latimes.com/business/story/2019-11-03/heloc-decline-americans-not-using-homes-as-piggy-banks.

is indubitably a cause for concern. With some 99 per cent of all jobs created between 2010 and 2016 having gone to workers with associate's degrees, bachelor's degrees or graduate degrees according to Georgetown University, it is not surprising that an ever-increasing number of Americans have felt the need to secure a tertiary educational qualification.[54] This sentiment is reflected in the unbroken growth in student loans since 2008, which, by December 2019, accounted for a greater percentage of household debt than any other category – except for mortgages. What is more, delinquency rates have typically been very high for student loans, and Brookings Institution estimated in 2018 that by 2023, 40 per cent of all student loans advanced since 2004 could be in default, leading to some $560 billion in unpaid debt.[55] And this was *before* the pandemic struck. As a consequence, a large number of young Americans are likely to have terrible credit scores in the future, and this will impair their chances of ever securing a home loan. Even without defaulting, the burden of a lingering student loan will make their debt-to-income ratio unattractive to potential lenders. Moreover, if this investment in education does not pay off in terms of significantly enhanced earnings, a whole generation of Americans will find their spending choices constrained beyond just their ability to acquire a home. As Farzon A. Nahvi, an emergency medicine physician, who had paid his medical school bills via a student loan, wrote in an opinion piece for the *New York Times* back in August 2018 itself:

---

[54] Carnevale, Anthony P., et al. 'America's Divided Recovery: College Haves and Have-Nots 2016.' Georgetown University Centre on Education and the Workforce, 30 June 2016, https://cew.georgetown.edu/cew-reports/americas-divided-recovery/#resources.

[55] Scott-Clayton, Judith. 'The Looming Student Loan Default Crisis Is Worse than We Thought.' *Brookings*, 11 January 2018, https://www.brookings.edu/research/the-looming-student-loan-default-crisis-is-worse-than-we-thought/.

> A career in medicine promised a better future ahead. But five years after graduating from medical school, that future still seems on a distant horizon. I cannot afford to buy a house, still ride my bicycle to work and continue to skimp on meals in order to cover more than $3,000 in monthly loan payments.[56]

Worryingly, nearly 45 million Americans who had outstanding student loans by early 2021 were either already in or could find themselves in a similar situation sooner rather than later.[57] That definitely does not bode well for the future growth of the US economy – where consumption spending accounts for almost 70 per cent of GDP.[58]

Now, it is the US government itself which has advanced most of these student loans through lending programmes that have gone through various iterations over the years, further adding to the ever-growing role of the federal government in the American economy. While student loans are an off-balance-sheet liability[59] for the administration, there are several 'entitlement programmes' where direct federal government spending serves as a bulwark for a large chunk of the population. An example of the same would be the Supplemental Nutrition Assistance Program (SNAP), or 'food

---

[56] Nahvi, A. Farzon. 'I Am a Doctor and Even I Can't Afford My Student Loans.' *New York Times*, 20 August 2018, https://www.nytimes.com/2018/08/20/opinion/medical-school-student-loans-tuition-debt-doctor.html.

[57] Friedman, Zack. 'Student Loan Debt Statistics in 2021: A Record $1.7 Trillion.' *Forbes*, 30 June 2021, https://www.forbes.com/sites/zackfriedman/2021/02/20/student-loan-debt-statistics-in-2021-a-record-17-trillion/?sh=38a7d7df1431.

[58] 'Shares of Gross Domestic Product: Personal Consumption Expenditures.' *FRED Blog*, 29 July 2021, https://fred.stlouisfed.org/series/DPCERE1Q156NBEA.

[59] Phillips, Matt. 'The US Government Has about $70 Trillion in Off-Balance Sheet Liabilities.' *Quartz*, 4 August 2013, https://qz.com/111454/the-us-government-has-about-70-trillion-in-off-balance-sheet-liabilities.

stamps' as it is known colloquially, on which some 40 million Americans depended to beat hunger by June 2019.[60] Other key entitlement programmes such as Medicare, Medicaid and Social Security have also grown enormously since 2008, and are the prime drivers behind an ever-increasing level of US gross national debt, which stood at $23.2 trillion at the end of 2019, representing over 106.6 per cent of GDP.[61] The massive stimulus given during the course of the pandemic saw this further balloon to $28.1 trillion or over 127.7 per cent of GDP by March 2021.[62]

'WORKS IN PRACTICE... DOESN'T WORK IN THEORY'

In general, monetary policy is deemed 'accommodative' when it seeks to make interest rates low enough to spur private spending and thereby economic growth, with the objective of either decreasing unemployment or to at least prevent it from rising further. Both households and the government have been sustaining very high levels of debt in the US, in no small part due to the low-interest-rate environment ushered in by the Fed's adoption of 'accommodative' monetary policies

---

[60] The Center on Budget and Policy Priorities. 'Policy Basics: The Supplemental Nutrition Assistance Program (SNAP).' 25 June 2019, https://www.cbpp.org/research/food-assistance/policy-basics-the-supplemental-nutrition-assistance-program-snap.

[61] United States, Department of Labor, Bureau of Labor Statistics. 'A Lesson in Measuring the Federal Debt.' *FRED Blog*, Federal Reserve Bank of St Louis, 9 December 2019, https://fredblog.stlouisfed.org/2019/12/a-lesson-in-measuring-the-federal-debt/?utm_source=series_page&utm_medium=related_content&utm_term=related_resources&utm_campaign=fredblog.

[62] US Department of the Treasury. 'Fiscal Service, Federal Debt: Total Public Debt [GFDEBTN].' *FRED Blog*, 2 June 2021, https://fred.stlouisfed.org/series/GFDEBTN and US Office of Management and Budget, et al. 'Federal Debt: Total Public Debt as Percent of Gross Domestic Product [GFDEGDQ188S].' *FRED Blog*, 29 July 2021, https://fred.stlouisfed.org/series/GFDEGDQ188S.

in the wake of the GFC. As we shall see, this accommodative monetary regime has created a path dependency and is now the new normal for the US economy.

But first, let us briefly recall the circumstances in which it was born.

As the GFC deepened, with the bankruptcy of heavyweight firms like Lehman Brothers and American Insurance General (AIG), and the US economy going into a recession by late 2008, the Fed's Federal Open Market Committee (FOMC) responded by reducing the target range for its key policy interest rate – called the effective federal funds rate (EFFR) – to 0 and 0.25 per cent in December 2008.[63] The EFFR is the weighted average of the rates at which US depository institutions (mainly commercial banks) extend overnight loans to each other on an uncollateralized basis to meet reserve requirements set by the Fed and other purposes. Commercial bank reserves are funds held in the account that a commercial bank has with the central bank, and the Fed requires US-based commercial banks to hold funds equal to around 10 per cent of their total deposit liabilities as reserves. Since the EFFR is the key rate on which all other bank lending rates in the US are based, its lowering is expected to lead to a decrease in borrowing costs across the board.

With the December 2008 EFFR cut, the Fed dropped its key policy rate to the so-called 'zero lower bound', or ZLB, which refers to a situation where a nominal interest rate, having already reached zero, cannot be lowered further, since lenders would then opt to hold cash, instead of a deposit 'paying' negative interest.[64] In practice, nominal interest rates can be reduced below zero, since there are costs involved in

---

[63] Isodore, Chris. 'Fed Slashes KEY Rate to near Zero.' *CNNMoney*, Cable News Network, 16 December 2008, https://money.cnn.com/2008/12/16/news/economy/fed_decision/index.htm.

[64] After all, it is better to hold a zero-interest-bearing currency note than a deposit where you pay the bank for holding your money.

holding and transacting large volumes of cash (currency). This is precisely why some central banks in the post-GFC era have been able to push their key policy rates into slightly negative territory. Indeed, economists now talk more in terms of the 'effective lower bound' or ELB – that is, the lowest level to which nominal rates can be reduced without compromising the efficacy of accommodative monetary policy.[65]

Back in 2008, it was generally believed that the ZLB and ELB were synonymous, and that most central banks would not find themselves in such a situation where they had to push their policy rates to such extremely low levels too often.[66] And this is why the Fed's decision to push the EFFR into ZLB territory was an indication of just how severe the economic crisis had become by the beginning of 2009. In particular, the Fed was worried about the prospect of serious deflation in the US economy.[67] Something that could have led to a deflationary spiral – wherein a fall in aggregate demand leads to prices decreasing, which, in turn, leads to a fall in aggregate supply that then causes loss of jobs, leading to even weaker demand, even lower prices, an even greater fall in supply and an even greater loss of jobs. Just how disastrous deflation of a significant magnitude can be is evidenced by the experiences during the Great Depression itself, when prices fell by 10 per cent year on year during the period 1929–32 and the US GDP contracted by some 15 per cent as unemployment soared.

---

[65] Having said that, the ELB cannot be appreciably below zero because there will come a point at which the cost of holding a deposit, where the lender pays the borrower, will outweigh the costs associated with holding cash directly.

[66] A notable exception was the Bank of Japan, which, as we shall see in chapter five, 'pioneered' the contemporary adoption of unconventional monetary policies, having had to face the ZLB for a very long time.

[67] Deflation refers to a general decline in the price level of goods and services in an economy, and if it is of a significant enough magnitude, it can ultimately lead to a major collapse in GDP through a deflation spiral.

But why was the Fed so worried about a major deflationary recession in early 2009, given that inflation, though falling, had not yet entered negative territory? As it turns out, the US economy during the GFC was characterized by the same additional source of deflationary pressure that contributed to the downward spiral during the Great Depression – over-indebtedness.

The GFC had created a situation where various US credit markets had become illiquid to the point of being frozen. A plethora of toxic assets were being directly held by commercial banks on their balance sheets – banks that were in no position to lend any more. Worse, the purchase of many of these assets had been financed by these banks, via short-term loans. The stage seemed set for what is hypothesized as a 'debt-deflation'. The broadest version of a debt-deflation is one where an increase in the real value of debt, on account of deflation, encourages default on the part of borrowers, leading to a wave of bank insolvencies. And this, in turn, leads to a fall in lending and then spending, resulting in further deflation. Subsequently, the deflationary spiral of economic contraction that has been detailed earlier ensues, with the deflationary pressure being sustained as the public looks to pay off debts by curtailing expenditure on goods and services. In fact, in the case of a debt-deflationary event, Irving Fisher – the originator of the theory – explained that the cause for the depression would be 'over-indebtedness to start with and deflation following soon after', instead of mere underconsumption (or overproduction).[68] And to quote Hyman P. Minsky, who developed Fisher's ideas further and found additional channels through which debt-deflation may work, 'Debt-deflation feeds upon debt-deflation.'[69]

---

[68] Fisher, Irving. 'The Debt-Deflation Theory of Great Depressions.' *Econometrica*, Volume 1, Number 4, October 1933, pp. 337–57.

[69] The entire quote is: 'In such processes the economic system's reactions to a movement of the economy amplify the movement – inflation feeds upon inflation and debt-deflation feeds upon debt-deflation.' See: Hyman

Fortunately for the US, the then chairman of the Fed, Ben Bernanke, had long been a student of the phenomenon of debt-deflation, having observed an additional channel through which it reinforced itself.[70] Specifically, his channel emphasized that since debt-deflation is operative in an environment of widespread bankruptcy, the process of credit intermediation in the economy itself gets impaired, and this ends up depressing aggregate demand on account of the credit contraction that follows. In a 2002 talk titled 'Making Sure It Doesn't Happen Again', Bernanke had even laid out a range of options for the Fed in case a Great Depression—like situation ever rose again. Specifically, he talked about various unconventional measures that could be adopted by the Fed in the event of conventional monetary policy failing to stimulate the economy even after the EFFR was dropped to the ZLB. The bottom line, as Bernanke put it, was:

> [T]he US government has a technology, called a printing press (or, today, its electronic equivalent), that allows it to produce as many US dollars as it wishes at essentially no cost. By increasing the number of US dollars in circulation, or even by credibly threatening to do so, the US government can also reduce the value of a dollar in terms of goods and services, which is equivalent to raising the prices in dollars of those goods and services. We conclude that, under a paper-money system, a determined government can always generate higher spending and hence positive inflation.[71]

P., Minsky. 'The Financial Instability Hypothesis.' The Levy Economics Institute Working Paper Collection, Number 74, May 1992, p. 2, https://www.levyinstitute.org/pubs/wp74.pdf.

[70] Bernanke, Ben. 'Nonmonetary Effects of the Financial Crisis in Propagation of the Great Depression.' *American Economic Review*, Volume 73, Number 3, June 1983, pp. 257–76.

[71] Bernanke, Ben. 'Deflation – Making Sure "It" Doesn't Happen Here (Remarks before the National Economists Club, Washington, D.C.).' *Federal Reserve Board*, 21 November 2002, https://www.federalreserve.gov/boarddocs/speeches/2002/20021121.

As fate would have it, the FOMC's adoption of the ZLB and various emergency liquidity measures was deemed inadequate to kick-start US credit markets and Bernanke got his chance to put his theory to the test. With desperate times calling for desperate measures, the Fed turned to the use of 'unconventional' monetary policy measures. Now, unconventional monetary policy is made up of three distinct approaches that can nevertheless be used together or on a stand-alone basis. They are:

1. Large-Scale Asset Purchases (LSAPs): An action popularly known as Quantitative Easing (QE), or balance sheet policy, since it involves the addition of assets on a central bank's balance sheet funded through newly created money.
2. Forward Guidance: This could be either the active management of expectations about the future course of the key policy rate (which for the Fed is the EFFR) when it has reached the ELB, or the active management of expectations with respect to future composition and/or the size of a central bank's balance sheet.
3. Negative Interest Rate Policy (NIRP): The act of pushing the key policy rate into negative territory (see chapter two for the European Central Bank's experience with NIRP).

The Fed's post-GFC move into unconventional territory involved QE in the main with forward guidance playing a complementary role.

QUANTITATIVE EASING

Though QE was not a novel approach – with variants having been used by the Fed itself during the 1930s and by the Bank of Japan in 2001 (see chapter five) – knowledge about its effects was very limited, especially when compared to traditional monetary policy. Be that as it may, the first round of LSAP, or QE1, which commenced in December 2008, had the following stated objective:

> Reduce the cost and increase the availability of credit for the purchase of houses, which in turn should support housing markets and foster improved conditions in financial markets more generally.[72]

In line with this goal, the Fed began to directly inject liquidity into the housing market, by buying $500 billion worth of mortgage-backed securities (MBS) financed by government-sponsored enterprises (GSEs), such as Fannie Mae and Freddie Mac, in December 2008.[73] In addition to this, it also bought $100 billion worth of agency debt securities (that is, direct GSE debt), issued by GSEs during the same period.[74] As credit conditions continued to worsen, the Fed expanded QE1 in March 2009 by purchasing an additional $750 billion of agency MBS, $100 billion of GSE debt and even, reportedly, $300 billion of treasury (government) securities, with long-term maturities.[75] Thus, besides attempting to reduce interest rates on MBS and GSE debt, QE1 also sought to push down long-term interest rates (that is, interest rates on long-maturity debt) for government borrowings.

With the US economy registering positive growth by the first quarter of 2010, its proponents credited QE1 with

---

[72] 'Federal Reserve Announces It Will Initiate a Program to Purchase the Direct Obligations of Housing-Related Government-Sponsored Enterprises and Mortgage-Backed Securities Backed by Fannie Mae, Freddie Mac, and Ginnie Mae.' *Board of Governors of the Federal Reserve System*, 25 November 2008, https://www.federalreserve.gov/newsevents/pressreleases/monetary20081125b.htm.

[73] Ibid.

[74] A security is a fungible, negotiable financial instrument that holds some type of monetary value.

[75] 'FOMC Statement.' *Board of Governors of the Federal Reserve System*, 18 March 2009, https://www.federalreserve.gov/newsevents/pressreleases/monetary20090318a.htm.

having saved the economy from severe debt-deflation by kick-starting key credit markets such as housing, which had become illiquid. This was followed by a reinvestment policy that began in August 2010, involving the replacement of maturing securities (including the treasury debt purchased earlier) to maintain the now enlarged size of the Fed's balance sheet.[76]

However, deflationary pressures remained operative in the US economy, with inflation as measured by the Personal Consumption Expenditures (PCE) Index excluding food and energy (core inflation) falling below the 1 per cent mark and headline unemployment almost touching 10 per cent by late 2010. It should be noted that since 1977, the US House of Representatives had entrusted the Fed with the dual mandate of price stability and maximum sustainable employment.[77] Since the 1990s, the Fed has interpreted its

---

[76] A typical central bank balance sheet is depicted in footnote 77. The purchase of assets leads to an increase in the left side of the balance sheet. This creates an equivalent increase on the right side, in the form of reserves of commercial banks.

[77] A central bank balance sheet:

Assets	*Liabilities and capital*
Net foreign assets	Reserve money
Net domestic assets	*Currency in circulation*
	Reserves of commercial banks
	Non-monetary liabilities
	Central bank securities
	Others
	Equity capital

Since 1977, the Fed has operated under a mandate from the US House of Representatives to 'maintain long run growth of the monetary and credit aggregates commensurate with the economy's long run potential to increase production, so as to promote effectively the goals of maximum employment, stable prices and moderate long-term interest rates'.

(*Source:* Section 2A of the 'Act to provide for the establishment of Federal reserve banks, to furnish an elastic currency, to afford means of rediscounting commercial paper, to establish a more effective supervision of banking in the United States, and for other purposes' as added by the

price stability mandate as requiring the maintenance of a symmetric 2 per cent core inflation target.[78]

The justification for pursuing this target is summarized as follows:

> Over time a higher inflation rate would reduce the public's ability to make accurate economic and financial decisions. On the other hand, a lower inflation rate would be associated with an elevated probability of falling into deflation... a phenomenon associated with very weak economic conditions. Having at least a small level of inflation makes it less likely that the economy will experience harmful deflation if economic conditions weaken.[79]

In 'normal' times, this 2 per cent target has been achieved via the manipulation of the EFFR, and that forms the crux of conventional monetary policy.

Implicit in this targeting framework is the assumption of a regime of monetary independence, wherein the Fed pursues its inflation target independent of the impact it will have on the government's financial position. Rather, it is the treasury that is expected to ensure that its spending is intertemporally sustainable, giving the Fed room to pursue its inflation target. Instead of this, if the treasury chose to be profligate, a situation could ensue where the Fed would

---

act of 16 November 1977 (91 Stat. 1387) and amended by the Acts of 27 October 1978 [92 Stat. 1897], 23 August 1988 [102 Stat. 1375] and 27 December 2000 [114 Stat. 3028].)

Available as: 'Section 2A. Monetary Policy Objectives.' Federal Reserve Act, passed on 16 November 1977. *Board of Governors of the Federal Reserve System*, https://www.federalreserve.gov/aboutthefed/section2a.htm.

[78] Symmetric here means that the inflation target is neither a floor nor a ceiling. The Fed would like to keep inflation around the 2 per cent mark, in a way that the length of time that the inflation rate is higher than 2 per cent is roughly the same as the length of time that it is lower than 2 per cent.

[79] 'FOMC statement.' *Board of Governors of the Federal Reserve System*, 14 December 2010, https://www.federalreserve.gov/newsevents/pressreleases/zmonetary20101214a.htm.

be forced to keep the policy rate low or make large-scale purchases of government debt despite an uptick in inflation in order to keep the government solvent in the interests of overall financial stability. This, in turn, would be considered a case of fiscal dominance.

With fears of a double-dip recession on the rise – in such a case an economy heads back into contraction after a few quarters of growth – the Fed decided to institute QE2 in November 2010, in order to 'promote a stronger rate of recovery and to help ensure that inflation, over time, is at levels consistent with its mandate'.[80] While QE1 was mostly aimed at stabilizing the financial sector, QE2 was more about jobs and growth. The latter, which went on till June 2011, saw the Fed purchasing long-term treasury securities worth $600 billion in pursuance of its dual mandate. With this action, the Reserve was seeking to 'flatten' the yield curve, which is obtained by plotting the yields of various treasury securities against their maturity terms on a graph.[81] A flattening of the yield curve simply means that the Fed was trying to reduce the yield on long-term treasury bonds relative to that of short-term treasury bonds. The Fed was ostensibly looking to reduce interest rates on long-term government securities, since they served as a benchmark for various kinds of long-term lending rates to the private sector, such as mortgages and corporate borrowings.

To further flatten the yield curve, the Fed initiated 'Operation Twist' from September 2011 to December 2012.[82]

---

[80] Ibid.

[81] US government bills and bonds of various maturities pay different interest rates. This spectrum of rates (or yields) from the shortest (overnight) to the longest (usually 30 years) is known as the term structure of interest rates. The yields curve is typically upward-sloping since lenders demand higher interest rates for longer-term loans. A flattening of the yield curve would mean that interest rates on long-term maturities were being lowered relative to the interest paid on short-term maturities.

[82] Goldstein, Jacob. 'Fed's "Operation Twist," Explained In 4 Easy Steps.'

This involved the swap of more than $600 billion associated with the purchase of treasury securities with maturities of six to 30 years and sales of those securities with maturities of three years or less. This would supposedly reduce duration risk for bond holders, since treasury debts of short duration are less risky than long-term treasury securities. A lowering of duration risk would induce investors to move into riskier assets (assuming their risk appetite remained as it was pre-Operation Twist), such as corporate bonds, and reduce interest rates on such assets as well.

However, the Fed was not done yet. In September 2012, due to continued weakness in the labour market, it began QE3, stating that:

> It will continue its purchases of agency MBS, undertake additional asset purchases, and employ its other policy tools as appropriate until such improvement [in the labor market] is achieved.[83]

The above statement meant that the duration of QE3 was not fixed and was contingent on the state of the US economy as perceived by the Fed. Accordingly, under QE3, the Reserve committed to buying $40 billion in MBS per month, instead of a predetermined amount, as was the case with the earlier QE rounds. Another $45 billion in monthly purchases of long-term treasury securities was added to this figure from December 2012, and QE3 continued at a rate of $85 billion per month till January 2014. And January 2014 onwards, there was a progressive reduction in bond purchases, with QE3 finally coming to an end in October 2014. Taken together, all three QE rounds rapidly expanded

---

NPR (National Public Radio), 21 September 2011, https://www.npr.org/sections/money/2011/09/21/140643696/operation-twist-explained-in-4-easy-steps.

83 'Federal Reserve Issues FOMC statement.' *Board of Governors of the Federal Reserve System*, 13 September 2012, https://www.federalreserve.gov/newsevents/pressreleases/monetary20120913a.htm.

the Fed's balance sheet, from $900 billion in December 2008 to $4.5 trillion by October 2014 – an expansion that was unprecedented in the history of the Reserve.[84] This growth in asset holdings was paid for by a process that has been summarized well by Bernanke himself:

> The Fed financed its purchases of securities from the private sector effectively by writing checks on itself. Sellers of securities deposited those checks in the banking system, and banks in turn added those funds to their reserves.[85]

The securities thus purchased became new assets on the Fed's balance sheet, and this expansion (that is, accretion in asset holdings) was 'financed' via electronically created liabilities in the form of additional commercial bank reserves.[86] This accretion of reserves by banks was also unprecedented in history, and led to commercial banks holding reserves far in excess of what the requirements mandated. By the end of QE3 in 2014, commercial banks were holding some $3 trillion in excess reserves as opposed to holding none before the GFC.

HYPERINFLATION?

This gargantuan accumulation of excess reserves by commercial banks did lead to warnings about impending hyperinflation in the US economy.[87] These fears arose out of

---

[84] An accumulation of assets is considered a balance sheet expansion.

[85] Bernanke, Ben. 'Should the Fed Keep Its Balance Sheet Large?' *Brookings*, 2 September 2016, https://www.brookings.edu/blog/ben-bernanke/2016/09/02/should-the-fed-keep-its-balance-sheet-large.

[86] Commercial bank reserves are funds held in the account that a commercial bank has with the central bank. The Fed requires US-based commercial banks to hold funds equal to around 10 per cent of their total deposit liabilities as reserves.

[87] Krugman, Paul. 'The Big Inflation Scare.' *New York Times*, 29 May 2009, https://www.nytimes.com/2009/05/29/opinion/29krugman.html.

a belief that banks could decide to engage in explosive credit creation by 'lending out' their excess reserves. Opponents of this view pointed out that banks don't actually 'lend out' reserves, and it was impossible for the national banking system as a whole to draw down reserves unless depositors began withdrawing their balances in currency.[88] While it is technically correct to say that banks don't 'lend out' reserves, what those fearing hyperinflation basically meant was that banks could begin a spate of loan creations in order to turn their excess reserves into required reserves.[89]

However, contrary to the expectations of those worried about hyperinflation, explosive credit creation never happened. Right when LSAP was initiated, the Fed was also authorized to start paying interest on excess reserves to commercial banks, just as it did for required reserves. This interest on 'all' reserves (IOR) gave banks the incentive to not engage in the kind of credit creation that was being feared in some quarters. Truth be told, in the post-GFC climate, banks had become increasingly circumspect about lending to businesses anyway, and were glad to hold on to these paying reserves as opposed to loading their balance sheets with many more potentially non-performing loans. For instance, by 2016, a loan application by small- and medium-sized businesses was considered to have an 80 per cent chance of being rejected by banks, as revealed by a Fed survey.[90] Since 2011, new regulations had also been put in

---

[88] Or sending it to overseas accounts.

[89] This would happen because every loan extended by a bank leads to the creation of a deposit for the borrower and thus increases deposits. All other things being the same would reduce the reserve deposit ratio, which is the basis for calculating required reserves.

[90] 'Easing the Sting of Bank Loan Rejection.' *PYMNTS*, 20 July 2016, https://www.pymnts.com/news/b2b-payments/2016/new-business-funders-sme-startup-small-business-bank-loan-rejection-application-approval-financing.

place that required banks to hold much greater liquid capital than before, and reserves served that purpose quite well.[91]

The reluctance of commercial banks to lend was mirrored by the lack of desire on the part of households and firms to engage in borrowed spending, if they could help it. Post-GFC, this depressed economic climate was reflected in a major decline in the velocity of money, which refers to the number of times a unit of money changes hands (that is, is spent) in an economy. By the middle of 2014, the velocity of money was only about a quarter of what it had been prior to the GFC. Now, traditional monetary theory says that the money supply multiplied by the velocity of money should equal nominal GDP, which is, simply put, the price-level multiplied by real GDP.[92] Given that real GDP grew at an anaemic rate during 2008–14, the huge increase in the monetary base should have caused a significant increase in the price-level, that is, inflation, had the velocity of money (with respect to the monetary base) not become a fraction of what it used to be. In fact, contrary to hyperinflationary fears, inflation remained well below the 2 per cent mark for most of the time that the multiple rounds of QE were in operation.

This then raises the question as to what effects these measures really had, given that the theory behind it isn't uncontested. After all, as Bernanke himself quipped in 2012, 'Well, the problem with QE is it works in practice, but it doesn't work in theory.'[93]

---

[91] A desire on the part of commercial banks to hold greater liquidity in an uncertain investment climate has also played a part.

[92] The standard expression is: MV = PQ, where M stands for some measure of money supply, V stands for the velocity of money (or the rate at which people spend money), P stands for the general price level and Q stands for the quantity of goods and services produced.

[93] Yu, Edison. 'Did Quantitative Easing Work?' *Economic Insights*, Volume 1, Number 1, January 2016, pp. 15–13, https://ideas.repec.org/a/fip/fedpei/00002.html.

A FEW (UNDOCUMENTED) BENEFITS OF QE

Evidence suggests that Bernanke's gambit succeeded to the extent that the various QE rounds *did* manage to reduce interest rates on MBS and treasury securities by a significant magnitude. Reduced MBS yields and mortgage rates certainly shored up the housing market, and helped both indebted households and banks repair their balance sheets through refinance. The drop in treasury yields helped the US government keep its ever-growing debt levels serviceable – a fact not lost on Washington, and a major reason why there will be pressure on the Fed to employ QE in the future as well.

These measures also helped inflate stock markets, as a combination of reduced yields on securities and ultra-low borrowing costs boosted speculative activity. Rather than invest in the real economy, US companies chose to use cheap money to engage in massive share buybacks to boost their bottom lines. While some members of the Fed congratulated themselves for supporting asset prices through 'recovery', critics blamed it for creating bubbles, where asset values diverged from fundamentals.

The Fed's accommodative monetary policies also created a massive pool of dollar liquidity that found its way to emerging market economies, causing all sorts of volatility – as epitomized by an event known as the 'Taper Tantrum' (see chapter three). As Stanley Fischer, vice chair of the Board of Governors of the Federal Reserve System, observed in 2014:

> There is little doubt that the aggressive actions the Federal Reserve took to mitigate the effects of the global financial crisis significantly affected asset prices at home and abroad as well as international capital flows.[94]

---

[94] Fischer, Stanley. 'The Federal Reserve and the Global Economy.' Per Jacobsson Foundation Lecture, Annual Meetings of the International Monetary Fund and the World Bank Group, Washington, DC, 11 October 2014.

Heightened capital outflows from the US during QE1 and QE2 weakened the dollar against other major currencies, and even sparked fears of a currency war.[95] A currency war refers to competitive devaluation between countries to shore up their exports. However, by July 2011, the dollar decline had reversed and the currency had begun to climb on trend against other currencies, without the decline having done that much to boost US exports.

Since neither corporate investment nor exports were boosted by QE, what impact did it then have on US output? Though various studies have found that the measures are associated with having had a positive impact on US GDP growth, estimates regarding the magnitude of its impact vary widely. Basically, it helped the US economy by ensuring that consumption did not collapse by keeping household borrowing costs low and by boosting the value of assets such as housing and stocks. QE also shored up the economy by accommodating the US government's fiscal expansion – although the Fed would say this was a by-product of its efforts, and not the real aim of the expansion at all. Overall, on the face of it, QE prevented the US economy from collapsing on itself, and also kept up a certain rate of inflation. And that is why it has become an essential part of the Fed's toolkit to fight deep recessions and Depression-like conditions.

ISSUES WITH QE

However, this does not mean that QE is a 'get out of jail (or in this case debt-deflation) free card' for the Fed, so to speak. Its employment creates a situation wherein the probability of the Fed experiencing a loss increases over time. This is because a sudden spike in inflation due to whatever reason

---

[95] Portes, Richard. 'Currency Wars and the Emerging Markets.' *VOXEU CEPR*, 4 November 2010, https://voxeu.org/article/currency-wars-and-emerging-markets.

could push interest rates up for the Fed's asset portfolio and reduce its value (since bond prices and interest rates are inversely linked) to a point where it might leave its liabilities in excess of its assets. This would mean that the Fed would start losing its capital. Central banks take such a possibility very seriously, because in the event of their capital entering negative territory, they would have to be recapitalized by the government, and that would directly affect whatever independence they have, at least in the eyes of the market. Theoretically, central banks can always discharge their monetary functions even with negative capital as long as it can be covered by the present discounted value of its future seigniorage earnings. This is even practically true as evidenced by the experience of a few central banks worldwide, but markets will tend to become jittery nonetheless. For the Fed, the stakes are much higher since it is the custodian of the almighty dollar, and overseas holders of the currency would take a very dim view of a situation where the Fed's capital is deep into negative territory. Unending QE also has implications for wealth distribution, inequality and financial stability.

Another fear that invariably lurks in any central bank is that it may have eased a little too much for too long. The Fed was always aware of the risks of holding a greatly enlarged balance sheet. It also knew that with so much liquidity sloshing around, it would have to tighten just in time – in order to avoid inflation significantly overshooting its 2 per cent target – in case there was a sudden rise in the velocity of money. Such a thing could happen if, for instance, the job market was to suddenly become tight enough to result in a wage-price spiral, wherein rising wages increase prices through increased spending; and this, in turn, leads to a demand for greater wages, greater spending and still higher prices.

NORMALIZATION?

By late 2015, headline (that is, U-3) unemployment fell to around the 5 per cent mark.[96] That was when the Fed decided to slowly start raising short-term interest rates in December that year, in a process called 'lift-off'. It was justified by the Fed in the following way:

> The Committee judges that there has been considerable improvement in labor market conditions this year, and it is reasonably confident that inflation will rise, over the medium term, to its 2 percent objective. Given the economic outlook, and recognizing the time it takes for policy actions to affect future economic outcomes, the Committee decided to raise the target range for the federal funds rate to ¼ to ½ percent. The stance of monetary policy remains accommodative after this increase, thereby supporting further improvement in labor market conditions and a return to 2 percent inflation.[97]

Opponents of the lift-off did not miss the fact that it was being justified on the basis of an improvement in the headline unemployment rate, which, as we have seen earlier, doesn't fully reflect the true conditions prevailing in the labour market. For them, the US economy was still not strong enough for even a minor drawdown in monetary easing. But the Fed also had an eye on asset prices, which were much higher than what average valuations would suggest. Some members of the Reserve even overtly alluded to this while responding to criticisms of the lift-off. At the same time, however, the Fed was not yet moving to 'normalize' the size

---

[96] 'The Employment Situation – November 2015.' *US Bureau of Labor Statistics*, 4 December 2015, https://www.bls.gov/news.release/archives/empsit_12042015.pdf.

[97] 'Federal Reserve issues FOMC statement.' *Board of Governors of the Federal Reserve System*, 16 December 2015, https://www.federalreserve.gov/newsevents/pressreleases/monetary20151216a.htm.

and nature of its balance sheet, and the declaration of the lift-off was accompanied by the following statement:

> The Committee is maintaining its existing policy of reinvesting principal payments from its holdings of agency debt and agency mortgage-backed securities and of rolling over maturing Treasury securities at auction, and it anticipates doing so until normalization of the level of the federal funds rate is well under way. This policy, by keeping the Committee's holdings of longer-term securities at sizable levels, should help maintain accommodative financial conditions.[98]

In any case, the Fed could not normalize its balance sheet through a QE 'exit' before the EFFR reached an appreciably higher level than it was right after the lift-off. The reason for this was simple. The three QE rounds taken together had poured in the same level of liquidity into the US economy as would have happened if the EFFR had been cut by 600 basis points, or 6 per cent.[99] Before exiting QE by a certain quantum, the Fed would have had to first raise the EFFR to a sufficiently high level, so that it could be cut by enough basis points before hitting the ZLB again – in the event that a QE exit led to deflationary pressures emerging in the economy.

With or without an abnormally large balance sheet, the Fed would not have liked to stay anywhere near the ZLB for longer than it absolutely needed to. Prior experience had shown that any major recession typically required the Fed to cut the EFFR by 530 basis points in order to provide sufficient monetary easing to shore up demand. Unfortunately for the Reserve, there was no possibility of it being able to raise the EFFR to that level any time in the future. To understand why this was the case, we must turn to the concept of neutral (also

---

98 Ibid.

99 One basis point is the same as 0.01 per cent (1/100th of 1 per cent) or 0.0001 in decimal form.

called 'natural') interest rates. A neutral interest rate, usually expressed in 'real' terms, that is, net of inflation, is one that is supposed to simultaneously keep the economy at maximum employment and at stable inflation.[100] Thus, the neutral rate is neither expansionary nor contractionary. By 2016, the real neutral rate of interest of concern to the Fed, which is the rate at which maximum sustainable employment and the 2 per cent inflation target are both simultaneously met, was likely hovering at around 1 per cent. For a target inflation rate of 2 per cent, the nominal neutral interest rate would have therefore been 3 per cent, given that the real neutral interest rate was 1 per cent. This is why publications from the Fed during the period 2015–17 talked about ultimately raising the EFFR to a 'normal level' of 3 per cent – given a 2 per cent inflation target.[101] If the EFFR increased above 3 per cent when inflation was at 2 per cent, it would mean monetary tightening, while anything below it would mean that the stance continued to be accommodative. So, 3 per cent was the maximum level to which the Fed could theoretically raise the EFFR, given its dual mandate. In practice, raising the EFFR to even 3 per cent was fairly difficult, given that inflation was persistently 'undershooting' (that is, staying below) the 2 per cent mark most of the time.

Prior to the GFC, the real neutral interest rate had been estimated to be under 3 per cent, which translates to a nominal neutral interest rate of under 5 per cent, with a 2 per cent inflation target.[102] The drop in the neutral interest

---

[100] Wessel, Michael. 'The Hutchins Center Explains: The Neutral Rate of Interest.' *Brookings*, 22 October 2018, https://www.brookings.edu/blog/up-front/2018/10/22/the-hutchins-center-explains-the-neutral-rate-of-interest/.

[101] Kaplan, Robert S. 'The Neutral Rate of Interest.' *Dallas Fed*, 24 October 2018, https://www.dallasfed.org/news/speeches/kaplan/2018/rsk181024.aspx.

[102] Roberts, John M. 'An Estimate of the Long-Term Neutral Rate of Interest.' *Feds Notes*, 5 September 2018, https://www.federalreserve.gov/

rate essentially tracked a drop in the potential growth rate of the US economy, which has consistently been projected by the Fed to be below 2.7 per cent since 2009. As an aside, the potential growth rate is the maximum rate at which an economy can grow sustainably without leading to major inflationary pressures. Factors such as adverse demographics and low-productivity growth reduce the potential growth rate of an economy, and thereby the real neutral interest rate. The US might be in the throes of both.

With the potential growth rate itself being so low, the possibility of the US economy falling into recession was also higher than before, since even a moderate external shock or a policy mistake could push GDP growth into negative territory. With headline unemployment fluctuating around the 5 per cent mark for most of 2016, it is not surprising that the Fed kept the target range for the EFFR at levels around those of December 2015 until 14 December 2016, and raised it by only 25 basis points after an FOMC meeting on that date.[103]

The increased probability of the US facing a recession meant that the probability of having to drop the EFFR to ZLB/ELB levels had also risen. As it happens, a 2017 study by economists with the Fed found that in the years ahead, the EFFR would be bound (that is, constrained) by the ZLB about 40 per cent of the time and would have to be kept there for at least two and a half years on average.[104] This estimate

---

econres/notes/feds-notes/estimate-of-the-long-term-neutral-rate-of-interest-20180905.htm.

[103] Cox, Jeff. 'Fed Raises Rates for the Second Time in a Decade.' *CNBC*, 14 December 2016, https://www.cnbc.com/2016/12/14/fed-raises-rates-for-the-second-time-in-a-decade.html.

[104] Kiley, Michael T., and John M. Roberts. 'Monetary Policy in a Low Interest Rate World.' Brookings Papers on Economic Activity, 23 March 2017, pp. 317-397, https://www.brookings.edu/wp-content/uploads/2017/08/kileytextsp17bpea.pdf

was based on the assumption that the nominal neutral rate of interest was 3 per cent.

Obviously, if the Fed found itself constrained by the ZLB this often, it would have to take recourse to unconventional monetary policy more often than not. And the main unconventional tool in its arsenal was QE. But this brought in its wake various risks, as delineated above. Moreover, QE was also subject to diminishing returns beyond a point. The usefulness of the tool when monetary policy was constrained by the ZLB, juxtaposed with the risks of a large balance sheet, meant that the best course of action for the Fed was to 'exit' QE when it could. And this would be in anticipation of having to use it again if and when the next crisis took place. As Patrick T. Harker, president of the Federal Reserve Bank of Philadelphia, explained in a May 2017 speech:

> Another factor of the 'why' is that we want our unconventional tools to be at their most effective. As productivity has dropped, it's taken the neutral funds rate with it, which means the zero lower bound is closer and we have less room for maneuver. That constricts the efficacy of using the fed funds rate. And if something were to happen, if another crisis were to occur, further asset purchases may prove less effective, or perhaps even more difficult to execute, with a large balance sheet still in place.[105]

Through the first half of 2017, headline unemployment showed a downward trend and touched 4.3 per cent, which was considered the 'full employment' mark, by May 2017.[106]

---

[105] Harker, Patrick T. 'Economic Outlook: The Labor Market, Rates, and the Balance Sheet.' *Market News International Connect Roundtable*, New York, 23 May 2017, https://www.philadelphiafed.org/publications/speeches/harker/2017/05-23-17-economic-outlook-the-labor-market-rates-and-the-balance-sheet.

[106] 'The Employment Situation – May 2017.' US Bureau of Labor Standards, 2 June 2017, https://www.bls.gov/news.release/archives/empsit_06022017.pdf.

Citing a strengthening job market, the Fed went about raising the EFFR target range in June 2017, thereby laying the ground for balance sheet reductions, something that is euphemistically called quantitative tightening (QT). The Fed was well aware that QT could cause volatility in secondary capital markets – given that, for years, bullish positions had been built up using the Fed's ultra-accommodative stance. And this is why, despite the calls for the process to proceed stealthily, the Fed made it a point to 'communicate' its intentions and mode of QT implementation in July that year, even though it was to begin in October 2017. Instead of an outright sale of assets it had purchased under QE, the Fed decided to execute QT via a process called 'roll-off', in which it would simply stop reinvesting in matured securities.[107]

The roll-off started at a time when the Trump administration was putting final touches on a major tax cut, which would provide the US economy with a massive, sugary high in 2018. In November 2017, the US Congress would pass the Tax Cuts and Jobs Act (TCJA), which was intended to boost investment and consumption, albeit at the cost of increasing the government's debt by another $1.9 trillion over the next 10 years.[108] Be that as it may, with the TCJA kicking in, the US economy would start registering quarterly growth rates in 2018 that were twice as high as potential growth.

With headline unemployment declining further and stock markets buoyant on the back of tax-cut-fuelled share buybacks, the Fed took the opportunity to raise the EFFR target range on a quarterly basis during 2018. QT proceeded

[107] The FOMC's statement on 14 July 2017 indicated that it intended to gradually reduce the Federal Reserve's security holdings by decreasing the investment of the principal payments it received from securities held in the System Open Market Account.

[108] Gale, William G. 'A Fixable Mistake: The Tax Cuts and Jobs Act.' *Brookings*, 25 September 2019, https://www.brookings.edu/blog/up-front/2019/09/25/a-fixable-mistake-the-tax-cuts-and-jobs-act/.

apace as well, alongside an increase in the EFFR, with the monthly roll-off target being raised by $10 billion for every successive quarter. Even with the target range for the EFFR having been raised to 2.25–2.50 per cent by 27 September 2018, the Fed's incumbent chairman, Jerome H. Powell, in October 2018 stated that there was still 'a long way' to go before it reached a 'neutral' level.[109] This comment, along with the fact that the Reserve had projected three rate hikes for the year 2019 during the last FOMC meeting, led to a major correction in US markets, worried as they were that the hikes would end up being contractionary. In a sign of just how much of a tightrope walk monetary policy has become during the era of secular stagnation, while delivering a speech on 28 November 2018, just a month later, Powell would change his stand and say that the EFFR was 'just below' neutral.[110] Given that the EFFR at the time of the speech was 2.20 per cent and PCE core inflation was 1.90 per cent, it meant that the Fed perceived the real neutral rate of interest to be well below 1 per cent by then.

Nevertheless, the FOMC would raise the EFFR target range by another 25 basis points on 20 December 2018, a move that reportedly made Trump 'irate'.[111] The President

---

[109] Cox, Jeff. 'Powell Says We're "a Long Way" from Neutral on Interest Rates, Indicating More Hikes Are Coming.' *CNBC*, 29 November 2018, https://www.cnbc.com/2018/10/03/powell-says-were-a-long-way-from-neutral-on-interest-rates.html.

[110] Condon, Christopher. 'Powell's "Just Below" Comment Seen as Suggesting Fewer Hikes.' *Bloomberg*, 28 November 2010, https://www.bloomberg.com/news/articles/2018-11-28/powell-sees-solid-economic-outlook-as-rates-just-below-neutral.

[111] Trump apparently told US Treasury Secretary Steven Mnuchin, 'I totally disagree with Fed policy. I think the increasing of interest rates and the shrinking of the Fed portfolio is an absolute terrible thing to do at this time especially in light of my major trade negotiations which are ongoing, but I never suggested firing Chairman Jay Powell, nor do I believe I have the right to do so.' (*Source:* David, Javier E. 'Mnuchin Says Trump Never Suggested Firing Fed Chairman Powell Despite "Absolute

had been firmly opposed to the Fed's EFFR target range hikes and QT, since those moves were increasing the cost of government borrowing at a time when his administration was widening the fiscal deficit with tax cuts and enhanced spending. He had also been publicly critical of Powell, his own nominee to the chairmanship of the Fed, and had even remarked that the latter 'almost looks like he's happy raising interest rates'.[112] US stock markets had finally begun to price in QT, which was also contributing to increasing the yield on treasury securities at a time when federal debt was expanding due to Trump's tax cuts. It wasn't very surprising then that the President was becoming even more vociferous against the Fed's normalization.

This state of affairs was a reason why the Fed's 20 December 2018 hike was also seen as an attempt to assert its independence from the treasury.[113] However, the Fed was not oblivious to changing sentiments, and the FOMC, after a meeting on 28 December 2018, pared down the projected number of rate hikes in 2019 from three to two, with recessionary fears growing amidst Trump's tariff war with China.

On the other hand, calls continued for the Fed to keep taking the EFFR up to a neutral level.[114] Indeed,

---

Terrible" Policy.' *Cnbc News*, 23 December 2018, https://www.cnbcnews.com/Business/Markets/Mnuchin-Says-Trump-Never-Suggested-Firing-Fed-Chairman-Powell-Despite-N951411.)

[112] Kemp, Ted. 'Trump Directly Attacks Fed Chairman Powell, Saying "Obama Had Zero" Interest Rates.' *CNBC*, 24 October 2018, https://www.cnbc.com/2018/10/24/interest-rates-trump-attacks-fed-chairman-powell-wsj-reports.html.

[113] Belvedere, Matt. 'Cramer: Fed Chief Jerome Powell Is Trump's Worst Re-Election Nightmare.' *CNBC*, 20 December 2018, https://www.cnbc.com/2018/12/20/cramer-fed-chief-jerome-powell-is-trumps-worst-re-election-nightmare.html.

[114] Cox, Jeff. 'Goldman Sachs: The Economy Needs to Slow Down to Avoid a "Dangerous Overheating."' *CNBC*, 5 November 2018, https://www.cnbc.com/2018/11/05/goldman-economy-needs-to-slow-down-to-avoid-a-dangerous-overheating.html.

some had even seen the US economy overheating during 2018 – since growth was running at twice its potential rate and Consumer Price Index or CPI-measured inflation had been rising, although core inflation had been undershooting the 2 per cent target for most months. But as Powell had observed in August 2018:

> The FOMC has been navigating between the shoals of overheating and premature tightening with only a hazy view of what seem to be shifting navigational guides.[115]

And those navigational guides had clearly begun to shift, with recessionary fears beginning to crystallize by early 2019. Factory output fell in February 2019, along with the news of a corporate earnings recession for the first time in two years. Worse, by the beginning of March 2019, the yield curve for securities underwent a near inversion, in that interest rates on short-term securities exceeded those on long-term securities. This caused considerable consternation in financial circles since an inverted yield curve is considered a strong indicator of an impending recession.[116]

Be that as it may, on 20 March 2019, the FOMC in a 'unanimous' decision decided to put off interest rate hikes for 2019, while keeping the target range for the EFFR unchanged, that is, 2.25–2.50 per cent. Most notably, it would also announce an end to QT by September 2019 – a decision that would send 10-year treasury yields to their lowest levels in the past 12 months. This move was a remarkable change from what was being projected just a few months ago, and

---

[115] Powell, Jerome. 'Monetary Policy in a Changing Economy.' Speech delivered at *Changing Market Structure and Implications for Monetary Policy*, a symposium sponsored by the Federal Reserve Bank of Kansas City, Jackson Hole, Wyoming, 24 August 2018, https://www.federalreserve.gov/newsevents/speech/powell20180824a.htm.

[116] Brettell, Karen. 'Countdown to Recession: What an Inverted Yield Curve Means.' *Reuters*, 28 January 2020, www.reuters.com/article/us-usa-economy-yieldcurve-explainer-idUSKBN1ZR2EX.

served to underscore the delicate dance that the management of secular stagnation had become for the Fed. Interestingly, this decision came on the back of the Fed warning about US corporate debt loads in its Financial Stability Report released in early May 2019, and the vulnerabilities and risks that posed for the overall financial sector.[117]

Subsequently, members of the Fed sought to downplay recessionary fears and the former Fed chairperson Janet Yellen publicly commented that not only did she not foresee a recession in 2019, but also that she saw no reason for the Fed to cut rates that year.[118] Of course, Yellen's forecast did not turn out to be quite correct, as we shall see.

First-quarter US GDP growth in 2019 was at 3.2 per cent, and this too served to 'cool' recessionary concerns. However, a closer look revealed that most of this growth had been due to a pile-up in inventories. Consumption, which was the main driver of the economy, had turned up weak numbers. Overall, the Fed's assessment was that growth for the year would be around the potential growth rate, that is, 2 per cent. This was an ill portent for Trump, who had promised that in his regime the annual GDP growth rate would be 3 per cent – instead of Obama's 2 per cent.[119] The only year that promise had been nearly met thus far was 2018, in large part due to the tax cut. But that move had also worsened the US's federal debt dynamics, and it wasn't surprising that

---

[117] 'Financial Stability Report.' *Board of Governors of the Federal Reserve System*, May 2019, https://www.federalreserve.gov/publications/files/financial-stability-report-201905.pdf.

[118] Mckee, Michael. 'Yellen Sees No U.S. Recession, Says Fed Won't Cut in 2019.' *Bloomberg*, 29 March 2019, https://www.bloomberg.com/news/articles/2019-03-29/yellen-sees-no-u-s-recession-says-fed-won-t-cut-rates-in-2019.

[119] Harwood, John. 'Trump and GOP Promised Economic Growth Much Better than Obama's. That's Not What Happened.' *CNBC*, 28 February 2019, https://www.cnbc.com/2019/02/28/trumps-economic-policies-failed-to-deliver-promised-3percent-growth-in-2018.html.

by the end of April 2019, Trump was adamantly calling not only for lowering the EFFR but also for a renewal of QE itself. This further served to underline that QE was now being seen by the American government as a major fiscal management device and not merely as a counter-cyclical monetary tool. This, in turn, meant that the whole issue of the Fed's independence was now front and centre.

The Fed, however, initially held its ground in the 1 May 2019 FOMC meeting, which kept the EFFR target range unchanged and reiterated the QT exit schedule. Although core inflation continued to undershoot the 2 per cent target, the Fed believed that it would rise with a lag due to the rising oil prices. This, along with low headline unemployment numbers, was cited to justify the no-cut stance.

But given that Trump's tariffs were beginning to have an impact on US consumption by pushing up the price of imported goods, the Reserve was still under pressure to cut rates. The moment of truth came at the end of July 2019, with the Fed announcing its first EFFR cut since the GFR, belying Yellen's forecast. But if people thought that this was it, they were mistaken.

In September 2019, the US Repurchase Agreement (repo) market – which is a key short-term credit market – faced a major liquidity crisis with borrowing rates registering a sudden jump to 5.25 per cent from 2.43 per cent.[120] Repo essentially means short-term borrowing in lieu of government securities with the promise to repurchase the same within a limited time frame at a certain premium. This premium drives the interest rate at which the loan is advanced. The Fed's QT, coupled with Trump's heightened spending, had created a situation wherein this market had many more

[120] Anbil, Sriya, et al. 'What Happened in Money Markets in September 2019?' *Board of Governors of the Federal Reserve System*, 27 February 2020, www.federalreserve.gov/econres/notes/feds-notes/what-happened-in-money-markets-in-september-2019-20200227.htm.

sellers of government securities than buyers, which led to the spike in interest rates. As a result, in October 2019, the Fed had to intervene by committing to purchase treasury securities to the tune of $60 billion a month to prevent this key market from becoming frozen, thereby putting paid to the roll-off for good.[121] Two more EFFR cuts followed in the remainder of 2019, bringing it down to the same level as it was in 2015 – before QT began. The exit had clearly failed. And that was even before the COVID-19 shock happened.

FOR BETTER OR FOR WORSE

The COVID-19 crisis saw the Fed open the veritable floodgates of liquidity. Apart from taking the EFFR down by 150 basis points to the ZLB in March 2020, it instituted a number of emergency lending facilities to the tune of some $2.3 trillion as a means for sustaining the flow of credit to businesses, local and state governments, households and various short-term credit markets (most notably, the repo market) which were at risk of seizing up. The Fed also started undertaking open-ended purchases of government bonds and asset-backed securities to ensure the smooth functioning of debt markets as well. All of these steps were of course right out of its post-GFC playbook.

However, since March 2020, the Fed has gone above and beyond what it did in 2008 by venturing into the purchase of privately issued securities, such as corporate bonds (including those that have junk ratings) in both primary (that is, directly from issuing companies) and secondary markets, as well as commercial paper.[122] In another unprecedented step, the Fed

---

[121] Marte, Jonnelle. 'Fed Launches Treasury Bill Buys in Bid for "Ample" Reserves.' *Reuters*, 2 October 2019, https://www.reuters.com/article/uk-usa-fed-bonds/fed-launches-treasury-bill-buys-in-bid-for-ample-reserves-idINKBN1WQ2TG?edition-redirect=in.

[122] Cheng, Jeffrey, et al. 'What's the Fed Doing in Response to the

has also advanced direct loans to mid-sized businesses and even non-profit organizations.[123] Essentially, it is now backstopping almost all kinds of credit extended in the US economy.

Now, a key learning from the historical use of such policies in both the US and Japan has been that they need to be deployed quickly during a crisis to ensure that various financial markets do not become completely illiquid. And, as we have seen earlier, in as much as preventing a financial collapse is concerned, such tools have been found to be quite useful. Hence, their prompt and confident use by the Fed to mitigate the immediate impact of the pandemic on the flow of credit in the American economy. The extensive lending has also given it a chance to address concerns about whether it was 'running out of bullets', in terms of being able to provide liquidity beyond taking down the policy rate to zero and buying government or quasi-government bonds. While answering a question about whether the Reserve had enough 'firepower' left to deal with the crisis, Powell, on a CBS show in May 2020, had this to say:

> Well, there's a lot more we can do. We've done what we can as we go. But I will say that we're not out of ammunition by a long shot. No, there's really no limit to what we can do with these lending programs that we have. So, there's a lot more we can do to support the economy, and we're committed to doing everything we can as long as we need to.[124]

Though there may be no theoretical limit to these lending programmes, the continuous enhancement of such a posture would mean that the Fed was taking even greater risk on to its balance sheet, for which the taxpayer would ultimately

---

COVID-19 Crisis? What More Could It Do?' *Brookings*, 3 June 2021, https://www.brookings.edu/research/fed-response-to-covid19.

[123] Ibid.

[124] Powell, Jerome. *60 Minutes*. Interview by Scott Pelley. *CBS*, May 2020, https://www.cbsnews.com/video/jerome-powell-federal-reserve-economic-crisis-coronavirus-pandemic-60-minutes/.

be liable. Indeed, despite these loans being advanced against supposedly good collateral, there is a possibility of the Fed facing substantial losses on account of the sheer quantum of the credit it is advancing in the wake of the pandemic. While it is true that the Fed's emergency liquidity facilities instituted during the GFC ultimately yielded a positive net income without any defaults, that experience cannot be a source of comfort now. This is because the pandemic-induced shock to the US economy is different from the GFC. While the latter had been a case of overborrowing by the financial sector spilling over into the real economy, the COVID-19 shock is the opposite. Back in 2008, once markets were becalmed via the Fed's injection of liquidity, creditworthy borrowers soon found themselves back in the reckoning for standard market-based credit and the Fed's liquidity provisioning could be wound down. In the post-pandemic scenario, the question is more of whether the supposedly solvent businesses that have been advanced emergency loans will continue to be solvent tomorrow. There is an inevitable balance sheet deterioration that is taking place due to the loss of economic activity on account of lockdowns, which are contingent on the state of the pandemic. Powell had himself outlined the issues at stake in a speech in April 2020:

> Many of the programs we are undertaking to support the flow of credit rely on emergency lending powers that are available only in very unusual circumstances – such as those we find ourselves in today – and only with the consent of the Secretary of the Treasury. We are deploying these lending powers to an unprecedented extent, enabled in large part by the financial backing from Congress and the Treasury. We will continue to use these powers forcefully, proactively, and aggressively until we are confident that we are solidly on the road to recovery. I would stress that these are lending powers, not spending powers. The Fed is not authorized to grant money to particular beneficiaries. The Fed can only make secured loans to solvent entities with the expectation

> that the loans will be fully repaid. In the situation we face today, many borrowers will benefit from these programs, as will the overall economy. But there will also be entities of various kinds that need direct fiscal support rather than a loan they would struggle to repay.[125]

When the first lockdowns were instituted in 2020, the number of such entities requiring direct fiscal support was immense. The sudden shutdowns had halted most economic activity, resulting in 22 million Americans being unemployed in the blink of an eye with thousands of heavily indebted firms teetering on the precipice of bankruptcy. The COVID-19 shock was so impactful that the U-3 unemployment rate hit 14.3 per cent in April 2020 (U-6 was a staggering 22.1 per cent for that month), surpassing the previous high of 12 per cent recorded at the height of the Great Depression in the 1930s. So, while the Fed has done what it can in terms of keeping the flow of liquidity going and preventing what it sees as solvent firms from collapsing because of illiquidity, it is the US government which has had to provide direct fiscal support to citizens such as Josiah Charles and firms that are in no position to avail of any further credit. Even the lending by the Fed has had to be guaranteed by the treasury, as Powell mentioned in April 2020, in the form of upfront equity investments and overall guarantees in the event of default.

All this has meant that the US government has been spending at a hitherto unheard-of rate even by its own standards. For instance, America's budget deficit in June 2020 was $863 billion as compared to just $8 billion for the same period in 2019. The Congressional Budget Office (CBO) estimates that the federal budget deficit was $2.7 trillion in

---

[125] Powell, Jerome. 'COVID-19 and the Economy.' Speech delivered at the Hutchins Center on Fiscal and Monetary Policy, Brookings Institution, Washington, DC, 9 April 2020, https://www.federalreserve.gov/newsevents/speech/powell20200409a.htm.

the first nine months of 2020, some $2 trillion more than the deficit recorded during the same period the previous year.[126] Naturally, the kind of borrowing needed to support this level of deficit spending would not have been possible without the Fed removing the sudden and massive oversupply of treasury securities from the market, as explained by John C. Williams, president and CEO of the Federal Reserve Bank of New York, during a speech in July 2020:

> As uncertainty about the coronavirus took hold; we saw disruptions in short-term funding markets. Markets for Treasury securities and agency mortgage-backed securities, which are normally highly liquid and form the bedrock of our financial system, nearly buckled under the strain of massive flows of funds in response to the pandemic.[127]

To prevent that buckling, the Fed began open-ended purchases of treasury securities and asset-backed securities in March 2020, tapered its purchases of the same in April and May 2020, before turning around to announce on 10 June 2020 that it would buy at least $80 billion of treasury securities per month along with $40 billion in residential and commercial MBS on the same periodic basis until further notice. As a result, its balance sheet had swelled to $7 trillion by August 2020, nearly 60 per cent more than the previous peak – attained prior to the roll-off in May 2015.

Importantly, in a speech in May 2020, Powell acknowledged that 'while the primary purpose of these open market operations is to preserve smooth market functioning

---

[126] United States Congressional Budget Office. 'Monthly Budget Review for June 2020.' *CBO*, 8 July 2020, https://www.cbo.gov/system/files/2020-07/56458-CBO-MBR.pdf.

[127] Williams, John C. 'Rising to the Challenge: Central Banking, Financial Markets, and the Pandemic.' Remarks at the 16th Meeting of the Financial Research Advisory Committee for the Treasury's Office of Financial Research, Federal Reserve Bank of New York, https://www.newyorkfed.org/newsevents/speeches/2020/wil200716.

and effective policy transmission, the purchases will also foster more accommodative financial conditions'.[128] Obviously, any US government going forward is going to hope that those accommodative financial conditions continue for a long time to come. Especially since more stimulus measures beyond CARES have had to be sanctioned, both by the erstwhile Trump administration in 2020 and the Biden presidency that succeeded it in January 2021.[129] Indeed, President Joe Biden's most important new legislative measure till date has been the 'American Rescue Plan' that he signed into law on 11 March 2021, which is a fresh stimulus package estimated to cost $1.844 trillion and includes $1,400 direct stimulus payments to eligible individuals.[130] As observed earlier, Washington's various COVID-19 shock mitigation measures had sent the US debt-to-GDP ratio to over 127 per cent by mid-2021, while the Fed had a balance sheet size of around $8.26 trillion as of August 2021.

The US economy grew by around 7 per cent in 2021 after suffering a contraction of 2.3 per cent in 2020.[131] Economic recovery from the pandemic shock began by the third quarter of 2020 itself, and a vaccination-boosted reopening subsequent to a terrible second wave allowed citizens to give vent to pent-up demand in 2021. As the shift towards demand for goods in lieu of services met pandemic-induced production bottlenecks and supply constraints there was a notable uptick in both inflation and inflationary

---

[128] Powell, Jerome. 'Coronavirus and CARES Act.' Testimony before the Committee on Banking, Housing, and Urban Affairs, US Senate, Washington, DC, 19 May 2020, https://www.bis.org/review/r200519a.htm.

[129] 'Policy Responses to COVID-19.' *IMF*, 2 July 2021, https://www.imf.org/en/Topics/imf-and-covid19/Policy-Responses-to-COVID-19#V. Accessed 18 August 2021.

[130] Ibid.

[131] 'June 16, 2021: FOMC Projections Materials, Accessible Version.' *Board of Governors of the Federal Reserve System*, 16 June 2021, https://www.federalreserve.gov/monetarypolicy/fomcprojtabl20210616.htm.

expectations during the course of 2021. This in turn sparked debate among mainstream economists as to whether Biden's stimulus, which probably boosted demand far beyond US potential output, would lead to a major inflationary episode on account of inflationary expectations getting unhinged. Concomitantly, there were concerns as to whether the Fed was in a position to continue its accommodative stance or not. Till mid-2021 the Fed stood its ground and its Monetary Policy Report for July 2021 observed that:

> Overall, an important part of the rise in inflation this spring appears to be due to a surge in demand, including the rebound in travel-related spending, running up against short-run production bottlenecks and hiring difficulties. As these extraordinary circumstances pass, supply and demand should become better aligned, and inflation is widely expected to move down toward the FOMC's 2 percent longer-run goal.[132]

The report also maintained that inflationary expectations would not be a dealbreaker either:

> In monitoring the inflation outlook, the FOMC considers a variety of financial and economic data in order to gauge whether inflation expectations are consistent with meeting its inflation objective. Recent readings on these measures indicate that inflation is expected to return to levels consistent with the Committee's 2 percent longer-run inflation objective after a period of temporarily higher inflation.[133]

As such, the FOMC decided in its 28 July 2021 meeting to keep the EFFR at ZLB levels and to continue purchases of government debt securities:

---

[132] 'Monetary Policy Report.' *Board of Governors of the Federal Reserve System*, July 2021.

[133] Ibid.

> The Committee expects to maintain an accommodative stance of monetary policy until these outcomes are achieved. The Committee decided to keep the target range for the federal funds rate at 0 to 1/4 percent and expects it will be appropriate to maintain this target range until labor market conditions have reached levels consistent with the Committee's assessments of maximum employment and inflation has risen to 2 percent and is on track to moderately exceed 2 percent for some time. Last December, the Committee indicated that it would continue to increase its holdings of Treasury securities by at least $80 billion per month and of agency mortgage-backed securities by at least $40 billion per month until substantial further progress has been made toward its maximum employment and price stability goals. Since then, the economy has made progress toward these goals, and the Committee will continue to assess progress in coming meetings. These asset purchases help foster smooth market functioning and accommodative financial conditions, thereby supporting the flow of credit to households and businesses.[134]

However, towards the end of 2021 the mood at the Fed had changed in the opposite direction. Inflation proved to be less transitory and more broad-based than earlier believed and in late November 2021 Powell himself told US lawmakers that it was time to retire the word 'transitory' to describe extant inflation.[135] And in December 2021, the FOMC decided to increase the pace at which it would taper asset purchases from what it had announced a month earlier, thereby bringing them to an end by early March 2022.[136] With US CPI

---

[134] 'FOMC Statement.' *Board of Governors of the Federal Reserve System*, 28 July 2021, https://www.federalreserve.gov/newsevents/pressreleases/monetary20210728a.htm.

[135] Cox, Jeff. 'Powell Says Fed Will Discuss Speeding up Bond-buying Taper at December Meeting.' *CNBC*, 30 November 2021, https://www.cnbc.com/2021/11/30/powell-says-fed-will-discuss-speeding-up-bond-buying-taper-at-december-meeting.html.

[136] 'Transcript of Chair Powell's Press Conference.' *Board of Governors of the*

clocking 7.5 per cent in January 2022 (as per data released in February 2022), its highest-ever level in forty years, the Fed seemed ready to begin a series of interest rate hikes through the course of 2022.[137] In fact, the impending rate hikes had been clearly indicated in the FOMC's statement subsequent to its 26 January 2022 meeting itself:

> The Committee seeks to achieve maximum employment and inflation at the rate of 2 percent over the longer run. In support of these goals, the Committee decided to keep the target range for the federal funds rate at 0 to 1/4 percent. With inflation well above 2 percent and a strong labor market, the Committee expects it will soon be appropriate to raise the target range for the federal funds rate. The Committee decided to continue to reduce the monthly pace of its net asset purchases, bringing them to an end in early March. Beginning in February, the Committee will increase its holdings of Treasury securities by at least $20 billion per month and of agency mortgage-backed securities by at least $10 billion per month. The Federal Reserve's ongoing purchases and holdings of securities will continue to foster smooth market functioning and accommodative financial conditions, thereby supporting the flow of credit to households and businesses.

The strong labour market alluded to here was based not just on the headline unemployment rate (that is, U-3) which stood at 3.9 per cent in December 2021, but also the fact that job openings were at a record high and far exceeded the number of job applicants at the time.[138] The US economy was also growing at a rate far higher than its potential

---

Federal Reserve System, 26 January 2022, https://www.federalreserve.gov/mediacenter/files/FOMCpresconf20220126.pdf.

[137] Mutikani, Lucia. 'U.S. Consumer Prices Post Largest Annual Gain in 40 Years as Inflation Becomes Widespread.' *Reuters*, 10 February 2022, www.reuters.com/business/us-consumer-prices-rise-strongly-january-weekly-jobless-claims-fall-2022-02-10/.

[138] 'Transcript of Chair Powell's Press Conference.'

growth rate, which was estimated to be around 2 per cent.[139] Accordingly, the picture painted by Powell during the press conference that followed the January FOMC meeting was of an economy that was 'very different' from the one that existed when the last lift-off was begun in 2015:

> [W]e know that the economy is in a very different place than it was when we began raising rates in 2015. Specifically, the economy is now much stronger. The labor market is far stronger. Inflation is running well above our 2 percent target, much higher than it was at that time. And these differences are likely to have important implications for the appropriate pace of policy adjustments.[140]

This to Powell's mind was justification for 2022 'to be a year in which we move steadily away from the very highly accommodative monetary policy that we put in place to deal with the – with the economic effects of the pandemic'.[141] The sequence for normalization was of course the same as the last time, first there was a tapering, which had been underway since December 2021, to be followed by the lift-off, and then a shrinking of the balance sheet via the run-off method, perhaps towards the end of 2022. Now, according to a Goldman Sachs prognostication, the number of such interest rate increases by the Fed in the course of 2022 could be as high as seven.[142] And given the sanctions regime being put on Russia as a result of its invasion of Ukraine that began in late February 2022, inflationary pressures transmitted via heightened energy and food prices may get exacerbated for a while.

---

[139] Ibid.

[140] Ibid.

[141] Ibid.

[142] Curran, Enda. 'Goldman Sees Fed Hiking Seven Times in 2022 instead of Five.' *Bloomberg*, 11 February 2022, www.bloomberg.com/news/articles/2022-02-11/goldman-sachs-now-predicts-fed-to-hike-seven-times-in-2022?cmpid=BBD021122_CAS&utm_medium=email&utm_source=newsletter&utm_term=220211&utm_campaign=closeasia.

Be that as it may, it is unclear as to how far the Fed would be able to take its lift-off (that is, interest rate hikes) before exceeding the neutral rate of interest for the economy and possibly pushing it towards a recession, howsoever mild. Bond markets for one certainly seemed to indicate that it wouldn't be very far given that the treasury yield curve was the 'flattest' it had ever been prior to a rate hike cycle and some analysts were projecting that the yield curve would invert by late 2022 itself.[143, 144] As has been mentioned before, an inverted yield curve is considered a strong indicator of an expected recession. Which means that bond markets do not believe that the Fed would be able to fight off inflation without causing a growth collapse.[145] Clearly, markets had a less rosy perspective of the US economy than Powell's comments would suggest. Indeed, the supposedly 'tight' situation in the US labour market that is being projected by the Fed in early 2022 could well change as millions of American workers who had left the workforce due to pandemic-related reasons return and immigration to America resumes in full force. America's labour force participation rate as acknowledged by the Fed was below February 2020 levels as of January 2022.[146] Illness, quarantine and caregiving had removed millions of

---

143 McCormick, Liz, and Michael Mackenzie. 'The Bond Market Is Sending a Worrying Message about the Economy.' *Bloomberg*, 17 February 2022, www.bloomberg.com/news/articles/2022-02-17/the-bond-market-is-sending-a-worrying-message-about-inflation-fed-and-economy.

144 McCormick, Liz. 'Fed Tightening May Usher in Yield Curve Inversion Late This Year, BofA Says.' *Bloomberg*, 22 February 2022, www.bloomberg.com/news/articles/2022-02-22/fed-tightening-may-usher-in-yield-curve-inversion-late-this-year.

145 McCormick, Liz, and Matthew Boesler. 'Fed Hikes Seen Starting with Yield Curve Flattest in Generation.' *Bloomberg*, 11 December 2021, www.bloomberg.com/news/articles/2021-12-11/fed-hikes-seen-starting-with-yield-curve-flattest-in-generation?cmpid=BBD121221_OAS&utm_medium=email&utm_source=newsletter&utm_term=211212&utm_campaign=openasia.

146 'Transcript of Chair Powell's Press Conference.'

individuals, especially women, from the workforce. But as the populace adopts to the new normal, a majority of such individuals are expected to return. A significant chunk of premature retirees may also rejoin. The 'great resignation' that was partly made possible due to rising asset prices will also recede with monetary tightening and its dampening effect on capital markets. Moreover, inflation was putting paid to the 'wait and watch' attitude of those who were looking for a better deal in the job market, banking as they were on the savings accrued due to the stimulus cheques. It is rather difficult to see a wage price spiral taking place in the US economy in the years ahead.

As Powell himself acknowledged in January, the growth stimulus from the US government was set to be negative in the course of 2022. This development, coupled with the Fed's own monetary tightening, could well end up dampening aggregate demand enough for growth to enter negative territory. Obviously, as is clear from the Fed's publications, at this point in time it was more focused on keeping the ship steady than attaining 'monetary space', that is, getting as far above the ZLB as possible. Indeed, stock markets themselves seem to believe that the Fed will be able to reach just under 2 per cent with its current tightening phase before it has to dial back.[147] Apparently, a trillion-dollar bet rides on this projection, and one can only imagine what were to happen if it did not come to pass.[148]

There will, of course, be neoliberal calls to let 'capitalism take its course', and allow mass bankruptcies to happen rather than prop up corporate zombies through easy money policies. But such calls will not be heeded. The Fed is not going to

---

[147] Bahceli, Yoruk, 'Analysis: A Trillion-Dollar Wager That Interest Rates Won't Rise Far.' *Reuters*, 2 December 2021, www.reuters.com/markets/europe/trillion-dollar-wager-that-interest-rates-wont-rise-far-2021-12-01.

[148] Ibid.

let the US economy crash into a major depression just so that creative destruction can take place. Instead, the Fed will likely attempt to make the landing as soft as possible. In any case, in late August 2020, Powell revealed a decision by the Fed to move to an 'average' inflation-targeting framework, wherein it would target inflation 'moderately above 2 per cent for some time', following a period of undershoot. Given that the Fed has witnessed years of undershoot with respect to its 2 per cent inflation target, this new framework may well be a justification for the Fed to pause its lift-off after a point if inflation still remained somewhat above target.

Though it may no longer be seen as a primary engine of global growth, the fact is America continues to possess the world's single largest consumer market in nominal terms and thereby a major opportunity for exporters around the globe. If inflation once again settles down, as the Fed expects it to post the lift-off, and America's financial markets remain open in terms of capital flows, it is unlikely that the dollar will be dethroned as the world's main reserve currency in the medium term. Especially given that its rivals such as the euro or the yuan simply cannot compete for the foreseeable future, as we shall find out subsequently. And despite the hype, digital currencies lacking a sovereign backer cannot oust the dollar either. Thus, the US, owing to its market size and global status, will be able to service its growing debt without private or foreign investors losing confidence – an exorbitant privilege, as it were. And this is something a country like Greece does not have, as we shall examine next.

TWO

THE GLOBAL FINANCIAL CRISIS OF 2008 BROUGHT IN ITS WAKE a credit crunch in the European banking system, and, by late 2009, fears arose as to whether Greece could finance its public outlays at all. The country had already been running high government deficits – having been hit by successive recessions in the recent past. In this context, disclosures by the Greek government that it had been understating its actual fiscal position catalysed a downgrade of the nation's sovereign rating by Standard & Poor's to 'junk' status in April 2010.[1] Finding no takers for its newly issued debt, this downgrade pushed the country over the precipice, as investors began to exit its secondary capital markets as well. Interest rates on the benchmark 10-year Greek government bond rose to over 13 per cent by late April 2010 – the highest level attained since 1996, and some 1,000 basis points higher than that on comparable German bonds – as there were few buyers left for Greece's government debt.[2]

Typically, such high rates push countries into a spiral of ever-increasing debt, coupled with the inability to find

---

[1] 'S&P downgrades Greece ratings into junk status.' *Reuters*, 27 April 2010, https://www.reuters.com/article/greece-ratings-sandp/sp-downgrades-greece-ratings-into-junk-status-idUSWNA964520100427#:~:text=NEW%20YORK%2C%20April%2027%20(Reuters,speculative%2C%20or%20junk%2C%20status.

[2] 'Greek/German Bond Yield Spread More than 1,000 Bps.' *Reuters*, 28 April 2010, https://www.reuters.com/article/markets-bonds-greece/greek-german-bond-yield-spread-more-than-1000-bps-idUSLDE63R0WU20100428.

enough buyers for newly issued government bonds to finance even the recurring interest payments on that debt. This leads to a situation where debt 'rollover', or the renewal of old debt, becomes impossible. Greece seemed to be heading towards a default, when the so-called Troika – the European Central Bank (ECB), the International Monetary Fund and the European Union – intervened at the request of the government with the first 'bailout' package in early May 2010, consisting of massive loans to allow the country to refinance its existing debt obligations.

However, this – and subsequent – bailouts would come with strings attached, in the form of 'conditionalities' that required the Greeks to curb public spending through the adoption of severe austerity measures, that included, among other things, pension freezes, reduction of government salaries, much lower healthcare spending, and higher taxes on fuel and alcohol. As can be imagined, these measures were highly unpopular, and were quite at variance with what the US did when hit by the GFC-induced recession, which was to increase public spending in order to shore up weak private consumption and investment. And in the initial period, the Fed's QE also led to a depreciation of the dollar against major currencies, making US exports cheaper in the world market. For Greece, however, austerity measures only contributed to a further weakening of demand in its economy, which ultimately plunged into a general Depression via a debt-deflationary spiral.

An interesting aside on this subject was captured by Ian Parker in his profile of Yanis Varoufakis, the former Greek minister of finance and noted economist, published in the *New Yorker.*[3] In March 2015, Varoufakis had met President Barack Obama at the White House in an informal setting. He is reported to have said: 'Mr President, of course one has

[3] Parker, Ian. 'The Greek Warrior.' *New Yorker*, 3 August 2015, https://www.newyorker.com/magazine/2015/08/03/the-greek-warrior.

to suffer costs in order to get the benefits, but the question is the balance. There has to be a positive balance… We are being asphyxiated for trying to simulate what you did, right?'

Obama's response was sensitive, if not very formal. 'I know,' he said. 'Austerity sucks.' In the opinion of Varoufakis, Obama was not quite referring to the 'unpleasantness' of austerity, but to its 'ineffectiveness'. The Greek minister interpreted it to mean that Obama agreed that austerity 'doesn't work – it creates misery, and it's self-perpetuating, and it's self-defeating'.

This 'self-defeating' deflationary spiral saw Greece's GDP fall by 23 per cent over 2008–13, before apparently stabilizing in 2014 – only to be followed by a double-dip recession that lasted till 2016.[4] Though the country's economy returned to very slow growth during 2017–19, the legacy of the huge fall in output between 2008 and 2013 had left around 35 per cent of Greece's youth without jobs,[5] even before the COVID-19 shock. The overall unemployment rate was also well over 16 per cent back in December 2019 itself.[6] It should be noted that Greece's unemployment figures have remained persistently high (the overall unemployment rate being 16.9 per cent in April 2021),[7] despite the fact that several Greeks

---

[4] 'GDP Growth (Annual %) – Greece.' *World Bank*, based on national accounts data and OECD National Accounts data files from 2007 to 2019, https://data.worldbank.org/indicator/NY.GDP.MKTP.KD.ZG?end=2019&locations=GR&start=2007.

[5] European Commission. 'December 2019: Euro Area Unemployment at 7.4%.' *Eurostat*, 21 January 2020 to 30 January 2020, https://ec.europa.eu/eurostat/documents/2995521/10159296/3-30012020-AP-EN.pdf/b9a98100-6917-c3ea-a544-ce288ac09675.

[6] 'Greek Unemployment Rate Eased to 16.3% in December.' *National Herald*, 5 March 2020, https://www.thenationalherald.com/greece_economy/arthro/greek_unemployment_rate_eased_to_16_3_in_december-256842/.

[7] 'Unemployment by Sex and Age – Monthly Data.' *Eurostat*, 13 August 2021, https://ec.europa.eu/eurostat/databrowser/view/une_rt_m/default/table?lang=en.

of working age have already left the country to find jobs elsewhere since the beginning of the crisis. The collapse of its GDP meant that though Greece had begun running annual budgetary surpluses (achieved through major spending cuts) prior to the COVID-19 crisis, its gross government debt-to-GDP ratio was still over 175 per cent in December 2019.[8] And Greece's debt-to-GDP ratio had no chance of meeting the target, that is – reaching 120 per cent of its GDP by 2020, mandated by the Troika. In May 2020, the European Commission (EC) forecasted that Greece's debt-to-GDP ratio would reach 196.4 per cent by the end of the year.[9] It is worth noting here that when the debt crisis first began, Greece had a debt-to-GDP ratio of 120 per cent.

WHY GREXIT NEVER HAPPENED

Prior to the pandemic, attempts to 'reflate' Greece via public spending had failed to materialize, despite its electorate having voted to power the far left anti-austerity Syriza Party in January 2015. The party's campaign had called for an outright retirement of at least half of the country's debt, short of which it believed that Greece's insolvency would have to be made official through a default. This could lead to a potential exit – 'Grexit' in popular parlance – from the

---

[8] Donnan, Shawn, and Jim Brunsden. 'Greece Faces "Explosive" Surge in Public Debt, IMF Warns.' *Financial Times*, 28 January 2017, https://www.ft.com/content/6b14c4a2-e4ec-11e6-8405-9e5580d6e5fb.

See also: 'Greece: 2019 Article IV Consultation—Press Release; Staff Report; and Statement by the Executive Director for Greece.' *IMF*, November 2019, https://www.imf.org/en/Publications/CR/Issues/2019/11/14/Greece-2019-Article-IV-Consultation-Press-Release-Staff-Report-and-Statement-by-the-48806.

[9] Amaro, Silvia. 'Greece Will Negotiate New Fiscal Targets with Europe for 2021 onward, Finance Minister Says.' *CNBC*, 2 June 2020, https://www.cnbc.com/2020/06/02/greece-staikouras-wants-new-fiscal-targets-to-be-discussed-with-europe.html.

19-country Eurozone, where the euro is the legal tender.[10] However, Grexit never happened, since Germany, which effectively has a veto in the Troika arrangement, gauged Greece's predicament correctly and got it to comply with bailout terms. As such, the Syriza regime had to accept the so-called 'Third Economic Adjustment Programme for Greece', a.k.a. the third bailout, on 12 July 2015. Let us take a brief look at how that came to be.

In the years since its debt woes began, Greece first attempted to return to financial markets to sell its debt in 2014 but the foray ended in failure within a few months. Unable to refinance its debt, and with interest rates on existing government securities beginning to rise sharply by early 2015, the newly elected Syriza government began demanding that the country's insolvency be officially accepted by the Troika and a debt haircut be given. It also called for a few austerity-reducing measures that would allow the provision of electricity and food stamps for Greece's rising poor and destitute population. The government also suggested that Greece be allowed to repay its debts as per a formula based on future growth rates for the country's economy.

The Troika, however, remained obdurate in the face of Greece's demands by withholding a new tranche of bailout money that the nation required to service €7.2 billion in debt repayments by mid-2015. And to put further pressure, the ECB also decided not to include Greek bonds when it launched a QE programme of its own in March 2015. The Troika demanded that Greece adhere closely to austerity measures agreed to by its pre-Syriza Eurocratic governments, besides a slew of new austerity measures, including public administration reforms, higher taxation rates and a crackdown

---

[10] The Eurozone is a subset of the 29-member European Union free trade area, and, besides Greece, includes Austria, Belgium, Cyprus, Estonia, Finland, France, Germany, Ireland, Italy, Latvia, Lithuania, Luxembourg, Malta, the Netherlands, Portugal, Slovakia, Slovenia and Spain.

on tax evasion. Matters almost came to a head in June 2015 when Syriza seemed to reject the bailout terms, with Greek Prime Minister Alexis Tsipras instead calling for a referendum to be held on 5 July 2015 to decide the matter. For a while, a Greek sovereign default seemed imminent.

The truth, though, was that managing such a default would not have been easy at all, as it would have been followed by the withdrawal of all the emergency liquidity assistance (ELA) facilities extended by the ECB which were keeping the Greek banking system afloat. Greece's Parliament would likely have had to pass emergency laws that would declare the reinstitution of a 'new' drachma as the legal tender. It would also have been followed by capital controls to ensure that whatever foreign investments remained in Greece did not flee overnight.

This new drachma would have debuted as a very weak currency in international markets and depreciated heavily against the euro – destroying the value of any bank deposits that might have been converted from euros to drachmas. This is precisely why Tsipras's call for a referendum immediately triggered panic withdrawals of deposits from Greek banks by the public, with people deciding that it was better to hold on to euros in cash.[11]

A weak new drachma would have also made key imports, such as food, fuel and medicines expensive. This meant that inflationary pressures would quickly build up in the economy. In fact, there was even a minor chance that runaway inflationary expectations could have taken hold, with people

---

[11] Yardley, Jim, and Anemona Hartocollis. 'Cash Withdrawals and Hoarding as Default Looms over Greece.' *New York Times*, 28 June 2015, https://www.nytimes.com/2015/06/29/world/europe/a-wary-athens-awaits-the-referendum-on-austerity.html?register=email&auth=register-email. See also: 'Debt Crisis: Split Greece Teeters on the Brink with Referendum.' *Hindustan Times*, 5 July 2015, https://www.hindustantimes.com/world/debt-crisis-split-greece-teeters-on-the-brink-with-referendum/story-yEpvF5wjRqDh50kcocWKoJ.html.

looking to spend whatever new drachma they had before it lost value. And this in turn could have, in theory, led to hyperinflation in the Greek economy, in a manner somewhat reminiscent of the German experience of 1923.[12]

To be sure, Grexit would not have been an easy event for the rest of the Eurozone either. For one, the default followed by Grexit would have meant that the country would not have repaid most of its €320 billion debt obligations, thereby leading to a condition similar to a haircut, but worse, since it would not have been orderly at all. After all, no country had left the EU until then – and no set procedure existed for overseeing the same. There were also fears that a Greek default would lead to an illiquidity contagion in the European banking system. Although by 2015 the chance of such an occurrence was much lower than what it was back in 2010, or even in 2012 for that matter, when the ECB chief, Mario Draghi, had said that he would do 'whatever it takes to preserve the euro'.[13]

So, both the Greeks and the Troika were perhaps playing a game of chicken, and the former blinked first. 'We tried, but we were defeated,' Euclid Tsakalotos, the country's finance minister, said, during a lecture in Paris in March 2019, while referring to his government's capitulation to the Troika in July 2015, and subsequent acceptance of the third bailout package.[14] It seems that Germany had correctly calculated that the pain of Grexit would be too much for Athens to bear. Of course,

---

[12] The reference here is to the Weimar crisis of 1923 that came about when Germany missed a reparations payment in November 1922.

[13] Draghi, Mario. 'Twenty Years of the ECB's Monetary Policy.' Address at the Global Investment Conference, European Central Bank, London, 26 July 2012, https://www.ecb.europa.eu/press/key/date/2012/html/sp120726.en.html.

[14] Tsakalotos, Euclid. 'Ongoing Lessons from the Greek Crisis for Europe.' Lecture at the Sciences Po Paris School of International Affairs, 13 March 2019, https://www.sciencespo.fr/evenements/?event=ongoing-lessons-from-the-greek-crisis-for-europe.

to soften the blow, Greece was promised concessions in repayment terms when the third rescue package ended.

Greece's exit from the third bailout in August 2018 would be a celebrated event for the Troika, with the country having returned to both a budgetary surplus and to sovereign debt markets. In fact, by May 2019, Greek bonds would be offering all-time low yields. It was, however, clear that the embrace of severe austerity had failed to lower Greece's debt-to-GDP ratio, which was supposed to be one of the main sustainability goals behind its adoption. Rather, the country had come out of the 'fiscal crisis' at great human cost. Large parts of its economy were lost forever; a very difficult unemployment situation continued to plague the nation. A whole generation of young people in Greece began calling themselves 'generation €592', referring to a popular sitcom about six unemployed friends, that drew its title from the monthly minimum wage rate for those under 25.[15] Worst of all, Greece's capacity to deal with a public health crisis was much lower than before.

Indeed, the COVID-19 shock could not have come at a worse time for Greece. Its healthcare system had been battered by the initial austerity-related cuts, with spending on the same being less by some 42 per cent in 2018 as compared to 2009.[16] This, despite public healthcare spending being on the 'rise' since 2014. Obviously, it meant that Greece was less prepared to handle the exigent circumstances than it would have been otherwise. In fact, even as Greece dealt with the pandemic, the lockdowns further pushed up unemployment numbers and put paid to any recovery led by key sectors in

---

[15] Chakrabortty, Aditya. 'Young, Educated Greeks Angry at Being Locked out of Their Lives.' *Guardian*, 3 August 2011, https://www.theguardian.com/world/2011/aug/03/young-educated-greeks-lives.

[16] Nikiforos, Michalis. 'Crisis, Austerity, and Fiscal Expenditure in Greece: Recent Experience and Future Prospects in the Post-Covid-19 era.' *Public Policy Brief Number 151*, Levy Economics Institute of Bard College, http://www.levyinstitute.org/pubs/ppb_151.pdf.

the economy, such as tourism and exports. As such, the IMF's 'World Economic Outlook' for 2020 projected that Greece's GDP would shrink by 10 per cent in 2020, and that it was likely to be the hardest-hit Eurozone economy.[17]

THE MAKINGS OF A GREEK TRAGEDY

Greece's woes stemmed from the fact that by agreeing to adopt the euro as its currency it had relinquished the ability to conduct any kind of independent monetary policy of its own. Hypothetically, if the country was still using the drachma, its central bank, the Bank of Greece (BoG), could have stepped in with large-scale purchases of government bonds in a bid to keep interest rates from soaring when the downgrade happened and thereby calm the country's public debt markets, as was done by the Fed both during the GFC and the COVID-19 shock.

But since it adopted the euro in 2002, the BoG, as a 'national central bank' (NCB) in the Euro system, has been secondary to the ECB, and could have purchased Greek debt using newly issued euros only at the direction of the latter – and that too in proportion to its capital key, that is, its shareholding in the ECB. When the debt crisis first began, the ECB did purchase some Greek sovereign debt under a programme called the Securities Market Programme (SMP). And though it may have temporarily reduced debt-service costs for the Greek government, its critics pointed out that the SMP and indeed the Troika bailouts were, to a great extent, designed to help French and German commercial banks offload their holdings of Greek sovereign debt, which had become toxic at the time. In that sense, the ECB's move was similar to what the Fed did in the US – by taking MBS

---

[17] 'World Economic Outlook, April 2020: The Great Lockdown.' *IMF*, April 2020, https://www.imf.org/en/Publications/WEO/Issues/2020/04/14/ weo-april-2020.

and agency debt off the balance sheets of commercial banks and other financial institutions. However, unlike the Fed's initial QE round, SMP did very little in terms of preventing Greece's exit from the sovereign debt markets, which happened in the wake of default fears in April 2010.

What's more, the ECB also made it clear that it was not a 'lender of last resort' for Greece, since EU rules require 'market forces' to bring about adjustments in the case of economic imbalances. So, in a situation quite opposite to that in the US, which handily borrows from the rest of the world in the dollar – owing to its status as the world's primary reserve currency – almost all of Greece's debt is denominated in the euro, a currency over whose supply it has little control.

On the other hand, because the Eurozone is not a fiscal union, but merely a monetary union, there was no 'EU federal' government stepping in to help Greece sustain public spending, which would have shored up consumer demand. Instead, the Troika compelled the country to undertake heavy austerity measures, which pushed it into a deflationary spiral at one end and a euro-denominated debt spiral at the other. Greece suffered the very debt-deflation that was avoided in the case of the US through the use of the unconventional monetary policies that we examined in chapter one.

Fortunately, in the wake of the COVID-19 shock, austerity was abandoned for once in the Eurozone, with even Greece increasing government spending to mitigate the impact of the crisis. And, this time around, the ECB stepped in with the early purchase of Greek debt, despite its junk status.[18] In late July 2020, a €750 billion stimulus plan was hammered out by members of the EU, with even Greece set to benefit from it.[19]

---

[18] Bahceli, Yoruk. 'Update-1: Greece Starts Sale of First Bond Since ECB Eligibility.' *Reuters*, 15 April 2020, https://www.reuters.com/article/eurozone-greece-debt/update-1-greece-starts-sale-of-first-bond-since-ecb-eligibility-idUSL5N2C325Z.

[19] Ward, Alex. 'What Alexander Hamilton Has to Do with the EU's $850 Billion Coronavirus Stimulus Plan.' *Vox*, 21 July 2020, https://www.vox.

Although this pandemic-recovery package was hailed as the first major move towards a fiscal union in Europe, it may not be that much of a watershed moment, as we shall see later in this chapter. In fact, while this development is noteworthy, it is important to remember that it will take much more for the Eurozone to stop being the zone of dysfunction that it has been ever since the GFC.

ZONE OF DYSFUNCTION

The reluctance of the Troika to give Greece a 'haircut', or a waiver for a significant chunk of its debt, was driven by the fact that the nation is but one of the several states that were afflicted by a debt crisis in the Eurozone subsequent to the GFC. Indeed, a whole group of European countries – including Portugal, Ireland, Italy, Greece and Spain (collectively referred to as PIIGS) – were each beset by debt crises, GDP contractions and massive unemployment in the wake of the GFC.[20] Starting in 2010, both Portugal and Ireland have also been recipients of bailout packages from the Troika, and their 'exit' from the same in 2014 was held up as an example of how austerity-led measures could restore stability. It is another matter that Portugal returned to slow growth only after it abandoned austerity in 2016.[21, 22] And

com/2020/7/21/21332541/coronavirus-eu-stimulus-merkel-billion-hamilton.

[20] Mehra, Mishita. 'A Look at Countries with Most Severe Austerity Measures and Ramifications.' *Economic Times*, 5 June 2012, https://economictimes.indiatimes.com/news/international/a-look-at-countries-with-most-severe-austerity-measures-and-ramifications/articleshow/13846767.cms?from=mdr.

[21] AFP/PTI. 'Portugal Adopts Anti-Austerity Budget despite Concerns.' *Business Standard*, 23 February 2016, https://www.business-standard.com/article/pti-stories/portugal-adopts-anti-austerity-budget-despite-concerns-116022400080_1.html.

[22] Alderman, Liz. 'Portugal Dared to Cast Aside Austerity. It's Having a

the high growth rates posted by Ireland (which is held up as a poster child for austerity) since it exited its own bailout are likely examples of accounting inventiveness than anything else, earning the country the sobriquet of 'leprechaun economy'.[23] As such, the so-called recoveries of both Portugal and Ireland were fragile even before the pandemic struck and continue to be subject to external factors, such as Britain's exit from the EU. Portugal, of course, witnessed a major contraction during 2020.[24] And though Ireland defied the Europe-wide trend of GDP contraction in 2020 and managed to grow in the pandemic-ridden year on account of heightened exports, structural weaknesses remain in place, as observed above.[25] As in the case of America, the headline unemployment rate had declined in both countries before the COVID-19 shock – even as labour force participation rates have shrunk and real wage growth has stayed below 1 per cent. Moreover, with sovereign debt-to-GDP ratios still quite high, neither country has much room for increasing government expenditure to renew their infrastructure.

Now, while Greece, Portugal or Ireland, or even all three taken together, are a relatively small component of the Eurozone economy, Italy and Spain are the third- and fourth-largest economies in Europe respectively. And giving either of them a haircut may not be something that the banking

---

Major Revival.' *New York Times*, 22 July 2018, https://www.nytimes.com/2018/07/22/business/portugal-economy-austerity.html.

[23] Broom, Douglas. 'Everything You Need to Know about Ireland's Economy.' *World Economic Forum*, 19 March 2019, https://www.weforum.org/agenda/2019/03/everything-you-need-to-know-about-ireland-s-economy/.

[24] Forecast for Portugal for Winter 2021. *European Commission*, 2021, https://ec.europa.eu/economy_finance/forecasts/2021/winter/ecfin_forecast_winter_2021_pt_en.pdf.

[25] O'Leary, Naomi. 'Ireland Only EU Economy to Grow in 2020.' *Irish Times*, 11 February 2021, https://www.irishtimes.com/business/economy/ireland-only-eu-economy-to-grow-in-2020-1.4482192.

system would be able to handle, stressed as it already is. Apart from Greece, Spain is the other Eurozone economy that has had a persistently high youth unemployment rate. Just to provide some perspective, as of December 2019, it stood at 30 per cent.[26] It worsened with the onset on the pandemic, reaching as high as 40.8 per cent in June 2020.[27]

Overall, Eurozone GDP grew at an average annual rate of only 0.81 per cent in the period 2008–19,[28] with the official unemployment rate being 7.4 per cent in December 2019 and the youth unemployment rate 15.3 per cent.[29] Obviously, the overall Eurozone figures did not indicate that the southern European countries were actually doing much worse than those in the north. For instance, while Spain had an overall unemployment rate of 13.7 per cent in December 2019, Germany's was a mere 3.2 per cent for that same period. Nevertheless, these figures are based on a narrow measure of unemployment, similar to America's U-3. So, even though they have fallen from the very high levels seen during the peak of the sovereign debt crisis in Europe, they do not convey the full picture about the state of the labour market in northern Europe prior to the COVID-19 shock. Subsequent to the pandemic-induced lockdowns, the

---

[26] It should be noted that Spain and Italy received bailout packages only in 2012.

[27] 'Spain Youth Unemployment Rate.' *Trading Economics*, August 2020, https://tradingeconomics.com/spain/youth-unemployment-rate#:~:text=Looking%20forward%2C%20we%20estimate%20Youth,according%20to%20our%20econometric%20models.

[28] Calculated from data available at: 'GDP Growth (annual %) – Euro Area.' *World Bank*, based on national accounts data, and OECD National Accounts data files, https://data.worldbank.org/indicator/NY.GDP.MKTP.KD.ZG?end=2019&locations=XC&start=2008. Accessed 25 September 2021.

[29] European Commission. 'December 2019: Euro Area Unemployment at 7.4%.' *Eurostat*, January 2020, https://ec.europa.eu/eurostat/documents/2995521/10493867/3-03032020-BP-EN.pdf/af09316f-78d0-037c-b27b-fa7844dc2c96.

Eurozone's official unemployment figures have not budged considerably from their December 2019 levels, on account of the fact that furloughed workers are not captured in unemployment data. The lockdown coincided with tens of millions of European workers being furloughed, rather than being retrenched outright as in the US, on account of state-subsidized pay cheque support programmes that were already in place.[30]

Moreover, the lowering of headline unemployment had not been mirrored by a consistent rise in inflation towards its target, which, in the case of the ECB, is 'something that is close to 2 per cent'.[31] In the immediate aftermath of the GFC, the ECB studiously avoided large-scale asset purchases or QE, though it did buy government bonds of countries in a debt crisis as mentioned previously. Instead, the ECB focused its accommodative stance on dropping the key policy rate close to zero, and keeping it there till the end of the first quarter of 2011. That year, there was a short-lived spurt in inflation, which led to mild increases in the policy rate by the ECB (though it stayed below 1 per cent throughout), only to have to reduce it again towards the end of the year as the Eurozone clearly entered disinflationary territory.

Given the generally depressed conditions, by the middle of 2012 the ECB had to drop its key policy rate to zero. It remained there till 11 June 2014, when the ECB deemed it necessary to show that the ZLB and ELB were not synonymous. Entering uncharted waters, the ECB pushed the deposit facility rate, which is its key policy rate, to –0.1 per cent, that is, into

---

[30] 'Europe's Economy Was Hit Hard Too, but Jobs Didn't Disappear Like in the U.S.' Narrated by Jim Zarrolli, *NPR* (*National Public Radio*), 23 April 2020, https://www.npr.org/2020/04/23/838085670/europes-economy-was-hit-hard-too-but-jobs-didn-t-disappear-like-in-the-u-s.

[31] 'The Definition of Price Stability.' *European Central Bank*, 8 July 2021, https://www.ecb.europa.eu/mopo/strategy/pricestab/html/index.en.html#:~:text=Reasons%20for%20aiming%20at%20below,reduce%20the%20risks%20of%20deflation.

negative territory, as inflation clearly seemed headed towards zero.[32]

The adoption of a Negative Interest Rate Policy, or NIRP, was not popular with the banks, since it led to a decline in their net interest margins, thereby impinging on profitability. However, forced to accept NIRP, European banks have since managed to increase profits from other sources of income, and this has meant that they did transmit the negative rates on to their loan customers. This, in turn, has apparently helped flatten the yield curve, and NIRP seems set to be an integral part of the ECB's unconventional toolkit.

Nonetheless, NIRP probably did not do enough in terms of monetary easing post its introduction in 2014. With the Eurozone officially in deflation by early 2015, the ECB finally undertook a QE programme of its own – starting in March 2015, as mentioned earlier. Importantly, besides purchasing government securities of EU member states, it also engaged in large-scale purchases of collateralized private bonds from commercial banks, since its charter allowed it to do so. Indeed, so dire was the need to revive private investment in Europe that the ECB undertook QE even as it was already making commercial banks pay an interest rate of 0.2 per cent for the reserves they held.

The ECB was, therefore, doing its best to ensure that commercial banks increased lending, given the huge reserve buffer it had injected into their balance sheets. However, its experience with the use of QE to combat deflation and disinflation has also proved to be a disappointment, and a major undershoot of the inflation target has been the norm. In December 2018, the ECB ended its Asset Purchase Programme (APP), after having increased its reserve liabilities by some €2.6 trillion.

---

[32] 'Key Interest Rate.' *European Central Bank*, 21 July 2021, https://www.ecb.europa.eu/stats/policy_and_exchange_rates/key_ecb_interest_rates/html/index.en.html.

However, this 'cessation of QE' did not last long. With US–China trade troubles and Brexit uncertainties taking their toll on the German economy, the ECB resumed QE in September 2019, amidst a marked slowdown in the overall Eurozone economy. It also pushed its deposit rate facility further into negative territory. (This has remained at –0.5 per cent since 18 September 2019.[33])

Then came the COVID-19 shock.

This saw the ECB instituting a number of emergency lending programmes, besides pushing the pedal on QE through the €1.35 trillion Pandemic Emergency Purchase Programme (PEPP), in order to complement the APP.[34]

It is safe to say that given the state of the Eurozone economy, even before the pandemic broke out, the ECB was likely to maintain an enlarged balance sheet for a very long time indeed; unless, of course, the EU itself disintegrates before that. Whether that happens or not will depend a lot on the outlook of the Eurozone's largest economy.

THE GERMAN QUESTION

One of the chief reasons for the delay in the ECB's institution of a QE programme back in the 2010s had been a reluctance on the part of Germany – the largest economy in the Eurozone – to cheapen the euro, amidst fears that it might stoke uncontrollable inflation. The Bundesbank, which was the only NCB to officially dissent against the APP even in 2014, was probably channelling memories of the hyperinflation experienced by Weimar Germany, which was still fresh in the minds of many citizens. Moreover, unlike the economies of the Eurozone countries, beset by a sovereign

---

[33] Ibid.

[34] 'Our Response to the Coronavirus Pandemic.' *European Central Bank*, 19 February 2021, https://www.ecb.europa.eu/home/search/coronavirus/html/index.en.html

debt crisis, Germany's economy was not threatening to fall into a deflationary spiral at the time.

Being an export-driven economy, the country no doubt stood to gain from a fall in the value of the euro – something that was likely to take place in the immediate aftermath of the ECB's QE, and indeed did happen. But then, the very adoption of the euro had given Germany a competitive edge, since the old Deutsche Mark would have been even stronger against other major currencies had it still been in circulation, given the country's massive external surplus. In any case, when the euro was first adopted, it is believed to have 'locked in' a 6 per cent competitive advantage for German exports in the Eurozone, since the Deutsche Mark was at that time rather undervalued vis-à-vis other European currencies.[35] This was a major reason behind the country managing to surge exports to other members of the Eurozone, taking advantage of its higher manufacturing productivity. German competitiveness was also supported by the country's wage-bargaining system, which keeps real wages muted and below productivity, and in turn keeps domestic consumption expenditure lower, making it a chronic over-producer and under-consumer.

Conversely, the countries of southern Europe had bid their own currencies up before converting to the euro, and they found their purchasing power higher than what their actual economic conditions would have allowed. The adoption of the euro and the concomitant removal of currency risk (since they would now all be trading in euros without being concerned about the direction in which bilateral exchange rates might move) also reduced borrowing costs for these countries on the European periphery, as it were. In the early days of the euro, that is, the beginning of the

---

[35] Ezrati, Milton. 'The German Swindle Built into the Euro.' *Forbes*, 23 January 2018, https://www.forbes.com/sites/miltonezrati/2018/01/23/the-german-swindle-built-into-the-euro/#4a2b783e27da.

twenty-first century, it was Germany that was in the throes of economic weakness, and, at the time, the ECB pursued an accommodative monetary policy to aid Berlin's recovery. For southern Europe, the availability of low-cost euro borrowing avenues induced a spending binge that pushed up private and public levels of debt in the run-up to the GFC. These countries engaged in credit-fuelled consumption and real estate growth, while German firms used their markets to enhance their efficiency, via expansion. Essentially, Germany over-produced while the PIIGS over-consumed.

Till the GFC broke out, the widening deficit of the European periphery with Germany was financed via capital flows from Western Europe. Accordingly, the TARGET2 intra-EU payments system did not show any imbalances, as money was flowing both ways.[36] This happy situation, however, would not survive the GFC. After the crisis, there was capital flight from the periphery to the core, even as the import of German goods by the latter continued unabated. Moreover, once QE began, financial entities in the European periphery that sold government bonds to the ECB immediately moved the proceeds to the EU core, especially Germany. The mechanics of this situation resulted in positive TARGET2 balances getting built up for the German Bundesbank, while correspondingly large negative balances accrued on the balance sheets of Banco de España and Banca d'Italia, besides others. The bottom line: Italy and Spain, alongside other countries like Portugal, owe Germany a considerable amount of euros. By the end of June 2021, Germany, Luxembourg, and the Netherlands had positive

---

[36] 'TARGET2 is a payment system owned and operated by the Eurosystem. It is the leading European platform for processing large-value payments, and is used by both central banks and commercial banks to process payments in euro in real time.' Taken from 'What is Target2?' *European Central Bank*, 29 June 2016, https://www.ecb.europa.eu/explainers/tell-me/html/target2.en.html.

TARGET2 balances of €1,101.9 billion, €319.8 billion and €13.8 billion respectively, while Italy, Spain and Portugal had negative balances of €521.5 billion, €503.9 billion and €84.3 billion respectively.[37]

Obviously, if there was no euro, such 'imbalances' would have been rectified through the relative appreciation or depreciation of individual currencies. But that 'luxury' was no longer available, and since the Eurozone is not supposed to be a 'transfer union' (Germany is adamant on this), there was no fiscal authority that could have ironed out the varying business cycles of different countries. In fact, the Eurozone does not meet the classic criteria for achieving a sustainable monetary union.[38] This was known when the euro was first adopted, but the refrain had been that the very creation of the Eurozone would lead to these criteria being eventually satisfied. That, however, has not been the case, and instead, what we have is a chronic build-up of TARGET2 imbalances.

For some time now, there have been warnings that this build-up would be a major risk for Germany if Italy or Spain were to leave the euro.[39] Post a hypothetical pull-out by either Spain or Italy, the central banks of these countries would not be able to make good on their liabilities (that is, what they owe) to the Bundesbank, what with their new currencies losing value against the euro. TARGET2 balance does not bear any interest, and this has fuelled allegations

---

[37] Statistical Data Warehouse. 'Target Data Balances.' *European Central Bank*, last updated on 2 August 2021, https://sdw.ecb.europa.eu/reports.do?node=1000004859.

[38] Blake, D. 'Target2: The Silent Bailout System that Keeps the Euro Afloat.' *City Research Online*, May 2018, https://openaccess.city.ac.uk/id/eprint/19674/.

[39] Turner, Philip. 'The ECB Must Reform Target2 to Make It Sustainable.' *Central Banking*, 12 June 2017, https://www.centralbanking.com/central-banks/financial-stability/fmi/3256376/the-ecb-must-reform-target2-to-make-it-sustainable.

that it represents a transfer from the core of Europe to the periphery. Overall, the prospect of facing a deadweight loss on its TARGET2 credit balances might be a reason why Germany may have to go the extra mile to keep the EU together.

Germany has, of course, already done that by some accounts. The bailouts themselves are an example of this. Also, back in 2015, when Germany realized that its exports to other states in the Eurozone had begun to contract due to a steady fall in their purchasing power, it did not obstruct QE beyond a point. The Eurozone QE lowered interest rates on government securities for its members, thereby making it easier for them to service their debt. Countries such as Italy and Spain saw yields on their 10-year maturity government bonds drop significantly once the ECB began QE in 2015.

As such, QE in the Eurozone is designed to be a 'neutral' policy which benefits each member equally and proportionally because the rate at which bonds are bought varies according to each country's share of GDP. Greece, however, was excluded from the ECB's first round of bond buying, as the latter made it clear that it wouldn't purchase the country's securities from commercial banks as long as it did not receive payment on Greek bonds set to mature by mid-2015. This move was part of a larger strategy to pressurize the country into undertaking more austerity measures. Behind the scenes, it was understood that the German government was driving the adoption of a harder stance vis-à-vis the Greeks.

More than any other Eurozone country (barring perhaps Greece itself now), the Troika's bailout had been most unpopular in Germany. Throughout the Greek debt crisis, German taxpayers remained the biggest contributors to its bailout package. And they have been rather unhappy with the interest waivers and repeated debt repayment extensions given to Greece as it is tantamount to reducing the principal that the country owes. An actual haircut of Greece's debt was (and still is) anathema to German voters, who will then have to bear an outright loss on loans made to Greece, which they see as a profligate country living beyond its means. But the truth is that Germany has gained immensely from the creation of the Eurozone; it led to the free movement of goods, but not of entire classes of labour. So, any bailout on Germany's part cannot be considered an act of altruism.

Since the Eurozone was meant to be an 'irrevocable' monetary union, any country leaving it unilaterally would also have to leave the EU as a matter of course. Thus, if countries start giving up on the euro, it will ultimately lead to an unravelling of the more-than-half-century-old EU project itself. A collapse of the Eurozone on its own would be highly detrimental to Germany, which would not only lose its low-cost advantage, but the end of the EU would mean that it could then also face tariff and other barriers given the loss of the free trade area. The impact of this on the German economy would be wholly negative, since over 37 per cent of German exports go to the rest of the Eurozone.[40] Europe's sole surviving 'strong' economy might, in that case, wither away.

As such, the entire Eurozone crisis has been a deeply polarizing issue, with northern European polities labelling the debt-afflicted southern Europeans as 'spendthrifts' and 'idlers', while the southern Europeans invariably accuse the Germans of trying to establish a neo-Nazi imperium, using debt as a weapon. Greece's Syriza-led government had pointed out that what it was asking for was no more and no less than the post-World War II debt waiver given to West Germany in 1953. It has even called for war reparations from Germany worth nearly €300 billion, based on the forced transfer of 476 million Reichsmarks in December 1942 from

---

[40] 'Facts about German Foreign Trade.' *Federal Ministry for Economic Affairs and Energy*, September 2019, https://www.bmwi.de/Redaktion/EN/Publikationen/facts-about-german-foreign-trade.pdf?__blob=publicationFile&v=9.

Greece to Nazi Germany as a loan which was never paid back. And this today amounts to what Greece is demanding, taking inflation and exchange rates into account.

A WAVERING CONSTRUCT

Although Germany may have been able to stare down Greece in the post-GFC period, it is not very clear whether it could have done the same with Italy, where deeply unpopular austerity measures, in the face of rising debt, brought to power an anti-austerity Euro-sceptic populist coalition government in 2018, which included the Five Star Movement and the Lega Nord.[41] Unsurprisingly, tensions between Rome and Berlin have been on the rise since then due to Italy's debt sustainability prospects.[42]

Italy's debt-to-GDP ratio stood at 134.8 per cent by the end of 2018 itself – a figure that was higher than what Greece had before it fell into a full-blown crisis.[43] By that time, Italy's $2.5 trillion sovereign debt load was also the third largest on the planet, behind only that of the United States and Japan. To be sure, QE had helped benchmark 10-year Italian bond yields at relatively low levels while it was in operation, but that changed once the first round of QE ended in 2018. Despite the ECB continuing to reinvest in maturing Italian bonds, yields for the 10-year benchmark bond had been on the rise and had jumped to 2.3 per cent by May 2019. To put

---

[41] D'Emilio, Frances. 'Populists Take Power in Italy, with Euro-skeptic Agenda.' *Associated Press*, 2 June 2018, https://apnews.com/15605caac2ac4963bc4d36d388067b14.

[42] In February 2021, a political crisis led to the formation of a government of national unity in Italy that continues to include both the Five Star Movement and the Lega Nord.

[43] 'Italy: Report Prepared in Accordance with Article 126(3) of the Treaty on the Functioning of the European Union.' *European Commission*, 10 March 2016, https://ec.europa.eu/economy_finance/economic_governance/sgp/pdf/30_edps/126-03_commission/com-2020-535-it_en.pdf.

things in perspective, the yield on comparable Greek bonds was 2.7 per cent during the same month. As an aside, Italian bond yields had declined considerably by June 2021 owing to the ECB's PEPP.

Back in the first half of 2019, rising bond yields was not auspicious news for the new regime in Rome, which had promised tax cuts and increased fiscal spending in order to support social assistance programmes, as well as build direly needed new infrastructure. Obviously, Italy did not have the fiscal space to accomplish this, which is why Rome had become rather receptive to overtures from outside the EU by early 2019. On 23 March 2019, Italy became the first major Eurozone economy and G-7 member to sign a memorandum of understanding (MoU) with China, signalling its participation in the latter's BRI, during a visit to Rome by Chinese President Xi Jinping. Another 29 separate deals, cumulatively worth $2.8 billion, would also be signed on the sidelines of the visit, with the most notable ones being related to Chinese investment in the Italian ports of Trieste, Genoa and Palermo, with a view to providing Chinese goods easier access to the European heartland. For instance, the port of Trieste boasts of direct rail links to various parts of Europe, besides offering exemptions from customs duties.

Italy's decision to participate in China's BRI was roundly criticized by the EU (headquartered in Brussels), which, in its EU–China strategy document released on 11 March 2019, had identified China as 'An economic competitor in pursuit of technological leadership and a systemic rival promoting alternative models of governance.'[44]

Joining the EC in condemnation of Italy's move would be Germany, France and the US, the last having already initiated

---

[44] 'EU–China – A Strategic Outlook.' *Joint Communication to the European Parliament, European Council and the Council*, European Commission, 12 March 2019, https://ec.europa.eu/commission/sites/beta-political/files/communication-eu-china-a-strategic-outlook.pdf.

a trade war with China by that time. Germany viewed Rome's move as diminishing 'EU unity' at a time when the bloc needed to stick together in order to avoid becoming dependent on rising global powers, such as China. 'We can only survive if we are united,' Heiko Maas, Germany's foreign minister, was reported to have said while referring to Italy's decision. As far as France was concerned, its relations with Italy were already at a low, with Paris having recalled its ambassador from Rome in February 2019, because in its view:

> For several months France has been the subject of repeated accusations, unfounded attacks and outrageous declarations that everyone knows and can have in mind. This is unprecedented since the end of the war. To have disagreements is one thing, to exploit the relationship for electoral purposes is another.[45]

Indeed, the new anti-immigrant Italian populist regime had been repeatedly blaming France for the geopolitical situation in Libya, which was leading to an influx of refugees into Italy, among other things. And, in January 2019, the then Italian deputy prime minister, Matteo Salvini, who was also the chairman of the Lega Nord, the main party in the populist coalition, even 'hoped' for the ouster of French President Emmanuel Macron, whose administration was already under severe pressure from the populist 'Yellow Vest' movement.

Given this state of affairs, it was not surprising that Italy summarily rejected criticism from France and Germany on its decision to endorse the BRI, and instead pointed out the deep economic ties that these two countries themselves have

---

[45] Davies, Pascale. 'France–Italy Row: Tajani Hits out at Di Maio after Paris Complains over Rome Attacks.' *Euro News*, 7 February 2019, https://www.euronews.com/2019/02/07/france-recalls-ambassador-to-italy-for-consultations-amid-unprecedented-attacks-from-rome.

with China. For instance, in 2017, France and China had announced a joint fund to invest in busy container ports in third countries, such as Rotterdam in the Netherlands. Moreover, China was already Germany's third-largest trading partner after the US and France, and Sino-German investment links were quite strong as well.

SYSTEMIC COMPETITORS

Italian sentiments about Franco-German 'hypocrisy' with respect to their ties with China would resonate with the 13 other EU member states that had endorsed China's BRI before it. Especially since most of these countries were already part of the 'Cooperation between China–Central Europe and Eastern Europe' (China–CEE) forum launched in 2012, which aims to promote trade and investment ties between China and the European countries that have joined this umbrella. China–CEE, popularly known as the '17+1' format, since it includes in its ambit 12 EU member states and some five Balkan countries, with China being the 'plus one', has been subject to increasing criticism from the EU since 2016.[46] Although suggestive of a multilateral approach, the 17+1 format is actually more about bilateral dealings between China and individual European states eager for infrastructure investment. While this may have diminished fears about 17+1 becoming a regional bloc within the EU, it has nonetheless led to accusations that Beijing is undermining European consolidation by turning CEE countries into 'Trojan Horses' for Chinese power projection. Indeed, there have been calls for China to adopt a 'One Europe' policy in a manner similar to the EU's endorsement of a 'One China' policy.

In recent years, there has been a definite hardening of stance regarding China's global policies in the EU. This has

[46] It was 16+1 till April 2019, when Greece joined and made it 17+1.

closely tracked the unveiling of the contours of Beijing's economic ambitions as encapsulated by the 'Made in China 2025' programme, which seeks to make China a player in 10 high-technology manufacturing sectors by 2025. It has also become apparent that Beijing wishes to use China–CEE and the overall BRI strategy to aid this goal by creating markets for home-grown products and resources alongside whatever projects it invests in overseas. Specifically, the country has been looking to entice small states into debt traps by getting them to accept loans for incongruously large projects that won't pay for themselves and will instead lead to China grabbing strategic assets in return for debt relief.

Indeed, while the chief concern of the last EU–China strategy, adopted in 2016, was the Chinese takeover of key European technology producers to aid the 'Made in China 2025' plan, it now seems to be turning towards the fact that Beijing is using European markets to assist its move up the industrial value chain. For example, while the emphasis of China–CEE has mostly been on infrastructure and logistics, the latest summit held in April 2019 talked a great deal about technology partnership.

China's drive to upgrade its industrial game comes when the Franco–German alliance is itself looking to craft a new industrial strategy – with the creation of European champions in sectors ranging from telecom to aerospace. Obviously, this requires scale, and China encroaching into European markets, to find scale for itself, is most unwelcome for the EU. As such, the main China–CEE project, the Belgrade–Budapest high-speed rail link, has come under scrutiny from the EU since it would not only be financed by Chinese public sector banks but would also see Chinese companies supply technology, materials and construction staff. This state of affairs militates against EU competition rules, which require such projects to be divided into small enough segments that can attract multiple bidders. The EU believes that China–CEE projects should be 'in line with EU law, rules and policies, and that the overall outcome is beneficial for the EU as a whole'.[47]

For CEE countries, which had been pushed by Berlin to sell some of their prime assets in the wake of the GFC, the above reeks of typical Franco-German hypocrisy vis-à-vis China. As the former Italian diplomat Alberto Bradanini, who had served as ambassador to China between 2012 and 2015, observed, while responding to German criticism of his country's move to join the BRI, 'In terms of port logistics, each European country tries to collect Chinese investments. It is logical and normal.'[48]

A prime example of the same would be the inland port of Duisburg, located in Germany's North Rhine–Westphalia province, which has become a key BRI logistics hub, where 35 freight trains from China come in every week to disgorge goods for further transhipment to European markets. Suffering due to the closure of old coal and steel factories, Duisburg's fortunes have turned after becoming a facilitator for the BRI. Incidentally, it would face competition from the Greek port of Piraeus, which is now owned by a Chinese company, COSCO, if the Belgrade–Budapest line were to become operational.

Even in terms of overall investments from China, Germany alone received around 20 per cent of the total investments made in the EU (excluding the UK) by Beijing between 2000 and 2019, while all the CEE countries put together received less than 10 per cent of that figure

---

[47] Hillman, Jonathan E., and Maesea McCalpin. 'Will China's "16+1" Format Divide Europe?' *Center for Strategic and International Studies*, 11 April 2019, https://www.csis.org/analysis/will-chinas-161-format-divide-europe.

[48] 'German Opposition to Italy's Belt and Road Deal with China "Unfair" Says Former Diplomat.' *Hellenic Shipping News*, 14 March 2019, https://www.hellenicshippingnews.com/german-opposition-to-italys-belt-and-road-deal-with-china-unfair-says-former-diplomat.

during the same period.[49] Moreover, the CEE states could also claim that they were more strident on issues of human rights and democracy in China than Germany. After all, the Czech Republic, along with Slovakia, Lithuania, Latvia and Estonia (all CEE members), is among a handful of countries worldwide that has a parliamentary support group for Tibet. The Czech Republic, in particular, also maintains close ties with Taiwan. On the other hand, Germany has faced criticism – from both within and without – in recent years, for being soft on China's excesses. This attitude is believed to stem from a certain 'China dependency' on the part of major German firms listed on the DAX (Germany's main stock exchange) that derive 15 per cent of their revenues from the country on average.[50] By 2016, China had emerged as Germany's largest trading partner and the latter's exports to the former grew at an average annual rate of around 12.7 per cent during 2006–18.[51] Needless to say, this expansion in exports to China provided great succour to Germany's manufacturing sector in the post-GFC period.

Be that as it may, in March 2019, Günther Oettinger, a German politician and the then EU commissioner for budget and human resources, openly called for the union to

---

[49] Brînză, Andreea. 'Central and Eastern Europe Is Not in Bed with China.' *Diplomat*, 3 July 2020, https://thediplomat.com/2020/07/central-and-eastern-europe-is-not-in-bed-with-china.

[50] 'German Firms Facing Perfect Storm as Chinese Growth Slackens.' *Handelsblatt Today*, 18 January 2019, https://www.handelsblatt.com/english/companies/red-scare-german-firms-facing-perfect-storm-as-chinese-growth-slackens-/23884056.html?ticket=ST-1801762-JZcFLwbWL9qFuTbOFP46-ap6.

[51] Poplawski, Konrad. 'Germany among the Biggest Losers of the US–China Trade War.' *Centre for Eastern Studies (OSW)*, 26 February 2020, https://www.osw.waw.pl/en/publikacje/analyses/2020-02-26/germany-among-biggest-losers-us-china-trade-war#:~:text=China%20is%20still%20the%20most,%25%20of%20total%20German%20trade).&text=In%202019%2C%20German%20exports%20to,%E2%80%932018%20was%20around%2012.7%25.

have the right to exercise a veto over Chinese investments in member states if they did not serve the interests of the EU as a whole.[52] It would seem that the dominant states in the EU wanted the benefits of a political union without its attendant costs.

However, the EU doesn't only have to worry about 'systemic competition' from China. The US has never quite been comfortable with the emergence of the euro as a reserve currency that could potentially rival the dollar, and commentators from across the Atlantic have repeatedly talked about the inherent weakness of the Eurozone. With the rise of Trump, however, the Transatlantic Alliance itself seemingly fell into jeopardy. After assuming office in 2017, Trump withdrew from the Paris Agreement on climate change and the Iran nuclear deal concluded in 2015 – both withdrawals being inimical to EU interests. What is more, after ending talks on the Transatlantic Trade and Investment Partnership (TTIP) with the EU soon after assuming office, the Trump administration, in 2018, imposed tariffs on European aluminium and steel. Worse, by February 2019, Washington was also threatening to put a 25 per cent tariff on automobile imports from the EU.

A Trump-led US was also adamant that NATO's European members must 'pay' for their security by raising defence expenditures to 2 per cent of GDP. Implicit in this was the suggestion that the raised defence spending be directed towards the purchase of American arms. Naturally, France and Germany were not enthused by these demands, given that they wished to protect their own defence-industrial bases. In recent years, the Franco-German alliance has also revived the idea of having a joint European force outside

---

[52] 'Chinese Investments in EUROPE: German EU Commissioner Floats EU Veto Right.' *DW*, 24 March 2019, www.dw.com/en/chinese-investments-in-europe-german-eu-commissioner-floats-eu-veto-right/a-48045932.

the NATO mandate, responsible for the defence of the EU. In November 2018, Macron called for the creation of a 'real European army' to protect the continent 'with respect to China, Russia and even the United States of America'.[53] The reference to the US as a potential adversary that Europe may need to defend itself against was unprecedented, and showed just how strained the old Euro–Atlantic Liberal Order had become.

But such calls likely played into the Trump administration's strategy with respect to the continent, which is to deepen ties with countries in Eastern Europe which were wary of any Franco-German neo-militarism, and would seek their own security assurances from the US. Basically, Trump's America intended to reshape its military commitments in the continent by drawing down its overall posture in defence of Europe, and instead focus on bilateral relationships that could yield geo-economic and geopolitical benefits. For instance, countries such as Poland were willing to offer the US political and financial incentives in lieu of guarantees vis-à-vis both Germany and Russia.

In fact, the changing US outlook in Europe led France and Germany to de-escalate tensions with Russia, which had soared after the Ukrainian conflict began in 2014. In June 2019, support from both France and Germany proved crucial in restoring Russia's voting rights at the Council of Europe, despite fierce calls from Ukraine to avoid doing so.[54] However, Russian energy resources remain important for Germany, and, given that the US sees Russia as a competitor

---

[53] Meixler, Eli. 'French President Emmanuel Macron Calls for a "European Army" to Defend against China, Russia and the U.S.' *Time*, 6 November 2018, https://time.com/5446975/emmanuel-macron-european-army-russia-us.

[54] Mounier, Jean-Luc. 'Russia's Undiplomatic Return to the Council of Europe.' *France 24*, 28 June 2019, https://www.france24.com/en/20190628-russia-undiplomatic-return-council-europe-ukraine.

for Europe's resource markets, keeping both countries as suppliers would be in the interests of Berlin.[55]

The Biden presidency has since tried to reset relations with the EU and there was apparently a renewed energy in diplomatic engagement during the first half of 2021. Reversing some of the Trump-engendered transatlantic dissonance, Biden cancelled Trump's troop pull-out plans from Germany in the early days of his presidency, besides signalling acceptance of Gazprom's Nord Stream 2 gas pipeline project for northern Europe in May 2021 by waiving sanctions on it.[56] In general, the Biden administration's decisions to rejoin the Paris Accord on Climate Change, renewed participation in various other multilateral fora, and restoration of funding to certain UN programmes were all welcomed by European capitals. On the trade front too, the EU and the US managed to make some forward movement, burying a 17-year-old trade battle that had involved the imposition of reciprocal tariffs on Europe's Airbus and America's Boeing. However, Biden has not abolished Trump's tariffs on steel and aluminium. Also, somewhat ironically, Biden has also reversed the one Trump decision that was popular with the Europeans – the removal of the travel ban from Europe. Citing concerns related to the Delta variant of the coronavirus, Biden has chosen to keep the travel ban in place, much to the chagrin of the Europeans who were freely allowing even unvaccinated Americans to travel to their soil by mid-2021.

Regardless of Biden's general efforts to improve ties, the EU will continue to seek alternative financial structures

---

[55] Russia's 2022 invasion in Ukraine has however seen Germany rethink energy ties with Moscow. Europe-wide the prevailing sentiment has shifted towards reducing dependence on Russia for oil and gas even as various sanctions 'carve outs' remain in place for continued supplies from the latter.

[56] Nord Stream 2 was shelved by Germany in February 2022 following Russia's recognition of two breakaway regions in Ukraine's Donbass.

of its own that are not susceptible to American sanctions. Back in August 2018, Heiko Maas had revealed that the EU had begun to work on an alternative payment settlement system to the US-controlled SWIFT (Society for Worldwide Interbank Financial Telecommunications), besides looking to create a 'European Monetary Fund' on the lines of the IMF. The catalyst for seeking an alternative to SWIFT was the US withdrawal from the Iran nuclear deal and the subsequent sanctioning of European firms that were engaged in business with Tehran. This alternative took the shape of the Instrument in Support of Trade Exchanges (INSTEX), set up as a European special purpose vehicle on 31 January 2019 to facilitate non-US dollar and non-SWIFT transactions with Iran.

However, a European alternative to SWIFT on its own will not be nearly enough to shield the EU, or any other entity for that matter, from America's sanction tactics. Almost any transaction involving US dollars is routed through American soil and is therefore vulnerable to secondary sanctions imposed by Washington. In the long run, the one way for countries to insulate themselves from this sanctions diplomacy would be to transact in currencies other than the dollar. For the EU, the answer would therefore lie in internationalizing the euro as a currency for settlements, invoicing and investment.

Unfortunately, the euro's internationalization has been stalled since the onset of the GFC. And post that event too, the euro has not shown the kind of stability that would attract more investors. To top that, it could be argued that for most of the 2010s there simply weren't enough highly rated euro-denominated securities that investors could buy – chiefly due to the fact that Germany had been running budget surpluses under a policy called Schwarze Null, or 'black zero'. In fact, prior to the pandemic, Germany had pushed its absolute general debt to a level below what it was in 2010, as a counterpoint to the anti-austerity crowd.[57] Germany had been the force behind the 1993 Maastricht Treaty, which forbids EU members to run annual budget deficits larger than 3 per cent of the GDP or debt above 60 per cent of the GDP. Failure to comply with the terms of the treaty could lead to so-called 'excessive debt measures' being instituted against a country, which would in turn lead to the imposition of fines.

Obviously, since the post-GFC era, the Maastricht Treaty has been observed more in its breach than otherwise. For that matter, even Germany had a debt-to-GDP ratio of 70 per cent in May 2019, despite running surpluses since 2016. Till date, no country has ever been penalized for being in breach of the treaty, although an EU finance ministers' meet was held on 9 July 2019 to decide whether to institute the 'excessive deficit procedure', or EDP, against Italy, which was set to breach the 3 per cent fiscal deficit mark, with its overall debt-to-GDP ratio expected to rise to 135 per cent by the end of 2019. Although the meet did not lead to an EDP being raised against Italy, it did not foster better relations between Italy and Germany either, with the latter seen as having instigated the move.[58]

In fact, in the run-up to the July 2019 finance ministers' meet, Italy's government had remained defiant and announced that it was considering floating an alternative currency to the euro, in the form of bills of treasury, just so that it could

---

[57] 'German General Government Debt Down in 2019 by €16 Billion to €2.05 Trillion–Debt Ratio Down from 61.9% to 59.8%.' *Deutsch Bundesbank Eurosystem*, 31 March 2020, https://www.bundesbank.de/en/press/press-releases/german-government-debt-829646#:~:text=General%20government%20debt%20in%20Germany,end%20of%202018%20to%2059.8%25.

[58] Reid, David, and Silvia Amaro. 'Germany's Scholz Says Rules Must Be Followed as Italy's Rising Debt Frustrates EU.' *CNBC*, 13 June 2019, https://www.cnbc.com/2019/06/13/scholz-says-rules-must-be-followed-as-italys-rising-debt-frustrates-eu.html.

pay off its debts. The Lega Nord, which along with other right-wing populist parties had done well in the European parliamentary elections held in May 2019, seemed in no mood to compromise on the anti-austerity stance. Instead, the Lega Nord's leader, Matteo Salvini, was looking to build a pan-European alliance of parties, with views similar to his, and talked of a new European axis comprising countries such as Hungary, Poland and Austria, alongside Italy, to counter the Franco-German alliance. Incidentally, Hungary and Poland, along with Slovakia and the Czech Republic, have a military alliance since 1991 – the Visegrád Group – which has also sought to deepen economic ties for some time now. Austria, though not a formal member of the Visegrád, is known to be close to the grouping. Visegrád also works closely with the US on defence matters. Salvini's statement therefore is suggestive of a larger political cleave emerging in the EU, with the Franco-German narrative of European integration being challenged.

Indeed, the decision to host hearings against Italy may not only have been motivated by fears that it was headed towards a default that would make the Greek debt crisis look like a picnic. Although it must be said that most Italian government debt is actually in the hands of domestic investors. Regardless, the growing confrontation between France and Germany on one side and Italy on the other, playing out in Brussels, is suggestive of a desire on the part of Berlin to punish Rome's populists for seeking to chart a dangerous path. This has echoes of the sentiments expressed in the EU since Brexit, wherein there is a desire to make Britain's exit somewhat painful for it.

Though Italy's populist government has mentioned in the past that it has no desire to leave the EU and has also limited the scope of Chinese involvement in sensitive sectors such as telecom, it is not clear whether its current politics could lead to a break in the future. Instead of threatening an 'Italexit' as it were, Rome seems to be playing a high-stakes game of trying to rebalance equations within the EU, with a view to diminish the Franco-German stronghold.

At the same time, Germany has not been too keen to tweak the model which has led to these imbalances in the first place. Despite some indications of rebalancing its economy away from an excessive dependence on exports and towards more domestic consumption, the fact remains that Germany continued to run both budget and external surpluses till the COVID-19 shock happened. This did nothing for its neighbours, which hardly benefitted from the size of the German market. Moreover, the country has consistently refused to turn the EU into a transfer union – wherein surplus regions would provide countercyclical support to deficit regions. In the past, Berlin did not express interest in Macron's suggestion of creating a union-wide budget and appointing a finance minister for the Eurozone.

Neither was it willing to make it easy for debt-ridden Eurozone members to borrow cheaply by allowing the issuance of joint European debt securities, since they would carry lower-risk premiums on account of Germany's much higher creditworthiness.

But then, the pandemic happened.

FUTURE IMPERFECT

When the novel coronavirus first began spreading across Europe in March 2020, the 'zone of dysfunction' began to resemble a 'zone of disintegration', as countries sealed borders, indulged in unbridled acrimony, and tried to corner medical supplies and equipment. The virus, it seemed, had emerged as a major centrifugal element in the EU.

Fiscal strings were loosened but only for national jurisdictions. Germany, in particular, had to give up on balancing budgets and opened the tap of spending in a bid to keep its already flagging economy from going under.[59] As did its anti-transfer union allies called the 'Frugals', a group of five north European countries – the Netherlands, Sweden, Austria, Denmark and Finland. But they weren't the only ones who needed to spend to stay afloat. The southern European economies simply could not continue with austerity during this crisis. In order to spend effective amounts, they needed to borrow commensurately, and for that, they needed at least some mutualization of the excessive risk brought on by the COVID-19 shock in the form of 'coronabonds', to be issued for the specific purpose of post-pandemic recovery. But the northern Europeans remained opposed to the idea. They instead proposed that the debt-ridden southern Europeans accept more ESF-style loans and the attendant conditionalities to tide over the crisis.

Italian mayors and politicians on their part reminded Germany of how Italy, Spain and other countries had chosen to forgive much of the debt Berlin owed them after World War II.[60] The impatience of Mediterranean Europe was palpable, with Italian President Sergio Mattarella stating in a televised address in April 2020 that the EC 'must act before it's too late'.[61] Portuguese Prime Minister António Costa was more blunt when he said that 'either the EU does what it has to do or it will end'.[62]

---

[59] Amaro, Silvia. 'The Coronavirus Crisis Has Changed the German Mindset – and This Matters for Markets.' *CNBC*, 6 July 2020, https://www.cnbc.com/2020/07/06/germany-massive-stimulus-reverts-years-of-austerity-mindset.html. See also: Varoufakis, Yanis. 'The EU Coronavirus Fund Will Take Europe Another Step towards Disintegration.' *Guardian*, 24 July 2020, https://www.theguardian.com/world/commentisfree/2020/jul/24/eu-coronavirus-fund-europe-recovery-package.

[60] Borrelli, Silvia Sciorilli, and Matthew Karnitschnig. 'Italy's Future Is in German Hands.' *Politico*, 4 February 2020, https://www.politico.eu/article/coronavirus-italy-future-germany/.

[61] Ibid.

[62] Ibid.

With the EU lurching towards disintegration, the Franco-German core seemed to realize that the same old wine wouldn't suffice this time over. 'We can make this moment of truth a moment of success,' said Macron, as he insisted on the need for a Europe-wide agreement on a recovery package. Germany, on its part, sought to convince the Frugals to avoid falling for the fallacy of composition, since the pain felt by the southern Europeans would eventually reach them through reduced access to markets. Managing to convince the Frugals, the Franco-German alliance was able to push through a €750 billion 'recovery fund' on 21 July 2020 after some 90 hours of negotiations. This fund was made up of €390 billion in grants and €360 billion in loans.[63]

Now, though the amount itself was not significant considering the number of recipients and their varied needs, what made it noteworthy was that it was meant to be raised by jointly issuing debt for the first time in the EU's history.[64] This, in turn, is being touted as a 'game-changing' development by Euro-boosters, who believe that it will serve as a harbinger of greater integration. However, even as this recovery fund was being agreed upon, the northern Europeans insisted that it would not mark the beginning of a mutualization of debt in the Eurozone and that they remained completely opposed to any sort of transfer union.

Moreover, the Frugals okayed this fund only after getting all members to agree that every national government would be allowed to scrutinize how its contributions were being

---

[63] Janse, Kalin Anev, and Iliyana Tsanova. 'What We Can Learn from Europe's Response to the COVID-19 Crisis.' *World Economic Forum*, 10 August 2020, https://www.weforum.org/agenda/2020/08/europe-response-covid-19-coronavirus-economic-crisis-euro-fiscal-monetary-policy-green-deal.

[64] Amaro, Silvia, and Christiane Wang. 'EU Leaders Reach $2 Trillion Deal on Recovery Plan after Marathon Summit.' *CNBC*, 20 July 2020, https://www.cnbc.com/2020/07/21/eu-leaders-reach-a-breakthrough-on-the-regions-recovery-fund.html.

spent, and, furthermore, reserve the right to put a stop to the said payments based on their scrutiny. Surely, given the extant acrimonious climate in the Eurozone, this was a recipe for trouble and further divisiveness.[65]

At the end of the day, the recovery fund will do little to address the original problem that has so divided the Eurozone. One is of course referring to the infliction of austerity on insolvent governments in the hope that they will magically turn around. In fact, the EC is still pushing for governments to balance their books in 2021 once again, when it expects an economic rebound to take place. Unfortunately, this is likely to spark yet another struggle between austerity and recession, even as the debt-to-GDP ratio of various southern European countries explodes. Quite clearly, the ECB will have its hands full trying to pass off debt management operations in the name of QE and extraordinary monetary easing.

The ECB's efforts will mean that the euro will not be seen as any better than the dollar, despite more 'highly rated' euro securities being made available to investors. In fact, given the state of the EU, the euro is in no position to contest the dollar. The Franco-German alliance is aware of this and is instead only looking to protect its turf as it were. This is evident in the EU's move to arm itself with new powers to regulate the operations of 'Big Tech' firms on European soil with respect to competition and content.[66] In extreme cases, the new rules that are sought to be introduced could lead to the total exclusion of targeted firms from the EU market. This is obviously not good news for America's tech titans. Indeed, the pandemic has not exactly served to draw the EU

---

[65] Varoufakis. 'The EU Coronavirus Fund Will Take Europe Another Step towards Disintegration.'

[66] Reuters. 'EU Seeks New Powers to Penalise Tech Giants.' *Economic Times*, 20 September 2020, https://economictimes.indiatimes.com/news/international/business/eu-seeks-new-powers-to-penalise-tech-giants-financial-times/articleshow/78213688.cms.

closer to the US, but has underlined the power differential between the two. A case in point would be the alleged diversion of medical supplies in April 2020 by the US from suppliers in East Asia – supplies that had been apparently intended for France and Germany. The episode witnessed the two countries volubly accusing the US of foul play, with the German interior minister calling it 'modern piracy'.[67]

This spat has also highlighted Europe's dependency on Asia in general and China in particular for medical supplies, among other goods. In fact, China too became a target of European indignation during the pandemic due to instances of substandard supplies and acts of price gouging. Particularly grating for the European capitals was China's so-called 'Wolf-Warrior' diplomacy, which sought to project Beijing's role in the pandemic in a grotesquely positive light, indicative of a thorough insensitivity to the global calamity.

As such, the EU is now focused on diversifying supply chains beyond just medical equipment and food, with a view to restarting production of previously offshored items on European soil.[68] This new diversification and limited localization strategy also extends to securing the supply of up to thirty critical materials used in the manufacture of items ranging from electric vehicles to solar cells. This would be done under the aegis of the Action Plan on Critical Raw Materials (AEST) unveiled by Brussels in September 2020.[69] China naturally finds numerous mentions in AEST's risk-

---

[67] Jeffery, Lynsey. 'German, French Officials Accuse U.S. of Diverting Supplies.' *NPR*, 4 April 2020, https://www.npr.org/2020/04/04/827321294/german-french-officials-accuse-u-s-of-diverting-supplies.

[68] 'EU Trade Chief Urges for More Diverse Supply Chains after Crisis.' *Reuters*, 16 April 2020, https://www.reuters.com/article/us-health-coronavirus-eu-trade-idUSKCN21Y27P.

[69] Van Leeuwen, Hans. 'Europe Looks to Cut Dependence on Chinese Commodities.' *Financial Review*, 4 September 2020, https://www.hellenicshippingnews.com/europe-looks-to-cut-dependence-on-chinese-commodities.

assessment document and it is clear that the EU is now quite wary of its dependence on China for rare-earths, lithium and solar cells.[70] Under a policy it calls 'open strategic autonomy', the EU is now also encouraging member states to vet Chinese investments more closely.

The move to moderate economic ties with China seemed to have also stiffened the German spine on the diplomatic front, at least somewhat. This was evidenced by the sharp German response to the Chinese foreign minister Wang Yi's threat to make the president of the Czech senate, Miloš Vystrčil, 'pay a heavy price' for officially visiting Taiwan in late August 2020 amidst protests from Beijing.[71] In response to this threat, Germany's foreign minister, Heiko Maas, publicly told Yi at a joint press conference held during a visit to Germany in September 2020 that 'threats have no place here'.[72] Speaking to the press after the conference, Maas went on to say that Europe 'would not allow itself to become a political football in the great-power rivalry between the US, Russia and China'.[73]

September 2020 also saw Germany's foreign ministry releasing a document called the 'Policy guidelines for the Indo-Pacific' which gave the impression that the country was going to take a stand against Chinese expansionism in the South China Sea. Against the run of play, however, on 30 December 2020, the EU and China agreed on principle to conclude a long-negotiated 'EU–China Comprehensive Agreement on Investment'. This gave rise to musings that the EU was once again looking to deepen ties with China.

---

[70] Ibid.

[71] Blanchard, Ben, and Yew Lun Tian. 'Czech Senate Speaker Will Pay "Heavy Price" for Taiwan Visit, China Says.' *Reuters*, 31 August 2020, https://www.reuters.com/article/us-taiwan-czech-china-idUSKBN25R059.

[72] Associated Press. 'Defying China's Wrath, Czech Senator Delivers Taiwan Speech.' *CNBC*, 1 September 2020, https://www.cnbc.com/2020/09/01/defying-chinas-wrath-czech-senator-delivers-taiwan-speech.html.

[73] Ibid.

However, in just a few months, this seeming rapprochement came unstuck. In March 2021, the EU sanctioned four Chinese officials over suspected human rights violations in China's far western region of Xinjiang. And in May 2021, the EC suspended efforts to ratify the proposed investment treaty after China imposed sanctions on several high-profile EU parliamentarians, functionaries and scholars on China. Meanwhile, Lithuania dropped out of the 17+1 formulation, calling for European solidarity instead. And in August 2021, Germany deployed a frigate to the South China Sea, signalling its intent to support the efforts of France to push back against Chinese revanchism in the global maritime commons.

Clearly, the EU has begun to draw a line with one of its 'Systemic Competitors'. However, the Franco-German alliance has some distance to go before it emerges as an independent pole in the emerging great-power competition of today. At the moment, the EU is mostly striving for strategic autonomy vis-à-vis the US and China by compartmentalizing competition and cooperation with either. The extent to which the EU will be able to manage this game remains to be seen. For the time being, however, excessive euro liquidity will join excessive dollar liquidity in creating greater spillover effects for emerging market economies, which will, yet again, find their own monetary policies constrained. This has been the case in the past too, from the time the floodgates of liquidity were first opened up by Western central banks after the GFC.

But despite some progress in creating joint mechanisms for mitigating the effects of unconventional monetary policies in the US and EU, the key pillars of the emerging world, such as India and China, have so far been unable to come together to create an alternative global financial architecture. Rather, growing divergences among them suggests that Western financial hegemony will continue for some time yet. This is what we shall examine next.

THREE

IN 2003, GOLDMAN SACHS CAME OUT WITH ITS NOW FAMOUS report, 'Dreaming with BRICs: The Path to 2050' (henceforth referred to as 'GS 2003').[1] The report built upon an earlier thesis by the investment bank's chief economist, Jim O'Neill, that the four economies, Brazil, Russia, India and China – or BRICs – could, given their land mass and population, surpass the Group of Six or G-6 association of 'developed' economies, namely, the US, Japan, Germany, France, the United Kingdom and Italy, in cumulative size by 2050, in dollar terms. 'GS 2003' projected that India and China could become the dominant producers of goods and services by the middle of the twenty-first century, even as Brazil and Russia held forth as the world's top raw-material suppliers, suggesting the possibility of a major global realignment, one that saw these four players draw closer.

In the wake of the GFC, 'GS 2003' certainly seemed prescient. By 2008, the four BRIC countries had moved to institutionalize their cooperation, with the first summit-level meeting happening a year later, in 2009, at the Russian city of Yekaterinburg in the Urals.[2] In 2010, the BRIC

---

[1] Wilson, Dominic, and Roopa Purushothaman. 'Dreaming with BRICs: The Path to 2050.' *Goldman Sachs*, 1 October 2003, http://www.goldmansachs.com/our-thinking/archive/archive-pdfs/brics-dream.pdf.

[2] Faulconbridge, Guy. 'Developing World Leaders Show New Power at Summits.' *Reuters*, 16 June 2009, https://www.reuters.com/article/us-summit/developing-world-leaders-show-new-power-at-summits-idUSTRE55F02F20090616?feedType=RSS&feedName=topNews.

countries also incorporated South Africa into their emerging geo-economic formation to create what is now known as the 'BRICS' grouping.[3] This happened despite Goldman Sachs having suggested in 2003 that the African country was too small to be in such a grouping. The inclusion of South Africa was clearly aimed at giving BRICS a more pan-global economic-south character, while also reflecting the importance of emerging Africa to any future alternative financial architecture that was not centred on the West.

In fact, with the US and Japan falling into recession in the immediate aftermath of the GFC, the GDP projections of 'GS 2003' with respect to the time when India and China would surpass the two G-6 nations in GDP terms began to look rather conservative. China and India continued to register positive GDP growth rates in the wake of the GFC, with the former's fiscal stimulus allowing it to register a real GDP growth rate of over 9 per cent in 2009.[4] This resulted in China surpassing Japan in GDP terms in 2010 itself, a full five years before 'GS 2003' had speculated it could happen.[5] Indeed, estimates made by other agencies in the post-GFC period suggested that India and China would cross the GDP-related milestones of 'GS 2003' much earlier than what the report had projected. In 2010, Standard Chartered predicted that China would surpass the US in nominal GDP by as early as 2020, as opposed to the 2043 date proposed by Goldman Sachs![6]

---

[3] P., J.P. 'Why Is South Africa Included in the BRICS?' *Economist*, 29 March 2013, https://www.economist.com/the-economist-explains/2013/03/29/why-is-south-africa-included-in-the-brics.

[4] 'GDP Growth (Annual %) – India, China, Brazil, Russian Federation, South Africa.' *World Bank*, based on national accounts data and OECD National Accounts data files from 1961 to 2019, https://data.worldbank.org/indicator/NY.GDP.MKTP.KD.ZG?locations=IN-CN-BR-RU-ZA.

[5] Tabuchi, Hiroko. 'Economy in Japan Fell 0.3% at Year End.' *New York Times*, 13 February 2011, https://www.nytimes.com/2011/02/14/business/global/14yen.html.

[6] Adam, Shamim. 'China to Exceed US by 2020, Standard Chartered Says.'

The other BRICS members, however, did not fare too well in the aftermath of the GFC. Brazil, Russia and South Africa all saw GDP growth enter negative territory in 2009.[7] Nonetheless, they posted recoveries the very next year, and seemed to be out of recession by 2011. With China and India leading the growth charge, and the rest of the BRICS group also posting modest growth rates, the stage seemed set for an inexorable shift in geo-economic influence and power towards the emerging entente of BRICS.

FOLLOW THE GROWTH

Enthused by the buoyant outlook for the BRICS economies and the global 'search for yield', due to the adoption of highly accommodative monetary policies by the Fed and other Western central banks which induced investors to look for better returns elsewhere due to the lowering of interest rates, international asset managers steadily increased their exposure to emerging market economies (EMEs) in general and to BRICS in particular from 2009–11. Indeed, this period could be characterized as a 'risk-on' period, a time during which investors feel confident enough to move into supposedly riskier but higher-yielding assets, such as EME stock and debt markets. Conversely, the GFC and its immediate aftermath would be a 'risk-off' period, wherein investors, worried about losing their 'riskier bets', abandon the same for low- or no-risk propositions, such as US treasury bonds or even outright cash.

Bloomberg, 15 November 2010, https://www.bloomberg.com/news/articles/2010-11-15/china-may-surpass-u-s-by-2020-in-super-cy5cle-standard-chartered-says.

[7] 'GDP Growth (Annual %) – India, China, Brazil, Russian Federation, South Africa.' *World Bank*.

The 'low for long'[8] forward guidance by the US Fed, however, was enough to bring on the mother of all risk-on episodes during the QE era, with investors desperate to benefit from continuing growth in places like India and China, even as growth had essentially stalled in the West. It is in an environment of growth that the demand for funds usually exceeds its supply, with the attendant rise in interest earnings from investment. Also, at a time of high economic activity, there are numerous investment classes and companies to choose from that can provide relatively high returns.

The BRICS countries, however, wanted to go a step further: use this tremendous Western interest in their growth stories to enable the reordering of international financial frameworks that would accommodate their rise. In the wake of 2008, they sought to have reforms instituted at key global economic governance bodies, such as the IMF and the World Bank. At the time, the West, led by the US, seemed amenable to this agenda, as signalled by the 2008 'Group of 20' (G-20) nations meet in Washington, where the need for a so-called 'Bretton Woods II' was agreed in principle, leading to Manmohan Singh, the then Indian Prime Minister, commenting that the summit was 'a clear indication that the balance of power is shifting in favour of emerging economies'.[9]

Following the 2008 summit, by December 2010, the IMF's Board of Governors had agreed to a slew of reforms that would see a modest increase in the representation of EMEs in the governance of the body.[10] The centrepiece of these reforms

---

[8] This meant the US Fed would keep interest rates low for an extended period of time—a form of 'forward guidance'. See also: chapter one.

[9] Chikermane, Gautam. 'Power Shift to New Economies, Says PM.' *Hindustan Times*, 17 November 2008, https://m.hindustantimes.com/business/power-shift-to-new-economies-says-pm/story-aA3g3jAiaWruOU9Lo265iN_amp.html.

[10] 'IMF Board of Governors Approves Major Quota and Governance Reforms.' *IMF*, 16 December 2010, https://www.imf.org/external/np/sec/

was an unprecedented doubling of quotas (that is, member contributions) accompanied by a 6 per cent shift in quota shares (which determine voting power) to dynamic emerging markets and developing countries from mostly advanced and oil-producing economies. The realignment of quota shares would see the four original BRICS countries become among the top 10 shareholding members of the IMF and, thereby, in the ranks of those with the greatest voting power in the body. Importantly, the reforms were also designed to protect the quota shares and voting power of the IMF's poorest members, leading to a situation where, of the 110 countries that would gain or maintain quota shares post the reforms, 102 would be emerging or developing ones. The IMF's board also supported an amendment to its articles of agreement that would facilitate a move to a more representative, all-elected executive board.

These reforms being pushed under the IMF's '14th General Review of Quotas', however, required the acceptance of at least three-fifths of the members, representing 85 per cent of the total voting power in the organization. This meant that the support of the US was key to seeing them through, since America, with its existing 16.75 per cent vote share in the IMF, had an effective veto over decisions such as quota reform. The Obama administration, which was said to be an enthusiastic supporter of these reforms, nonetheless required the support of the US legislature to vote in favour of the 14th Review. And that support had to be garnered from the US Congress before December 2012, which was the initial deadline set for member nations to take the final decision.

Till around 2012, the BRICS economies believed that they would get their due at the IMF, and this was reflected in their willingness to enhance contributions to the body on the sidelines of an informal meeting of the grouping's

---

pr/2010/ pr10477.htm.

leaders in Los Cabos that year. The official statement released stated clearly:

> These new contributions are being made in anticipation that all the reforms agreed upon in 2010 will be fully implemented in a timely manner, including a comprehensive reform of voting power and reform of quota shares.[11]

The contributions were made as part of the IMF's New Arrangements to Borrow (NAB) credit system, which allows it to borrow funds from members over and above their quota contributions during exigencies such as the GFC.[12] Indeed, despite its position as the world's lender of last resort, the IMF at the time had a corpus of only $370 billion from its quota contributions, and the NAB contributions made by the BRICS members played a major role in the international stabilization efforts of the IMF post-2008. The understanding was that the new contributions being made under the NAB would be converted into quota contributions once the 14th Review reforms were adopted by the IMF. Essentially, the BRICS nations were already advancing the additional sums to the IMF that they would have to give once the quota contributions were doubled as a part of the 14th Review reforms package.

However, by 2013, it had become clear to BRICS that the US political process was not really in favour of these reforms, as the Obama administration failed to convince the US Congress of the necessity and usefulness of this to

---

[11] PTI. 'BRICS Leaders Pledge $75 Billion to IMF's Euro Zone War Chest.' *The Hindu Business Line*, 19 June 2012, http://www.thehindubusinessline.com/economy/brics-leaders-pledge-75-billion-to-imfs-euro-zone-war-chest/article3546228.ece.

[12] 'Where the IMF Gets its Money.' *IMF*, 31 March 2020, https://www.imf.org/en/About/Factsheets/Where-the-IMF-Gets-Its-Money. See also: 'IMF Standing Borrowing Arrangements.' *IMF*, January 2018, https://www.imf.org/en/About/Factsheets/Where-the-IMF-Gets-Its-Money.

America.[13] Opposition in the US Congress basically centred on the fact that the US would have had to double its quota contributions to the IMF, even as its relative voting power would reduce in the face of reallocated quota shares. Similar concerns were also being echoed in European capitals, which had long been accustomed to a disproportionate voice at the IMF despite having only a very small fraction of the world's population. The real US worry could have also stemmed from the fact that as per the new vote-share distribution, BRICS, if operating as a bloc, would have almost 15 per cent of the votes, which would mean that the US would no longer be the sole wielder of a de facto veto over major decisions in the IMF. This fear probably crystallized as BRICS started to move beyond talking shop, and began to institutionalize their interactions.

TAPER TANTRUMS

Even as the IMF reforms remained stalled, the US Fed announced in early 2013 that it was beginning to 'taper' its bond-buying programme under QE. This almost doubled the yield on benchmark 10-year US treasury bonds in a span of three months, during late spring 2013, leading to these suddenly becoming attractive again in the risk-return space for investors, who started deserting emerging market bonds and equities for the apparently 'safer' climes of the US bond market.[14] The result was tremendous volatility in the BRICS debt and currency markets, as 'hot money' that had been borrowed from US markets at near-zero rates flew back there. India, Brazil and South Africa seemed particularly affected by

---

[13] Stuenkel, Oliver. 'The Death of IMF Reform?' *Diplomat*, 22 February 2014, http://thediplomat.com/2014/02/the-death-of-imf-reform.

[14] US Government. 'Daily Treasury Yield Curve Rates.' *US Department of the Treasury*, 2013, https://www.treasury.gov/resource-center/data-chart-center/interest-rates/pages/TextView.aspx?data=yieldYear&year=2013.

the Taper Tantrum, with Morgan Stanley including them in a club of the 'fragile five', countries with currencies most vulnerable to capital outflows.[15]

The episode served to underline to the BRICS countries just how dangerous the so-called 'carry trade' involving the investment of dollar funds borrowed at very low rates in the West into their debt and equity markets had become. At a mere signal from the Fed, there could be vast outflows from their economies, putting pressure on exchange rates, which in turn would make foreign currency debt owed by their domestic corporations that much harder to service. The Fed was effectively the world's de facto central bank, although one that could be counted upon to respond only to the requirements of the US economy.

And EMEs were particularly vulnerable to capital flow reversals as they typically have more unhedged foreign currency borrowings than advanced economies (AEs).[16] This exacerbates the issue of currency mismatch, which refers to a situation – to explain a complex issue somewhat simply – where domestic firms may have more foreign currency denominated liabilities than assets. A depreciation in the exchange rate following a sudden stop invariably leads to a tightening of financial conditions for such firms, and this is reflected in far lower spending by them. Asset markets, such as real estate, also suffer due to the withdrawal of liquidity from the system. Moreover, export finance in dollars also dries up. What is worse, since EME exports are usually invoiced in dollars, the fall in the exchange rate may not boost their exports – at least in the near term. What all this

[15] Global Emerging Markets Equity Team. 'Elections 2014: How Fragile Are the "Fragile Five"?' *Morgan Stanley*, 3 December 2013, https://www.morganstanley.com/public/Tales_from_the_Emerging_World_Fragile_Five.pdf

[16] That is, not protected against loss by balancing or compensating contracts or transactions.

means for an EME is that an exchange rate depreciation does not necessarily boost growth by way of greater exports, as it would for an AE, and can indeed hurt output growth due to a tightening of domestic financial conditions. The fall in the exchange rate can, however, lead to greater inflation, due to pass-through from imported inputs on to fuel and food prices, which in turn could lead to second-order effects on inflation. This is on account of greater wage demands. After all, food and fuel constitute a major part of the retail inflation basket in EMEs such as India. The spillover effects for EMEs just described, where the effect of a depreciation on exports (that is, output) and inflation may not be in the same direction, had become more pronounced since the GFC. This was because both foreign currency borrowings by EME corporations as well as the participation of foreign investors in their capital markets had grown considerably since 2008, owing to both the availability of cheap money in the AEs and the concomitant global search for yield.

Thus, the 2008 meltdown notwithstanding, the BRICS countries were still feeling the force of America's pre-eminent position in the international financial system. In fact, far from getting greater say at the IMF, which in any case had been blocked by the US Congress, BRICS found that multilateral financial institutions were once again being driven by West-centric agendas. For instance, emerging economies were not happy with the nature and magnitude of the bailout packages being given to Greece by the IMF ever since its sovereign debt crisis began. It seemed to BRICS that the international body was being party to a barely concealed effort to save the euro and foster further privatization of the Greek economy in a way that helped Western corporations.[17] Interestingly, the

---

[17] India had argued at the IMF back in 2010 itself that what Greece needed was a part cancellation of its debt liabilities rather than recurrent refinancing coupled with austerity measures that would only serve to make its debt burden worse and put it in need of further bailouts. This assessment, as we saw in the previous chapter, turned out to be correct.

Greek crisis had all the shades of IMF lending behaviour from the 1980s, when it imposed severe loan conditionalities on African countries, which were stuck in an external debt trap.[18] India and China were not necessarily opposed to the bailout packages given to Greece, but they wanted a say in the way the money was being advanced to it.

By February–March 2014, relations between Russia and the West had begun to deteriorate rapidly due to the former's annexation of Crimea and the conflict in Ukraine. In March 2014, a first round of Western sanctions would be imposed on Russia, which would push it towards a financial crisis, as foreign capital began to flee. In fact, Russia would have to literally burn through its foreign exchange reserves in a bid to support the rouble, as even domestic retail investors began to switch their rouble deposits to dollars.

Meanwhile, apart from the effects of the Taper Tantrum, the economies of Brazil and South Africa were getting weighed down by a general fall in the prices of metals, minerals and other commodities that had begun around 2013–14. It was this 'end to the commodity super-cycle' as it were that spelled trouble for the two countries as well as Russia, and all three needed investments that would help them lower costs in their key resource sectors, besides catalysing the diversification of their economies as well.[19]

The stage was therefore set for BRICS to draw closer and erect two tangible pillars of their engagement with the signing of the Contingency Reserve Arrangement (CRA) treaty and establishment of the BRICS Development Bank

---

[18] Hanlon, Joseph. 'Wolfowitz, the World Bank, and Illegitimate Lending.' *Brown Journal of World Affairs*, Spring/Summer 2007, Volume 13, Issue 2, https://www.brown.edu/initiatives/journal-world-affairs/sites/brown.edu.initiatives.journal-world-affairs/files/private/articles/13.2_Hanlon.pdf.

[19] 'Africa: End of the Commodity Super-cycle Weighs on Growth.' *World Bank*, 13 April 2015, https://www.worldbank.org/en/news/press-release/2015/04/13/africa-end-of-the-commodity-super-cycle-weighs-on-growth.

(now called the New Development Bank, or NDB), during the Sixth BRICS Summit held at Fortaleza, Brazil, in July 2014.[20]

A NEW DEVELOPMENT

The CRA is a $100 billion reserve pooling arrangement meant to provide emergency liquidity to member countries during a balance of payments crisis, with 41 per cent of it being funded by China, 18 per cent each by Brazil, India and Russia, and the remaining 5 per cent being contributed by South Africa.[21] However, in the event of an emergency liquidity situation, China would be able to call upon only half its contribution, Brazil, India and Russia could request an amount equal to their contributions, while South Africa would be able to seek more than twice its contribution.[22] The overall voting power in the CRA decision-making process is not on an equal basis either. While just 5 per cent of the total voting power is spread equally among the participants, the remaining 95 per cent is distributed proportionately, to the value of each participant's commitment to the CRA.[23,24]

---

[20] The CRA's objective was to provide emergency dollar liquidity to members during risk-off episodes such as the Taper Tantrum, whereas the NDB was a new multilateral bank tailored to provide financing for the infrastructural needs of emerging economies. See also: Government of India. 'Sixth BRICS Summit – Fortaleza Declaration.' *Ministry of External Affairs*, 15 July 2014, https://www.mea.gov.in/bilateral-documents.htm?dtl/23635/Sixth+BRICS+Summit++Fortaleza+Declaration.

[21] 'Treaty for the Establishment of a BRICS Contingent Reserve Arrangement.' *University of Toronto*, BRICS Information Centre, 15 July 2014, http://www.brics.utoronto.ca/docs/140715-treaty.html.

[22] Ibid.

[23] Ibid.

[24] The CRA would essentially allow BRICS to provide short-term liquidity to each other through dollar swaps under the aegis of an interbank agreement between the countries' central banks that would lay down the operational procedures for extension of support when requested. Thus, the

At $100 billion, the CRA may seem to be a fraction of the stabilization funds available to the IMF, but then it is also spread amongst far fewer parties in this case. To be sure, the individual emergency funds that can be drawn aren't that big by themselves, relative to the requirements of the respective BRICS economies, but the very presence of the CRA serves as a 'precautionary instrument' in the light of 'potential short-term balance of payments pressures' as the agreement itself underlines. Besides, in the years ahead, the CRA's scope could well expand, and it is, in any case, open to new members as well.[25]

As mentioned above, the 2014 Fortaleza Summit also saw the agreement for the NDB being signed, which was formed with the express purpose of:

> [M]obilizing resources for infrastructure and sustainable development projects in BRICS and other emerging economies and developing countries, complementing the existing efforts of multilateral and regional financial institutions for global growth and development.[26]

---

participating countries would retain possession of committed resources until a request for assistance by one party was granted and a currency swap actually took place. The dollar swap itself would involve the exchange of the requesting country's currency for US dollars, to be repaid at a later date, with the exchange rate for both the transaction and repurchase being the spot market rate a couple of days prior to the date on which the respective central banks' accounts are credited. Interest will be paid on the dollars obtained by the requesting party, but not on the requesting party's currency by the providing party.

[25] Of course, the fact that just 30 per cent of the maximum amount a party is entitled to request will be made available subject to the approval of the other participants, with the remaining 70 per cent being contingent on the conclusion of a conditionality-based agreement with the IMF, seems to also detract from its efficacy in providing appreciable short-term liquidity in a simple manner. However, this IMF linking criterion could also change in the future.

[26] 'Agreement on the New Development Bank – Fortaleza, July 15.' *New Development Bank*, 15 July 2015, https://www.ndb.int/wp-content/

However, unlike global multilateral financial institutions, such as the World Bank, but in a manner akin to some regional initiatives like the Corporación Andina de Fomento (CAF), the NDB was initially capitalized on an equal share voting basis. And thus, each BRICS country guaranteed $10 billion for a total authorized capital base of $50 billion, which is to be doubled to the full authorized capital level of $100 billion in the years ahead.[27] Also, unlike the World Bank, the presidency of the NDB is on a rotational basis, with each founding member getting to elect a president for a five-year term.[28]

Clearly, the NDB's charter was drafted in a manner that would seem to posit it as more democratic and equitable than the Bretton Woods twins. Of course, there were those who derided it as a 'BRICS club', although there is every likelihood that someday new members would join. Nevertheless, back in 2014, it took considerable bargaining from India to make China accept the equal shares principle. India was also adamant that no member be allowed to increase its share in due course without the concurrence of the four other members. This too was agreed upon.[29]

---

themes/ndb/pdf/Agreement-on-the-New-Development-Bank.pdf.

[27] Ibid.

[28] 'The Bank shall have an initial authorized capital of US$ 100 billion. The initial subscribed capital shall be US$ 50 billion, equally shared among founding members. The first chair of the Board of Governors shall be from Russia. The first chair of the Board of Directors shall be from Brazil. The first President of the Bank shall be from India. The headquarters of the Bank shall be located in Shanghai. The New Development Bank Africa Regional Center shall be established in South Africa concurrently with the headquarters.' Taken from 'About Us.' *New Development Bank*, https://www.ndb.int/about-us/essence/history/.

[29] 'Victory for Modi, India as BRICS Summit Clears Setting Up of a New Development Bank.' *India Today*, 16 November 2015, http://indiatoday.intoday.in/story/modi-victory-brics-summit-clears-a-new-development-bank/1/372582.html.

What, however, was not agreeable to the other members, apart from India, was its proposal to have the NDB headquartered in New Delhi. Rather, the Chinese desire to have it located in Shanghai was more to the liking of Russia, Brazil and South Africa. After all, each of these countries had seen their exports to China rise considerably since the beginning of the new millennium. And now, with the end of the commodity super-cycle, they were becoming even more beholden to China as a customer, besides looking towards it for fresh investments that could help them increase the competitiveness of their economies. The People's Republic, which alone accounted for two-thirds of cumulative BRICS' GDP, already boasted of gleaming infrastructure on its eastern seaboard, and at the time seemed more in need of making loans than taking them. So, even though China's economy had already entered a structural slowdown, it was still being seen as the 'shining city on a hill' among the BRICS countries.

On the other hand, India–China trade, which too had risen greatly since the 2000s, was heavily skewed in Beijing's favour.[30] Indeed, India's trade deficit with Beijing had become a major sticking point in bilateral relations. Xi Jinping's visit to India in April 2014, on the eve of which he had announced that China would invest some $100 billion in India in the coming years, had also been marred by a border incident.

Moreover, by mid-2014, India's economic environment was on the mend, with a putative acceleration in growth. Its strengthening economic fundamentals suggested that it could no longer be considered a part of the 'fragile five', as

---

[30] Though bilateral India–China trade has also grown by several multiples in the new millennium, it has leaned in Beijing's favour. Indeed, it was China that benefitted at India's expense, with the bilateral trade deficit amounting to $37.8 billion in 2014 out of a total trade volume of $70.59 billion. Which means that India's trade deficit with China itself accounted for more than half of its total trade!

it had been in 2013. This would soon be attested to by the IMF's then India mission chief, Paul A. Cashin, who observed in October 2014:

> India is the odd man out from the emerging markets and BRICS economies that were being called the Fragile Five last year… But the story for India changed quickly… India is better prepared for shocks today than when the U.S. Fed's tapering started and more prepared than other emerging markets.[31]

An improving environment would actually allow India to beat China's annual GDP growth rate for the first time in several years in 2014.

As such, India was wont to be seen helping China leverage the 'multi-polar' BRICS framework for furthering its own geopolitical agenda. At the same time, it was also imperative that the Western order be shown that an alternative financial architecture can and will be developed. The reconciliation of these two objectives in New Delhi's mind took the form of its insistence on the equal shares principle, which meant that BRICS would be a consensus-driven body.

Though India's insistence on this principle was criticized by some as having prevented the capital base of the NDB from attaining a size it could have, since China would have put in more authorized capital, the size was nonetheless considerable. For instance, based on its capital subscription, it was estimated in 2014 that the NDB could lend up to $35 billion annually over the next two decades, exceeding the $31.6 billion lent by the World Bank on an annual average basis during the period 2009–13. This is perhaps why Joseph Stiglitz remarked at the time of the NDB's creation that it

---

[31] Mehra, Pooja. 'India off Fragile Five List, Says IMF.' *The Hindu*, 26 October 2014, https://www.thehindu.com/business/Economy/india-off-fragile-five-list-says-international-monetary-fund/article6535530.ece.

represented a 'fundamental change in global economic and political power'.[32]

Truth be told, for several years, the World Bank's lending potential had become suspect at a time when the investment needs of emerging economies across the globe had already grown. By 2008 itself, emerging economies were investing in infrastructure at a rate that was twice that of mature economies, and this had accelerated further as more populations grew out of low-income status and demanded better electricity, transport, telecommunications and water services.[33] According to the World Bank itself, there was an annual 'trillion dollar infrastructure investment gap' in emerging economies and existing development banks could at best fill 40 per cent of that requirement.[34]

With the US Congress missing the revised deadline of end 2014 set by the IMF's board for it to accept the 14th Review reforms package,[35] BRICS went ahead in bringing the CRA and NDB agreements into force at the Ufa Summit held in July 2015. India's veteran banker K.V. Kamath was appointed the first president of the NDB as a quid pro quo for China getting to set up the NDB's headquarters in Shanghai.[36] Further underlining the balance of power within

---

[32] Stiglitz, Joseph. 'Nobel Economist Joseph Stiglitz Hails New BRICS Bank Challenging U.S.-Dominated World Bank & IMF.' *Democracy Now*, 17 July 2014, https://www.democracynow.org/2014/7/17/nobel_economist_joseph_stiglitz_hails_new.

[33] Dobb, R., et al. 'How the Growth of Emerging Markets Will Strain Global Finance.' *McKinsey & Company*, December 2010, http://www.mckinsey.com/global-themes/winning-in-emerging-markets/how-the-growth-of-emerging-markets-will-strain-global-finance.

[34] 'Global Infrastructure Facility.' *World Bank*, 2016, https://www.worldbank.org/en/programs/global-Infrastructure-facility/brief/global-infrastructure-facility-gif-opens-for-business.

[35] Yukhananov, Anna. 'U.S. Congress Will Not Pass IMF Reforms This Year.' *Reuters*, 10 December 2014, http://www.reuters.com/article/us-usa-congress-imf-idUSKBN0JO1UC20141210.

[36] PTI. 'KV Kamath Appointed BRICS Bank President.' *Business Today*,

the grouping would be the fact that the inaugural chairman of the Board of Directors would come from Brazil, and the inaugural chairman of the Board of Governors would be from Russia.[37]

Thus, despite the shades of rivalry, the NDB emerged as an example of geo-economic congruence between India and China. Since the early 2000s, both countries had chosen, on occasion, to cooperate on global economic issues, keeping aside their border dispute and geostrategic competition. Examples range from their coordination of national positions during global climate change talks to jointly bidding for oil and gas assets in third countries, as part of a consortium. In the case of the NDB, the need to close ranks against continued Western intransigence in letting the world financial order evolve provided the necessary coincidence for the two Asian giants. For Russia, being able to act as a facilitator between the two rising countries of the East, that were already serving as large markets for its military technology and natural resources, strengthened its hand in the face of its dramatically deteriorating relations with the West, led by the US.

This convergence of interests between India and China extended to the Asian Infrastructure Investment Bank (AIIB) as well, though it had an essentially Chinese heart.[38] Launched at an elaborate ceremony in Beijing in October 2014, with its treaty of agreements coming into force in December 2015, the AIIB had also been set up to fill the 'infrastructure financing gap' that had cropped up in emerging economies, but it would be focused on lending to the Asia–Pacific region, rather than on a global scale. In 2015, it was believed

---

11 May 2015, https://www.businesstoday.in/current/economy-politics/kv-kamath-named-head-of-new-development-bank-brics-nations/story/219147.html.

[37] Ibid.

[38] 'Who Will Pay for Asia's $8 Trillion Infrastructure Gap?' *Asian Development Bank*, 30 September 2013, http://www.adb.org/news/infographics/who-will-pay-asias-8-trillion-infrastructure-gap.

that Asia alone required $8 trillion for new investment in infrastructure by 2020.

Also headquartered in Shanghai, like the NDB, the AIIB is, in some ways, China's answer to the US–Japan-centric ADB, and it signalled the country's rise to prominence in the Asia–Pacific when juxtaposed with the influence of those two countries. This is underlined by the fact that voting power in the AIIB is decided by the economic size of the member countries and not on the basis of their contributions to the bank's authorized capital. China's shareholding is 30.34 per cent and it has retained 26.06 per cent of the voting rights, alongside veto powers for certain key decisions.[39]

Though the AIIB had been posited as a 'regional initiative' due to its lending geography and the fact that Asian members would at all times own more than three-quarters of the bank, its ranks of founding members included the four largest European economies, that is, Germany, Britain, France and Italy. This fact, of course, caused a fair deal of consternation in the US, which tried to prevent these countries from joining the AIIB. In the case of Britain, the Obama administration's open message to the country to not join the bank, which was ignored, ended up becoming a major foreign policy loss for Washington and an image gain for China.

On the other hand, Japan's decision to not participate showed that it did not wish to be 'structurally' relegated to second place in the AIIB vis-à-vis China (since voting power is decided by the size of the economy), with the latter also holding a veto on certain matters. From its perspective, the country's overseas lending was better deployed through the ADB, where the US and Japan have 15.6 per cent and 15.7 per cent stake respectively, while China has just 6.5 per cent.

---

[39] Aneja, Atul. '50 Nations in, AIIB Takes Shape.' *The Hindu*, 30 June 2015, http://www.thehindu.com/news/national/india-signs-articles-that-determine-each-countrys-share-in-asian-infrastructure-investment-bank/article7368050.ece.

Plus, the bank invariably has a Japanese president.[40] With Japan not participating in the AIIB, India, as Asia's third-largest economy in nominal terms, became the second-largest stakeholder, with 8.52 per cent of the shares and a voting share of 7.5 per cent. The AIIB was evidently 'multilateral' enough for India to participate in, even though it was a China-led initiative. It was also in keeping with New Delhi's emerging doctrine of shaping multinational institutions from 'within', if it could.

But the constrictions of multilateralism, while useful from the perspective of underlining China's official posture – that it did not wish to upend the existing order – were obviously not acceptable for a country which believed that the time had come for it to put in motion a major self-centric 'going out' plan. A plan that was intended to help China turn itself into an 'indispensable nation', much as the US already fancied itself to be.[41]

A BELT AND A ROAD

During a visit to Kazakhstan in September 2013, Chinese President Xi Jinping talked about a 'New Silk Road Economic Belt' (SREB) linking China and Europe through Central and West Asia. And while on a state visit to Indonesia in October 2013, he spoke about the '21st Century Maritime Silk Road' (MSR) that would connect China to Southeast Asia, Africa

---

[40] Qin, Chen, and Takehiro Masutomo. 'Why Japan Dominates Leadership of Asian Development Bank.' *CNBC*, 3 April 2013, https://www.cnbc.com/id/100614728. See also: 'Past ADB Presidents.' *Asian Development Bank*, https://www.adb.org/about/management/past-presidents.

[41] In 2014, Hillary Clinton used the phrase in her memoir *Hard Choices*, giving it popular currency again. For a history of the phrase, see also: Zenko, Micah. 'The Myth of the Indispensable Nation.' *Foreign Policy*, 6 November 2014, https://foreignpolicy.com/2014/11/06/the-myth-of-the-indispensable-nation.

and then Europe.[42] These alignments were supposed to be a throwback to the ancient trade routes that connected China to the global economies during the early medieval era – when it was the world's largest economy. Taken together, the SREB and the MSR constituted what was called the One Belt One Road (OBOR) initiative, which was elevated to the level of a 'national strategy' during a Communist Party of China (CPC) Central Committee plenary session in November 2013. In 2015, Beijing released a 'Belt and Road action plan' and, since 2016, OBOR has simply been called the Belt and Road Initiative in the English documents used by the People's Republic of China. In fact, the BRI was incorporated into China's 13th Five-Year Plan (2016–20) in 2016, and made a part of the Party Constitution the year after that.

A map released by China's National Development and Reform Commission in a March 2015 document titled 'Vision and Actions on Jointly Building the Silk Road Economic Belt and the 21st Century Maritime Silk Road' gives an inkling of the sheer extent of the country's ambitions. Now, as per the '13th Five-Year Plan for Economic and Social Development of the People's Republic of China (2016 to 2020)', the stated objectives of the BRI are:[43]

1. Increasing commerce along the BRI networks:
   We will improve the bilateral and multilateral co-operation mechanisms of the BRI focusing on

---

[42] Qian, Xiao. 'Belt and Road Benefits Indonesia, the World.' *Jakarta Post*, 5 April 2019, https://www.thejakartapost.com/academia/2019/04/05/belt-and-road-benefits-indonesia-the-world.html. See also: Jinping, Xi. 'Speech to Indonesian Parliament.' *ASEAN–China Center*, 2 October 2013, http://www.asean-china-center.org/english/2013-10/03/c_133062675.htm.

[43] People's Republic of China, National Development and Reform Commission. '13th Five-Year Plan for Economic and Social Development of the People's Republic of China (2016 to 2020).' Translated by the Compilation and Translation Bureau, Central Committee of the Communist Party of China, *Central Compilation & Translation Press*, 2016, https://en.ndrc.gov.cn/policies/202105/P020210527785800103339.pdf

policy communication, infrastructure connectivity, trade facilitation, capital flow, and people-to-people exchanges.[44]

2. Creating free trade areas along the BRI routes:
   We will speed up efforts to implement the free trade area strategy, gradually establishing a network of high-standard free trade areas. We will actively engage in negotiations with countries and regions along the routes of the BRI on the building of free trade areas.[45]
3. Heightening financial integration to fund infrastructure:
   We will strengthen co-operation with international organizations including international financial organizations and institutions, work actively to promote the development of the Asian Infrastructure Investment Bank and the New Development Bank, put the Silk Road Fund to effective use, and attract international capital for the creation of a financial co-operation platform that is open, pluralistic, and mutually beneficial.[46]
4. Securing natural resources:
   We will strengthen international co-operation on energy and resources and production chains, and increase local processing and conversion.[47]
5. Improving communications infrastructure in the BRI corridors:
   We will advance the development of multi-modal transportation that integrates expressways, railways, waterways, and airways, build international logistics thoroughfares, and strengthen infrastructure development along major routes and at major ports of entry. We will work to develop Xinjiang as the core region for the Silk

---

[44] From chapter 51, section 1. 'Cooperation Mechanisms', 13th Five-Year Plan, p. 147.

[45] From chapter 52, section 2. 'Regional and Bilateral Free Trade Systems', 13th Five-Year Plan, p. 149.

[46] From chapter 51, section 1. 'Cooperation Mechanisms', 13th Five-Year Plan, p. 147.

[47] From, chapter 37, section 1. 'Development of the Western Region', 13th Five-Year Plan, p. 104.

Road Economic Belt and Fujian as the core region for the 21st Century Maritime Silk Road.[48]

6. Enriching cultural exchanges:
We will conduct extensive international co-operation in the areas of education, science, technology, culture, sports, tourism, environmental protection, health care and traditional Chinese medicine.[49]

Along the land-based stretch, that is, the 'belt', China has been pushing investment in contemporary rail and road infrastructure, and power transmission and generation as well as optical fibre networks that would create a structural superhighway facilitating the movement of goods, services, people and information across the length of Eurasia. On the infrastructure side of things, the MSR has naturally seen greater focus on modern port projects and other measures to improve seaborne connectivity. The idea, according to Chinese state-run media, was to create an economic cooperation area 'that stretches from the Western Pacific to the Baltic Sea'.[50]

The BRI sits well with China's need to find an outlet for the massive overcapacity it currently has in its infrastructure-related sectors, such as cement, steel, engineering equipment, construction and even in newer industries such as solar photovoltaics. Thus, China aims to export its 'redundant capacities' in these sectors and also preserve, to whatever extent possible, the current levels of employment being generated by them, at least in the medium term. Because along with the material that will flow into these projects, so will Chinese manpower.

---

[48] From chapter 51, section 2. 'Economic Corridors', 13th Five-Year Plan, p. 147.

[49] From chapter 22, section 6. 'Lower Business Costs in the Real Economy', 13th Five-Year Plan, p. 63.

[50] Tiezzi, Shannon. 'China's "New Silk Road" Vision Revealed.' *Diplomat*, 9 May 2014, https://thediplomat.com/2014/05/chinas-new-silk-road-vision-revealed.

The alignment of these undertakings also sits well with securing key commodity flows for China, given the resource profile of the countries involved, especially those in the Eurasian heartland and the Persian Gulf. But the BRI is much more than the creation of tighter connectivity for trade flows. Alongside these new transport corridors, Beijing aims to encourage investment from the mainland into new industrial development that will leverage the productivity-enhancing infrastructure slated to be built, in order to manufacture competitive goods and provide services for both local markets as well as export. Indeed, this is supposed to be a key attraction for many of the countries along the OBOR alignments. Resource exporters hit by the post-GFC downturn (and by the pandemic-induced lockdowns in 2020, although prices have rebounded in 2021) in commodity prices, such as the Central Asian Republics and Russia, have been rather keen to diversify their economy by increasing the share of manufacturing output, and generating much-needed employment.

⋆

Securing specific resources will be crucial to China's rise up the industrial value chain that is being pursued under the aegis of the 'Made in China 2025' (MIC 2025) industrial policy, which focuses on 10 sunrise sectors. These sectors are: next-generation information technology (IT), new materials, new energy and energy-saving vehicles, maritime engineering equipment and high-tech ships, biomedicine and high-performance medical equipment, agricultural machines, high-end computerized machines and robots, aerospace equipment, advanced railway transportation equipment and power equipment.[51] China's ambition is to not just become 'self-reliant' in these sectors but to actually

---

[51] 'Made in China 2025: Circular of the State Council.' *Lexis Nexis*, 8 May 2015, https://hk.lexiscn.com/law/law-english-1-2588408-T.html.

lead them by 2049.[52] Naturally, BRI countries will be seen as outlets for the country's output as it tries to attain global scale in them.

But Beijing intends to do more than that. All of the MIC 2025 sectors will leverage the key emerging digital technologies of this era, such as artificial intelligence, and will ultimately depend on ultra-fast telecommunication links with physical movement mapped through precise geographic information systems. It is no wonder that China has been offering to share its technological innovations with BRI countries in key industries via the 'Digital Silk Road' (think 5G networks and equipment) and 'Space Silk Road' (think Beidou Satellite Navigation Systems) tracks. This offer is ultimately part of an overall strategy to make BRI investment recipients align themselves with Chinese manufacturing standards that will emerge out of Beijing's MIC 2025 plan. In the age of digitally networked industries, whoever sets the standards will occupy the commanding heights of the supply chain for that industry. This is because standards decide what components – whether it be on the hardware or software side – of an industrial system are interoperable with each other. Unsurprisingly, in April 2020, it was reported that Beijing was set to unveil a 15-year plan called 'China Standards 2035' in its bid to define global standards in emerging industries.[53]

Naturally, a 'cobalt to computers' China-led ecosystem, as Beijing may have envisaged under the BRI, would need closer financial integration underlying all the physical (and virtual) connectivity. Since 2015, China has sought to catalyse that integration by deploying some of its foreign exchange reserves via the 'Silk Road Fund', which, along

---

[52] Congressional Research Service. '"Made in China 2025" Industrial Policies: Issues for Congress.' *Federation of American Scientists*, 11 August 2020, https://fas.org/sgp/crs/row/IF10964.pdf.

[53] Kharpal, Arjun. 'Power Is "Up for Grabs": Behind China's Plan to Shape the Future of Next-Generation Tech.' *CNBC*, 27 April 2020, https://www.cnbc.com/2020/04/27/china-standards-2035-explained.html.

with Chinese development banks and two of the large state-owned commercial banks, is a key source for supporting investments in BRI projects. Beijing has long been looking for better returns for its foreign exchange (FX) reserves, a large part of which is currently invested in US treasuries and other low-risk assets that have been generating very low or even negative yields as the Western economies pursue loose monetary policies. At the same time, however, inward investment in China has still been notching up appreciable yields. Generally speaking, the rate of return on China's foreign liabilities has been 4 per cent higher than that on its outbound investments.[54]

In general, the BRI aims to diversify China's capital exports towards higher-return ventures and is intended to serve as a way for it to internationalize its financial sector, through the deployment of domestic economic surpluses. China's savings rate has consistently exceeded its level of domestic investment (high as that might be), and both corporate and retail investors in the country are looking for more foreign openings. And this is especially so because its underdeveloped financial market and non-comprehensive social welfare system cannot satisfy the needs of an ageing demography. But the internationalization of China's financial sector cannot happen on the basis of dollar-denominated loans alone. It will require the internationalization of China's official currency, the Renminbi (RMB), whose basic unit is simply called the yuan, with RMB and yuan being used interchangeably in international parlance.

RMB INTERNATIONALIZATION

As such, Chinese banks involved in financing the BRI have for quite some time been raising yuan-denominated funds

---

[54] Yi, Chen. 'Financial Logic Explains China's Capital Exports.' *Global Times*, 12 March 2015, http://www.globaltimes.cn/content/911662.shtml.

for the same in addition to dollar borrowings. For instance, the Bank of China (BOC), which intended to invest $100 billion in BRI projects during 2016–18, issued a 'Silk Road' multi-currency bond across world markets in 2015. And though it ended up raising most of its borrowings in dollars, it also gathered a significant yuan component.[55] The BOC is actually aiming to be the chief conduit for cross-border yuan-denominated transactions, and intends to support this by establishing branches in at least 50 per cent of the countries that will be a part of the BRI alignments. The BOC and other Chinese banks have also been increasing 'dim sum bonds' issued from offshore RMB hubs such as Doha in the name of investing the funds raised in BRI initiatives. These moves are quite in keeping with China's ambition of issuing higher amounts of RMB-denominated debt for BRI projects.

The internationalization of China's financial sector thus entails the internationalization of the yuan as an investment currency because that significantly reduces costs and eliminates currency risks. And since China envisions the BRI as a region of 'more capital convergence and currency integration', it would also want other countries that are a part of the initiative to begin using the yuan as an investment currency. More so as yuan liquidity is made available internationally via yuan payment for increasing Chinese imports, currency swaps and through access to China's capital markets. Even the Silk Road Fund, after all, has no upper limit in its capital raising, and allows participation by foreign entities. Russian banks, for instance, have already been rather active in issuing RMB-denominated corporate bonds once they were frozen out of Western markets due to sanctions. Back in November

---

[55] Karekar, Rupali. 'Bank of China Issues Global Silk Road Bond, Includes $500 Million Tranche.' *Straits Times*, 25 June 2015, http://www.straitstimes.com/business/banking/bank-of-china-issues-global-silk-road-bond-includes-500-million-tranche.

2014 itself, Russia's largest bank, Sberbank, became the first in the country to issue RMB-denominated credit guarantees.[56] Since then, several Russian commercial banks have opened accounts for settlements in yuan, besides also offering such accounts for ordinary depositors. And since 2015, there have been intermittent reports that the Russian government has been considering the issuance of RMB-denominated bonds as well.

The flow of energy resources to China from hydrocarbon-rich states along the BRI is meant to serve as a means for Beijing to get economic entities in these countries to use the yuan for cross-border transactions amongst themselves as well. If China chooses to run current account deficits with its BRI partners, especially the ones that are commodity exporters, very soon large pools of yuan liquidity will get built up, given the scale of trade likely to be involved. If this were to be coupled with the Chinese financial entities extending FX subsidies for yuan settlements between other BRI countries, it could lead to a 'deeper' internationalization of the currency – where a non-China-related financial interaction too might be settled in yuan.

Moreover, given that China is likely to be the top consumer of oil and gas from the hydrocarbon-rich countries along the BRI, it will also push for the commodities to be priced in yuan and not just paid for in the currency. Such a move would completely eliminate exchange risk from these key transactions for China. Its strategy is to therefore grow the network for the yuan through bilateral relationships, to an extent that it makes sense for others to start using it as well.

To get and give a sense of the potential size of this network, China has, since the unveiling of the BRI, held two

[56] Kujundzic, Petar. 'Russia's Largest Bank Issues First Credit Guarantees in Yuan.' *Russia Today*, 5 June 2015, https://www.rt.com/business/265318-sberbank-yuan-credit-guarantees.

international 'forums', in 2017 and 2019, to bring together countries from across the globe that are willing to partner in its new going-out strategy. And at present, there are over 70 countries participating in the BRI. The first BRI forum held in May 2017 saw the participation of 28 heads of state, with officials from some 130 countries and 70 international organizations being present in all.[57]

UNRAVELLING

But there was a notable exception. Fellow BRICS member India declined to send even a junior official to the 2017 forum. This was in the offing, given that the China–Pakistan Economic Corridor (CPEC), first envisaged in 2013,[58] had emerged as a flagship project of the BRI with the signing of a $46 billion Sino-Pakistani agreement in April 2015.[59] India had objected to the CPEC back then itself, on the grounds that it impinged on India's sovereignty, given that the CPEC alignment passed through the Gilgit–Baltistan region which India claims as a part of the erstwhile princely state of Jammu and Kashmir (that acceded to India in 1947).[60] In the lead-up to the 2017 forum, India made it clear to China that it was impossible for New Delhi to participate in the BRI given

[57] 'The First "Belt and Road" Forum: Developing New Silk Roads.' *OBOReurope*, 16 May 2015, https://www.oboreurope.com/en/first-belt-road-forum/#:~:text=On%20May%2014%20and%2015,delegations%20from%20nearly%2060%20governments.

[58] Mardell, Jacob. 'The BRI in Pakistan: China's Flagship Economic Corridor.' *MERICS*, 20 May 2020, https://merics.org/en/analysis/bri-pakistan-chinas-flagship-economic-corridor.

[59] Stevens, Andrew. 'Pakistan Lands $46 Billion Investment from China.' *CNN Business*, 20 April 2015, https://money.cnn.com/2015/04/20/news/economy/pakistan-china-aid-infrastucture.

[60] Razdan, Nidhi. 'Before PM Narendra Modi's Trip, India Objects to $46 Billion China Pakistan Economic Corridor.' *NDTV*, 12 May 2015, https://www.ndtv.com/india-news/before-pms-trip-india-objects-to-chinas-46-billion-economic-corridor-with-pak-762533.

this scenario.[61] Beyond the sovereignty issue, New Delhi was naturally discomfited by the potential for the CPEC to foster a greater China–Pakistan strategic collusion to the detriment of Indian interests.

Moreover, the CPEC was only the northernmost element of what India increasingly saw as Chinese encroachment into its traditional sphere of influence in South Asia – with Bangladesh, Myanmar, Nepal, the Maldives and Sri Lanka all being enmeshed in the BRI by 2017. Sri Lanka, in particular, was a major cause of concern for New Delhi, since it was compelled to lease the port of Hambantota to the Chinese in July 2017 for a period of 99 years in lieu of a payment of $1.1 billion. That amount would essentially allow it to repay loans from the Export–Import Bank of China that it had taken for the development of the port itself.[62] By the time of the handover, Hambantota was considered a part of the MSR and was seen by New Delhi as a potential naval base for China, whose ships and submarines had been making regular calls to other Sri Lankan ports since the 2010s.

Sharing India's concerns about Hambantota was the US military, which had always eyed the BRI with suspicion. This was the case despite the fact that till about mid-2017 the US government itself had made neutral or mildly favourable noises regarding the initiative. However, by the second half of 2017, the Trump administration had shed its initial benevolent ambivalence towards the BRI, what with China refusing to yield on trade issues and not leaning on North Korea hard enough to check its nuclear build-up. And, in October 2018, the US claimed that Hambantota was going

---

[61] Haidar, Suhasini. 'Why Did India Boycott China's Road Summit?' *The Hindu*, 20 May 2017, https://www.thehindu.com/news/national/why-did-india-boycott-chinas-road-summit/article18516163.ece.

[62] Abi-Habib, Maria. 'How China Got Sri Lanka to Cough up a Port.' *New York Times*, 25 June 2018, https://www.nytimes.com/2018/06/25/world/asia/china-sri-lanka-port.html.

to be used as a military base by the Chinese, something that Colombo vociferously denied at the time.[63]

Sri Lanka's predicament was also being taken note of by other BRI partner countries, which began scaling back projects, realizing what lay in store for them if they chose to ignore the fiscal sustainability implications of BRI initiatives. In 2018, Malaysian Prime Minister Mahathir Mohamad, while cancelling several projects in his country worth billions of dollars, famously remarked that 'there is a new version of colonialism happening', although he subsequently denied that this was said in reference to China.[64] In fact, he even participated in the second BRI forum in 2019, and Malaysia agreed to restart a key BRI project it had cancelled earlier, on renegotiated terms, with the total outlay for the project significantly reduced.[65] With the onset of the pandemic, the China–Myanmar Economic Corridor (CMEC), arguably of greater strategic import for China than even the CPEC, is also dwindling in scope. Though Beijing had initially looked to invest around $100 billion in the CMEC, it is now increasingly apparent that the actual figure will be a fraction of that. Till August 2020, Myanmar had approved only nine out of a total of 38 projects proposed by China as part of the CMEC.[66] Myanmar had also considerably scaled down the

---

[63] 'Sri Lanka Rejects US Claims, Says No Chinese Military Base at Port.' *Economic Times*, 11 October 2018, https://economictimes.indiatimes.com/news/defence/sri-lanka-rejects-us-claims-says-no-chinese-military-base-at-port/articleshow/66163389.cms.

[64] Hornby, Lucy. 'Mahathir Mohamad Warns against "New Colonialism" during China Visit.' *Financial Times*, 20 August 2018, https://www.ft.com/content/7566599e-a443-11e8-8ecf-a7ae1beff35b.

[65] 'Hits and Misses: Highlights of Xi Jinping's Second Belt and Road Forum.' *Business Standard*, 20 April 2019, https://www.business-standard.com/article/international/hits-and-misses-highlights-of-xi-jinping-s-second-belt-and-road-forum-119042800205_1.html.

[66] Roy Chaudhury, Dipanjan. 'Myanmar's Pushback against China-Funded Economic Corridor Inspired by Debt Trap in S Asian States.'

financial scope of even the approved projects with its deputy minister of planning and finance openly warning about the need for his country to avoid a 'Chinese debt trap'.[67] Since the February 2021 military coup in Myanmar, however, there have been reports that the ruling Junta has reorganized various leading committees that oversee BRI projects with a view to providing renewed momentum to the CMEC.[68] Nevertheless, it remains to be seen as to how much actually gets implemented, given China's own new-found wariness about post-coup instability in Myanmar.

Even in the African continent, where China is deeply entrenched as an investor – having helped countries ameliorate their erstwhile aid dependency on the Western bloc – the pandemic has brought to the fore a growing resentment against Beijing's presence. A case in point would be Zambia, where three Chinese workers were allegedly murdered by locals in May 2020 at a warehouse in Lusaka.[69] Rising anger in the country against an increasing number of Chinese workers at one end, and the creeping takeover of the African nation's key economic sectors the other served as a backdrop for this incident. Reports suggest that there is a high possibility that Zambia may have to cede control of its main airport, roads, electric utilities and even the national broadcaster to China on account of being unable

---

Economic Times, 22 August 2020, https://economictimes.indiatimes.com/news/international/world-news/myanmars-pushback-against-china-funded-economic-corridor-inspired-by-debt-trap-in-s-asian-states/articleshow/77688207.cms.

[67] Ibid.

[68] Roy Chaudhury, Dipankar. 'Myanmar's Military Junta Revives Scope of BRI Projects.' *Economic Times*, 26 July 2021, https://economictimes.indiatimes.com/news/international/world-news/myanmars-military-junta-revives-scope-of-bri-projects/articleshow/84739776.cms.

[69] Liu, Hongjie. 'Three Chinese Nationals Murdered in Zambia.' *China Daily*, 25 May 2020, https://www.chinadaily.com.cn/a/202005/25/WS5ecbc80aa310a8b24115854d.html.

to repay loans worth $8.7 billion.[70] In November 2020, Zambia became the first African country to default in the pandemic era, and the country has been on the lookout for an IMF bailout since.[71] Unhappy with the economic mismanagement that had saddled Zambia with $12 billion in external debt (mostly owed to China) and creeping authoritarian tendencies, Zambia's electorate voted out the incumbent government in Lusaka led by Edward Lungu in August 2021.[72] And it is not just smaller African nations where the innate problems with the BRI have come to the fore. The pandemic-induced downturn has also spawned a major backlash in Kenya, East Africa's largest economy, over concerns related to the viability and environmental sustainability of key China-funded infrastructure projects.[73]

Even though the popularity of China's debt-oriented diplomacy started waning not too long after the first BRI forum in 2017, America hasn't done much since then to consolidate its strategic partnerships with vigorous economic diplomacy either. For example, the Trump-era trade friction with American allies and partners, besides the broad use of sanctions as a geopolitical tool, as reflected in the passing of

---

[70] 'Zambia Risks Losing Sovereignty to Beijing Due to Debt-trap Diplomacy.' *Mizzima*, 18 August 2020, http://mizzima.com/article/china-monitor-zambia-risks-losing-sovereignty-beijing-due-debt-trap-diplomacy.

[71] Hill, Matthew, and Taonga Clifford Mitimingi. 'After Five Attempts, Hichilema Is Poised to Win Zambian Vote.' *Bloomberg*, 15 August 2021, https://www.bloomberg.com/news/articles/2021-08-15/zambia-s-hichilema-nears-big-win-in-vote-denounced-by-president.

[72] Marima, Tendai. 'Young Zambians Hope for Brighter Future as Hichilema Wins Vote.' *Al Jazeera*, 16 August 2021, https://www.aljazeera.com/news/2021/8/16/young-zambians-hope-for-brighter-future-as-hichilema-wins-vote.

[73] Cheatham, Amelia. 'Belt and Road in Kenya: COVID-19 Sparks a Reckoning with Debt and Dissatisfaction.' *Council on Foreign Relations*, 12 April 2021, https://www.cfr.org/blog/belt-and-road-kenya-covid-19-sparks-reckoning-debt-and-dissatisfaction.

the Countering Adversaries of America Through Sanctions Act (CAATSA) in July 2017, meant that India remained committed to the creation of a multipolar order. Such impulses lay behind the so-called 2018 'Wuhan reset', in which India and China agreed to mend relations that had been set back due to the Doklam dispute of 2017 and India's opposition to the BRI. Nevertheless, New Delhi remained wary of the initiative, with the CPEC becoming an ever bigger sticking point. And this was a prime reason why India would ignore the second BRI summit held in 2019 as well. On top of that, as we shall see in chapter seven, India refused to join the Regional Comprehensive Economic Partnership (RCEP) later that year, which is a purported China-led trade bloc with objectives complementary to the BRI.

Meanwhile, American hostility towards the BRI also strengthened through the course of 2019, in step with the growing US–China trade war. During a June 2019 visit to India, Mike Pompeo, the US Secretary of State, had this to say:

> There are a myriad of opportunities that lay before us in the Indo-Pacific region. Countries... which have signed on to the Belt and Road projects have found Beijing's deals come not with strings attached, but with shackles.[74]

With the onset of the pandemic, US pushback started taking the form of Washington actively dissuading its allies from joining the BRI. In May 2020, Pompeo created a bit of a flutter by suggesting that Australia may be disconnected from the coveted 'Five-Eyes' intelligence-sharing network, comprising the US, UK, Canada, Australia and New Zealand, due to the participation of the Western Australian state of Victoria in the BRI.[75] Washington also began pressurizing its

[74] 'China Slams Mike Pompeo for His Criticism of BRI during India Visit.' *Economic Times*, 27 June 2019, https://economictimes.indiatimes.com/news/international/world-news/china-slams-mike-pompeo-for-his-criticism-of-bri-during-india-visit/articleshow/69974085.cms.

[75] Tillett, Andrew. 'US Backtracks over Intel Sharing Threat.' *Financial*

closest allies, such as Israel, against getting too close to China economically. Of course, the Washington establishment has known for a while now that mere political rhetoric and threats to downgrade old security relationships will not suffice to counter the BRI. Which is why the so-called Blue Dot Network (BDN), first announced in November 2019 at the Indo-Pacific Business Forum in Bangkok along with Japan and Australia, was revived by the Biden administration in June 2021.[76] Although the BDN's core objective is to assess and certify infrastructure projects to a standard that makes them market-driven, transparent and financially sustainable, it is likely to serve as a means to attract private capital to such projects in developing countries. The International Development Finance Corporation (IDFC), set up by the US in December 2019 with a funding portfolio ceiling of $60 billion, is supposed to serve as the main financial vehicle for the BDN. Taking things a step further, July 2021 also saw the G-7 group of nations led by the US unveil a programme called 'Build Back Better World' or B3W, which is:

> An Affirmative Initiative for Meeting the Tremendous Infrastructure Needs of Low- and Middle-Income Countries. President Biden and G7 partners agreed to launch the bold new global infrastructure initiative Build Back Better World (B3W), a values-driven, high-standard, and transparent infrastructure partnership led by major democracies to help narrow the $40+ trillion infrastructure need in the developing world, which has been exacerbated by the COVID-19 pandemic.[77]

Review, 24 May 2020, https://www.afr.com/politics/federal/pompeo-belts-victoria-over-china-infrastructure-deal-20200524-p54vv3.

[76] 'US, Japan, Australia Reviving "Blue Dot" to Provide Alternative to China's BRI.' *ANI News*, 9 June 2021, https://www.aninews.in/news/world/us/us-japan-australia-reviving-blue-dot-to-provide-alternative-to-chinas-bri20210609220153.

[77] 'FACT SHEET: President Biden and G7 Leaders Launch Build Back Better World (B3W) Partnership.' *The White House*, 12 June 2021, https://

And unlike the BRI, which has been mostly focused on physical infrastructure:

> Through B3W, the G7 and other like-minded partners will coordinate in mobilizing private-sector capital in four areas of focus – climate, health and health security, digital technology, and gender equity and equality – with catalytic investments from our respective development finance institutions.[78]

Moreover,

> B3W will be global in scope, from Latin America and the Caribbean to Africa to the Indo-Pacific. Different G7 partners will have different geographic orientations, but the sum of the initiative will cover low- and middle-income countries across the world.[79]

Naturally, the B3W will try to posit itself as a high-quality initiative since it 'will be guided by high standards and principles, such as those promoted by the updated Blue Dot Network, relating to the environment and climate, labour and social safeguards, transparency, financing, construction, anticorruption, and other areas'.[80]

Obviously, the US has to bring to the fore an inclusive and forward-looking approach if it has to reinvigorate its existing alliance network. Especially since allies such as Japan and Australia are themselves quite cognizant of the broader Chinese geopolitical aims. Australia, despite its critical dependence on the Chinese market, was the first country to proscribe Huawei's 5G equipment, and also stop Chinese moves to acquire utilities and large farms on its soil. This

---

www.whitehouse.gov/briefing-room/statements-releases/2021/06/12/fact-sheet-president-biden-and-g7-leaders-launch-build-back-better-world-b3w-partnership.

[78] Ibid.

[79] Ibid.

[80] Ibid.

pushback has not been without a price, and the pandemic era has seen Sino-Australian relations nosedive.[81] As we have seen before, the Europeans have also grown quite wary of China. In September 2020, France, Germany and the UK submitted a joint 'Note Verbale' to the UN challenging the legality of China's revanchist maritime claims in the commons of the South China Sea.[82] In pursuit of those claims, Chinese ships rammed fishing vessels from Vietnam and the Philippines in disputed waters during the course of 2020, besides engaging in a month-long standoff with a Malaysian oil exploration platform. Chinese fighter jets also violated Taiwanese airspace on a regular basis.

Truth be told, by 2019 itself, that is, even before the COVID-19 shock, China no longer had the financial strength to pursue the BRI on the grand scale that it had envisioned, as evidenced by Beijing openly calling for global partners to buy into the initiative in March 2019.[83] To that end, the second BRI forum, in April 2019, witnessed an attempt by China to rebrand the initiative by promising to 'clean' and 'green' it. Xi Jinping himself vowed 'zero tolerance' towards corruption in BRI projects, while Yi Gang, governor of the People's Bank of China, said that it would 'build an open, market-oriented financing and investment system'.[84] Further

---

[81] Jacob, Meera. 'Explained: How China–Australia Relations Collapsed.' *Week*, 20 July 2021, https://www.theweek.in/news/world/2021/07/20/explained-how-china-australia-relations-collapsed.html.

[82] Roy Chaudhury, Dipanjan. 'France, UK, Germany Submit Joint Note in UN against China's South China Sea Claims.' *Economic Times*, 20 September 2020, https://economictimes.indiatimes.com/news/defence/france-uk-germany-submits-joint-note-in-un-against-chinas-south-china-sea-claims/articleshow/78191913.cms.

[83] 'China Seeking Global Partners to Fund Its BRI Projects.' *Economic Times*, 18 March 2019, https://economictimes.indiatimes.com/news/international/business/china-seeking-global-partners-to-fund-its-bri-projects/articleshow/68464869.cms.

[84] Ibid.

underlining the need for reform was IMF chief Christine Lagarde, who said, 'BRI 2.0 can also benefit from increased transparency, open procurement with competitive bidding, and better risk assessment in project selection.'[85] However, events since then probably belie such hopes, and in January 2020, a survey of European firms revealed that very few were participating in the BRI with the rest staying away on account of concerns about a lack of transparency.[86]

The COVID-19 shock has served as a further setback for the BRI, as numerous projects have been getting stalled with several partner countries looking for debt waivers – something that China has had to contend with for some time now. By the second quarter of 2018 itself, non-performing assets in BRI projects already totalled more than $101.8 billion, according to data from the Organization for Economic Cooperation and Development (OECD).[87] This figure is becoming much worse now with the effects of the pandemic. Even China admitted in June 2020 that one-fifth of BRI projects had been 'severely affected' by the pandemic, with another 30–40 per cent 'somewhat affected'.[88]

Mirroring the pandemic-induced stress in BRI projects was a decline in overall investments during the first six

---

[85] Lagarde, Christine. 'BRI 2.0: Stronger Frameworks in the New Phase of Belt and Road.' *IMF*, Speech at Belt and Road Forum, Beijing, 26 April 2019, https://www.imf.org/en/News/Articles/2019/04/25/sp042619-stronger-frameworks-in-the-new-phase-of-belt-and-road.

[86] 'China's Belt and Road Projects Lack Transparency, Say European Firms.' *Business Standard*, 16 January 2020, https://www.business-standard.com/article/pti-stories/lack-of-transparency-in-china-s-belt-and-road-projects-eu-firms-120011600166_1.html.

[87] Kung, Chan, and Yu (Tony) Pan. 'How China's Belt and Road Initiative Went Astray.' *Diplomat*, 7 May 2020, https://thediplomat.com/2020/05/how-chinas-belt-and-road-initiative-went-astray.

[88] 'One-fifth of Belt and Road Projects "Seriously Affected" by Covid-19: China.' *Business Standard*, 19 June 2020, https://www.business-standard.com/article/international/one-fifth-of-belt-and-road-projects-seriously-affected-by-covid-19-china-120061900604_1.html.

months of 2020. Total investment in the initiative's projects was about 50 per cent lower in the first six months of 2020 as compared to the same period in 2019, and 60 per cent lower as compared to the first half of 2018.[89] Reduced investments are getting reflected in the number of projects taking off under the BRI aegis worldwide. For example, in Central and Eastern Europe, only some 10 per cent of announced projects had been completed by October 2020.[90] The CPEC flagship too is not exactly sailing steadily, with growing concerns about the security of the projects on account of terrorist attacks.[91]

Given these trends, it is quite reasonable to assume that China will become more 'focused' with respect to its selection of projects, while the geopolitical orientation of the BRI will grow. The failure of these projects in today's pandemic-ridden times will naturally impinge on the ability of its smaller-sized participants to repay Chinese debt, thereby paving the way for the acquisition of their national assets by Beijing. According to AidData, an international development body at America's William & Mary University, there are already in excess of 40 low- and middle-income countries which owe more than 10 per cent of their nominal yearly GDP to China.[92] The situation is particularly fraught

---

[89] Wang, Christoph N. 'Brief: Investments in the Chinese Belt and Road Initiative (BRI) in 2020 during the Covid-19 Pandemic.' *Green Belt and Road Initiative Center*, 31 July 2020, https://green-bri.org/investment-report-belt-and-road-initiative-bri-2020-covid19.

[90] Varano, John. 'China's 17+1 Initiative Stalls amid Security Concerns and Broken Promises.' *Strategist*, 22 October 2020, https://www.aspistrategist.org.au/chinas-171-initiative-stalls-amid-security-concerns-and-broken-promises/.

[91] 'Protests, Suicide Attacks: Backlash Grows against China's Belt & Road Projects in Pakistan.' *Times of India,* 21 August 2021, https://timesofindia.indiatimes.com/world/pakistan/protests-erupt-in-gwadar-against-chinas-belt-and-road-plan/articleshow/85506861.cms.

[92] 'China: Is It Burdening Poor Countries with Unsustainable Debt?' BBC News, 6 January 2022, https://www.bbc.com/news/59585507.

for Djibouti, Laos, Zambia and Kyrgyzstan, which each have debts to Chinese lenders greater than 20 per cent of their annual GDP.[93] Indeed, Laos became an early example of the 'relinquish national assets for Chinese debt relief' scenario, when its failure to honour BRI loan commitments forced it to hand over majority control of its electricity grid to a Chinese company in September 2020.[94] This particular acquisition may actually confer an added lever to China over Vietnam, given that the latter – itself faced with domestic shortages – is now a major importer of electric power from Laos.[95]

Be that as it may, the main crutch supporting the RMB's internationalization, that is, the BRI, is now under duress and has also served to drive a wedge between the BRICS nations. Post China's border incursions in April–May 2020, India took various steps to decouple itself from the Chinese economy, such as attempting to substitute imports of intermediate inputs and banning Chinese mobile applications, besides introducing new measures to restrict and regulate investments from the country. New Delhi reportedly even mused about a clouded future for the BRICS 2020 summit in Russia, with a view to applying pressure on China for withdrawing its intrusions in eastern Ladakh.[96] This was a far cry from late

---

[93] Ibid.

[94] Zhai, Keith, and Kay Johnson. 'Exclusive: Taking Power – Chinese Firm to Run Laos Electric Grid Amid Default Warnings.' *Reuters*, 4 September 2020, https://in.reuters.com/article/china-laos/exclusive-taking-power-chinese-firm-to-run-laos-electric-grid-amid-default-warnings-idINL4N2G122S.

[95] Minh, Anh. 'Vietnam to Import More Electricity from Laos.' *VN Express*, 9 December 2019, https://e.vnexpress.net/news/business/industries/vietnam-to-import-more-electricity-from-laos-4024344.html#:~:text=Vietnam%20will%20import%20an%20additional,at%20a%20meeting%20on%20Saturday.

[96] Bhaumik, Anirban. 'India Hopes Stand-off with China Will End Soon, Not Overshadow BRICS, SCO Summits in Russia.' *Deccan Herald*, 9 August 2020, https://www.deccanherald.com/national/india-hopes-stand-off-with-china-will-end-soon-not-overshadow-brics-sco-summits-in-

2019, when India, Russia and China were jointly exploring ways to reduce their dependence on SWIFT for mutual financial transactions.[97]

To be sure, India will stay invested in finding a means to circumvent US 'sanctionomics' (for instance, CAATSA) with respect to its strategic dealings with Russia. It will also not disconnect from multipolar institutions such as BRICS, which continues to seek future quota reviews at the IMF. But it will want BRICS institutions to shape themselves in a pattern that is more to its liking. For instance, in August 2021, India's commerce minister, Piyush Goyal, stated during the Fifth Meeting of BRICS Industry Ministers:

> The horizon of NDB should be expanded and resources be utilized for strengthening social infrastructure, especially for funding service delivery in [the] education and health sector[s], besides promotion of [the] infrastructure and industrial sector[s].[98]

India will also remain invested in the AIIB as long as it manages to keep a modicum of multilateralism intact and doesn't become a major source of finance for BRI projects. Indeed, New Delhi continued to avail of AIIB infrastructure loans even during the ongoing standoff with China.[99]

---

russia-871442.html.

[97] Roy Chaudhury, Dipanjan. 'India-Russia-China Explore Alternative to SWIFT Payment Mechanism.' *Economic Times*, 14 November 2019, https://economictimes.indiatimes.com/news/economy/foreign-trade/india-russia-china-explore-alternative-to-swift-payment-mechanism/articleshow/72048472.cms.

[98] ENS Economic Bureau. 'Piyush Goyal: Horizon of NDB Should Be Expanded to Strengthen Social Infra.' *Indian Express*, 19 August 2021, https://indianexpress.com/article/business/piyush-goyal-horizon-of-ndb-should-be-expanded-to-strengthen-social-infra-7460458.

[99] 'Modi Govt Took Loans Worth over Rs 9k Crore from China-Based AIIB: Anurag Thakur in Lok Sabha.' *News 18*, 16 September 2020, https://www.news18.com/news/india/modi-govt-took-loans-worth-over-rs-9k-crore-from-china-based-aiib-anurag-thakur-in-lok-sabha-2882683.html.

However, India is unlikely to contribute financial capital to enhance the role of institutions that are perceived to be led by China. Instead, New Delhi is likely to redirect its resources towards emerging constructs, such as the B3W, BDN and the India–Japan Asia Africa Growth Corridor, besides winning back neighbourhood influence through its own limited version of chequebook diplomacy, as it has done in the Maldives.[100, 101] No longer will India–China economic relations remain compartmentalized from the border dispute and military competition between the two nations.

So, China certainly cannot expect any buy-in from India at a time when its strength to go it alone on these initiatives stands diminished. In fact, Beijing has now itself become a recipient of emergency lending from both the AIIB and NDB.[102] So, in the post-pandemic era, we find a BRI that is made up of a patchwork of projects, many of which are of questionable value, leaving behind a trail of bad debt that will affect not just the debtors but the creditor as well. Moreover, the BRI is now also going to face a coordinated pushback by a network of democracies in the Indo-Pacific arena. None of this is particularly auspicious for a plan that was supposed to help China create a credible rival global economic architecture to that of the West.

But why did China opt for such a plan in the first place, and why was it in a hurry to internationalize the RMB? To

---

[100] 'Asia–Africa Growth Corridor: Partnership for Sustainable and Innovative Development.' *ERIA*, 26 May 2017, https://www.eria.org/Asia-Africa-Growth-Corridor-Document.pdf.

[101] HT Correspondent and Sohini Sarkar. 'India Provides Soft Loan of $250 mn to the Maldives.' *Hindustan Times*, 20 September 2020, https://www.hindustantimes.com/india-news/india-provides-soft-loan-of-250-mn-to-the-maldives/story-yEtwD2LBZX9RszJnTSmDtO.html.

[102] Patranobis, Sutirtho. 'After China, BRICS Bank Loans $1 Billion to India to Fight Covid-19 Pandemic.' *Hindustan Times*, 13 May 2020, https://www.hindustantimes.com/world-news/after-china-brics-bank-loans-1billion-to-india-to-fight-covid-19-pandemic/story-pqQYj7CrFiHBo1FNibPwUM.html.

understand this, we will need to turn to history – specifically Japan's rise on the world stage as an industrial power and its ultimate inability to emerge as a true Asian financial rival to the US. The origin story of Japan's modern-day economic journey, which has lessons for all Asian countries, is what we shall examine next.

FOUR

In 1793, George Macartney, the first British envoy to China, arrived in the imperial capital city of Beijing. He sought an audience with the Qianlong emperor of the Manchu-led Qing dynasty, to whom he would convey a formal request from the British government to relax trade restrictions, open new ports to British trade (besides Guangzhou), allow a British mission in Beijing and even lease an island in China's southern region for British use.[1] However, according to some accounts, since Macartney refused to kowtow to the emperor, which involved him kneeling three times and bowing so deeply that his head touched the floor, he was refused an audience in the imperial court. Macartney was eventually received by the emperor in a more informal setting on the outskirts of the capital, and Macartney and the other Englishmen were allowed to get away by simply bending their knees, as they would to their own sovereign.[2] The Qianlong emperor, while rejecting all of Macartney's requests, had this message for the British king:

---

[1] Hevia, James L. 'A Multitude of Lords: Qing Court Ritual and the Macartney Embassy of 1793.' *Late Imperial China*, Volume 10, Number 2, 1989, pp. 72–105.

[2] Gillingham, Paul. 'The Macartney Embassy to China, 1792–94.' *History Today*, Volume 43, Issue 11, November 1993, https://www.historytoday.com/archive/macartney-embassy-china-1792-94. See also: Bartlett, Beatrice S. 'A New Edition of Macartney Mission Documents: Problems and Glories of Translation.' *Études chinoises*, Volume XIV, Number 1, Printemps 1995, https://www.persee.fr/doc/etchi_0755-5857_1995_num_14_1_1228.

> Hitherto, all European nations, including your own country's barbarian merchants, have carried on their trade with our Celestial Empire at Canton. Such has been the procedure for many years, although our Celestial Empire possesses all things in prolific abundance and lacks no product within its own borders. There was therefore no need to import the manufactures of outside barbarians in exchange for our own produce.[3]

Such an attitude was prevalent not only in the Middle Kingdom but in the other realms of East Asia as well – a region known for its restrictive approach to trade – in the late eighteenth century. Korea's diplomatic ties were, for instance, restricted to sending tributary delegations to Beijing, and receiving its own tributary delegations from the Japanese principality of Tsushima in Pusan. Chinese and Japanese subjects were the only outsiders allowed to enter Korea, with Pusan being the only port open to the Japanese.[4] It is not for nothing that Korea was called the 'hermit kingdom'.

And what of Japan? Even as the 'Macartney Embassy', as that mission came to be called, was being snubbed in China, Japan was into its 160th year of a policy of isolation, known as *sakoku*, or 'locked country', that did not let any Japanese leave the country or any foreigner enter it without special permits and provisions, violations attracting the penalty of death. Of course, that did not mean that Japan was completely sealed off from the rest of the world. Trade was allowed with five different entities through four different gateways, including

---

[3] Gentzler, Mason J. 'Two Edicts from the Qianlong Emperor, on the Occasion of Lord Macartney's Mission to China, September 1793.' *Changing China: Readings in History of China from Opium War to the Present.* Praeger Publishers, 1977. Asia for Educators, http://afe.easia.columbia.edu/ps/china/qianlong_edicts.pdf.

[4] Kočvar, Jan. 'The Opening of Korea until 1876.' In Aleš Skřivan and Arnold Suppan, eds. 'Prague Papers on the History of International Relations', pp. 195–210, Institute of World History, 2009, http://usd.ff.cuni.cz/?q=system/files/kocvar%20korea.pdf.

the port of Nagasaki, from where trade with Western agencies, such as the Dutch East India Company, was allowed. The overall *sakoku* policy was, among other things, broadly aimed at keeping Western Christian influence out of the country – something that was seen as a potentially destabilizing force, and could have even paved the way to outright colonization. However, the restricted trade also served to reinforce the power of the Tokugawa *shogunate*, the hereditary military dictatorship that ruled feudal Japan at the time. The emperor was a mere titular head, nominally presiding over subordinate feudal lords, who could possibly pose a challenge to the *shogun*, the hereditary military dictator, by building up their military and economic power through trade.[5]

The beginning of the end of the *sakoku* system came one day in July in 1853, when Commodore Matthew Calbraith Perry of the United States Navy, commanding a fleet of four 'black ships', as they came to be known among the Japanese, sailed into the Edo (later known as Tokyo) bay aboard the frigate *Susquehanna*. Perry was on a mission from the US government to open Japanese ports to American trade, and he decided to use the Paixhans shell guns on board his ship to air his views.[6] The blanks fired from these guns and from those aboard the other ships under his command were part of a 'demonstration of force' by Perry to get the Japanese to convey the letter he was carrying from then US president Millard Fillmore to the *shogun* in his palace in Edo. Naturally, the letter contained a list of demands on the trade front. Once Perry had successfully accomplished this, besides being granted permission to make a landing on Japanese soil in what is today Yokosuka, he sailed away from the island nation,

---

[5] For a detailed look at this period, see: Cullen, L.M. *A History of Japan, 1582–1941: Internal and External Worlds*. Cambridge University Press, 2003.

[6] Williams, S.W. *A Journal of the Perry Expedition to Japan (1853–54)*. Kelly & Walsh, 1910. *Internet Archive*, https://archive.org/stream/journalofperryex00swel#page/12/mode/2up.

promising to return in a year's time to hear an official reply to Fillmore's letter.

Perry ended up returning to Japan in February 1854, earlier than he had said he would, hastened by reports of other Western powers as well as the Russians trying to get the Japanese to accept similar demands from their end. Upon return, he found that the Japanese had essentially agreed to all the demands made in Fillmore's letter, and despite some delay in the choice of a suitable venue to officially accede to US terms, Tokugawa Japan signed the Convention of Kanagawa with the US being represented by Perry. As a result of this Kanagawa Treaty, the ports of Shimoda and Hakodate were thrown open to American ships. Japan also agreed to provide care for shipwrecked US sailors and allowed the establishment of an American consulate in Shimoda.[7] Subsequently, Russia, Britain, France and the Netherlands would all follow the 'Perry model' to coerce Japan into signing treaties to regularize similar concessions. Moreover, these fleets were also combined on occasion to defeat Japanese feudal lords who refused to recognize the concessions made by the *shogunate*.

Japan was isolated no longer.

All this, however, served to greatly diminish the standing of the Tokugawa *shogunate*, as their inability to deal with modern Western military threats became clear to the Japanese people. Moreover, the opening of trade brought in its wake inflation and monetary instability – due to the infusion of foreign currency into the economy and a change in the price structure. Farmers producing tea and silk, as well as traders dealing in these commodities, suddenly found new markets overseas and were now much better off, while the samurais and urban dwellers reeled under price rise. The country was thrown into a 15-year period of political turmoil, torn between the questions of international openness and support

---

[7] Ibid.

for the existing feudal system.[8] This naturally resulted in the weakening of the *shogunate* and its feudal allies, with their ultimate defeat in the Boshin War paving the way for the Meiji Restoration of 1868. Power in Japan became centralized under a group of ministers drawn from powerful samurai 'Hans', with the emperor serving as a symbolic head.

FUKOKU KYOHEI

The Meiji government in Japan embarked on a policy of *fukoku kyohei*, which roughly translates into 'enrich the state, strengthen the military'.[9] To achieve this aim, Meiji Japan strived to bring the Industrial Revolution to its soil through the import of Western machinery, ideas, concepts, financial systems and training personnel. Concomitantly, certain key features inherited from the Tokugawa period, such as nationally unified markets, transportation and distribution networks, were upgraded with modern road, rail and communication infrastructure. The Tokugawa period had also created a populace with a relatively high level of literacy, and subsequently a promotion of Western-style research and development activities in agriculture and engineering was built up.[10]

On the industrial side, the Meiji modernizing zeal initially focused on the textile industry, especially the cotton sector. At the time, cotton textiles were one of the largest manufacturing sectors in the world. Japan, since the opening up of trade, had become mostly an importer of English cotton

---

[8] Cullen, *A History of Japan*.

[9] Ohno, Kenichi. 'The Industrialization and Global Integration of Meiji Japan.' *East Asian Growth and Japanese Aid Strategy*, trans. from Japanese by Anjali Patel, National Graduate Institute for Policy Studies, 2003.

[10] Ohno, Kenichi. *The Economic Development of Japan: The Path Travelled by Japan as a Developing Country*. National Graduate Institute for Policy Studies, 2006, p. 35. Grips Development Forum, https://www.grips.ac.jp/forum/pdf06/EDJ.pdf.

fabric and garments, and an exporter of raw cotton. Looking to climb up the value chain rapidly in this sector, the country adopted a policy of import substitution in cotton yarn, fabrics and garments, supported through the importation of spinning and weaving machinery from the West. And it began by serving the domestic market for finished garments using imported cotton yarn. Even as the share of domestic production in finished cotton products sold in the home market grew, Japan first became a net exporter of cotton yarn and a net importer of raw cotton, through the adaptation of imported spinning machines by 1900.

Subsequently, the island nation started exporting finished cotton products, which were being produced using imported weaving machinery, to other parts of Asia, even as it became the top importer of raw cotton from India. Japanese textile companies, in order to become a monopsonistic buyer of Indian cotton, decided to use only a Mitsubishi group–owned shipping line called Nippon Yusen to bring Indian cotton to Japan.[11, 12] Its competitiveness in cotton textiles thereafter rose to a level wherein not only did Japanese firms dominate their home market but they actually managed to drive out British cotton textiles, at least to an extent, from major Asian markets such as India and China.[13]

By the end of the Meiji period in 1912, just two years before the beginning of World War I, Japan had become industrialized in light manufacturing, led by cotton textiles. Interestingly, throughout this period, the country promoted exports as a way to pay for imports of capital machinery, intermediate inputs and raw materials from abroad to earn foreign exchange. As a result, Japan managed to avoid serious balance of payments problems.[14]

---

[11] Ibid., p. 65.

[12] Monopsony refers to a situation where a single buyer dominates the market.

[13] Ohno, *The Economic Development of Japan*, pp. 60–61.

[14] Balance of payments refers to the net sum of the external accounts

Silk yarn followed by tea, cereals, seafood, minerals, coal and other commodities were the major Japanese exports to the West, exchanged in lieu of cotton yarn and machinery. As import substitution progressed in light industries, Japan started exchanging consumer goods – cotton textiles, glass products, clocks, umbrellas, etc. – with the rest of Asia, in lieu of raw materials. Raw silk, however, remained its top export right up to the beginning of World War II, and served its role as the chief foreign exchange earner for a country ever hungry to source Western technology.[15] So, from a policy of isolation, Japan transformed its outlook to one where trade provided key support for industrialization.

Though Japan's industrial push focused on light industry, it simultaneously paid attention to those sectors of heavy industry that would enable military and infrastructure development. Interestingly, Meiji modernization of heavy industry had a decidedly 'emergency character' to it, focused as it was on shipbuilding, mining, railroad rolling stock, explosives and, naturally, armaments.[16] Development of the consumer goods machinery sector did not see the same level of priority given to it, as evidenced by the fact that

---

of a country, in terms of outflows (money to the rest of the world) and inflows (money flowing into the country) over a particular period of time. So, basically, it is captured by the following equation: current account (difference between annual exports and imports) = capital account (the difference between outward and inward investments) + change in the forex holdings of a country.

A country must pay for any imports over and above what it exports by either importing capital or by running down its reserves, or both. The opposite holds true in the case of exports being greater than imports, with the country being in a position to either increase outward investments or accumulate more reserves or both.

[15] Ohno, *The Economic Development of Japan*, p. 59.

[16] Yoshio, Ando. 'The Formation of Heavy Industry: One of the Processes of Industrialization in the Meiji Period.' *Developing Economies*, Volume 3, Issue 4, December 1965, pp. 450–70, https://www.ide.go.jp/library/English/Publish/Periodicals/De/pdf/65_04_04.pdf.

Japan continued to import cotton textile machinery till as late as 1910 and even beyond.[17] Machine tools for military-related industries were developed, however, by adapting and improving imported Western baselines. The iron and steel industry too was developed as a means to meet the requirements of shipbuilding, railroads and armaments, and became a major focus area in the early twentieth century.

The Meiji government was determined not to fall prey to colonialism subsequent to its opening up to the rest of the world. As it is, the 'opening up' of Japan had come on unequal terms. As per the treaty conditions with various Western powers, Japan neither had the right to set tariff rates on imports nor the jurisdiction to try foreign offenders in its courts.[18] So even though fears about outright colonization diminished as the regime consolidated itself, there was this clear ambition to become a 'first rank nation' that would overturn all unequal treaties, and perhaps begin imposing unequal treaties of its own.

This emerging sentiment was on display as early as 1876, when Japan raced ahead of Western powers to bring about the forcible opening up of Korea and the beginning of the end of the latter's tributary status to Qing China. The terms imposed by the Japanese on Korea in the Treaty of Ganghwa Island (1876) were startlingly similar to those imposed on Japan by other Western powers at the time: the opening of new ports, aid to stranded sailors, etc., and the most egregious of all – immunity to Japanese citizens from Korean courts.[19] This 'right to extraterritoriality' was the most reviled of all Western impositions on subjugated Asia at the time, and Japan had now become the first Asian country to use it on its neighbours.

Fukoku kyohei, after all, required the import of raw materials from the neighbourhood, relevant to Japan's military build-

---

[17] Ibid.

[18] Ohno, *The Economic Development of Japan*, p. 42

[19] Kočvar, 'The Opening of Korea until 1876.'

up – such as higher-quality ferrous ores and coal than what could be mined in Japan. While the country's own substantial Kamaishi mines sufficed for the beginnings of an iron and steel industry, it was only with the establishment of the Yawata Iron Works in 1901, using Chinese Ta Ya iron ore, that the domestic iron and steel industry really took off.[20] Yawata's significance can be gauged by one fact: in the very first year of operation, it accounted for 53 and 82 per cent of all domestic pig iron and rolled steel production respectively.[21] And by this time, Japan had also become a major importer of raw cotton from other parts of Asia.

The country, therefore, looked to its near abroad to create a zone of influence, which would serve as a base for resource extraction on the supply side and as an outlet for Japanese manufactures on the demand side. Besides, this zone of influence would also serve as a buffer against other imperial powers, such as Russia or Britain. This bid for imperial expansion served as a mutually reinforcing paradigm, with the development of military-industrial capability. A clear parallel to China's twenty-first century revanchism in the South China Sea can be drawn here.

By the 1890s, Meiji Japan's modernization, despite a yet-underdeveloped metallurgical sector, had advanced sufficiently for it to score a victory over Qing China in the First Sino-Japanese War of 1894–95. The Treaty of Shimonoseki, which ended the war, saw China ceding Formosa/Taiwan, the Penghu islands in the Taiwan strait and the Liaodong peninsula in Manchuria to Japan, besides agreeing to pay the latter a massive war indemnity, opening up four new ports to Japanese trade, and granting Japan the 'most favoured nation' status.[22]

---

20 Yoshio, 'The Formation of Heavy Industry: One of the Processes of Industrialization in the Meiji Period.'

21 Ibid.

22 See: 'Treaty of Shimonoseki, April 17, 1895.' *Treaties between China and Foreign States*, Second Edition, 1917, Volume 2, pp. 590–96, *USC US–China Institute*, http://china.usc.edu/treaty-shimonoseki-1895.

Once they secured the cession, the Japanese first defeated the Chinese forces garrisoned in Penghu, thereby destroying any hopes of the forces left in Formosa of getting reinforcements from the mainland. Subsequently, the Japanese mounted a full-scale invasion of the island, making short work of the hastily declared Republic of Formosa that had been set up by the people there to sidestep the cession of the territory by the Qing Empire.[23] Japan also used this opportunity to capture the Senkaku/Daioyu group of islands that have today become a flashpoint between China and Japan.

However, still barely seen as a 'regional power' by the West and Russia, the 'Triple Intervention' of Russia, France and Germany, under the threat of military action, forced Japan to relinquish its new-found rights to the Liaodong peninsula and settle for more war indemnity instead. Indeed, even though the war brought on the collapse of Chinese influence in Korea, it ended up benefitting the Russians disproportionately. They pressurized Qing China for more concessions, and, in concert with other European powers, denied Japan the spoils. Realizing that a clash with the Russians was in the offing, the First Sino-Japanese War served to hasten Japan's build-up of land and sea capabilities, backed by a major expansion of iron and steel production. This, in turn, was tested during the Russo-Japanese War of 1905, which the latter won convincingly, much to the surprise of the West.[24]

The terms of peace following the war, as enshrined in the Treaty of Portsmouth, were again not as favourable to Japan as they could have been – which subsequently led to unrest

---

[23] 'False Issues: The Short-lived Republic of Formosa.' *The Du Xiang-guo Papers, Special Collections – Selects of Invasion of Taiwan in 1895*, Archives of Institute of Taiwan History, Academia Sinica, http://archives.ith.sinica.edu.tw/collections_con2_en.php?no=177.

[24] In India, this development became a source of inspiration to many, since it was the first time that an Asiatic country had defeated a major European power in war. It was an oft-cited example within the Indian freedom movement.

among its populace. However, the country, by its defeat of Russia, had shown how an Asian nation could 'catch up' with Europe in terms of industrial and military capability through public policy aimed at national modernization. Meiji Japan's way served to emphasize the twin benefits of industrialization – productivity and security. Industrial development and the attendant increase in output per worker, through the employment of energy-driven machines, leads to wage rise and creates conditions for the growth of a middle class, able to purchase a basket of goods and services. With this also comes factory-scale metallurgical capability that is crucial to building modern weapons systems required to defend sovereignty. The imperial struggles of East Asia served to highlight, yet again, that there could be no independent policymaking in a nation that relies on external sources for the means to defend itself.

AN EAST ASIAN MODEL

Regardless of the stigma attached to the behaviour of imperial Japan towards its immediate neighbours, the said neighbours – who had, for centuries, trasmitted attitudes, customs and know-how to the Japanese – now had to take note of the country's trajectory, especially with respect to the role of the state in industrial development. Japan was a pioneer in an Asian form of state-led capitalism, wherein a flexible mix of public and private strategies was used to sequence industrial development as part of what is called 'industrial policy'. For instance, the first cotton textile mills, which were set up using imported Western machinery, were actually set up by the Meiji state owned enterprises (SOEs).[25] Though they weren't commercially successful, they served as 'proof of concept', and helped create the human resources needed for much bigger textile mills set up by large private conglomerate-type entities.

[25] Ohno, *The Economic Development of Japan*, p. 75.

And these groups themselves had come into being through the no small role played by the Meiji government. In the 1880s, the government sold off, at very low prices, several mines and factories that it had either set up or acquired from Tokugawa-era fiefs.[26] This paved the way for the emergence of the *zaibatsu*, or financial cliques of Japan, which grew into massive, vertically integrated family-holding groups, with a wholly owned banking subsidiary at the core.[27] The four big *zaibatsu* of pre–World War II Japan were of course Mitsubishi, Mitsui, Sumitomo and Yasuda, with the first three brands widely recognized even today. They were reorganized as *keiretsu* groups in post–World War II Japan, wherein the old family core of the *zaibatsu*, system was dissolved and replaced by myriad cross-holdings between companies even as the old names were retained.[28]

Even though the Meiji government let the private sector focus on light manufacturing and mining, the SOEs continued to dominate heavy industries, persisting with the 'emergency character' discussed earlier. Armament manufacturing, shipbuilding and early iron and steel works were organized as military arsenals under army and navy management in the run-up to Japan's pre–World War II conflicts with China and Russia. Moreover, even after the progressive privatization of, say, shipbuilding and other heavy industry enterprises, state hand-holding in the form of subsidies and tariff protection was rife. Private shipyards came under the purview of the 'Law of Encouragement

---

[26] Yoshio, 'The Formation of Heavy Industry'.

[27] Ohno, *The Economic Development of Japan*, p. 45.

[28] *Kereitsu* is basically an informal grouping or alliance of companies attained through cross-shareholding and other interlocking business relationships between them. So, the various companies under the old *zaibatsu* system evolved their relationship into this format instead of revolving around a family at the core.

for Shipbuilding', and received protection as well as secure markets in the form of government procurement.[29]

The Japanese state, from the Meiji period, would typically nurture sunrise sectors before handing them over to capitalist enterprises. For example, in 1900, the first indigenous Japanese locomotive was produced through an alliance between an SOE and the private sector, with the former supplying the blueprints.[30] Such synergy was typical of the country's industrial policy, wherein the government would transfer technology to private firms, help them absorb the same, continue extension services in production process management and training, and then promise to procure assured numbers once series production kicked in.

As such, *zaibatsu* cliques were great beneficiaries of industrial policy and their domination of Japan's emerging industrial economy further fuelled the country's imperial expansionary zeal. After all, any growth in Japan's military-industrial complex meant more assured procurement for them. Also, expansion served their own trading and investment interests, whether it was for commodities or currencies.

On the other hand, the fact that every military victory by Japan yielded only truncated geo-economic returns for it, on account of established powers calibrating its gains, essentially served to push the country further down the path of militarization. This, in turn, sharpened the focus of industrial policy, which identified sectors that were needed to increase comprehensive military power. For instance, prime movers – that is, the main propulsion machinery – for warships was an area where Japan initially either licence-produced or reverse-engineered designs before beginning to churn out improved versions. But then it began coming up with engines that displayed remarkable original innovation.

---

[29] Yoshio, 'The Formation of Heavy Industry'.

[30] Ohno, *The Economic Development of Japan*, p. 80.

THE WAR AND AFTER

By World War II, Japan's military character had assumed a logic of its own, and for the purpose of the war effort, many *zaibatsu*-owned enterprises were nationalized. However, this nationalization also helped instil a certain regimentation and discipline in the country's industrial workforce that was earlier known for springing from one industrial concern to another.[31] Due to wartime embargos, a long-standing gap in Japan's industrial estate, that of having geographically concentrated ancillaries supporting major industries, was overcome. During the war, components were not available for import. And the standard practice by the big firms of the day – of producing many components or production machinery in-house – simply would not suffice for the greatly enhanced rate of production the times demanded. So, the World War II period saw the emergence of local outsourcing and the creation of supply chains in Japan.

After its defeat in World War II, the Allies first sought to demilitarize and dismantle Japan's industrial policy architecture, and the *zaibatsu* were identified for dissolution, since they were seen as a key facet behind the country's peculiar rise. However, fears about communism soon prompted the Americans to change course, and they allowed the *zaibatsu* credo to be reconstituted in the *keiretsu* format, as they encouraged the reindustrialization of Japan, which had seen its factory-scape bombed into oblivion by the US during the war.[32]

Not only was post-war Japan allowed to import the latest machinery from the West, but it was also given access to the American market. What is more, it was allowed to retain the commercial side of its industrial policy ethos. Thus, turning the devastation of their industrial estate into an opportunity,

---

[31] Ibid., pp. 79–80.

[32] Ibid., pp. 154–55.

the Japanese imported the latest machinery and tools to kick-start a second wave of industrialization – albeit this time they focused on heavy industry, sans any overt military underpinnings. Ironically, since all this new machinery was more productive than the legacy factories being operated in the West at the time, a period of 'catch-up growth' for the country was set off, based on increasing the share of manufacturing in its GDP. Manufacturing, owing to its more capital-intensive nature, can lead to an overall increase in the total factor productivity (TFP)[33] of an economy, with the potential to lift its long-term trend growth rate in the process. And this is precisely what the Japanese sought to do, once again. But this time, they focused on certain heavy industries, rather than light industries, for economic development.

In keeping with its industrial policy of identifying 'sectors likely to win', the new democratic Japanese state focused on consumer durables, diversified iron and steel, chemical industries and electrical equipment.[34] It promoted an export orientation and intense competition between domestic firms – although it would be a while before the country started delivering consistent current account surpluses, as we shall see later. Since the Meiji restoration, Japan had encouraged, among its youth, an image of being a country of *monozukuri*, or 'making things/production/craftsmanship',[35]

---

[33] TFP is a measure of technical progress in an economy, and growth economists believe it accounts for half of all economic growth.

[34] A point to note here: Japan could be considered a 'managed democracy' during this period, and further down the road as well, given that it has been dominated by a single party for most of its post–World War II state.

[35] Zokai, Keivan, et al. 'Recapturing Monozukuri in Toyota's Manufacturing Ethos.' *MIT Sloan Management Review*, 11 March 2014, https://sloanreview.mit.edu/article/recapturing-monozukuri-in-toyotas-manufacturing-ethos/. See also: Babu, Venkatesha. 'Japan's Culture of Craftsmanship.' *Business Today*, 24 April 2016, https://www.businesstoday.in/magazine/features/what-indian-manufacturing-can-learn-from-monozukuri/story/230748.html.

and that ethos, along with a now regimented workforce, paved the way for the country's miracle growth years. The fact that Japan was effectively a single-party state during this period, and even later, helped in fostering a homogeneous national ethos geared towards development.

Between 1955 and 1970, the nation saw an average annual growth rate of 9.7 per cent, something rarely seen anywhere else before.[36] During this period, Japan moved from import substitution to export promotion in a number of industries, which had become competitive with those in the West. Again, the Japanese government's role in serving as an intermediary for securing technology for firms through MITI – the Ministry of International Trade and Industry – and in helping industry-wide diffusion of the same through short-patent periods and direct support for technology absorption, as was done during the Meiji period, cannot be understated here. However, within three decades or so, the country's re-emergence on the world stage as a competitor to the US – albeit as an economic entity this time – would generate considerable dissonance through the late 1970s, and particularly in the 1980s, as we shall see next.

'YELLOW PERIL'

In June 1987, three sledgehammer-wielding US Congressmen smashed a Toshiba radio to pieces on the steps of Capitol Hill in Washington, DC.[37] This symbolic protest had come in the wake of disclosures that Toshiba Machine, a subsidiary of Toshiba Corporation, had sold advanced machine tools

---

[36] Fukumoto, Tomoyuki, and Ichiro Muto. 'Rebalancing China's Economic Growth: Some Insights from Japan's Experience.' *Bank of Japan*, July 2011, https://www.boj.or.jp/en/research/wps_rev/wps_2011/data/wp11e05.pdf.

[37] Tolchin, Martin. '"Japan-bashing" Becomes a Trade Bill Issue.' *New York Times*, 28 February 1988, https://www.nytimes.com/1988/02/28/weekinreview/the-nation-japan-bashing-becomes-a-trade-bill-issue.html.

to the Baltic Shipyard in Leningrad (now St Petersburg) earlier in the decade. These new milling machines had helped the Soviets manufacture much quieter propellers for their nuclear submarines, leading to an alleged reduction of sonar detection range by a factor of twenty. The Pentagon estimated that it would have to spend billions of dollars in order to reopen a technology gap in submarine stealth with the Soviets.[38]

The Toshiba transfer was in violation of the rules enshrined in the Coordinating Committee for Multilateral Export Controls (COCOM), a group set up specifically to regulate high technology from Western bloc countries to the Soviet Union.[39] However, these very restrictions meant that the Soviet bloc was willing to pay handsomely for imports of advanced precision machining equipment, something that Japan, by the 1980s, led the world in. Toshiba Machine had received three times the market price for its sale, even as it had played down the actual capabilities and end-use significance of this equipment to a Japanese bureaucracy ever eager to boost exports in order to obtain the necessary export licences. While COCOM rules mandated that only two-axis machine tools could be exported to the Soviet bloc, Toshiba Machine had sold four sets of five-axis and nine-axis milling machines each.[40]

Also implicated in this transfer was Norway's state-owned Kongsberg Vaapenfabrikk, which provided the software and numerical control devices that would operate Toshiba's machine tools. As a result, the scandal came to be known

---

[38] Kelly, S.D. 'Curbing Illegal Transfers of Foreign-Developed Critical High Technology from CoCom Nations to the Soviet Union: An Analysis of the Toshiba Kongsberg Incident.' *Boston College International and Comparative Law Review*, Volume 12, Issue 1, pp. 181–223, 12 January 1989. Digital Commons @ Boston College Law School, https://lawdigitalcommons.bc.edu/iclr/vol12/iss1/8.

[39] Ibid.

[40] Ibid.

as the Toshiba–Kongsberg incident. Be that as it may, for US legislators this incident was much more about Toshiba than Kongsberg. Coming at a time when US polity was already concerned about Japan's outward push in terms of exports and overseas investments, the incident foregrounded the 'Yellow Peril' that was increasingly replacing the 'Red Menace' in the xenophobic American psyche.

Japan, since the mid-1960s, had been running consistent trade surpluses with the US, leading to heightened friction and politicization of commercial ties. By the 1980s, it was not enough to merely call this 'friction'; a Japan phobia seemed to have gripped the political class as Japanese investors increasingly bought up high-visibility US businesses, such as Columbia Pictures.[41] This wave of Japanese investment into the US came in the wake of the 1980 reform of Japan's Foreign Exchange and Foreign Trade Control Law (FEFTCL), which eased the movement of capital to and from the country.[42] But for many American politicians, it was more a case of Japanese capital flowing in to 'buy up America', rather than vice versa; in their view, Japanese firms continued to be protected from takeovers by foreigners through various means, including the traditional practice of cross-shareholdings, despite the official removal of foreign direct investment or FDI restrictions for most sectors. High-profile acquisitions coupled with a worsening trade deficit fashioned the political rhetoric in the US, which claimed that 'Americans were paying Japan to buy them out'.

In this environment, Toshiba's transfer of sensitive technology to the Soviet Union was, to the Americans, at best symptomatic of Japan's mercantilist policies, and at worst

---

[41] Richter, Paul. 'Sony to Pay $3.4 Billion for Columbia Pictures: Japanese Firm Willing to Offer High Price to Get Film, TV Software for Video Equipment It Makes.' *Los Angeles Times*, 28 September 1989, https://www.latimes.com/archives/la-xpm-1989-09-28-mn-361-story.html.

[42] See chapter five.

an example of how the country was looking to translate its economic rise into global influence by undermining the US. Either way, American economic nationalism was pushing back hard against Japan, just as it is pushing back against China today.

REBALANCE

By the early 1970s, Japan's investment-driven model had started running out of steam, as the return to capital began to fall appreciably. Years of 'catch-up methods' using manufacturing technology imported from the West, which were then improved upon in terms of quality and cost, had delivered miracle growth from the mid-1950s to the early 1970s. However, with Japan no longer 'capital scarce', there was a slowdown in the productivity growth of capital as diminishing returns began to set in. On the other hand, the mass migration of people from the countryside to the towns had also become a thing of the past as the country's urbanization process drew to a close. This had the effect of plateauing demand growth in a variety of consumer durables industries – sectors that accounted for a large share of Japanese manufacturing growth during its miracle years.

At the economy-wide level, the nation's investment push had been financed through a rising domestic savings rate that touched 40 per cent of GDP by 1970. In the early years after World War II, Japan had a savings rate of only around 10 per cent, and successive administrations since then had encouraged the populace to save more through the *maruyu* system of tax breaks for savings and other promotional activities. The post-war Japanese practice of providing a large fraction of employee compensation in the form of semi-annual bonuses did no disservice to the cause of savings either, nor did the convention of working even on Saturdays.

These factors, during the high-GDP-growth phase, supplemented specific socio-economic aspects that encourage a high savings rate. This included the desire to bequeath wealth to future generations, precautionary motives related to uncertainties about future income and concerns about retirement spending, since Japan had a very rudimentary pension benefit system at the time and a lack of consumer finance, much as China did till recently. In any case, the attention given to manufacturing had left the country's non-traded sectors, such as urban services, rather underdeveloped, thereby limiting the opportunities available for spending anyway, even as income was rising rapidly with the growth of the economy. Overall, Japan during its high-growth era was also a much younger country than it is today, and according to the 'life-cycle' hypothesis, this leads to a high savings rate since people tend to save more when they are young, hedging for an uncertain future.

Now, it wasn't as if the Japanese people had an array of financial products to choose from either during the high-growth phase, to serve as a destination for their savings. It seemed as if the entire financial system had been essentially designed to transfer their savings via bank intermediation into industrial investments, in sectors chosen by the country's economic planning agency in coordination with MITI, which naturally facilitated the diffusion and absorption of technology. The mobilization of increasing levels of domestic savings through the banking sector helped keep the cost of capital below the return to capital during Japan's high-growth phase, and greatly contributed to incentivizing rapid capital accumulation, leading to capital 'deepening' in the economy.[43]

This low cost of borrowing, however, received an upward push with the oil shock of 1973, when inflation soared to

---

[43] This means the amount of capital per worker (that is, if you divide the total amount of capital by the total number of workers in Japan) was increasing. In other words, production was becoming more mechanized and capital-intensive.

25 per cent the very next year.[44] Naturally, this led to monetary tightening by the Bank of Japan, and a hike in interest rates owing to inflationary pressure. This meant that the gap between the return to capital and the cost of capital narrowed considerably in the years immediately following 1973, which was when the country's investment rate, after hitting a historic high of 36.4 per cent, began to fall.[45] The oil shock also put permanent upward pressure on real wages as workers aggressively demanded pay hikes, which they now received since their bargaining power had gone up significantly by that time, owing to Japan having gone past its Lewis turning point. The Lewis turning point for a country refers to a situation where there is no surplus labour left in the villages that can be moved to cities to hold real wages down.

Japanese workers, till around that time, had actually been receiving real wages less than their productivity and now wanted a fairer share of the output, as it were. A combination of higher energy prices, higher wage rates and increased cost of borrowing at a time of lower capital productivity and a weakening domestic demand for the extant manufacturing basket contributed to lowering profitability expectations from domestic investment in manufacturing. It also meant that from thereon the share of employment in sectors such as manufacturing and mining would not rise beyond the peak attained on the eve of the 1973 oil shock.

Japan realized that rapid capital accumulation in manufacturing would not serve as a solitary growth engine any more. Further, promotion of rapid investment in industry could lead to unmanageable excess capacity and an accumulation of non-performing assets (NPAs) that would portend a banking crisis, since the country's industrial investment was mostly financed by loans via the 'main

---

[44] Fukumoto and Muto, 'Rebalancing China's Economic Growth: Some Insights from Japan's Experience.'

[45] Ibid.

bank' system. The Japanese therefore sought to transition to a potentially slower-growth model, driven by a mix of investment, consumption and exports. And even though consumption was now, in principle, supported by higher disposable income, it would still take time for it to become a primary growth engine in a country characterized by heavy savings, an underdeveloped services sector and an inflationary environment that could put a check on the rise in real wages.

So, the obvious choice for evening out the rebalancing was an even greater focus on the export option, given that Japanese manufacturing had become internationally competitive by the 1970s. The country's products, such as the smaller cars from Toyota and Nissan, guzzling lesser fuel than American muscle cars from General Motors and Ford, were arguably better suited for the double-digit inflationary environment the West had entered post the oil shock of 1973, which would be reinforced by more oil shocks later in the decade.[46] And similar to this was a range of Japanese-made household electrical appliances that saved on electricity bills. Meanwhile, the island nation began to heavily innovate in energy efficiency and factory processes to keep its industries competitive, besides promoting structural changes in its manufacturing ecosystem towards emerging industries such as computer hardware and consumer electronics, much of which it would dominate in the 1980s. It wasn't only that Japan was making products that were cheaper to buy and use, it was also pioneering the development of new consumer electronics, such as the Sony Walkman and VHS recorder that would enter nearabout every home in the West at some point.

Japanese industrial policy thus continued its strategy of constant 'restructuring' of the manufacturing sector by continuing to guide the now lower levels of investment

---

[46] Macalister, Terry. 'Background: What Caused the 1970s Oil Price Shock?' *Guardian*, 3 March 2011, https://www.theguardian.com/environment/2011/mar/03/1970s-oil-price-shock.

towards sunrise sectors, even as it exited older industries. Investments were also made towards cost reduction measures that enhanced competitiveness. And these investments certainly helped with the aim of capturing market share internationally, which ensured that there was no major fall in the share of total employment from manufacturing, since capacity utilization levels remained high.

Indeed, the success of this export orientation could be gauged from the fact that an ever more capital-intensive Japanese manufacturing sector continued to account for around a quarter of total employment in the early 1990s. This availability of manufacturing employment throughout the 1980s not only tied in well with Japan's social contract of maintaining low levels of unemployment, but it also ensured that the economy retained highly productive, well-paying jobs in the industrial sector, which sustained middle-class incomes. This was all the more important since the country was still developing the relatively inefficient non-tradable sectors of its economy, which generated jobs that required lower skills and paid less. But it was the labour-intensive, non-tradable sectors which made up for the collapse in agricultural employment, as Japan became an overwhelmingly urban country. And that urbanization naturally led to heightened real estate activity, a key services sector, which picked up the slack not just from declining rural employment but also from the controlled demise of sunset industries in Japan, such as coal and textiles.[47]

For the competitive industries, however, the country's market dynamic, that saw corporations vying to retain market share even if products had to be offered below cost, a practice known as 'excessive competition', provided lessons in grabbing market share overseas. Indeed, complaints against Japanese corporations 'dumping' their wares on international markets skyrocketed during this period. Beginning in 1970

---

[47] Ohno, *The Economic Development of Japan*, p. 177.

itself, the country had begun notching up overall current account surpluses, a trend that would continue throughout the next two decades, except for years such as 1973 and 1980, when oil shocks hit overseas demand and led to a spike in the oil import bill.

Moreover, post-1973, the general drop in the investment rate also meant that savings now began to exceed investment and Japan emerged as a net exporter of capital with the progressive liberalization of overseas investment norms, that culminated in the 1980 reform of the FEFTCL.[48] Some of these savings went abroad as 'developmental assistance' channelled through the Asian Development Bank (ADB) set up in 1967. Just as China's AIIB and Silk Road Initiative today, ADB assistance was, from the very early days, tied to buying products from Japan, or for securing access to natural resources in target countries, besides exporting national industrial standards.

But increased exports and foreign investments were not the only tools needed for smoothening out the nation's rebalance away from rapid domestic investment. The oil shocks had left domestic demand rather weak, and even with current account surpluses, Japan was now typically notching up economic growth rates of around 4 per cent instead of the 8 per cent it had entered the 1970s with. In a bid to shore up overall demand, the government began to run up deficits from the mid-1970s, by expanding public works as well as increasing social security payments. The need to finance these deficits in an environment increasingly vitiated by trade friction with the US set in motion the liberalization of Japan's finance sector. This would culminate in a rather tragic turn of events for Japan's economy – a story that serves as a cautionary tale for our times.

That is the story of the next chapter.

---

[48] See chapter five.

FIVE

AS WE SAW IN THE PREVIOUS CHAPTER, THE NEED TO FINANCE the large deficits Japan had begun running by the early 1970s became a key driver behind the financial liberalization of its economy. Post-1973, the Japanese government was keen to use domestic savings to finance public spending via government bonds. This need was in a way first felt back in the mid-1960s itself, when there were premature fears of an economic slowdown, and it was in 1965 that a government bond market was first set up.[1] Post-1973, however, the need had become very real, as Japan had begun to run up very large fiscal deficits.

Nevertheless, the government was able to undertake some fiscal consolidation in the early 1980s, due to fast-growing exports, and Japan's current account surplus expanded to record levels.[2] But around that time, the monetary stance was loosened once more by the Bank of Japan (BoJ), since inflation had been brought under check – in large part due to investments in energy efficiency paying off. The monetary loosening was ostensibly done to shore up the investment climate and boost consumer credit in aid of Japan's rebalance towards greater reliance on consumption. But what it also did was make it easier for the big banks to advance loans to

[1] 'Securities Market in Japan 2014.' *Japan Securities Research Institute*, 2014, http://www.jsri.or.jp/publish/english/pdf/english_07.pdf.

[2] Ueda, Kazuo. 'Perspectives on the Japanese Current Account Surplus.' In Stanley Fischer, ed. *NBER Macroeconomics Annual 1988*, Volume 3, MIT Press. Macroeconomics Annual Book Series.

riskier borrowers in the real estate sector, as well as to small and medium enterprises (SMEs), that were earlier deprived of main bank finance. These were the new 'borrowers' that big banks were targeting, since the aftermath of the FEFTCL reform alluded to in the previous chapter had stripped them of their traditional corporate clients. By paving the way for major Japanese corporations to raise money through overseas bond issues, this reform also led to the progressive deregulation of the domestic bond market, because that was the only way in which it could survive the opening up of overseas bond markets for Japanese companies. Throughout the 1980s (and even in the 1990s) there was constant concern in the country about the so-called 'hollowing out' of the domestic bond market in the sense that there was not enough bond supply (that is, issuance of securitized debt) from Japanese companies. These organizations instead preferred to issue bonds overseas due to the higher issuance costs at home, and Japanese investors in turn preferred buying these overseas bonds rather than buy those issued on the country's soil.[3]

Euro–yen markets, which did not have collateral requirements or mandatory prospectus issues, while also offering swaps and other hedging mechanisms not found in Japan at the time, were the arena of choice for Japanese funds looking to raise money quickly and cheaply. By 1985, bond issues in the euro–yen market supplied more than half of all bond finance for Japanese funds and a third overall for the country's corporate finance. This process continued despite Japanese investors being forbidden by fiat from buying such overseas corporate bonds within three months of the date of issuance. London-based underwriting securities companies helped Japanese investors circumvent this restriction by

[3] Takahashi, Wataru. 'The Japanese Financial Sector's Transition from High Growth to the "Lost Decades": A Market Economy Perspective.' *Research Institute for Economics and Business*, 24 October 2011, https://www.rieb.kobe-u.ac.jp/academic/ra/dp/English/DP2011-29.pdf.

selling them Eurobonds issued by Japanese corporations on a subscription basis. By 1989, overseas markets accounted for over 60 per cent of all bonds issued by the country's entities.[4]

Thus, the opening up of new direct financing opportunities through bond issues both at home and abroad led to major Japanese corporations moving away from the indirect financing option of bank loans. Large manufacturing firms also began to increase the use of internal funds (that is, retained profits after paying off dividends to shareholders) for investment purposes. Indeed, internal accruals became the chief source of financing for them by the 1980s.[5] But the share of loans in corporate investment was also taken away by stocks and, by the late 1980s, bank loans would account for a smaller share of funding for major companies than either internal funds, bonds or equity.[6] Thus, liberalization paved the way for the rapid transformation of the Japanese financial sector – moving it away from being bank-based to a progressively securitized one.

Major corporate borrowers moved away from the main bank system due to a mix of factors that included easier borrowing conditions overseas, competitive coupon rates (that is, the yield paid by a fixed income security) and a lessening of the hold their erstwhile 'close' banking partners had on corporate decision-making. It has also been proposed that since many of the corporate bonds issued in the 1980s

---

[4] Hattori, M., et al. 'A Financial System Perspective on Japan's Experience in the Late 1980s.' Paper presented at the 16th International Conference hosted by the Institute for Monetary and Economic Studies, Bank of Japan, May 2009, https://www.imes.boj.or.jp/english/publication/edps/2009/09-E-19.pdf.

[5] Horiuchi, Akiyoshi. 'An Evaluation of Japanese Financial Liberalization: A Case Study of Corporate Bond Markets.' In Takatoshi Ito and Anne O. Krueger, eds. *Financial Deregulation and Integration in East Asia*, NBER-EASE, Volume 5, January 1996, https://www.nber.org/chapters/c8562.pdf.

[6] Ibid.

were 'convertible' in nature – which meant they could be converted into equity – they conferred greater discretionary ability on the part of the management to undertake expenditure on perquisites.[7] Convertible bonds are usually issued by newer firms looking to obviate the risk associated with loans, but in Japan's case only large corporations were allowed to issue convertibles during the 1980s, and this fact had been advanced to support the 'perquisite expenditure' theory mentioned above.

Meanwhile, faced with the fact that they had lost their prime customers, big banks directed their lending efforts towards real-estate-linked sectors as well as SMEs, which till then had been dependent on smaller regional banks, agri-cooperatives and credit unions for finance. The real estate sector in particular emerged as a favourite destination for the massive expansion in credit and bank lending that Japan would see through the 1980s. Unable to properly assess the risk faced by the new borrowers in real-estate-linked sectors, Japanese banks agreed to lend to many less creditworthy entities on the basis of real estate collateral.[8] Land scarcity in an urbanized country gave rise to a sense that real estate prices would only rise over time, especially since falling property prices had been witnessed very rarely during the high-growth era. This led to the notion that real estate was good collateral to hold on to.

The real estate sector was also being supported through both taxation and regulation by the government. This sector is, after all, a way to kill many 'political economy' stones when growth is tepid as it generates demand for the domestic steel and cement sectors, which increasingly become overcapacity

---

[7] Ibid.

[8] Shiratsuka, Shigenori. 'Asset Price Bubble in Japan in the 1980s: Lessons for Financial and Macroeconomic Stability.' *Discussion Paper Number 2003-E-15*, Institute for Monetary and Economic Studies, Bank of Japan, 2003, https://www.imes.boj.or.jp/research/papers/english/03-E-15.pdf.

once the heady days of rapid industrialization end. It also serves as an outlet for laid-off blue-collar workers, provides the 'sites' for 'rebalancing' to new services sectors – such as non-bank finance, retail, etc. – besides catering to electoral promises of affordable housing. Unfortunately, the turn to real estate to support growth, rather than have growth sustain real estate activities, doesn't end too well for economies. Urbanization by itself is not a sustainable growth driver. This is something Japan would soon find out. And China may be finding out now as we shall see in the next chapter.

DID SOMEBODY SAY PLAZA?

The FEFTCL reform was also undertaken to ward off pressure from the Americans who were raising a red flag about Japanese protectionism. But, as we saw earlier, this did not quite satisfy US interests; they wanted much deeper and wider financial reform that would lead to the decontrol of interest rates in the Japanese economy. The narrative as far as the Americans were concerned was one of Japanese financial repression leading to lower-than-normal interest rates, making it unattractive for investors to put their money in Japan.[9] After all, there were times during the 1960s and 1970s when real interest rates on deposits offered by Japanese banks were in the negative territory.

In addition to this, the 'narrow' Japanese financial sector also lacked enough diversity of instruments that could be invested in, much as the Chinese financial sector does today. As far as the Americans were concerned, only broad-based financial deregulation that would raise interest rates and investment opportunities would lead to dollar investments in the Japanese economy, put upward pressure on the yen and thereby correct the worsening trade deficit with the

---

[9] Takahashi, 'The Japanese Financial Sector's Transition from High Growth to the "Lost Decades"'.

country. The Japanese decided to engage the Americans on these views by setting up the Yen–Dollar (YD) Committee in November 1983, to coincide with then US President Ronald Reagan's visit to Japan.[10]

This clarion call for financial deregulation by the Americans was enthusiastically supported by the big Japanese banks that wanted to tap into a wider base of clientele, as well as expand their own investment and financing options. For instance, they wanted an easing of regulations for their participation in stock markets – something they got after the YD Committee reached an agreement in May 1984 concerning the 'liberalization of Japan's financial markets, yen internationalization, and the lowering of barriers to market access for foreign financial institutions in Japan'.[11] But the various structural reforms that were set in motion following the YD Committee would not be enough to satiate America's crusade against an 'undervalued' yen. This is almost a direct parallel to the way America labels China as a 'currency manipulator' today.

The relentless American pressure on Japan to 'do something' about persistent trade imbalances culminated in the Plaza Accord of 1985 that was agreed upon by the G-5 group of top industrialized economies, which comprised France, Germany, Japan, the United Kingdom and the US.[12] Though ostensibly designed to bring about a convergence of policies and performance among the G-5 and develop a more appropriate pattern of exchange between them, the

---

[10] Ibid.

[11] Osugi, K. 'Japan's Experience of Financial Deregulation Since 1984 in an International Perspective.' *BIS Economic Papers, Number 26*, Bank for International Settlements, January 1990, http://www.bis.org/publ/econ26.pdf.

[12] 'Announcement by the Ministers of Finance and Central Bank Governors of France, Germany, Japan, the United Kingdom, and the United States (Plaza Accord), 22 September 1985.' *Managing the Dollar: From the Plaza to the Louvre*, Institute for International Economics, 1988.

Plaza Accord was mostly about getting Japan to let the yen appreciate with respect to the dollar. To a lesser degree it was also about getting the Deutsche Mark to appreciate against the dollar, since Germany too had been running trade surpluses with respect to America.

Accordingly, through heavy coordinated intervention in foreign exchange markets, the yen appreciated 11.8 per cent in the week following the Plaza Accord.[13] Japan had after all been accruing dollar reserves for some years now to hold the yen down vis-à-vis the dollar, and in the weeks following the Plaza Accord it would sell dollars to buy yen. And to support this new 'stance', the BoJ also indicated that it would not compensate for the yen appreciation by loosening its monetary position, thereby prompting a sharp rise in Japanese interest rates.

The yen rose from 250 to a dollar just before the Plaza Accord to 160 to a dollar soon after, and would continue to appreciate for the next few years.[14] The result of this sharp appreciation was expectedly a slowdown in Japanese exports. To counter this, the Japanese government increased public spending, besides initiating tax cuts to boost consumption. However, these measures were not enough to compensate for the hit taken by exports. Overall, growth slowed from 5.2 per cent in 1985 to 3.3 per cent in 1986.[15] Manufacturing profits in 1986 fell sharply as compared to the year before, and there was a slight decrease in manufacturing employment as well. Most secondary sectors were badly hit. Thus, the first *endaka*

---

[13] Ito, Takatoshi. 'The Plaza Agreement and Japan: Reflection on the 30th Year Anniversary.' *Baker Institute for Public Policy*, 2015, https://www.bakerinstitute.org/media/files/files/0eb0ad16/WorkingPaper-Plaza-Ito-092815.pdf.

[14] Ibid.

[15] 'GDP Growth (Annual %).' Real GDP growth rates estimated based on World Bank national accounts data and OECD national accounts data files from 1961 to 2019, *World Bank*, 2015, https://data.worldbank.org/indicator/NY.GDP.MKTP.KD.ZG.

fukyo, or 'high yen recession', lasting up to early 1987 was experienced by Japan.[16] In a bid to shore up flagging demand, the BoJ loosened its monetary stance once more.

BUBBLING OVER

However, monetary easing didn't do much to revive manufacturing investment. What it did do, though, was push even more credit into the already 'hot' real estate sector, as evidenced by the fact that construction kept booming throughout the first *endaka* recession. It also pushed the Nikkei Stock Index towards record highs. Japan's asset markets had now firmly entered bubble territory. A bubble which came to be called the Hesei boom, since Japan had by then entered the Hesei era, which marked the reign of Emperor Akihito, who succeeded his father Hirohito a day after the latter's demise on 8 January 1989.[17] Of course, as we saw earlier, the Hesei boom had been in the making ever since the beginning of serious financial liberalization in Japan, as marked by the FEFTCL reform, which made banks reorient lending towards less creditworthy firms operating in real-estate-linked sectors, including construction, wholesale and retail, on the basis of real estate collaterals.

The banks' push for increased lending to the real estate sector was made easier by the increased liquidity that became available to them in the 1980s, even as their main customers, that is, major Japanese corporations, moved away. Ironically,

---

[16] The term *endaka fukyo* was first used by the Japanese themselves while describing the severe economic downturn faced by their country during 1992–95. The term here has been used retrospectively since the 'growth recession' from 1985–87 was actually the first significant high-yen-induced slowdown.

[17] Hamada, Koichi. 'The Heisei Recession: An Overview.' *ESRI International Forum*, the Social and Economic Research Institute, Cabinet Office of Japan, 18 September 2003, http://www.esri.go.jp/jp/workshop/030918/030918hamada.pdf.

it was these very same corporations that provided much of the increased liquidity to their erstwhile lenders by way of investing in time deposits offered by the big banks at market-based interest rates. With a strengthening yen limiting export possibilities and a tight domestic market, Japanese corporations rather than investing in new factories decided instead to engage in a 'carry trade' that would prove hugely profitable as long as the bubble lasted. And this 'carry trade' was enabled by the fact that these firms' post-deregulation could raise money by issuing securities (mainly bonds) to new lenders outside the Japanese banking system, such as foreign investors and life insurance companies, at relatively low borrowing costs. Following this, they would make profits by drawing on the higher market-based interest rates that banks now offered via time deposits. So, in a reversal of roles, the big Japanese corporations now became creditors to their old lenders and effectively joined the financial intermediation sector by emerging as 'shadow banks', bringing in new funds from foreign investors, life insurance companies and even retail investors.

As eligibility norms for issuing corporate bonds were gradually relaxed through the 1980s, more and more firms started to behave as 'shadow banks' by engaging in this 'carry trade'. By 1988, the number of Japanese companies eligible for issuing unsecured straight bonds had increased to around 300, while around 500 firms could now issue convertible bonds.[18] And beginning November 1987, companies in the country were also allowed to raise funds by issuing corporate paper, a key short-term instrument that further fuelled their 'carry trade' through time deposits in the banks.[19] With greater liabilities in the form of these new time deposits, as a result of arbitrage-seeking behaviour by Japanese firms,

---

[18] Hattori, M., et al. 'A Financial System Perspective on Japan's Experience in the Late 1980s.'

[19] Ibid.

banks were pushed to expand their assets by lending to their new less creditworthy customers on the basis of real estate collateral that led to a classic price-lending spiral. Large Japanese banks were keen to protect market share despite lowered profitability expectations, and felt that they had hedged against risks adequately by accepting real estate as collateral. Their borrowers, that is, real-estate-linked firms as well as SMEs, were also keen to grow quickly. And this was in no small measure due to the need to find more 'positions' in their concern for employees demanding advancement, while being protected from lay-offs due to social pressure that demanded 'long-term employment' for workers.

In the second half of the 1980s, land prices would rise by an average 50 per cent across Japan.[20] In metropolitan centres such as Tokyo, land prices would actually triple during this period, hitting their peak in early 1991.[21]

Banks also expanded their balance sheets by lending to brokerage houses and other firms for stock market activity, besides dabbling in the market themselves. Stock market speculation was the other kind of 'carry trade' that large Japanese non-banking firms were engaging in. In a practice known as *zaitech*, major Japanese corporations would arbitrage between capital gains in stock prices and the cost of lending via securities.[22] This is reflected in the fact that there was considerable accumulation of financial assets by non-banking companies during this period. *Zaitech* saw many Japanese

---

[20] Otsubo, S.T. 'Post-War Development of the Japanese Economy.' PPT prepared for students in the EDP&M Program, Economic Development and Policy Management Program, Nagoya University, April 2007, https://www.gsid.nagoya-u.ac.jp/sotsubo/Postwar_Development_of_the_Japanese%20Economy(Otsubo_NagoyaU).pdf.

[21] Ibid.

[22] Engdahl, William. 'Will Japan's "Zaitech" Bring a Market Crash?' *EIR*, Volume 14, Number 38, 25 September 1987, http://www.larouchepub.com/eiw/public/1987/eirv14n38-19870925/eirv14n38-19870925_006-will_japans_zaitech_bring_a_mark.pdf.

companies recycle capital raised on markets to push up stock prices. As stock prices rose, these companies were able to issue convertible bonds at very low coupon rates even as the capital gains, which were shown as corporate profits, boosted stock prices due to a perception of increasing profitability. Moreover, the banks were also doing their bit to raise the stock prices of companies that had time deposits with them.

As the bubble expanded, so did the profits from *zaitech*, leading to some estimates suggesting that almost half of all corporate profits by 1989 were derived through this practice.[23] Speculative activity in an environment of easy liquidity pushed the Nikkei Stock Exchange to unprecedented levels of market capitalization, with the index tripling between 1985 and 1989 to touch an all-time high of almost 39,000 in 1989.[24] At this point, the Nikkei Stock Exchange would account for a third of worldwide market capitalization.[25] Thus, the securitization of the Japanese financial sector that was set off by deregulation ultimately led to tremendous asset price inflation, even as the consumer price index (CPI) remained tepid. Indeed, low consumer inflation contributed to the BoJ maintaining an accommodative monetary stance. On the other hand, a return to strong growth in 1987, the continuation of fiscal stimulus to support domestic demand and the conclusion of the Louvre Accord by the G-5 that year (1987), which looked to reverse the recessionary impact of the 1985 Plaza Accord, probably led to a sense of euphoria about future growth prospects.[26] This euphoria would 'justify'

---

[23] Ibid.

[24] Barsky, R.B. 'The Japanese Bubble: A "Heterogenous" Approach.' *National Bureau of Economic Research*, Number 15,052, June 2009, http://www.nber.org/papers/w15052.pdf.

[25] 'Listing, not Keeling.' *The Economist*, Tokyo, 26 November 2011, http://www.economist.com/node/21540306.

[26] 'Statement of the G6 Finance Ministers and Central Bank Governors (Louvre Accord).' *The G-8 Path: Ministerial and Other Meetings*, 22 February 1987, http://www.g8.utoronto.ca/finance/fm870222.htm.

the wild increase in asset prices in the minds of Japanese investors.

Unfortunately, the 'good times' would draw to a close rather quickly for the country's finance firms. By 1989, the BoJ accepted that there was a dangerous bubble in Japan's asset markets and decided to pull the liquidity plug as it were. The central bank, in a series of steps, increased the discount rate from 2.5 per cent in May 1989 to 6 per cent in August 1990.[27] The impact of this monetary tightening began to be felt by early 1990, when the Nikkei index began its rapid downward slide to fall by some 50 per cent before the end of the year. With the stock exchange on a downhill slide, the real estate market followed suit within a year. *Zaitech* now worked in reverse, with speculating firms facing huge losses and an erosion of capital leading to the withdrawal of liquidity from the banking system. The Japanese government also tightened norms for lending to the real estate sector, and land prices started falling rapidly by 1991. The bursting of these bubbles had a deleterious impact on Japan's real economy, with the GDP growth rate falling by more than half to 2.4 per cent in 1992 and then to just 0.5 per cent in 1993.[28] The first of Japan's 'lost decades' had begun.

LOST DECADES

Once the Hesei boom was over, Japan's banking system found itself buried under a mountain of non-performing loans (NPLs) that, according to some estimates, amounted

---

[27] Jinushi, T., et al. 'Monetary Policy in Japan Since the Late 1980s: Delayed Policy Actions and Some Explanations.' *Japan's Financial Crisis and its Parallels to US Experience*, Special Report 13, edited by Ryoichi Mikitani and Adam S. Posen, Institute for International Economics, September 2000, pp. 115–48. *Peterson Institute for International Economics*, https://piie.com/publications/chapters_preview/319/6iie289X.pdf.

[28] 'GDP Growth (Annual %).' *World Bank*, 2015.

to 25 per cent of GDP by 1995.[29] The profitability of many borrowing firms had depended greatly on real estate prices, which, as we know, had halved and were still falling. With mounting losses, most of these corporations were unable to repay their debts, with many defaulting. On top of that, the falling real estate prices meant that the collateral held by banks was now worth much less. Before the bubble burst, borrowers could draw up to 90 per cent of their real estate collateral, but by 1998, only 50 per cent of the loan was considered under collateral coverage, leaving 40 per cent of such loans uncovered.[30] So, basically, the broken balance sheets of a multitude of borrowing firms now lay as toxic assets on the balance sheets of their creditor banks. Securities underwriting firms and the purchasers of Japanese corporate securities, such as life insurance companies, were badly hit as well.

Faced with the prospect of serial bankruptcies and defaults, banks in the country with the support of the Japanese government decided to pursue a policy of 'forbearance lending' by rescheduling loan repayments for their debtors even as they continued lending to them, in order to forestall their filing for bankruptcy. The government favoured such an approach in order to keep unemployment levels down. For banks, this policy served to mask the severity of the losses that they had incurred on the NPLs held by them. Overall, the forbearance policy was encouraged in the fond hope that an economic recovery would remedy the situation with the borrowing firms getting back into the black. That, however,

---

[29] Though the official estimates were only about 10 per cent at the time. See also: Geevers, Peiter. *The Heisei Boom and Its Aftermath: Lessons for the US Federal Reserve System*. Master's Thesis, University of Amsterdam, 19 March 2009.

[30] Kanaya, Akihiro, and David Woo. 'The Japanese Banking Crisis of the 1990s: Sources and Lessons.' *Essays in International Economics*, Number 222, International Economics Section, Princeton University, June 2001, https://www.princeton.edu/~ies/IES_Essays/E222.pdf.

did not happen and the policy only served to add to the credit problems Japan would face for much of the 1990s, with 'zombie firms' allowed to continue trading through forbearance lending.

Importantly, as a result of this policy, banks became rather reluctant to advance new loans as they had in reality suffered a major erosion of capital and were now facing shortages. At the same time, most firms chose to pay down existing debts rather than make new investments in Japan. The economy was moving from very low inflation to deflationary territory, which had two effects: it made their existing debts more difficult to service and greatly reduced the incentive for making new investments. Thus, the credit bust led to the drying up of private investment, which contracted by an average rate of 2 per cent in the first half of the 1990s, in Japan.[31] The impact on consumption was also pronounced. While in the 1980s those who owned property had taken to conspicuous consumption buoyed by a sense of 'wealth' on account of rising asset prices, now they held off on spending due to precautionary reasons. Japan's rebalance did not turn out to be as smooth a process as envisioned after all.

Perhaps the only reason why banks had initially thought that there might be a recovery was the massive spending programme undertaken by the government in the wake of the downturn. Onwards of 1992, successive Japanese administrations started running large budget deficits on account of tax cuts and massive spending on public works, but this failed to revive strong economic growth in the 1990s. There is, however, a view that without repeated fiscal stimulus, things would have been much worse for the Japanese economy.

---

[31] Araki, Haruka. 'The Causes of the Japanese Lost Decade: An Extension of Graduate Thesis.' *Soka University*, 26 May 2017, http://daigakuin.soka.ac.jp/assets/files/pdf/major/kiyou/16_keizai3.pdf.

This view probably stems from the fact that monetary policy was an even bigger failure in reviving demand in the economy. Since 1994, the BoJ, in a bid to do its part to revive investor sentiment, adopted a very loose monetary stance keeping the discount rate below 1 per cent, but this did not lead to any revival of investment sentiment in the Japanese economy through the rest of the 1990s.[32] The lack of monetary transmission, as it were, in the decade could be attributed to the forbearance policy, which kept large NPLs on bank balance sheets and kept them from taking the risk of extending cheap new loans, even when they could borrow quite cheaply from the BoJ's discount window. Rather than this policy of forbearance, the Japanese government could have instead injected fresh capital into these banks and allowed them to write off their bad debts. However, such a move was deemed unpopular with the Japanese electorate, which held the banks chiefly culpable for the Hesei boom and its aftermath. Besides, it would have also resulted in greater unemployment in a milieu where the political economy was wired to expect low levels of joblessness, as is the case with China today.

It was a case of delaying the inevitable, and making it worse. The 1997 Asian Financial Crisis (AFC), which saw the yen declining sharply against the dollar, led to a wave of bankruptcies in the Japanese banking system, including the closure of two very old and prominent financial institutions – Hokkaido Takushoku Bank and Yamaichi Securities.[33] Their closure was on account of NPLs and a plunge in the value of equities held by them, making it impossible for them to bear the erosion of capital any longer. It was only after the insolvency of institutions such as these that the government

---

[32] Jinushi, 'Monetary Policy in Japan Since the Late 1980s: Delayed Policy Actions and Some Explanations.'

[33] Otsubo, 'Post-War Development of the Japanese Economy.'

could step in to recapitalize Japan's banks and allow them to dispose of NPLs.

In 1999, the Bank of Japan would officially adopt a Zero Interest Rate Policy (ZIRP) and in 2001 it would begin the world's first post–World War II QE programme that would see it purchase bank assets in order to directly infuse funds into the banking system.[34] The QE programme was intended to make it easier for banks to deal with NPL disposal and feel confident about future lending. These measures, along with the recapitalization of Japanese banks with public money, did manage to stabilize the financial system to a large extent, with some 70 per cent of legacy NPLs being successfully retired between 2002 and 2007.

Monetary easing was also undertaken with the expectation that it would push up prices and lead to growth. But this growth remained rather elusive for the Japanese economy, which, after contracting for two years in the wake of the AFC, barely remained in positive territory in the early 2000s. It is noteworthy that the decline of the yen around the time of the AFC failed to push up Japanese exports.[35] Overall, the economy remained in deflationary territory and this first phase of QE was pursued relentlessly till 2006.[36] And this was done because at the other end, the Japanese government kept pump-priming the economy through an infrastructure build-up.

The righting of the banking system through recapitalization, massive public spending and pouring of

---

[34] Harari, Daniel. 'Japan's Economy: From the "Lost Decade" to Abenomics.' *Standard Note: SN06629*, Economic Policy and Statistics, Library of the House of Commons, United Kingdom, 24 October 2013, http://researchbriefings.files.parliament.uk/documents/SN06629/SN06629.pdf.

[35] Ito, Takatoshi. 'Japan and the Asian Financial Crisis: The Role of Financial Supervision in Restoring Growth.' *The International Centre for the Study of East Asian Development*, Volume 99, Number 10, Kitakyushu, July 1999, http://en.agi.or.jp/workingpapers/WP1999-10.pdf.

[36] Harari, 'Japan's Economy: From the "Lost Decade" to Abenomics.'

seemingly unlimited liquidity into the banking sector via unconventional monetary policies saw the country's renewed business investment oriented towards manufacturing exports. With some renewed investment and strong exports, the economy managed to notch up a 1.7 per cent average annual real GDP growth rate from 2003–07, even though domestic prices kept falling all the way until 2006.[37] Nevertheless, this return to weak trend growth gave the BoJ a sense that the Japanese economy was out of the woods at last, with the government also drawing down on deficit spending, leading to a fall in the fiscal deficit from 8 per cent in 2003 to 2 per cent in 2007. As such, the BoJ announced an end to the first round of its QE policy in 2006.

Alas, the GFC hit soon thereafter, sparking the deepest recession in Japanese post-war history, with the economy contracting by over 1 per cent in 2008, followed by another 5.4 per cent in 2009.[38] Though this fall in output was partially made up by mid-2010 due to a rebound in exports and yet another humongous fiscal stimulus, the country's economy was firmly in deflationary territory. In 2010, the BoJ joined the US Fed in instituting ZIRPs once again, and a new round of QE was announced with the explicit target of attaining a 'price stability' inflation band of 0–2 per cent. This round of QE, besides stuffing banks with liquidity, so that they extended loans for new business activity, saw a major increase in government bond-buying activity by the Japanese central bank.

The March 2011 Great East Japan earthquake and tsunami put paid to any notion of a recovery, and Japan's real GDP contracted in 2011.[39] The Japanese government

---

[37] Real GDP growth rates estimated using 2010 dollars by the World Bank. 'GDP Growth (Annual %).' *World Bank*, 2015, https://data.worldbank.org/indicator/NY.GDP.MKTP.KD.ZG?end=2019&locations=JP&start=1991.

[38] Ibid.

[39] Ibid.

responded with more spending and announced a 10-year reconstruction package. Nevertheless, the economy hasn't really budged since then and, as of the end of 2020, Japan's nominal GDP in dollar terms was barely above what it was at the end of 2008.[40]

And all this happened despite the efforts made by former Prime Minister Shinzo Abe, since he took power in 2012, to resuscitate the Japanese economy via a very loose monetary stance, short-term stimulus and 'structural reforms', which together constitute the so-called 'three arrows of Abenomics'.[41] The first two are of course par for the course for any Japanese government since the end of the Hesei boom, and the last is easier said than done. Indeed, one of the reasons why repeated fiscal stimulus has been unable to put Japan back on a decent growth path is that it has been mostly of the pork barrel variety, focused on keeping otherwise excess capacity in core industries such as cement and steel in business. Now, given that diminishing returns to capital set in for Japan a long time ago, it isn't surprising that public spending has not achieved much besides 'building roads to nowhere' and preventing a major contraction.

Public spending certainly hasn't been a harbinger for restructuring or remoulding the country's economy into newer, more productive sectors or towards a so-called innovation economy. Indeed, secular Japanese stagnation has been accompanied by a decline in total factor productivity. So there has been little 'crowding in' as far as the experience of countercyclical fiscal policy is concerned. Japanese corporations in the main have looked to invest abroad in pollution havens and low-cost locations as part of their global

---

[40] Based on an inspection of World Bank data.

[41] Yoshino, Naoyuki, and Farhad Taghizadeh-Hesary. 'Three Arrows of "Abenomics" and the Structural Reform of Japan: Inflation Targeting Policy of the Central Bank, Fiscal Consolidation, and Growth Strategy.' *Asian Development Bank Institute*, Number 492, August 2014, http://hdl.handle.net/11540/1254.

supply model. Between 1991 and 2018, the economy grew by an average rate of just under 1 per cent on an annual basis, with real GDP in 2018 being less than 30 per cent higher than real GDP in 1991.[42]

Periodic pump-priming of the economy, coupled with very low to no or negative nominal GDP growth, caused Japan's gross government debt-to-GDP ratio to rise from 67 per cent in 1990 to 236 per cent in 2018,[43] the highest by far among the G-7 group of countries.[44] The country has managed to sustain such a high debt-to-GDP ratio thus far on account of being able to borrow in yen, borrow at home and borrow cheap. Japan's risk-averse investors exhibit a pronounced 'home bias', whereby the country's large stock of yen-denominated private savings has consistently found its way into Japanese government bonds (JGBs) since 1990, that is, when fixed capital investment opportunities started dwindling. And with post-bubble Japan being in the grip of deflation, the very low rates of interest paid on 'safe' JGBs did not seem so bad after all.[45] As such, the country's banks, non-banking finance companies, pension funds and insurance firms have all channelized domestic private savings into long-term Japanese government debt since 1990, helping keep debt-service costs very low. In fact, the nation's net interest-payment-to-GDP ratio is lower than the average for OECD economies.[46] Overall, with 90 per cent of Japanese

---

[42] Calculated by the author from annual GDP (constant LCU) data for Japan using World Bank data.

[43] 'IMF Executive Board Concludes 2015 Article IV Consultation with Japan.' *IMF*, 23 July 2015, https://www.imf.org/external/np/sec/pr/2015/pr15352.htm.

[44] Lennard, Carrie. 'Lessons for G7 Economies from Japan's Super High Public Debt-to-GDP Ratio.' *Euromonitor International*, 31 August 2015, http://blog.euromonitor.com/2015/08/lessons-for-g7-economies-from-japans-super-high-public-debt-to-gdp-ratio.html.

[45] They also help banks fulfil their collateral obligations.

[46] Lennard, 'Lessons for G7 Economies from Japan's Super High Public Debt-to-GDP Ratio.'

government debt held by onshore entities, the possibility that a foreign speculative attack on its debt will succeed is insignificant for the time being.[47]

This is especially because the BoJ has been pushing JGB bond yields down to nothing through its continued massive purchases of long-term Japanese government debt, ever since it began the so-called 'Quantitative & Qualitative Easing' (QQE) programme in March 2013. Introduced soon after the current BoJ governor, Haruhiko Kuroda, assumed office, QQE was intended to be a step beyond whatever QE the central bank had done till then, as Kuroda himself explained in July 2016:

> QQE has two key elements that enable the bank to move beyond the previous monetary policy measures. The first is the bank's strong and clear commitment to achieving the price stability target of 2 per cent at the earliest possible time, which is underpinned by a large-scale monetary easing, thereby drastically converting the deflationary mindset among people and raising inflation expectations. The second is to put downward pressure on the entire yield curve through massive purchases of Japanese government bonds (JGBs), financed by an equally massive increase of the monetary base (Chart 1). These two elements together have reduced real interest rates and thus have produced strong easing effects.[48]

However, the BoJ wanted to maintain those 'strong easing effects' for a long time, since inflation showed no signs of

---

[47] 'Japan's Debt Mountain: How Is It Sustainable?' *Economic Times*, 10 June 2020, https://economictimes.indiatimes.com/news/international/business/japans-debt-mountain-how-is-it-sustainable/articleshow/76298563.cms.

[48] Kuroda, Haruhiko. 'Re-anchoring Inflation Expectations via "Quantitative and Qualitative Monetary Easing with a Negative Interest Rate."' Remarks at the Economic Symposium of the Federal Reserve Bank of Kansas City, held on 'Designing Resilient Monetary Policy Frameworks for the Future', Bank of International Settlements, 27 August 2016, https://www.bis.org/review/r160831a.pdf.

approaching its target value. To indicate the same, the central bank had pushed its key short-term policy rate into negative territory in January 2016 itself, a move that was called 'QQE with negative interest rate'. And in September 2016, 'QQE with negative interest rate' was upgraded to 'QQE with yield curve control' (QQE-YCC), which was still in place at the time of writing. In a July 2019 speech, Kuroda explained the logic underlying QQE-YCC:

> Under yield curve control, the Bank aims to control both short- and long-term interest rates, setting the target level of 10-year Japanese government bond (JGB) yields at around zero per cent. The previous policy framework that set the amount of JGB purchases as the operating target was simple to operate in practice. However, there was a problem that the degree of downward pressure on the yields could change to a large extent, depending on economic and market conditions at the time. In contrast, under yield curve control, the Bank sets the specific target level of interest rates and conducts JGB purchases so as to achieve this target. In exerting monetary easing effects stably for a long time, the Bank judges that yield curve control is a better framework in terms of both controllability and sustainability.[49]

Forget about a speculative attack from foreign shores, QQE-YCC has ushered in an era of BoJ dominance of the JGB market, with anybody trying to 'short' Japanese government debt meeting a swift and sure end. In fact, the central bank is now called the 'widow maker' by traders who have essentially abandoned the JGB market. The writing on the wall was apparent to foreign dealers even before QQE-YCC was introduced, with major Western banks such as the Royal Bank of Scotland leaving the JGB market in 2014–15 itself.

---

[49] Kuroda, Haruhiko. 'Overcoming Deflation: Japan's Experience and Challenges Ahead.' Speech at the 2019 Michel Camdessus Central Banking Lecture, International Monetary Fund, 22 July 2019, https://www.boj.or.jp/en/announcements/press/koen_2019/ko190723a.htm/.

Basically, the BoJ's purchase of various classes of JGBs has reduced market liquidity to such an extent that there are sometimes just not enough bonds to trade. Its bid to reflate the Japanese economy has also made it the dominant player in the exchange traded funds (ETFs) market.[50] Beginning in 2010, the BoJ started buying ETFs in order to provide further liquidity to the economy and this process was stepped up in the QQE era through its various iterations. By December 2018, the central bank 'owned' over three-quarters of the ETF market and some 5 per cent of all outstanding shares in the main Japanese stock exchange by extension.[51] The market liquidity situation was so bad that the BoJ actually offered to loan ETFs to traders, just so that trades could happen. For the time being, the combination of accumulated Japanese private savings and the BoJ's QQE-YYC is ensuring that bond and stock prices remain high, while interest rates stay rock-bottom. For the Japanese government, these ultra-low interest rates have made it easy to achieve debt turnover despite the massive debt pile.

However, this happy situation may not last forever if the country's overall stock of savings begins declining on trend as it did till about 2012 before seemingly reversing course. An ageing population is bound to catch up with the Japanese economy's overall savings position at some point. That, as per the life-cycle hypothesis, will mean future declines in its household savings rate. Also, the fact that wages in cash

---

[50] Investopedia says, 'An exchange-traded fund (ETF) is a type of pooled investment security that operates much like a mutual fund. Typically, ETFs will track a particular index, sector, commodity, or other asset, but unlike mutual funds, ETFs can be purchased or sold on a stock exchange the same way that a regular stock can.'

Chen, James. 'What Is an Exchange Traded Fund?' *Investopedia*, 2 February 2022, https://www.investopedia.com/terms/e/etf.asp.

[51] Kihara, Leika. 'Kuroda Defends Japan Central Bank's ETF Buying, Sees No Near-Term Exit.' *Reuters*, 7 December 2018, https://www.reuters.com/article/us-japan-economy-boj/kuroda-defends-japan-central-banks-etf-buying-sees-no-near-term-exit-idUSKBN1O602Q.

terms were actually 10 per cent less in 2011 as compared to 1987 hasn't helped either.[52] Moreover, Japanese corporations are once again looking to use retained earnings to build up their capabilities in areas such as energy storage and artificial intelligence. This would mean that demand for JGBs from their end – either directly or via their deposits in Japanese banks – may also decline in the years ahead. At the moment, of course, both households and corporations are likely to save what they can, given the uncertainty brought upon by the pandemic. However, to service future debt, Japan may find it difficult to depend mostly on domestic savings and might have to increasingly turn to foreign lenders instead.

'OH, JUST MONETIZE IT ALL'

For the foreseeable future though, the Japanese economy will remain in the grip of 'powerful monetary easing' and the government has little to worry about with respect to debt rollover. Even before the COVID-19 shock pushed Japan's economy into a depressed state by April 2020, on account of various restrictions and a decline in exports, the BoJ was already adding some 80 trillion yen worth of JGBs on to its balance sheet on an annual basis, and had planned to continue with this practice for an 'extended period of time', which, as revealed by Kuroda in 2019, meant at least till spring 2020.[53] With the pandemic, the BoJ is now into an open-ended JGB-buying programme that does not seem to have an end in sight.[54] Indeed, this has left room for the Japanese government to deliver a much bigger stimulus package than it did in the wake of the GFC. The BoJ is also going all in

[52] Harari, 'Japan's Economy: From the "Lost Decade" to Abenomics.'

[53] Kuroda, 'Overcoming Deflation: Japan's Experience and Challenges Ahead.'

[54] Amamiya, Masayoshi. 'Japan's Economy and Monetary Policy.' Speech at the Japan National Press Club, Bank of International Settlements, Tokyo, 29 July 2020, https://www.bis.org/review/r200803c.pdf.

with corporate financing, what with its massive purchase of various kinds of corporate debt.

So, QQE-YCC will continue well beyond the date set, given the headwinds in the global economy on account of first the US–China trade war and now the pandemic. Indeed, any hope Kuroda had of tapering off JGB purchases stand dashed, with the economy likely to be buffeted by global trade tensions and post-pandemic weakness. In any case, with Japan back in deflationary territory thanks to COVID-19, it is far from reaching the core inflation target rate of 2 per cent. Worse, the years of deflation and stagnant real wages have created an ethos where consumers neither expect nor want general inflation, faced as they are with rising food and energy prices, which are of course not considered while calculating core inflation. Firms on their part are wary of raising prices, lest they lose customers.

The BoJ, while recognizing these issues and admitting that neither households nor firms may be particularly 'moved' by its accommodative stance, believes that salvation may yet lie in QQE-YCC. However, this operation of QQE-YCC over an 'extended period of time', resulting in the existence of a bloated BoJ balance sheet, was leading to the charge that Kuroda is in essence 'monetizing' Japanese government debt – something that he has hotly denied in the past.

Now, what exactly constitutes debt monetization is a somewhat controversial subject. The mere purchase of government securities on secondary markets or even in the primary market cannot be construed as debt monetization, as that is part and parcel of how central banks implement policy even in normal times. Rather, allegations of debt monetization arise whenever the size of the central bank balance sheet seems to increase (by purchasing government securities) in tow with a major growth of public debt – as was the case after the GFC and now in the wake of the pandemic. This simultaneous increase is posited as evidence that the central bank is enabling the growth of public debt as it were. Central banks, however, counter this by saying that these balance sheet enlargements are undertaken in pursuit of their mandated objectives of price stability and support to growth, since they are merely 'temporary' measures that will be withdrawn once those objectives are met. The argument being that 'true' debt monetization results only where money creation by the central bank serves as a 'permanent source' of financing for government spending. And balance sheet measures implemented during exigent circumstances should not be viewed as permanent monetary financing of the government's expenditure. The overall argument is that as long as it is the central bank, and not the treasury, which drives the balance sheet expansion, with the former doing so in pursuit of its mandate, it can't be called monetization.

Indeed, ever since the GFC, major central banks have sought to retain market confidence in their money by pointing out that they buy government debt only from the secondary market and not directly from the administration itself. In fact, all of them, including the BoJ, are forbidden by law from doing so. Although, in the wake of the pandemic shock, the Bank of England (BoE) decided to keep the option of buying bonds directly from the government open. The attempts to normalize balance sheets by some major Western central banks (most notably the Fed) in the decade of the 2010s were also partly in aid of burnishing their credibility in terms of their faithfulness to price stability mandates.

Unfortunately, the BoJ's balance sheet has seen a secular increase for a period of over a decade since the GFC with no end in sight. The question naturally arises as to just how long a major balance sheet expansion can last before it is said to have taken on a permanent character. The BoJ on its part has repeatedly stressed that it isn't monetizing Japanese government debt, and that its price stability mandate remains the driver behind QQE-YCC. Moreover, Abe's move to increase the consumption tax from the current 8 per cent to 10 per cent in October 2019, in aid of fiscal consolidation, was supposed to provide further confidence that unlimited money printing was not on the cards.[55]

MODERN MONETARY THEORY?

Nevertheless, the consumption tax was considered painful even before the pandemic and created space among domestic Japanese advocates for a theory that suggests it (that is, the hike) was not needed at all. The theory in question is Modern Monetary Theory (MMT), a heterodox construct that first came into prominence in America in recent years, before being talked about in Japan. With the post-pandemic explosion in fiscal deficits, MMT is now being actively debated in academic circles not just in the US or Japan but around the world.

Though the MMT 'school' has a range of features proposed by a varied set of authors, most notably from the University of Missouri-Kansas City and the Levy Economics Institute of Bard College, at its core the approach posits that a sovereign government that issues its own currency can never go broke. Thus, it does not face a budget constraint the way a private individual, a corporation or a local government could or Greece could for that matter, since it can always issue more currency to repay whatever it owes at all times. In this view of things, the only check on otherwise unfettered government spending 'accommodated' by the central bank is inflation, a drop in the exchange rate or a rise in interest rates.

And since Japan has been under deflationary pressure for years on end, despite intermittent pump-priming, with debt turnover aided by the BoJ's ultra-accommodative monetary stance, its example is being held up by adherents of the theory as a validation of the same. To leading MMT subscribers, such as economist Stephanie Kelton, QQE-YCC seems a

---

[55] 'Japan Delivers Long-Delayed Consumption Tax Hike.' *BBC News*, 1 October 2019, https://www.bbc.com/news/business-49849484.

lot like the theory's prescription of making the central bank hold interest rates on government debt at zero through the creation of reserves in the commercial banking system.

MMT emerged in a post-GFC world where massive monetary stimulus by the central banks of advanced economies was seen to have disproportionately benefitted the wealthy by propping up asset prices, while doing little to boost aggregate demand, inflation or even inflation expectations for the future. Quite apart from the MMT spectrum, it was a widely held view, even prior to the pandemic, that monetary policy has run its course, and fiscal policy has to step up to boost aggregate demand, sustain full employment and prevent advanced economies from falling into deflation. As such, MMT gained major visibility in the US after Congresswoman Alexandria Ocasio-Cortez of New York began speaking about its usefulness as a means for boosting public spending on welfare and the creation of 'good' jobs. Ocasio-Cortez is a rising star in the US Democratic Party firmament, which has been lurching to the left, and may be on the lookout for intellectual support for sustaining entitlement spending and providing tax cuts for the US middle class. With its view that taxation is more a means of regulating aggregate demand in the economy than being needed to meet government expenditure, MMT seems well suited for that role. As does MMT's belief that the government should adopt a 'functional finance' view of things, in that its expenditure should be oriented towards achieving specific outcomes rather than worrying about budgetary impact. And the chief outcome it should aim for is of course full employment.

In Japan, however, where Abenomics is committed to long-term fiscal consolidation and the maintenance of primary balances, extraordinary measures have been taken to denounce MMT. For instance, back in May 2019, finance ministry officials distributed documents containing both data that militated against the MMT and the views of some

17 well-known economists who critiqued the theory.[56] The then Japanese finance minister, Tarō Asō, also publicly dismissed MMT on more than one occasion and indicated that he saw it as 'very dangerous'. Asō's view was echoed by the BoJ, with a prominent board member stating that 'it would cause [runaway] inflation for sure'. In fact, Kuroda himself told the Diet (the Japanese parliament) in April 2019, 'It's wrong to assume there will be no hyper-inflation even if you boost fiscal spending recklessly, as long as it's financed by the central bank.' He further added, 'Japan has deployed economic stimulus policies. But the government believes it's important to restore fiscal health and make fiscal policy sustainable.'[57]

As such, Kuroda believed that 'it's wrong to say Japan is resorting to MMT', a view shared by others. After all, unlike MMT's 'passive and persistent' purchase of government debt by the central bank at zero interest rates, the BoJ has been 'actively' maintaining QQE-YYC. Moreover, MMT sees interest rates as useless to control inflation, and believes that raising them may even boost spending by putting more purchasing power in the hands of savers. Conversely, negative interest rates are sometimes seen as contractionary in an MMT world since they hurt the income of savers. In the MMT world, control of inflation is achieved through regulation of market pricing power and the discretionary use of taxation to temper surging aggregate demand. Most importantly, both the BoJ and the Japanese treasury, wary of a sovereign downgrade by ratings agencies, have been looking towards fiscal coordination to put a check on unfettered

---

[56] Kasai, Tetsuya. 'Finance Ministry Raises Red Flag Over Modern Monetary Theory.' *Asahi Shinbun*, 7 May 2019, http://www.asahi.com/ajw/articles/AJ201905070039.html.

[57] Kihara, Leika. 'BOJ Chief Rejects Idea of Japan as "Modern Monetary Theory" Model.' *Reuters*, 9 May 2019, https://in.reuters.com/article/us-japan-economy-boj/boj-chief-rejects-idea-of-japan-as-modern-monetary-theory-model-idINKCN1SF05A.

debt growth. This is obviously at variance with the MMT prescription given the country's deflationary tendencies, which would warrant continued public expenditure.

Overall, as per the theory, fiscal dominance is absolute, with the central bank giving up its traditional role – given that all it would do is help maintain zero interest rates on government expenditure. Obviously, this is not a world the BoJ or any central bank would want to live in. Central banks in advanced economies pride themselves for having tamed inflation – that great nemesis of both investors and the poor alike – by managing inflationary expectations. In fact, they can claim to have been so successful in this sphere that before the pandemic's disruptive effect on supply-networks they were finding it difficult to raise expectations about inflation. Having said that, they will definitely not want to err so much in the direction of raising expectations that they become unhinged and the economy ends up in a hyperinflationary regime.

For the time being, the BoJ maintains that it still has room for further monetary easing by continuing to purchase assets other than JGBs, and sets store in manipulating interest rates to boost demand. Although in the wake of the COVID-19 shock more extreme measures may be proposed by some quarters if Japan finds itself locked in deflationary territory. One such measure is the so-called 'helicopter money' option, which is essentially an overt 'permanent' monetization of deficit spending achieved through the creation of non-interest-bearing liabilities by the central bank. While it has different variants, it involves either a tax cut or heightened spending that is directly financed by the central bank, something that the BoJ is forbidden by law from doing. Since the exercise has to give a 'permanent character' to the monetization, the implementing central bank can do so by buying a zero coupon perpetual bond from the government. Another way to do this would be by registering a negative entry on the liability side of its balance sheet while funding government expenditure. However, doing so has the potential of pushing the central bank's capital into negative territory – something that markets will frown upon. This is why the perpetual bond option will be preferred. Be that as it may, the emphasis is on 'permanent', since the idea is to perpetually rid the government of any liabilities arising from its expenditure. Moreover, permanent monetization is also meant to convey to the private sector that it need not fear future tax increments to offset the same. The 'inflation tax' on the private sector would also be limited, since in depressed conditions additional spending is likely to be taken up more by output growth than price rise.

Incidentally, helicopter money has been discussed by the BoJ, among others, in the past and has been rejected on the grounds that it still had a ways to go before it got to this 'last-ditch' attempt to boost inflation. But were matters to come to a head, helicopter money is the more likely option to be pursued than the wholesale adoption of MMT. Helicopter money, of course, has its own issues, as we shall see in chapter eight. For the moment, even with global fuel and raw material inflationary pressures which have created so much concern elsewhere, Japan's core inflation rate remains below 1 per cent as of end 2021, with the economy having contracted by 4.8 per cent in 2020 on account of the COVID-19 shock.[58, 59] With rising exports, and even the Tokyo Olympics providing some succour, Japan of course returned to economic growth in 2021.[60] However, Kuroda, who stated in September 2021 that Japan was still stuck in a 'deflationary mindset', subsequently vowed to stay the course

---

[58] "Japan's December Consumer Inflation Hovers at Near 2-Year High." *CNBC*, 21 January 2022, https://www.cnbc.com/2022/01/21/japans-december-consumer-inflation-hovers-at-near-2-year-high.html.

[59] 'Japan's Economy Shrinks 4.8% in 2020 Due to COVID.' *BBC News*, 15 February 2021, www.bbc.com/news/business-56066065.

[60] Hornyak, Tim. 'Tokyo Olympics: How Japan Is Seeing Economic Benefits.' *Time*, 11 August 2021, time.com/6089274/tokyo-olympics-economic-benefits.

on ultra-accommodative policies in early 2022.[61,62] Meanwhile, due to the pandemic, Japan's debt-to-GDP ratio rose to 259 per cent during 2021.[63]

The Land of the Rising Sun has come a long way in the last 150 years – from being the first Asian country to industrialize, to becoming an imperial power, to being devastated by war, to then rising as a techno-economic entity, and then finally ending with the lost decades. It is a cautionary tale, which, strangely enough, has lessons not only for those countries in decline – that is, the West – but also for those that still see themselves as rising. Japan's example certainly seems to have taught China the importance of creating a stake for itself in the world financial order while it still has structural advantages, such as accounting for a large share of global GDP and trade. This is especially important since the incumbent superpower of the day wouldn't be keen to allow a geopolitical competitor to rise in an uncalibrated manner, as the current US–China tensions demonstrate. However, is it already too late for China, given that its internal strength is not as great as it seems from the outside and its external position does not yet rival that of the US, despite over a decade of effort since the GFC? It is therefore time for us to examine the travails of this main challenger to Western power at this point in time, and the next chapter will be devoted to the story of China.

---

[61] Kawanami, Takeshi, et al. 'After 20 Years, Japan Still Stuck in Deflationary Mindset: Kuroda.' *Nikkei Asia*, 8 September 2021, https://asia.nikkei.com/Economy/After-20-years-Japan-still-stuck-in-deflationary-mindset-Kuroda2.

[62] Kihara, Leika. 'BOJ Kuroda Vows to Keep Ultra-Easy Policy in Wake of ECB's Hawkish Shift.' *Reuters*, 4 February 2022, https://www.reuters.com/markets/asia/bojs-kuroda-vows-keep-ultra-easy-policy-support-growth-2022-02-04.

[63] 'Japan: Staff Concluding Statement of the 2022 Article IV Mission.' *IMF*, 27 January 2022, https://www.imf.org/en/News/Articles/2022/01/27/mcs012722-japan-staff-concluding-statement-of-the-2022-article-iv-mission.

SIX

SHANGHAI, 24 AUGUST 2015: BY THE END OF TRADING DAY, the 'A' shares listed on the Shanghai Stock Exchange (SSE) Composite Index had lost almost 8.5 per cent of their valuation, registering the biggest-ever single-day loss in percentage terms since March 2007.[1] Several hundred billion dollars in investor wealth was destroyed in this plunge, and not just in China alone. The rout in Shanghai reverberated across the world as the stocks of companies with significant exposure to the country were hammered down in trade. London's Financial Times Stock Exchange (FTSE) 100 Index saw the shares of major British companies losing £75 billion in valuation, while in New York, Dow Jones collapsed by 1,000 points right after opening, though it somewhat recovered later on.[2]

On the night of this stock blowout, since then dubbed as 'Black Monday' by the international media, officials of the China Securities Regulatory Commission (CSRC) seemed uncharacteristically sanguine about the development – in marked contrast to their response to the country's stock

---

[1] 'China Stocks Suffer Biggest One-Day Loss In Eight Years.' *Al Jazeera*, 24 August 2015, http://www.aljazeera.com/news/2015/08/china-stock-markets-150824092716245.html.

[2] Egan, Matt. 'After Historic 1,000-Point Plunge, Dow Dives 588 Points at Close.' *CNN Money*, 25 August 2015, http://money.cnn.com/2015/08/24/investing/stocks-markets-selloff-china-crash-dow/. See also: Thompson, Mark, and Thomas Riley. 'World Markets Plunge as China Stocks Crash.' *CNN Money*, 24 August 2015, https://money.cnn.com/2015/08/23/investing/world-stock-markets/index.html?iid=EL.

market downturns even in the very recent past.[3] During the last major fall, just a few weeks before this, on 27 July 2015, the CSRC had scrambled to calm investors by calling a late-night press conference, where it announced its intention to keep encouraging state-backed entities to 'buy into' the market.[4]

Indeed, Black Monday was no one-off. Chinese bourses (that is, stock markets) had been crashing with alarming regularity since June 2015. From the all-time high reached in that month, the SSE had already lost over 30 per cent of its peak value by the time Black Monday happened.[5] In the intervening period, the country's officialdom had responded with a range of 'extraordinary measures' to stem the decline in the bourses.[6] These 'extraordinary measures' included, among other things, an unprecedented $480 billion stock purchase programme via a CSRC arm called China Securities Finance, effectively ordering major brokerages to buy shares worth tens of billions of dollars and making them

---

[3] This is not the first time a stock market crash has been dubbed 'Black Monday', of course. In the world of finance, Black Monday is usually a reference to the worldwide stock market crash of 17 October 1987 led by a meltdown in Dow Jones, which fell by over 22 per cent in a single session. The term is also retrospectively used to describe the stock market crash of 19 October 1929, which heralded the Great Depression. The Shanghai-led crash was the first Black Monday of the twenty-first century, as it were.

[4] Su, Mo, and Yuan'an Zhang. 'CSRC Said to Greet Latest Stock Market Crash with Calm.' *Caixin Online*, 25 August 2015, http://english.caixin.com/2015-08-25/100843467.html.

[5] Warner, Jeremy. 'The Really Worrying Financial Crisis Is Happening in China Not Greece.' *Telegraph*, 9 July 2015, https://www.telegraph.co.uk/finance/china-business/11725236/The-really-worrying-financial-crisis-is-happening-in-China-not-Greece.html.

[6] Timmons, Heather, and Lily Kuo. 'A Complete List of the Chinese Government's Stock-Market Stimulus (That We Know about).' *Quartz*, 28 July 2015, http://qz.com/445454/a-complete-list-of-the-chinese-governments-stock-market-stimulus.

pledge to not resell them until the market rebounded to a relatively high level. It also included putting a four-month moratorium on initial public offerings (IPOs) and urging state-owned enterprises (SOEs) to not dilute their stake in publicly listed arms. At one point, the CSRC even suspended trading for half the companies on China's mainland exchanges. There was a major clampdown on short selling, with anybody selling large amounts of stock on the spot or in futures markets running the risk of being identified as a 'malicious short seller' by a police investigation. As it is, major shareholders, executives and directors of companies had been banned from selling stakes for a period of six months. At the same time, rules for insurers to buy blue chips and the repayment terms for money that had been borrowed by investors to buy shares were both relaxed. This easing of rules indicated a desire on the part of Chinese authorities to boost the stock markets by whatever means possible.

However, these numerous interventions were seen by some foreign observers as an example of how China was going back on its pledge during the Third Plenum of the 18th Chinese Communist Party Congress in November 2013 to give the market a 'decisive role' in the economy, with the government making a mockery of laissez-faire, even in stock markets.[7] Several foreign investors exited the country's financial markets following the government's interventions and, at one point in time, the IMF is reported to have actually urged the Chinese authorities to wind down

---

[7] Ong, Ryan. 'The Third Plenum of the 18th Chinese Communist Party Congress: A Primer.' *China Business Review*, 16 September 2013, https://www.chinabusinessreview.com/the-third-plenum-of-the-18th-chinese-communist-party-congress-a-primer. See also: 'Communiqué of the Third Plenary Session of the 18th Central Committee of the Communist Party of China. (Adopted at the Third Plenary Session of the 18th Central Committee of the Communist Party of China on November 12, 2013).' *China.org.cn*, 15 January 2014, http://www.china.org.cn/china/third_plenary_session/2014-01/15/content_31203056.htm.

these measures eventually, in the interest of allowing prices to be determined by market forces.[8] Though it seemed the IMF wasn't linking the country's short-term 'extraordinary measures' to the yuan's eligibility for Special Drawing Rights (SDR) status, a decision on which was due later in the year, the Chinese probably did not want to get tagged with a 'de-liberalizing' image.[9] So perhaps it was to stem the view that Beijing wasn't really committed to financial openness and the development of its capital markets that the CSRC sought to project a stand-offish attitude for once, that is, right after Black Monday.[10] Besides, the very occurrence of Black Monday meant that the 'extraordinary measures' of the recent past hadn't really worked. Neither had an announcement on the Sunday before Black Monday that domestic pension funds would be allowed to invest 30 per cent of their total net assets in stocks.[11]

But the bears in Shanghai were not done yet. The day after Black Monday, the SSE fell by another 7 per cent – 'Black Tuesday' as it were – with the impact once again felt across the world.[12] This nearly 16 per cent fall in the SSE over a period of two days led to renewed pressure on the Chinese government to once again 'do something' to shore

---

[8] Mayeda, Andrew. 'IMF Said to Urge China to Exit Measures to Prop up Stocks.' *Bloomberg*, 24 July 2015, http://www.bloomberg.com/news/articles/2015-07-24/imf-said-to-urge-china-to-exit-measures-to-prop-up-stock-market.

[9] See chapter three.

[10] Warner, 'The Really Worrying Financial Crisis Is Happening in China Not Greece.' *Telegraph*.

[11] Inman, Phillip. 'China to Allow Pension Fund to Invest in Stock Market for First Time.' *Guardian*, 23 August 2015, https://www.theguardian.com/world/2015/aug/23/china-to-allow-pension-fund-to-invest-in-stock-market-for-first-time.

[12] Khan, Mehreen. 'Markets Live: FTSE Bounces Back as China Injects Fresh Stimulus after Stocks Crash in Country's "Black Tuesday".' *Telegraph*, 25 August 2015, http://www.telegraph.co.uk/finance/markets/11819812/Black-Monday-live-FTSE-100-China-global-markets-rate-cut.html.

up markets. The all-time high reached by the Shanghai index before the meltdown started in June 2015 had been the apogee of a boom that emerged in mid-2014. The seeds for this boom had been laid by the Chinese government itself, through its removal of restrictions on the ability of investors to purchase stocks using borrowed money. This led to an explosion of margin trade in the bourses,[13] with margin debt touching a record 2.3 trillion yuan ($359 billion) at the peak of the boom (a rise of several multiples since mid-2014).[14] It would become the chief cause of the crash as traders exited bets they had made with borrowed money.

The Chinese administration's embarrassment was compounded by the fact that state-run media had also played a major role in talking up the stock markets and endorsing equity investment, something that had led to several middle-class citizens flocking to the bourses as retail investors. By mid-2015, the country's stock markets had more than 90 million small investors – a number that exceeded the total membership of the Communist Party of China (CPC).[15] In fact, the need to retain the confidence of this constituency was a key driver behind the government's interventions in the first place. By buying up stocks, the government was essentially trying to help domestic retail investors and some foreign players recover a part of their losses, before they exited Chinese stocks too.

Renewed efforts to shore up market confidence after Black Tuesday started with a People's Bank of China (PBOC) announcement on interest rate cuts, and a reduction of the

---

[13] That is, speculation in stocks and shares using borrowed money.

[14] Verhage, July. 'Macquarie: Chinese Margin Debt Has Much, Much More Room to Run.' *Bloomberg Markets*, 24 June 2015, http://www.bloomberg.com/news/articles/2015-06-24/macquarie-chinese-margin-debt-has-much-much-more-room-to-run.

[15] Allen, Katie. 'Why Is China's Stock Market in Crisis?' *Guardian*, 8 July 2015, https://www.theguardian.com/business/2015/jul/08/china-stock-market-crisis-explained.

reserve requirement ratios (RRRs) for commercial banks. But these actions to increase liquidity were seen as part of a wider move to support the economy, rather than being specifically directed at the bourses. As such, the rate cuts didn't do much on their own, and a rebound of 5.3 per cent in the SSE a couple of days after Black Tuesday was attributed to secret purchases of equities by the Chinese government, thereby marking a return to direct intervention.[16] The secret purchases were apparently also made to boost public sentiment in the run-up to the Seventieth Anniversary of Victories in the Chinese People's War of Resistance against Japanese Aggression and the World against Fascism on 3 September 2015, which would be marked by a massive parade.[17] Beijing did not want weak bourses to be a dampener for this gala during which it would go on to unveil a range of new weapons systems designed to counter US influence in the Asia–Pacific.[18]

China's 'extraordinary measures' before Black Monday, its stand-offish attitude during the event itself and the next day, and then the return to direct stock buying, albeit secret, all taken together, was seen as an example of policy flip-flop by those who were fashioning their bets on the country's stock markets, based not on macro-fundamentals but on the government's commitment to propping them up. Indeed,

---

[16] 'China Intervened Today to Shore up Stocks Ahead of Military Parade.' *Bloomberg News*, 27 August 2015, http://www.bloomberg.com/news/articles/2015-08-27/china-said-to-intervene-to-shore-up-stock-market-before-parade-idtyzfdu.

[17] 'Grand Reception Commemorating 70th Anniversary of Victory of Chinese People's War of Resistance against Japanese Aggression and World Anti-Fascist War Held in Beijing.' *Ministry of Foreign Affairs*, 3 September 2015, https://www.fmprc.gov.cn/mfa_eng/topics_665678/jnkzsl70zn/t1294320.shtml.

[18] Erickson, Andrew S. 'Showtime: China Reveals Two "Carrier-Killer" Missiles.' *National Interest*, 3 September 2015, http://nationalinterest.org/feature/showtime-china-reveals-two-carrier-killer-missiles-13769.

commentators had long been saying that the stock market boom, which saw the SSE's capitalization rise 150 per cent between June 2014 and June 2015, was not backed by the 'fundamentals' of a Chinese economy, that had clearly slowed down from its miracle years.[19] Crashing bourses reinforced this assessment of emerging economic weakness, and, in the wake of Black Monday, many analysts sought to draw a link between the crash and negative macroeconomic trends.

For instance, one of the main reasons advanced for the fall on Black Monday was the surprise devaluation of the yuan two weeks prior, on 11 August 2015, when the yuan was allowed by the PBOC to experience its greatest-ever proportional fall against the dollar since 1994.The devaluation came on the back of months of declining exports and was accompanied by news of much slower manufacturing activity, as indicated by the early Caixin China Purchasing Managers' Index, which registered its lowest level in six and a half years in August 2015.[20] For the government, a stock market meltdown, which it could not prevent, being linked to fundamental economic weakness, reflected poorly on its ability to manage the 'new normal' that China's economy was having to navigate after the GFC brought severe weakness in its wake to the country's key external markets.

Though intervening in stock markets ran contrary to its avowed commitment to financial openness, which it needed to internationalize the RMB, this consideration was clearly overshadowed by the need to maintain the perception that the CPC had things under control. Indeed, the Chinese government probably felt that 'weakness in

---

[19] Lee, Timothy B. 'China's Stock Market Crash, Explained in Charts.' *Vox*, 26 August 2015, https://www.vox.com/2015/7/8/8911519/china-stock-market-charts.

[20] 'China August Manufacturing Activity Hits Lowest Level since 2009.' *Wall Street Journal*, 20 August 2015, http://www.wsj.com/articles/chinas-caixin-manufacturing-pmi-falls-to-77-month-low-1440123262.

economic management' was more detrimental to the yuan's internationalization prospects than a perception of moving away from marketization in the short term.

In the months following Black Monday, authorities also began arresting stock market 'manipulators' – a term that included even journalists, who had suggested the government may draw down its interventionist stance to support stock markets![21] The arrests were presented as an example of how the administration was taking resolute action against those 'culpable' for the downturn. Clearly, the agenda was to find scapegoats who could be blamed to deflect the public's attention and anger from the management of the complex economic transition under way in China.

EATING DINNER DURING LUNCH

It was in December 2004, during the annual Central Economic Work Conference, that China, for the first time, officially endorsed the need to transition away from a growth path that was investment-driven and export-led to one that relied on boosting domestic consumption.[22] By the 2007 National People's Congress, the then Chinese premier, Wen Jiabao, was of the opinion that 'the biggest problem with China's economy is that the growth is unstable, unbalanced, uncoordinated, and unsustainable', thereby conveying a tone of urgency to rebalance the Chinese economy towards consumption, from an over-reliance on investment and exports.[23]

---

[21] Yan, Sophia. 'Hundreds Arrested as Beijing Launches Stock Market Crackdown.' *CNN Money*, 31 August 2015, http://money.cnn.com/2015/08/31/investing/china-arrests-markets-crash/.

[22] 'China's Central Economic Work Conference from 2004–2008 (Sourced from *Xinhua*).' *People's Daily*, 8 December 2009, http://en.people.cn/90001/90778/90862/6834832.html.

[23] 'IMF Survey: China's Difficult Rebalancing Act.' *IMF*, 12 September 2007, http://www.imf.org/external/pubs/ft/survey/so/2007/car0912a.htm.

Jiabao's concern wasn't unfounded, because not soon after, the 2008 GFC would occur, putting paid to any notion that China could continue to forever rely on an investment-driven, export-led path to deliver rapid growth. In the wake of the crisis, chronic demand weakness in the Western economies – the main outlets for China's exports – made it clear to the administration that it would have to set into motion steps to rebalance the economy towards consumption at home, in order to sustain growth over the longer term. This was just as the Japanese had had to do after the end of the miracle phase of their growth story. And while the Japanese had rebalanced their economy towards consumption over a period of two decades, spanning the 1970s and 1980s, it was unclear at the time whether China could afford to do so at the same pace.

And in the immediate aftermath of Lehman Brothers' collapse in September 2008, an event that marked the full-blown onset of the GFC, China had to adopt a set of 'countercyclical' measures in the face of sharply declining exports. These measures would actually boost the share of investment in its GDP for the next few years, even as the share of exports in the GDP would go down. Besides re-pegging the yuan to the dollar to arrest its steady nominal appreciation against the latter since 2005, China also announced a gargantuan RMB 4 trillion ($586 billion) fiscal stimulus package in November 2008 – one that was equal to 12.5 per cent of China's nominal GDP in 2008.[24] This fiscal package, scheduled for execution till the end of 2010, focused primarily on infrastructure development, reconstruction and affordable housing post the 2008 Sichuan earthquake. The idea was to boost domestic demand through greater fixed asset investment over and above what was already planned, given

---

[24] Naughton, Barry. 'Understanding the Chinese Stimulus Package.' *China Leadership Monitor*, Spring 2009, Issue 28, 8 May 2009, http://www.hoover.org/sites/default/files/uploads/documents/CLM28BN.pdf.

the huge hit exports had taken, in order to prevent economic collapse and massive unemployment. Moreover, the nature of this investment was supposed to be of the 'crowding in' variety, which would encourage simultaneous non-public investment by providing the enabling infrastructure. At that point, little did people realize, or even care, that the means being chosen to save the economy would become a slowly tightening noose in the years ahead.

Only around 30 per cent of the RMB 4 trillion stimulus package was direct central government expenditure, with the majority of that amount being sent as 'block grants' towards centrally approved projects proposed by local administrations.[25] Indeed, most of the November 2008 stimulus package was meant to be executed by provincial, county and municipal governments in China, with Beijing essentially providing seed capital out of its 30 per cent direct outlay. Accordingly, the majority of the funding for the overall stimulus package had to be garnered by local governments from sources other than the central budget.

In aid of this endeavour, local governments floated thousands of SOEs, known as local government financial vehicles (LGFVs), in order to circumvent legal provisions that otherwise restrict the issuance of public debt by them. Simultaneously, Beijing relaxed the paid-in capital requirements for such LGFVs, besides allowing them to raise corporate debt via bond issue.[26] Beijing also instituted a special programme for the extension of extra-long-term, concessionary interest rate bank loans to LGFVs by state-owned policy banks, led by the China Development Bank (CDB).[27] These concessionary long-term loans were allowed to serve as their equity paid-in capital for investment

---

[25] Ibid.

[26] 'Paid-in' capital simply refers to the amount of equity investment received by an economic entity.

[27] Naughton, 'Understanding the Chinese Stimulus Package.'

projects, thereby paving the way for China's mostly state-owned commercial banking system to extend shorter-term credit to such LGFVs in an environment where they were being encouraged by Beijing to do so anyway. Some of the debt raised by these financial vehicles, via corporate bond issue, was also allowed to add to their paid-in capital, thereby strengthening their balance sheets further.[28] As a result, over 60 per cent of the funding for the November 2008 stimulus package would come from bank credit received by these LGFVs. The extra-long-term loans were extended by holding land as collateral, for which the rights to sell or develop had been conferred upon the local governments that had floated them. It is important to note that the only means for LGFVs, which were 'off balance sheet' entities, to repay their loans or get the funds for new investments, besides new borrowing, were either by means of land sales or the proceeds from the projects that they developed on the lands allotted to them.

The funding mechanism of the stimulus essentially institutionalized a channel for moving both bank and non-bank credit to sectors such as infrastructure and real estate, via LGFVs. By 2010, these financial vehicles on their own accounted for 15 per cent of bank borrowing and their debt equalled three-quarters of explicit public debt in China, which by that year stood at 43.5 per cent of GDP.[29] But the explosive rise of bank credit that accompanied stimulus spending during 2009 and 2010 was not only directed towards such LGFVs. In a highly politicized environment of economic pump-priming, China's mostly state-owned commercial banking sector also lent to large SOEs, which used these funds to play in the real estate sector (since further expansion of their bread-and-butter businesses, such as

---

[28] Ibid.

[29] Perkowski, Jack. 'China's Debt: How Serious Is It?' *Forbes*, 21 January 2014, https://www.forbes.com/sites/jackperkowski/2014/01/21/chinas-debt-how-serious-is-it/#6291c782547e.

telecommunications and mining, weren't exactly attractive right after the 2008 downturn). This kind of activity naturally boosted the already hot real estate sector, which had been growing at an annual rate of just under 30 per cent since 2003.

As such, bank credit growth during 2009 was three times that of the year before, and almost 40 per cent of the new lending went to businesses.[30] The PBOC played its part by adopting an accommodative monetary stance, which saw it reduce both the benchmark one-year lending and borrowing rates to encourage credit growth, while protecting bank profitability by keeping the spread (that is difference) between the two the same as before.

With annual exports once again rising to their old levels, albeit with monthly volatility, and the stimulus having delivered 9.4 per cent real GDP growth in 2009, by the end of 2010, China seemed to signal that it was ready to make a concrete move to rebalance its economy towards consumption.[31] The yuan was de-pegged from the dollar, and the Twelfth Five-Year Plan (TWFYP), spanning the period 2011–15, called for reducing income inequality, increasing domestic consumption, improving social infrastructure and expanding social security – all of which indicated a desire to turn to a less capital-intensive path for development.[32]

---

[30] Zhuo, Chen et al. 'The Financing of Local Government in the People's Republic of China: Stimulus Loan Wanes and Shadow Banking Waxes.' *Asian Development Bank*, No. 800, January 2018, https://www.adb.org/sites/default/files/publication/396826/adbi-wp800.pdf.

[31] 'GDP Growth (Annual %) – China.' Based on national accounts data and OECD national accounts data files from 2006 to 2019, *World Bank*, 2019 https://data.worldbank.org/indicator/NY.GDP.MKTP.KD.ZG?end=2019&locations=CN&start=2006.

[32] Sano, Janya. 'Key Targets in the 12th Five-Year Plan and Policies for their Realization – Reasons for the 7% Growth Target.' *Pacific Business and Industries*, Volume XI, Number 42, 2011, The Japan Research Institute Limited, https://www.jri.co.jp/MediaLibrary/file/english/periodical/rim/2011/42.pdf.See also: Casey, Joseph and Katherine Koleski. 'Backgrounder: China's 12th Five-Year Plan.' *U.S.–China Economic and*

After all, Chinese households had not benefitted sufficiently from the country's investment-driven path, which had led to a declining share for labour in national income, given that household income had risen less rapidly than overall GDP.[33] Moreover, this reliance on investment to drive growth had led to China's industries becoming increasingly capital-intensive, leading to a reduction in the employment intensity of its GDP growth.[34]

Despite the seeming endorsement of a transition to a services-based consumption economy, TWFYP also called for achieving an average annual GDP growth rate of 7 per cent during the plan period, as well as very ambitious infrastructure and affordable housing targets.[35] Obviously, domestic consumption expenditure was in no position to deliver that level of growth on its own, and the credit-inflated infrastructure boom that had been set in motion by the stimulus was allowed to continue by planners through means other than a direct expansion of bank credit. Even though bank credit growth slowed to more 'normal' levels after 2010 (though it was still over 15 per cent year-on-year), due to new loan restrictions and directed lending norms by Beijing, non-bank credit, or so-called 'shadow banking', rose twice as rapidly.[36]

The LGFVs, which were drawing a lowered quantum of loans from commercial banks due to the new restrictions,

---

Security Review Commission, 24 June 2011, https://www.uscc.gov/sites/default/files/Research/12th-FiveYearPlan_062811.pdf.

[33] Ibid.

[34] Fukumoto, Tomoyuki and Ichiro Muto. 'Rebalancing China's Economic Growth: Some Insights from Japan's Experience.' *Bank of Japan*, July 2011, https://www.boj.or.jp/en/research/wps_rev/wps_2011/data/wp11e05.pdf.

[35] 'Key Targets of China's 12th Five-Year Plan (Sourced from Xinhua).' *China.org.cn*, 5 March 2011, http://www.china.org.cn/china/NPC_CPPCC_2011/2011-03/05/content_22059883.htm.

[36] Non-bank financial intermediaries, whose governance lies outside normal banking regulations.

greatly increased their borrowings, via the issue of corporate bonds and equity-like instruments, to support their binge on infrastructure and housing projects.[37] A large part of this increased 'securitized' borrowing by LGFVs came through finance from shadow-banking entities, such as trust loans and wealth management products (WMPs). Trust loans, of course, also made direct loans to LGFVs. These trends were reflected in data from China's National Audit Office, which showed that by 30 June 2013, bank loans accounted for 57 per cent of direct and contingent liabilities of LFGVs, down from 79 per cent at the end of 2010, even as the share of bonds in financing rose from 7 to 10 per cent, and that of trust financing from 0 to 8 per cent.[38] Other shadow-banking channels accounted for the remaining 25 per cent share in borrowing.[39] In comparison to a 67 per cent rise in total debt, bank loans to LGFVs registered a growth of only 19 per cent between end 2010 and 30 June 2013.[40]

Meanwhile, small and medium enterprise (SME) real estate developers, who would have had difficulty accessing commercial bank credit due to risk exposure, also became recipients of credit from shadow-banking activities. Beijing's direct lending norms and loan restrictions made the developers a natural destination for shadow banks in search of high-yielding investments. Indeed, the rapid growth of shadow banking in China was fuelled by the fact that domestic investors were on an 'internal search for yield', given that in an environment of financial repression bank deposits could give almost none to negative real returns.

---

[37] Zhuo, et al., 'The Financing of Local Government in the People's Republic of China: Stimulus Loan Wanes and Shadow Banking Waxes.'

[38] 'Shadow Banking Risks Exposed by Local Debt Audit: China Credit.' *Bloomberg*, 6 January 2014, https://www.bloomberg.com/news/articles/2014-01-06/shadow-banking-risks-exposed-by-local-debt-audit-china-credit.

[39] Ibid.

[40] Ibid.

Many of these shadow-banking products had the direct or indirect involvement of commercial banks. While many WMPs were sold by banks themselves, several trust loans were marketed by them; thus, giving the false illusion to investors that they had implicit bank guarantees. Hence, like Japan in the 1980s, commercial banks in China greatly increased their exposure to the real estate sector and to small- and medium-sized firms that were riskier prospects for investment, albeit by using non-transparent 'off the book' methods, instead of direct bank-based intermediation. The vast flow of credit to the real estate sector naturally served to push prices up, and an index of prices in 40 Chinese cities showed a gain of 60 per cent between 2008 and August 2014.[41] Prime residential properties in Shanghai and Beijing actually closed in on the prices of those in New York and Paris by that time. Between 1998 and 2013, the share of real estate investment expenditure as a share of GDP rose from 4 per cent to 12.5 per cent.[42]

This credit-inflated boom in infrastructure and real estate pushed China's total debt to 28.2 trillion yuan by mid-2014, or to 282 per cent of China's GDP from about 158 per cent in 2008, according to McKinsey.[43] LGFV debt alone accounted for close to 40 per cent of GDP by 2014.[44] Moreover, even though much of this rise in debt seemed backed by 'assets',

---

[41] Dobbs, Richard, et al. 'Debt and (Not Much) Deleveraging.' *McKinsey Global Institute*, February 2015, https://www.mckinsey.com/~/media/McKinsey/Featured%20Insights/Employment%20and%20Growth/Debt%20and%20not%20much%20deleveraging/MGI%20Debt%20and%20not%20much%20deleveragingFullreportFebruary2015.pdf.

[42] Dollar, David. 'China's Rebalancing: Lessons from East Asian Economic History.' John L. Thornton China Center, October 2013, http://www.brookings.edu/~/media/research/files/papers/2013/10/02-china-economic-rebalancing-dollar/china-economic-rebalancing-dollar.pdf.

[43] Dobbs, et al., 'Debt and (Not Much) Deleveraging'.

[44] Investment Strategy Group. 'Walled in: China's Great Dilemma.' *Goldman Sachs*, January 2016, http://www.goldmansachs.com/what-we-do/investment-management/private-wealth-management/intellectual-capital/isg-china-insight-2016.pdf.

many of the assets themselves were of questionable value. The rapidity with which China had executed the November 2008 stimulus had been largely a result of the fact that local governments in the country had long been compiling a list of 'shovel-ready' pet projects on their land banks. They saw Beijing's stimulus programme as a godsend for them to surmount the disadvantage they faced in the centre–province tax distribution structure – something that had long hamstrung them from implementing public projects in their domain. While Beijing got to keep more than 50 per cent of tax revenue collected by local governments, the latter were responsible for 80 per cent of their expenditure. With the floodgates of borrowing opening to them, LGFVs pushed through as many projects as they could. And thus, counties with small-sized populations built airports, municipalities built ghost towns, and provinces built bridges and highways to nowhere.

In fact, as had become apparent by 2013, many WMPs floated by Chinese banks were actually their own LGFV loans and those made by trust loans to LGFVs that had turned 'bad'. Banks were thus acting as middlemen to refinance a slew of 'bad' LGFV loans. One audit of local governments in 2014 showed that up to 20 per cent of new borrowing by these financial vehicles was for debt servicing or loan repayment.[45] Thus, banks in China had, in effect, already started zombie lending, albeit in an 'off the books' fashion. 'Extend and pretend' was becoming a way of life in the country.

China's overall debt had also become subject to the vagaries of the real estate sector. By the second half of 2014, almost half of China's cumulative debt had direct or indirect exposure to the real estate sector. A third of this was on account of loans outstanding to SME developers, who accounted for an overwhelming majority of the real estate sector's revenue. What is more, much like Japanese SMEs

---

[45] Dobbs, et al., 'Debt and (Not Much) Deleveraging.'

in the 1980s, Chinese real estate SMEs had also borrowed mostly on the basis of real estate collateral. Their ability to repay their debt was therefore highly contingent on the continuation of the real estate boom in the country. As was that of various SOEs in steel and cement, which had also borrowed heavily during the boom, sending corporate debt levels soaring by 2014.

However, the rise of NPLs as a result of China's credit-inflated building boom is hardly surprising, since the return on capital in the country – as a result of an ever-increasing capital–output ratio and near-stagnant total-factor productivity (TFP) – had been steadily declining since 2008. Between 2009 and 2013, the addition to GDP from every additional unit of capital investment declined from 0.25 to 0.16 even as growth in TFP became ever so slow.[46] The declining return on capital was one of the chief reasons for rebalancing the Chinese economy from over-reliance on investment anyway. However, the 2008 GFC had created a situation wherein the opposite had happened. And the country would miss its official growth target for 2014, even as its debt load continued to grow much faster than its GDP. The old Chinese saying 'Eating dinner during lunch leaves one hungry' did not seem so out of place at all.

A NEW NORMAL FOR CHINA

With China officially missing its 7.5 per cent growth target for 2014,[47] Chinese Premier Li Keqiang, speaking at the Annual National People's Congress in March 2015,

---

[46] Brandt, Loren. 'China's Productivity Slowdown and Future Growth Potential.' *Trade and Investment Global Practice*, World Bank Group, June 2020, http://documents1.worldbank.org/curated/en/839401593007627879/pdf/Chinas-Productivity-Slowdown-and-Future-Growth-Potential.pdf.

[47] Yao, Kevin, and Pete Sweeney. 'China's 2014 Economic Growth Misses Target, Hits 24-Year Low.' *Reuters*, 20 January 2015, http://www.reuters.com/article/us-china-economy-idUSKBN0KT04920150120.

acknowledged that the downward pressure on China's economy was intensifying, with 'deep-seated problems in the country's economic development becoming more obvious' and that the difficulties China was facing that year could be bigger than those of the year before.[48]

This was as clear an admission as any that the credit-fuelled investment binge was showing diminishing returns as far as growth was concerned. Keqiang further declared a 'new normal' for the Chinese economy, signalling the onset of an era of much slower growth than what was registered before 2008. But he also used the occasion to reiterate the Chinese Communist Party's commitment to 'developmentalism', as evidenced by the following, 'In order to defuse problems and risks, avoid falling into the "middle income trap", and achieve modernization, China must rely on development, and development requires an appropriate growth rate.'[49]

Unfortunately, post-2008, some form of stimulus seems to have been Beijing's only answer to achieve that 'appropriate' growth rate. Even after the November 2008 fiscal package, China repeatedly used fiscal and monetary stimulus whenever it felt that its target growth rates may not be met. And so, even as the 'new normal' was proclaimed, Beijing announced that it would boost central government expenditure to $2.74 trillion in 2015, a rise of over 10 per cent from the previous year.[50] This announcement was accompanied by the PBOC's third interest rate cut in 2015, as well as an easing of reserve requirements. By the end of 2015, the central bank would go on to reduce interest rates three more times.

This round of pump-priming in 2015 was a reflection of the fact that China's economy had hardly rebalanced during the TWFYP. According to Goldman Sachs, the country's

---

[48] Qing, Koh Gui, and Kevin Yao. 'China signals "New Normal" with Higher Spending, Lower Growth Target.' *Reuters*, 5 March 2015, http://www.reuters.com/article/us-china-parliament-idUSKBN0M103W20150305.

[49] Ibid.

[50] Ibid.

private consumption expenditure in 2015 stood at 38.2 per cent of GDP, which, as a share of GDP, was actually lower than the 38.3 per cent it had been just prior to 2007 – when the then Premier, Wen Jiabao, expressed concerns about the unbalanced nature of growth.[51] Which is why even eight years after his statement, China's President Xi Jinping had this to say in a September 2015 *Wall Street Journal* interview:

> What China needs is a higher quality and efficiency of economic development by successfully addressing the problem of unbalanced, uncoordinated and unsustainable development, so that our economy will be put on a more solid basis and go forward more steadily.[52]

Clearly, domestic consumption had a lot of distance to cover before it could deliver fast-paced growth for the Chinese economy. Of course, the country could always devalue the yuan to see if it could tap a greater proportion of consumption in other countries than it was already doing. After all, the yuan had gained 45 per cent in real (inflation-adjusted) terms since 2005 against the dollar, and given falling exports in 2015 and slower growth, it would have been an unsurprising thing for China to do.[53] And that is how its August 2015 devaluation was noted by many foreign observers, when the normally stable yuan was allowed to lose nearly 5 per cent of its value vis-à-vis the dollar in international trade over a period of just two days.[54]

---

[51] Investment Strategy Group. 'Walled in: China's Great Dilemma.'

[52] 'China Strongly Committed to Deepening Reform on All Fronts: President Xi.' *Global Times*, 22 September 2015, http://www.globaltimes.cn/content/943839.shtml.

[53] Prasad, Eswar. 'China's Efforts to Expand the International Use of the Renminbi.' *Brookings Institution*, 4 February 2016, https://www.brookings.edu/wp-content/uploads/2016/07/RMBReportFinal.pdf.

[54] Sweeney, Pete, and Lu Jianxin. 'China Lets Yuan Fall Further, Fuels Fears of "Currency War".' *Reuters*, 12 August 2015, https://www.reuters.com/article/us-china-markets-yuan-idUSKCN0QG04U20150812.

At the time, China, however, sought to allay fears that the fall in the yuan's value was the beginning of a prolonged period of currency weakening. The official line was that a devaluation would not aid the process of rebalance as it would mean diminished purchasing power for domestic consumers. It could also spark competitive devaluations by other nations, leading to a potential currency war, something that Keqiang had publicly stated that the country wished to avoid. Instead, the devaluation was portrayed as an example of how China was looking to let market forces have a greater say in determining the yuan's value, rather than follow a policy of shadowing the dollar – which had been strengthening against other major currencies. In principle, it was true that a yuan that did not track the dollar closely would have greater chances of being seen as an alternative investment currency by investors, and this could also support its case for SDR inclusion – the decision on which was due later that year. The IMF, which in May 2015 had already declared that it did not consider the yuan to be undervalued any more, essentially welcomed the new methodology Beijing had used to effect the devaluation. In a statement a day after China changed its opening trade fixing mechanism, the IMF said:

> The new mechanism for determining the central parity of the Renminbi announced by the PBC appears as a welcome step as it should allow market forces to have a greater role in determining the exchange rate. [...] Regarding the ongoing review of the IMF's SDR basket, the announced change has no direct implication for the criteria used in determining the composition of the basket. Nevertheless, a more market-determined exchange rate would facilitate SDR operations in case the Renminbi were included in the currency basket going forward.[55]

---

[55] 'IMF Welcomes China's New Yuan Mechanism, No Impact on SDR Push.' *Bloomberg News*, 12 August 2015, https://www.bloomberg.com/news/articles/2015-08-12/imf-welcomes-china-s-new-yuan-mechanism-no-impact-on-sdr-push.

Though a freer floating yuan would, in theory, make it more attractive for investors, a major devaluation would actually have run quite contrary to the cause of internationalizing the RMB.A devaluation could easily have triggered expectations of further weakness in the future, given China's extant economic environment, and that would have led to investors exiting yuan-denominated assets, thereby weakening the currency, thus serving as a self-fulfilling prophecy. Unsurprisingly, that is precisely what happened, and the PBOC would have to burn through a considerable amount of its foreign exchange reserves after the August 2015 devaluation, in order to belie market expectations about any rapid weakening in the yuan's value and to reduce capital flight risk.

The PBOC's interventions on the side of the yuan, however, were particularly heavy, since considerable capital had been flowing out of China anyway. Monetary easing (that is a lowering of interest rates) meant that investors were now unhappy with the returns they were getting in Chinese assets, given the perceived risk profile of the same. Slowing growth and instability in asset markets were serving to considerably reduce any optimism investors may have had about the economy's future. Moreover, capital was also flowing out of the country because many wealthy Chinese households were parking their wealth abroad, fearful of the anti-corruption campaign that was under way, in addition to their own perceptions about the weakness of the economy. August 2015 alone would see $94 billion flow out of China, a record at the time.[56] Such large outflows had, of course, been made possible by the fact that in the run-up to its bid for securing SDR status for the yuan, Beijing had removed many of the capital account restrictions of the past. And though individual households were barred from moving

---

[56] Prasad, Eswar. 'The Renminbi's Ascendance in International Finance.' *Social Science Computing Cooperative*, 5 November 2015, https://www.ssc.wisc.edu/~mchinn/FRBSFConfPaper_EswarPrasad.pdf.

more than $50,000 abroad annually, China's liberalization of current account payment transactions in goods and services in 2012 meant that households could send money overseas using time-tested methods to skirt capital controls – such as over invoicing.[57]

In this context, the August 2015 devaluation of the yuan was probably more a reflection of the fact that China was finding it difficult to defend the currency's rate before 11 August 2015, given the outflows that were taking place and which were bound to continue in an environment of monetary easing. The move to a weaker yuan was therefore a shift to a more defensible rate for the currency, and a move to stem the attrition in foreign exchange reserves that was taking place.[58]

But monetary easing would have to continue for the time being, given the fact that China's local governments and corporations were already sinking under the highest debt-service load in the world, and the nation was still in the process of modifying the term structure of their debts from short-term loans to longer-term interest-bearing bonds. By 2015, the PBOC's monetary easing probably served more to reduce debt-servicing costs for China's economy than provide a stimulus, and that is precisely why Beijing was again raising fiscal spending to try and boost the economy. And since the increase in central government expenditure came on the back of official moves to wind down borrowing by LGFVs, some analysts took it as a sign of further confirmation that the country had finally decided to rein in unsustainable local government spending.

---

[57] Lee, Yimou. 'As African "Chinese" Park Money in Hong Kong, Beijing Targets "Naked" Officials.' *Reuters*, 27 January 2014, https://in.reuters.com/article/hongkong-china-investment/as-african-chinese-park-money-in-hong-kong-beijing-targets-naked-officials-idINL3N0KO1OO20140127.

[58] One-time devaluations are sometimes engineered by central banks as a means to get ahead of speculators sequentially hammering down a currency.

Earlier, in October 2014, the China State Council had issued Rule No. 43, a document that laid down new guidelines to limit local government debt.[59] It called for shutting down non-standardized financing channels, such as LGFVs, for provincial administrations, and also made it clear that these governments were not liable for all the debt owed by the financial vehicles. This move created considerable consternation and uncertainty in China's corporate bond market, since investors did not know which part of the LGFV debt did not actually have the sovereign guarantee. In early 2015, Beijing began restructuring local government debt loads by allowing LGFVs to repackage some of their short-term bank loans into long-term municipal bonds, which bore lower interest rates.

But 'the call of growth' was so strong that in May 2015, just two months after the annual National People's Congress (NPC), China relaxed some of the provisions of Rule No. 43. A joint directive from the Chinese finance ministry, central bank and financial regulator was issued instructing banks to continue extending loans to LGFVs for existing projects that had commenced prior to the end of 2014, and to even renegotiate debt where necessary to ensure project completion. This move naturally confounded those who believed that the country had become serious about getting over its addiction to pumping in credit to fuel growth. And, as we shall see soon, there was no reason for them to put a check on their bewilderment.

Meanwhile, even as China was kicking the can down the road with regard to dealing with local government debt, it seemed to be in 'extend and pretend' mode as far as rising corporate indebtedness was concerned. Since at least 2012,

---

[59] Xun, Wu. 'An Introduction to Chinese Local Government Debt.' *MIT Golub Center for Finance and Policy*, October 2015, http://gcfp.mit.edu/wp-content/uploads/2013/08/Policy-Report-of-Chinese-Local-Government-Debt-final.pdf.

working capital had been drying up with interest coverage ratios worsening in a range of overcapacity industries, such as steel, cement and aluminium, that had had a preponderance of SOEs. This process had accelerated considerably by 2015, with the country's first-ever corporate bond default taking place the year before.[60] Some SOEs, for instance, were continuing to produce merely to generate enough income to be able to pay the interest they owed to their lenders, chiefly publicly owned banks. To support this activity, they had been receiving subsidies, debt rollovers and even fresh credit, besides other aid, such as tax refunds. And local governments had been actively encouraging such practices. Many smaller firms were being merged with large entities, in a bid to enable them to get credit on inputs and cheap loans from their parent companies.

The corporate debt situation was getting worse and an increasing number of firms were not even in a position to meet interest payments on the debt they owed – much less being in the position to ever be able to repay their debt. In 2015, some six Chinese companies defaulted in the corporate bond markets, with four of them unable to pay interest on their bonds.[61] More such defaults would have been likely without the bailouts orchestrated by the Chinese government in a not-so-transparent manner. Indeed, while on one side the CSRC was tightening bond market rules, making it difficult for lower-rated firms to service existing debt, the government was at the other end, standing with a de facto guarantee over large parts of this very market. It

---

[60] Yan, Sophia. 'China Has First Corporate Default.' *CNN Business*, 7 March 2014, https://money.cnn.com/2014/03/07/investing/china-solar-default/index.html.

[61] Zhang, Shuncheng, et al. 'China Corporate Bond Market.' *Fitch Ratings*, October 2019, https://your.fitch.group/rs/732-CKH-767/images/china-corporate-bond-market-blue-book_fitch_10083315.pdf. See also: 'Pricing Risk.' *Economist*, 28 November 2015, https://www.economist.com/finance-and-economics/2015/11/28/pricing-risk.

was an example of how policymakers were having to adopt seemingly contradictory policies in yet another financial market, given slowing growth and low profitability. And with banks being encouraged to lend to a range of insolvent SOEs, it was clear that China's era of 'zombie lending' – in a manner similar to Japan in the 1990s – was well under way. Only, this time, it had been ushered in by the state itself in a rather direct way.

Low corporate profitability was one of the reasons why Beijing had propped up the stock market. The idea was to give China's big SOEs an alternative source of income, even as they were being made to absorb many smaller firms. Perhaps the intention was also to encourage *zaitech* (share buybacks) with 'Chinese characteristics'. Bond market tightening was also aimed at pushing more investors towards the equity market. But, as we saw earlier, it was not to be, and the unravelling of the stock market pushed wealthy and upper-middle-class households back into WMPs and other shadow-banking products, which were offering higher returns.

Throughout 2015, debt distress seemed on the rise, with some 45 per cent of new corporate loans being taken to service interest payment on existing loans, rather than make investments. The LGFV debt restructuring programme would also be expanded several times, to touch 4 trillion yuan by the end of the year. Much of this distress was on account of the massive exposure that both Chinese corporate and local government debt had to the real estate market, which had cooled off nationwide, except for certain Tier I cities on account of curbs introduced by Beijing in 2013. However, with a slowing economy, the central government had started rolling back some of those curbs by the end of 2014 itself, even as it tried to develop equity markets as an alternative to real estate for Chinese investors. With the collapse of the stock market boom by mid-2015, Beijing started to ease restrictions on mortgage borrowing, in a sign that it was once again looking to warm up the real estate market.

However, wealthy Chinese homes seemed to have become more interested in real estate abroad, especially in the Anglosphere. For instance, taken together with Hong Kong and Taiwan, mainland Chinese accounted for $28.6 billion of investment into American real estate between April 2014 and March 2015.[62] Chinese households were also buying bitcoins onshore, and then selling them on exchanges abroad, besides purchasing insurance products in Hong Kong.

The country's companies too continued to purchase overseas assets, hastened by the prospect of further weakening in the value of the yuan. As such, capital continued to flow out of China, and the PBOC's foreign exchange reserves would stand at $3.23 trillion by January 2016 – having fallen by more than half a trillion dollars during the course of 2015.[63] And this was due to heavy interventions from its side made in a bid to keep the currency within its trading band vis-à-vis the dollar.

January 2016 would see yet another fall in the Shanghai stock market, exaggerated by the CSRC's hasty bid to introduce circuit breaker mechanisms, which were subsequently withdrawn. With China also reporting its slowest GDP growth rate in 25 years in 2015, negative perceptions about the country's economic trajectory, reinforced by the communist government's inability to manage the development of stable financial markets, would continue to trigger large capital outflows throughout 2016, necessitating heavy PBOC intervention in favour of the yuan.[64]

---

[62] Frank, Robert. 'Wealthy Foreigners Bought $100 Billion in US Real Estate.' *CNBC*, 22 June 2015, https://www.cnbc.com/2015/06/22/wealthy-foreigners-bought-100-billion-in-us-real-estate.html.

[63] 'China FX Reserves Fall Almost $100B to Lowest since May 2012.' *Reuters*, 7 February 2016, https://www.cnbc.com/2016/02/07/china-fx-reserves-fall-almost-100b-to-lowest-since-may-2012.html.

[64] 'China Economic Growth Slowest in 25 Years.' *BBC News*, 19 January 2016, https://www.bbc.com/news/business-35349576.

Indeed, the expectation of capital flows putting downward pressure on the yuan's exchange rate with the dollar led to speculators pushing even more bets against the former in offshore markets. And this selling pressure on the offshore yuan meant that the PBOC was finding it increasingly difficult to maintain the trading band for the onshore yuan, because of arbitrage possibilities. With the spread between onshore and offshore exchange rates for the currency reaching 2 per cent, the central bank sought to make the yuan dearer offshore by drying up its liquidity.[65] Besides direct interventions, wherein the PBOC sold dollars in offshore yuan markets – chiefly Hong Kong – it also increased reserve ratios for offshore yuan bank accounts. At one point in January 2016, China even warned billionaire George Soros, known as the man who broke the pound, against betting on a yuan slide.[66] Soros, who had been predicting a 'hard landing' for the Chinese economy since 2015, was held to be responsible by authorities for short-selling pressure on the yuan in offshore markets. Instead of worrying about how to send capital abroad, via vetted channels for influence and RMB internationalization, Beijing was now increasingly worried about vast uncontrolled capital outflows that could damage its plans for the currency.

A BRIDGE TOO FAR

In February 2016, China gave a bigger push to reheating the real estate sector by loosening property curbs, even as monetary easing continued. This move was, of course, part of the country's continuing emphasis on a desirable rate of economic growth, as enumerated in the Thirteenth Five

[65] Reuters Staff. 'Spread between Onshore, Offshore Yuan Widest since September 2011.' *Reuters*, 5 January 2016, https://in.reuters.com/article/us-china-yuan/spread-between-onshore-offshore-yuan-widest-since-september-2011-idUSKBN0UJ0PG20160105.

[66] https://fortune.com/2016/01/26/china-goes-after-george-soros.

Year Plan unveiled in 2015. As a part of this plan, China announced its desire to double household income by 2020, as compared to the levels seen in 2010, something that would require an average annual growth rate of at least 6.5 per cent between 2016 and 2020. With this, Beijing would be true to Xi Jinping's 2015 slogan to 'comprehensively build a moderately prosperous society'.[67] While once again making it easier to lend to the real estate sector, China also went on to announce a bigger fiscal outlay for 2016 than it did in 2015, pushing up the deficit from 2.3 per cent to 3 per cent for the year.

The fact that the government was giving a bigger stimulus to meet a lower growth target than the year before only served to underline the declining effectiveness of the same. Even if official figures were considered, in 2015, China's credit growth was larger than the reported growth rate by a factor of two. If a so-called 'augmented' credit criterion were to be considered, the country's credit creation growth rate in 2015 actually touched 25 per cent, or a level close to what was seen right after the 2008 stimulus programme. And in 2016, this would rise even further – all in aid of meeting a certain targeted growth rate.

At these rates, China was being projected to reach a debt-to-GDP ratio of well over 300 per cent by 2020 (which it reached, by some estimates, in October 2019 itself), which would greatly increase the chances of a financial crisis occurring in the country.[68] Taken together with other criteria observed during credit-inflated booms in emerging markets that go bust, some analysts were predicting that a financial

---

[67] 'China's Xi Jinping Unveils New "Four Comprehensives" Slogans.' *BBC News*, 25 February 2015, https://www.bbc.com/news/world-asia-china-31622571.

[68] Tiftik, Emre, and Khadija Mahmood. 'Global Debt Monitor: COVID Drives Debt Surge – Stabilization Ahead?' *Institute of International Finance*, 17 February 2021, https://www.iif.com/Portals/0/Files/content/Global%20Debt%20Monitor_Feb2021_vf.pdf.

crisis was just five years away for the country. Yet others felt that this would be a crying shame, since they believed that China could easily grow at 2–3 per cent annually by concentrating on reforms, even as it took its foot off the credit accelerator. However, there were still others who felt that 2–3 per cent was probably closer to the nation's actual GDP growth rate, even with all the credit infusion. If this were indeed the case it would signal a much more acute debt-deleveraging dilemma for Beijing – in which the fear of an economic contraction was leading to continued encouragement of credit growth that would inevitably lead to an even bigger debt reckoning later.

With Beijing announcing a debt-restructuring package for SOEs – similar to what it was doing for LGFVs – major Western credit rating agencies began to express their concerns about China's financial stability through a ratings downgrade. Moody's downgraded China's outlook from stable to negative in March 2015, with Standard & Poor's following soon thereafter. The country's reaction to the ratings downgrades by Western agencies was fierce, with finance minister Lou Jiwei accusing them of 'bias'. Addressing a press briefing after a G-20 meeting in Washington on 20 April 2016, he observed, 'Historically, the market performance of most of China's sovereign debt was higher than the assessment of the credit-rating agencies. That means there's bias.'[69]

The accusation of a prejudice on the part of Western credit rating firms towards China is, of course, not new, and was a catalyst for Beijing to set up its own credit rating agencies. But Western agencies weren't the only entities sounding the alarm on the country's debt levels. In April 2016, the IMF itself expressed a sense of foreboding about

---

[69] 'China's Finance Minister Accuses Credit Rating Agencies of Bias.' *Bloomberg News*, 16 April 2016, http://www.scmp.com/news/china/economy/article/1936614/chinas-finance-minister-accuses-credit-rating-agencies-bias.

China's plans to securitize corporate NPLs. In a blog post on the institution's official website, IMF staffers, pointing out the perils of China's plan at a time when corporate debt had touched 160 per cent of its GDP, wrote:

> While such techniques can play a role in addressing these problems and have been used successfully by other countries, they are not comprehensive solutions by themselves. Unless they are carefully designed and part of a sound overall framework, they could actually worsen the problem, for example, by allowing 'zombie' firms (non-viable firms that are still operating) to keep going.[70]

The post added, 'Banks generally also don't have the expertise to run or restructure a business and debt–equity conversions could create conflicts of interest – banks may keep lending to a now-related party.'

Interestingly, Chinese banks themselves were concerned about the debt-swap plan and did not want to end up exchanging their bad loans for bad equity. Perhaps to quell such doubts, Zhang Yi, chairman of the State-owned Assets Supervision and Administration Commission (SASAC), while speaking at a central and local enterprise work conference, reportedly said that his agency will 'basically resolve the problem of unproductive zombie firms over the next three years'.[71] His vow came in the wake of the fact that SOEs had on average seen their profits dip by 9.5 per cent in the first 11 months of 2015, with SASAC-controlled firms seeing an even greater dip in profitability of 10.4 per cent during the same period.[72]

---

[70] Daniel, James, et al. 'Tackling China's Debt Problem: Can Debt–Equity Conversions Help?' *IMF Blog*, 26 April 2016, https://blogs.imf.org/2016/04/26/tackling-chinas-debt-problem-can-debt-equity-conversions-help/.

[71] 'China to Clean-Up "Zombie" Companies by 2020: Xinhua.' *Reuters*, 17 January 2016, http://www.reuters.com/article/us-china-companies-idUSKCN0UV0GH.

[72] Ibid.

This 'promise' to resolve the fate of zombie SOEs would be followed by more musings about the danger posed by a failure to do so. An article appearing in the CPC's mouthpiece, *People's Daily*, on 9 May 2016, written by a supposedly 'authoritative insider', warned that 'excessive credit growth could plunge China into financial turmoil, even wiping out the savings of the ordinary citizens'.[73] This was followed by the publication of a speech by none other than Xi himself the next day, in which he unveiled his vision for the Chinese economy based on what he called 'supply-side structural reform', of which a key element would be 'deleveraging campaigns'. This meant direct efforts to cut down corporate borrowing. Some observers saw this as disapproval of Keqiang's support to greater credit injection for fuelling growth.

The realization that the situation may spin out of control was coming at a time when China's NPL problem only seemed to be getting worse. In a report released in April 2016, the IMF estimated that 15.5 per cent of Chinese banking loans, worth about $1.3 trillion, were at risk of turning sour – a figure that was nine times higher than the official 1.75 per cent NPL ratio estimated by the China Banking Regulatory Commission (CBRC) in March 2016.[74] Charlene Chu, an analyst who had made a name for herself by being prescient on China's debt situation, estimated NPLs to be around 22 per cent of total

---

[73] 'China Debt-Fueled Stimulus May Lead to Recession – People's Daily.' *Reuters*, 9 May 2016, https://www.reuters.com/article/us-china-economy-trend/china-debt-fueled-stimulus-may-lead-to-recession-peoples-daily-idUSKCN0Y003W.

[74] 'China May Have $1.3 Trillion of Risky Loans, IMF Report Shows.' *Bloomberg*, 15 April 2016, https://www.bloomberg.com/news/articles/2016-04-15/china-may-have-1-3-trillion-of-risky-loans-imf-report-shows. See also: Reuters Staff. 'UPDATE 1-China's Non-performing Loans Hit 11-Year High – Regulator.' *Reuters*, 12 May 2016, https://in.reuters.com/article/china-economy-loans/update-1-chinas-non-performing-loans-hit-11-year-high-regulator-idUSL3N18935N.

loans outstanding and believed that a massive bailout would be required.[75] CLSA, a long-time brokerage and investment firm, stated that Chinese bank NPLs were in the 15 to 19 per cent range, and estimated that the country may need up to $1 trillion to clean up bad debts laden with its banks.[76]

With the Chinese corporate-debt-to-GDP ratio touching what was then the highest-ever level of 166.9 per cent in the second quarter of 2016, Beijing would accelerate its deleveraging campaigns to curtail corporate borrowing.[77] This effort was mounted even as the PBOC kept tightening capital controls during 2016 to stem the steady depreciation of the yuan.

A mix of capital controls, interventions in the foreign exchange market and the fact that the yuan was at long last included in the SDR basket by the IMF in October 2016 would help it regain some ground against the dollar during the course of 2017. The corporate-debt-to-GDP ratio too would decline to about 160 per cent by the close of 2017 on account of the deleveraging campaigns.[78] But these firefighting measures were not nearly enough given the sheer enormity and nature of China's structural debt problems. Indeed, in October 2017, mounting corporate and household debt problems would lead the PBOC governor, Zhou Xiaochuan, to overtly sound the alarm about the

---

[75] Shaffer, Leslie. 'China's Debt Avalanche is the Biggest Worry.' *CNBC*, 29 January 2016, https://www.cnbc.com/2016/01/29/chinas-debt-avalanche-is-the-biggest-worry.html.

[76] Cheung, Francis. 'China's Bad Debt Epidemic.' *CLSA*, 20 May 2016, https://www.clsa.com/idea/chinas-bad-debt-epidemic.

[77] 'China Deleveraging Is Going into Reverse, New BIS Data Show.' *Bloomberg News*, 26 September 2018, https://www.bloomberg.com/news/articles/2018-09-26/china-s-deleveraging-is-going-into-reverse-new-bis-data-show.

[78] Taplin, Nathaniel. 'Why China's Deleveraging Has Faltered.' *Wall Street Journal*, 23 November 2018, https://www.wsj.com/articles/why-chinas-deleveraging-has-faltered-1542964998.

possibility of the country experiencing a 'Minsky moment', which refers to a situation wherein asset prices suddenly crash on account of excessive debts and/or currency pressures (that is, a declining currency leads to capital flight from asset markets and a concomitant fall in values).[79]

As things would turn out, the yuan's recovery against the dollar proved to be short-lived. Early 2018 saw the commencement of the US–China trade war, with Trump imposing a 30 per cent duty on US solar panel and washing machine imports in January of that year.[80] This was followed by other measures, including tariffs of 25 per cent on steel and 10 per cent on aluminium, in March 2018.[81] While the tariffs on solar panels, washing machines, steel and aluminium were not specific to China per se, the gloves would be off for good with the imposition of 25 per cent tariffs on Chinese technology goods worth $50 billion – including machinery, semiconductors, autos, aircraft parts and intermediate electronics components – being imposed in July and August 2020 as part of a probe into China's intellectual property practices.[82]

While China retaliated with protectionist measures of its own, it was not long before the yuan once again began to slide against the dollar by April 2018. Trump's tariffs may have hurt the American consumer, but it made matters worse for

---

[79] Reuters Staff. 'China Central Bank Warns against "Minsky Moment" Due to Excessive Optimism.' *Reuters*, 19 October 2017, https://www.reuters.com/article/us-china-congress-debt-minskymoment-idUSKBN1CO0D6.

[80] Reuters. 'Trump Imposes Steep Tariffs on Imported Solar Panels and Washing Machines.' *Guardian*, 23 January 2018, https://www.theguardian.com/environment/2018/jan/23/trump-imposes-steep-tariffs-on-imported-solar-panels-and-washing-machines.

[81] 'Factbox: Tariff Wars – Duties Imposed by Trump and U.S. Trading Partners.' *Reuters*, 6 May 2019, https://in.reuters.com/article/us-usa-trade-tariffs-factbox/factbox-tariff-wars-duties-imposed-by-trump-and-u-s-trading-partners-idUSKCN1SB0SA.

[82] Ibid.

the credit-addled Chinese manufacturing landscape as well. Barring a precipitous fall in the wake of the GFC, Chinese exports to America had actually risen just under 60 per cent during 2007–17.[83] Though American exports to China had more than doubled during the same period, that could not prevent the US–China deficit from widening to around $375 billion at the end of 2017 from just over $258 billion at the end of 2007.[84]

With industrial unemployment on the rise, Beijing had to dial down on its deleveraging campaigns, and the corporate-debt-to-GDP ratio would resume its upward trajectory in 2018, thereby reversing the improvements seen in 2017.[85] In any case, indications are that it was private enterprises, especially small ones, in the country that had mostly been at the receiving end of the effort to rein in spiralling corporate debt, with SOEs being allowed to continue with their 'lend and spend' ways. This can be seen by the fact that a record number of bond defaults during 2017 had been concentrated in the private sector, with errant SOEs continuing to be the recipients of 'extend and pretend' largesse from commercial banks. Not a happy state of affairs, given that the private sector accounts for around 60 per cent of China's GDP, and is the dominant job creator.[86]

The deleveraging campaigns, however, did manage to shut the shadow-banking tap for LGFV bonds. That, combined with Beijing's studious refusal to extend any

---

[83] Calculated from: United States, Department of Commerce. 'Foreign Trade.' *Census Bureau*, https://www.census.gov/foreign-trade/balance/c5700.html#2007.

[84] Ibid.

[85] It had risen to 164 per cent by early 2018. See: Taplin, Nathaniel. 'Why China's Deleveraging Has Faltered.' *Wall Street Journal*, 23 November 2018, https://www.wsj.com/articles/why-chinas-deleveraging-has-faltered-1542964998.

[86] 'China's Private Sector Contributes Greatly to Economic Growth: Federation Leader.' *Xinhua*, 6 March 2018, http://www.xinhuanet.com/english/2018-03/06/c_137020127.htm.

sovereign guarantees to the same, saw these bond yields spike, leading to a significant number of defaults. This was hardly surprising, given that LGFVs needed to find new creditors from wherever they could simply to stay afloat. Just how badly they needed to be refinanced can be gauged from the fact that by early 2019, 78.7 per cent of LGFV bonds were being used to repay or refinance maturing debt, or swap for other debt instruments, up from just 19.3 per cent in 2013.[87]

However, with overall LGFV debt already having reached a cumulative value of some 60 per cent of GDP, Beijing could not stand by idly either while its own deleveraging campaign pushed the economy towards debt deflation. As such, Beijing extended the bond-swap programme and also directed the China Development Bank to extend soft loans to LGFVs. But these could only go so far and the main reason why more LGFV bond defaults were not happening was the general monetary easing being undertaken by the PBOC, which had already cut the RRR four times since 2018.

With the trade war taking its toll and even official data showing that the economy was stumbling, monetary easing was once more in the offing with deleveraging taking a back seat.[88] In the first week of January 2019, Keqiang publicly announced that further action to bolster the economy, including RRR cuts and more reduction in taxes and fees, was in the offing.[89] As if on cue, the PBOC cut the RRR

---

[87] Carfagno, Bart, et al. 'Local Government Debt: Running Faster Just to Stand Still.' *Rhodium Group*, 15 May 2019, https://rhg.com/research/local-government-debt-lgfv-running-faster-just-to-stand-still.

[88] Chinese exports to the US managed to register growth in 2018 despite the trade war. This was chiefly on account of the yuan's slide and Trump's tax cuts, which boosted domestic US consumption, thereby fuelling imports. However, by early 2019, Chinese exports to America had begun to slide and they would fall from 2018 levels during the course of the year.

[89] Yao, Kevin, and Lusha Zhang. 'China Slashes Banks' Reserve Requirements again as Growth Slows.' *Reuters*, 4 January 2019, https://in.reuters.com/article/china-economy-rrr-cut/china-slashes-banks-reserve-requirements-again-as-growth-slows-idINKCN1OY0RV.

for the fifth time since 2019 not soon after. And then, in late January 2019, Xi himself issued a long communiqué in which he 'stressed' the need to 'balance stabilizing growth and guarding against risks', while reminding China's officialdom, 'Effective steps should be taken to stabilize employment, the financial market, foreign trade, foreign investment, domestic investment and expectations to keep economic growth within a reasonable range.'[90]

Clearly, deleveraging had run its course.

COMMAND AND CONTROL

The PBOC's rate cuts since early 2018 did not mean that the floodgates of monetary stimulus were being opened. And there was no point either, given that studies suggested that China's credit multiplier was already zero, in the sense that further growth of credit to the usual unproductive sectors was unlikely to result in significant growth.[91] However, it also wasn't the case that the country had given up on credit growth altogether. The new mantra was 'targeted lending' – the focus was on getting credit to those who 'needed it'; that is, to productive and job-creating sectors. This was very much in keeping with Xi's call in the January 2019 speech in which he asked for concrete measures to make financing for medium-sized, small and micro firms easier and affordable, and to stabilize and support employment.[92]

But that was easier said than done. Despite the PBOC's consistent RRR cuts, interest rates for these medium and

---

[90] 'Xi Urges Major Risk Prevention to Ensure Healthy Economy, Social Stability.' *Xinhua Net,* 22 January 2019, September 2020, http://www.xinhuanet.com/english/2019-01/22/c_137763248.htm.

[91] Chen, Sophia, et al. 'Credit and Fiscal Multipliers in China.' IMF, 12 December 2017, https://www.imf.org/en/Publications/WP/Issues/2017/12/12/Credit-and-Fiscal-Multipliers-in-China-45460.

[92] 'Xi Urges Major Risk Prevention to Ensure Healthy Economy, Social Stability.' *Xinhua Net.*

small enterprises remained as stubbornly high as ever. After all, China's main banks, laden with bad debt as they were, were not really in the mood to transmit rate cuts to riskier lenders – unless of course they belonged to the all-important real estate sector.

Knowing that monetary transmission was not happening, and in a belated acknowledgement of the actual position of Chinese banks, the PBOC moved to bail out major banks in January 2019 by swapping non-interest-bearing perpetual bonds issued by them with central bank bills, even though the headline goal was to improve their 'liquidity'. As the PBOC press release of 25 January 2019 states:

> To improve the liquidity of banks' perpetual bonds (including capital bonds without fixed terms) and to encourage banks to replenish capital through perpetual bond issuance, the People's Bank of China (PBC) decides to launch Central Bank Bills Swap (CBS). Primary dealers of open market operations can trade their perpetual bonds issued by qualified banks for central bank bills with the PBC. And banks' perpetual bonds with ratings at no lower than AA will be included as qualified collateral for medium-term lending facility (MLF), targeted medium-term lending facility (TMLF), standing lending facility (SLF) and central bank lending.[93]

To be fair, the press release did state that the other aim of the move was to 'replenish capital'. Nevertheless, it is noteworthy that this somewhat coy bailout was also done in a way that did not lead to a flood of liquidity into the markets. Be that as it may, just a few months later, in May 2019, Baoshang Bank, a major regional credit provider, became the first bank to fail in China in over two decades.[94] This time around, the

---

[93] 'PBC Launches Central Bank Bills Swap to Support Liquidity of Banks' Perpetual Bonds.' *People's Bank of China*, 4 September 2020, http://www.pbc.gov.cn/english/130721/3753025/index.html.

[94] 'China's First Bank Seizure since 1998 Shows Hidden Loan Risk.' *Bloomberg*, 27 May 2019, https://www.bloomberg.com/news/articles/ 2019-05-27/china-s-first-bank-seizure-since-1998-shows-hidden-loan-risks.

PBOC had to step in overtly. Baoshang's failure shook up financial markets as it was considered a 'star city commercial bank', and, according to the last annual report it published, its NPL ratio was a mere 1.68 per cent at the end of 2016 – registering a minor rise from just 1.41 per cent at the end of 2015.[95] Furthermore, its capital adequacy at the end of 2016 was also a healthy 11.69 per cent, while it registered a sizeable profit.[96] Clearly, all that glisters is not bullion when it comes to the country's banking sector.

Further revealing just how undependable both official statistics and commercial banks' own reports had become in the era of 'extend and pretend', Baoshang was followed by the failure of more 'star performers' – such as Jinzhou Bank from China's rust-belt province of Liaoning as well as Hengfeng Bank, based in Shandong.[97] While the PBOC maintained its distance from these entities, Beijing had to get other policy banks to step in temporarily.

Meanwhile, even as the administration grappled with the undeniable crisis in its banking sector through 2019, the PBOC cut the RRR three more times by October 2019, following the January 2019 cut. The latest RRR reduction, in September 2019, released some $126 billion in liquidity.[98] For the economy, as a whole, this monetary easing was serving

---

[95] Lopez, Linette. 'There Are 3 Reasons China Just Took Over a Bank for the First Time in 20 Years, and 2 of Them Are a Huge Deal.' *Business Insider*, 29 May 2019, https://www.businessinsider.in/latest/there-are-3-reasons-china-just-took-over-a-bank-for-the-first-time-in-20-years-and-2-of-them-are-a-huge-deal/articleshow/69550502.cms.

[96] Ibid.

[97] Tang, Frank. 'China Calls on Local Governments to "Defuse the Bomb" of Troubled Small Banks.' *South China Morning Post*, 30 August 2019, https://www.scmp.com/economy/china-economy/article/3025122/china-calls-local-governments-defuse-bomb-troubled-small.

[98] Chen, Yawen, and Kevin Yao. 'China Cuts Banks' Reserve Ratios, Frees up $126 Billion for Loans as Economy Slows.' *Reuters*, 6 September 2019, https://www.reuters.com/article/us-china-economy-rrr-cut-idUSKCN1VR13X.

more to enable debt turnover and assist firms beleaguered by the trade war to cut costs rather than boosting growth.

Of course, the PBOC tried to channel credit towards the 'deserving', but the measures adopted for this purpose – such as the targeted medium-lending facility – at best generated mixed results. On the other hand, shadow-banking credit resumed its earlier upward trajectory, further underlining the inability of the central bank to implement targeted lending in the economy.

Unsurprisingly, most of the SMEs that did benefit from the PBOC's attempts to channel credit were in the real estate sector. And so did ordinary households and speculators looking to buy into the home market, which had gotten hotter since the bank began its easing process. This despite efforts being under way to prevent margin speculation and guidance by the PBOC to lenders to not reduce mortgage rates on housing. Concerned about rising home prices, a Politburo meeting held in July 2019 observed:

> We should adhere to the principle that housing is used for living, not for speculation, implement the long-term mechanism for real estate, and will not use real estate as a short-term means of stimulating the economy.[99]

Obviously, given the already high prices that were shutting out many potential households from the market, even as unsold inventory piled up in smaller towns and cities, Beijing could not risk a major debt-fuelled bubble, whose uncontrolled explosion would take the banking sector down with it.

Such a debacle would require the central bank to pour a massive amount of liquidity into the economy, which in turn would lead to a serious depreciation of the RMB and to

---

[99] 'RPT-UPDATE 1: China Will Boost Economy but Won't Use Property Market for Stimulus – Politburo.' *Reuters*, 31 July 2019, https://www.reuters.com/article/china-economy-politburo/rpt-update-1-china-will-boost-economy-but-wont-use-property-market-for-stimulus-politburo-idUSL4N24W03E.

capital flight. Though one of Beijing's responses to the US-inflicted trade war had been to let the currency depreciate in order to provide succour to its beleaguered exporters who were getting shut out of the North American market, it had, thus far, been a controlled affair. Capital controls instituted since the 2015–16 uncontrolled yuan fall and the PBOC's reserves of around $3 trillion were adequate to stave off an attack on the currency. However, all bets would be off if a Minsky moment were to take place in China. And the initial burst of consumer inflation led by energy and food prices that could follow would also do no justice to the imperative of rebalance, since people would have that much less to spend on things other than those commodities.

Indeed, the other reason why Beijing wanted to keep real estate prices from runaway growth was the fact that land and housing were precisely the sectors in which Chinese households were investing. Household borrowings were mainly in the form of outstanding mortgage loans, which stood at $3.92 trillion by the end of June 2019, accounting for 54 per cent of all household debt.[100] And both the household-debt-to-GDP ratio and the household-debt-to-disposable-income ratio had been consistently rising since the GFC. Though the former was around 55 per cent in mid-2019, and less than that in the Western economies, it had actually trebled since 2008.[101] More worryingly, the household-debt-to-disposal-income ratio was already 85 per cent, and higher than that of many Western economies.[102]

---

[100] Tang, Frank. 'China to Survey 30,000 Households about Debt Levels as Financial Risks Continue to Rise.' *South China Morning Post*, 29 September 2019, https://www.scmp.com/economy/china-economy/article/3030831/peoples-bank-china-survey-30000-households-about-debt-levels.

[101] 'Financial Stability Review.' *Reserve Bank of Australia*, October 2019. https://www.rba.gov.au/publications/fsr/2019/oct/pdf/financial-stability-review-2019-10.pdf.

[102] 'Chinese Household Debt at 85% of Disposable Income, Fitch Says.'

Obviously, the debt load coupled with the disruption caused by the trade war was taking its toll on consumer spending, with precautionary savings on the rise. The result was that the Chinese economy had failed to rebalance significantly since the GFC, with consumption still accounting for less than 40 per cent of the GDP. Unfortunately for Beijing, a significant fall in real estate prices would not aid the cause of rebalancing either, since households would feel less wealthy and curtail spending further. A real estate crash would, of course, lead to a wave of foreclosures. This would probably be because many Chinese took out mortgages with the expectation of price rise, not to mention the fact that the financial sector would definitely see a Japanese-style bust.

So, even before the COVID-19 shock, China was walking on a tightrope, trying to keep real estate prices just right. With the sector itself accounting for a quarter of the country's GDP, it had become simply too big to fail. As Xi had himself noted in January 2019, 'It is necessary to introduce a long-term mechanism to maintain the sound development of the real estate market in a steady manner.'[103]

But that was easier said than done, especially when keeping things 'just right' became that much harder on account of the pandemic.

IS IT JUST A MATTER OF TIME?

The COVID-19 shock brought in its wake further monetary easing by the PBOC, chiefly in the form of RRR cuts

---

Star, 19 July 2019, https://www.thestar.com.my/business/business-news/2019/07/19/chinese-household-debt-at-85pct-of-disposable-income-fitch-says#:~:text=Chinese%20household%20debt%20at%2085%25%20of%20disposable%20income%2C%20Fitch%20says,-Business&text=KUALA%20LUMPUR%3A%20Chinese%20household%20debt,%2D2018%2C%20Fitch%20Ratings%20says.

[103] 'Xi Urges Major Risk Prevention to Ensure Healthy Economy, Social Stability.' *Xinhua Net*.

and some very minor interest rate reductions. This form of monetary easing, coupled with a relaxation of urban residential curbs, helped China's real estate sector avert a major slump during 2020. Overall, property sales in the country declined by only 2.1 per cent in the first seven months of the year, in comparison to the same period in 2019, with the reduction in sales being concentrated in the first five months.[104] Real estate investment – that is, the purchase of new properties – also returned to growth quite soon after the end of the Chinese lockdowns in May 2020. Taken together with a sharp rise in property sales in July 2020, some analysts began warning about a new bubble in specific Chinese cities on account of easier borrowing conditions.[105] Perhaps motivated by similar fears, Beijing tightened financing norms for property developers in August 2020, in what has come to be known as the three redlines policy.[106] The introduction of the three redlines policy once again underlined the delicate dance involved in keeping the real estate sector in a Goldilocks state – not too hot, not too cold.[107]

The lockdowns that followed the outbreak of the virus led to a 6.9 per cent contraction in the country's GDP

---

[104] Liu, Pearl. 'China Residential Property Sector a "Slow Growth Market" Now, as Sales and Profits Decline, Beijing Steps up Cooling Measures.' *South China Morning Post*, 30 August 2020, https://www.scmp.com/business/china-business/article/3099440/china-residential-property-sector-slow-growth-market-now.

[105] 'Property Investment Increases 11.7% in China in July.' *Economic Times*, 14 August 2020, https://realty.economictimes.indiatimes.com/news/industry/property-investment-increases-11-7-in-china-in-july/77545098.

[106] Future access to financing will be predicated on developers' adherence to strict criteria including liability to asset ratio (excluding advance receipts) of less than 70 per cent, net gearing ratio of less than 100 per cent, and cash to short-term debt ratios of more than 1x. See: 'China's Three Red Lines.' *UBS*, 11 January 2021, https://www.ubs.com/global/en/asset-management/insights/china/2021/china-three-red-lines.html.

[107] Liu, 'China Residential Property Sector a "Slow Growth Market" now'.

during the first quarter of 2020, and by April 2020, there were reports that suggested that some 2,47,000 firms had filed for bankruptcy during January–February 2020 alone.[108] With that many firms filing for bankruptcy, there was bound to be a rise in the NPL ratio even in China's official statistics; however, it followed the usual 'understated' flavour of this metric in the country.[109] But, as we have seen earlier, the actual NPL ratio was likely far higher even before the COVID-19 shock, given the entrenched 'extend and pretend' dynamics of the nation's banking sector. One can only guess what the true NPL ratio might be in the pandemic era. Since the onset of the pandemic, signs of growing stress have been getting publicly flagged, with the China Banking and Insurance Regulatory Commission (CBIRC) issuing an explicit statement back in August 2020 that NPLs among small and medium enterprises were close to reaching a 'pre-set tolerance limit' beyond which interventions would be necessary.[110] In March 2021, the CBIRC stated that there was bound to be a surge of bad loans due to the pandemic.[111]

When the pandemic first struck, Beijing asked banks to perform a 'national service' by way of reducing lending rates and rescheduling loan repayments, besides encouraging them

---

[108] 'Coronavirus Crisis: 2.47 Lakh Chinese Firms Go Bankrupt in Jan–Feb.' *Economic Times*, 23 September 2020, https://auto.economictimes.indiatimes.com/news/industry/coronavirus-crisis-2-47-lakh-chinese-firms-go-bankrupt-in-jan-feb/75108045.

[109] 'China to Accelerate Non-Performing Loans Settlement.' *Xinhua Net*, 17 June 2020, http://www.xinhuanet.com/english/2020-06/17/c_139146249.htm.

[110] Yingzhe, Guo, and Wu Xiaomeng. 'China Is Approaching Its Limit on Bad Small Business Loans.' *Caixin Global*, 24 August 2020, https://www.caixinglobal.com/2020-08-24/china-is-approaching-its-limit-on-bad-small-business-loans-101596468.html.

[111] Tang, Frank. 'China on Guard for "Inevitable" Rise in Bad Loans Following Covid-19 Shock.' *South China Morning Post*, 3 March 2021, https://www.scmp.com/economy/china-economy/article/3123785/chinas-top-banking-regulator-sees-surge-bad-loans-2021.

to lend.[112] This discharge of national service saw China's five largest banks report their biggest-ever declines in profitability in the first half of 2020 with bank credit peaking in May 2020. Cognizant of the state of its banking sector health, Beijing started dialling back on credit growth by the end of 2020 itself and introduced curbs on both mortgage lending and consumer loans, apart from discouraging borrowing by the real estate sector via the three redlines policy. Riding on the back of a stimulus- and exports-fuelled recovery in the economy, China's banks would turn around to post profits during the first half of 2021. Of course, once the coronavirus-related forbearance policy for debtors expired in late 2021, these banks saw a major rise in their bad assets.[113] And though they have increased their capital buffers several times since the COVID-19 shock, a requirement for future bailouts cannot be ruled out.

That Beijing could at all dial back on credit growth during 2021 was on account of the fact that China had become the only major economy to grow in 2020, even if it was by a mere 2.2 per cent.[114] It had bucked the global contractionary trend owing to a stimulus package estimated to be about $521 billion in low-return infrastructure projects channelled

---

[112] Lee, Yen Nee. 'China's Mega Banks Lost Billions of Dollars in Profit as Bad Loans Rise During Coronavirus Pandemic.' *CNBC Markets*, 31 August 2020, https://www.cnbc.com/2020/08/31/profit-declines-for-chinas-big-banks-in-first-half-of-2020-due-to-bad-loans-during-coronavirus.html.

[113] 'Chinese Banks to See Doubling of Bad Property Loan Ratio, Warns S&P.' *Reuters*, 15 December 2021, www.reuters.com/markets/rates-bonds/chinese-banks-see-doubling-bad-property-loan-ratio-warns-sp-2021-12-15/. Accessed 28 February 2022.

[114] Wang, Orange. 'China's 2020 Economic Growth Revised down with Beijing Braced for Headwinds.' *South China Morning Post*, 17 December 2021, https://www.scmp.com/economy/economic-indicators/article/3160028/china-gdp-2020-economic-growth-figure-revised-down-22.

through SOEs and LGFVs[115] as well as a rise in exports. Being the first country to exit the lockdown mode, China's factories hummed with orders as competitors remained shuttered. What is more, the country also managed to avert further waves and major lockdowns during the course of 2020, even as the rest of the world's industrial landscape struggled. With people locked up around the world, demand was particularly pronounced for manufactured goods even as spending on services suffered. This was in addition to the hugely increased demand for medical supplies ranging from masks to ventilators. Naturally, with its vast industrial capacity, China was in a position to take advantage. But various headwinds to growth would soon start showing up.

A combination of stimulus-fuelled investments, surging factory orders driven by export demand and pandemic-induced bottlenecks, started boosting prices of commodities and raw materials by 2021. This in turn boosted factory gate prices and there was some talk of China exporting inflation since this got reflected in the prices of finished goods exported from the country. Rising factory gate prices coupled with weak consumer demand and the effects of the three redlines policy on the real estate market started taking its toll on growth by the second quarter of 2021 itself, when the year-on-year figures for the quarter came in lower than expected.[116] Worse, even as the rest of the world started to reopen, China had to go into lockdown mode to prevent the spread of the Delta variant. Since the onset of the pandemic, China had adopted a so-called zero-COVID policy which in general aimed for 'control and maximum suppression' of any

---

[115] Larsen, Kate, et al. 'It's Not Easy Being Green: Stimulus Spending in the World's Major Economies.' *Rhodium Group*, 2 September 2020, https://rhg.com/wp-content/uploads/2020/09/Its-Not-Easy-Being-Green-Stimulus-Spending-in-the-Worlds-Major-Economies.pdf.

[116] 'China's Economy Grows Slower than Expected in Second Quarter.' *Reuters*, 15 July 2022, https://www.reuters.com/business/view-chinas-economic-growth-more-than-halves-second-quarter-2021-07-15/.

outbreak via a 'find, test, trace, isolate and support' formula.[117] And despite high vaccination rates, it could not control the Delta variant without imposing strict restrictions on economic activity. However, this lockdown made things even more difficult for debt-addled firms which had to absorb higher costs since Chinese consumers were in no mood to absorb higher prices.

Truth be told, Beijing's three redlines policy had perhaps been a little too successful, thereby illustrating how the margin for error had got further constricted since the COVID-19-shock. Not only had Beijing wanted to dial back on credit offtake by the real estate sector, it probably wanted to cool commodity prices (prices of coal, steel, aluminium etc.) as well, given that real estate was the most commodity- and credit-intensive sector. But in trying to do so, Beijing had taken the wind out of the sales (pun intended) of the real estate sector which entered a period of decline starting with a sharp fall in sales during July 2021.[118] What is more, China's regulatory crackdown on various segments of its own once-ballyhooed 'tech sector' had turned investor sentiment against Chinese bourses. Led by heavy selling of the shares of China's internet giants, the last week of July 2021 would witness a record crash in Chinese stock markets.[119] Incidentally, in July 2021, China's banking regulator yet again sounded the

---

[117] Llupià, Anna, et al. 'What Is a Zero% COVID Strategy and How Can It Help Us Minimise the Impact of the Pandemic?' *IS Global*, 27 November 2020, https://www.isglobal.org/documents/10179/7943094/26_ISGlobal+COVID19+y+COVIDCero+o+Maxima+Supresion+EN/0a4e83bb-6257-4f5d-8960-16c323b464b2.

[118] 'China Home Sales Slump Deepened in January in Blow to Economy.' *Bloomberg*, 31 January 2022, https://www.bloomberg.com/news/articles/2022-01-31/china-home-sales-slump-deepened-in-january-in-blow-to-economy.

[119] 'Investors Lose $1 Trillion in China's Wild Week of Market Shocks.' *Economic Times*, 30 July 2021, https://economictimes.indiatimes.com/markets/stocks/news/investors-lose-1-trillion-in-chinas-wild-week-of-market-shocks/articleshow/84895480.cms?from=mdr.

alarm and warned that the 'current economic recovery is unbalanced and lacks a solid foundation'.[120]

The remainder of 2021 would justify the banking regulator's alarm, with China's real estate sector entering a period of dangerous decline, beset as it was by falling sales, weakening prices and default contagion among developers.[121] While the plight of Evergrande Group, China's largest real estate player, tottering on the brink of insolvency, had been making headlines for most of the year, by late 2021 it was undeniable that the Chinese real estate sector itself was in a wide-ranging debt crisis.[122] Beyond Evergrande, a range of offshore bonds issued by Chinese developers (including those who had borrowed more heavily abroad than Evergrande) were losing value, as foreign investors sought to exit while they could.[123] Weighed down by a worsening debt crisis and falling home sales, China's real estate and construction sectors would each register their first year-on-year contractions since the start of the pandemic in the third quarter of 2021.[124] Even more troubling for Beijing was the fact that individual investors had begun protesting for the losses they were

---

[120] 'UPDATE 1-China's bank regulator warns of rising bad loans due to uneven recovery', *Reuters*, 14 July 2021, https://www.reuters.com/article/china-banks-idCNL1N2OQ0G4.

[121] 'China Home Sales Slump Deepened in January in Blow to Economy.' *Bloomberg*.

[122] He, Laura. 'China's Evergrande Downgraded by Fitch.' *CNN*, 15 December 2021, edition.cnn.com/2021/12/15/economy/china-omicron-economy-intl-hnk/index.html.

[123] Wilkins, Rebecca Choong. 'China Bond Rout Shifts from Evergrande to Other Big Developers.' *Bloomberg*, 8 November 2021, www.bloomberg.com/news/articles/2021-11-08/china-bond-rout-shifts-from-evergrande-to-other-big-developers?srnd=premium-asia.

[124] 'China's Property Sector Shrinks For 1st Time Since Pandemic.' *Bloomberg*, 19 October 2021, https://www.bloomberg.com/news/articles/2021-10-19/china-s-property-sector-contracts-for-first-time-since-pandemic.

incurring on the WMPs sold to them by developers.[125] In doing so, they had joined homebuyers who had already been protesting outside Evergrande's offices, faced as they were with the prospect of being left with unbuilt dwellings that they had already paid for.[126]

Not only was real estate China's most commodity-intensive and credit-intensive sector, it continued to be a prime driver of growth, accounting for a third of the country's GDP growth in recent times, claims of decoupling notwithstanding.[127] Amplifying the impact of the real estate slowdown were electricity shortages that were curbing the output of sectors such as steel, cement, aluminium and even fertilizers.[128] In fact, electricity shortages, weak demand, Omicron-related containment measures which were more stringent than what was employed for Delta, and Beijing's desire to keep the skies clear during the 2022 Winter Olympics all contributed to China's industrial output showing a steady decline in growth during the course of the second half of 2021 leading into 2022.[129]

---

[125] 'Furious Investors Test China's Resolve to Crack down on Property.' *Bloomberg*, 11 November 2021, www.bloomberg.com/news/articles/2021-11-11/china-evergrande-crisis-furious-property-investors-demand-government-action?cmpid=BBD111221_CAS&utm_medium=email&utm_source=newsletter&utm_term=211112&utm_campaign=closeasia.

[126]

[127] Magnus, George. 'From Economic Miracle to Mirage – Will China's GDP Ever Overtake the US?' *Guardian*, 28 December 2021, www.theguardian.com/business/2021/dec/28/from-economic-miracle-to-mirage-will-chinas-gdp-ever-overtake-the-us.

[128] 'China Power Cuts: What Is Causing the Country's Blackouts?' *BBC News*, 30 September 2021, https://www.bbc.com/news/business-58733193.

[129] 'China Jan Factory Activity Growth Slows, Demand Wanes as COVID Surges.' *Reuters*, 30 January 2022, https://www.reuters.com/markets/asia/china-jan-factory-activity-growth-slows-demand-wanes-covid-surges-2022-01-30.

Unsurprisingly, the impact on China's growth rate became pronounced. In the third quarter of 2021, China's GDP would grow by a mere 4.3 per cent.[130] By late 2021, speculation was already rife among analysts as to whether Beijing would resort to a panic stimulation of the economy.[131] It was mused whether China would set a 'floor' for the GDP growth rate given Jinping's 2020 statement that 'It is entirely possible to reach the high-income country status by current standards by the end of the 14th Five-Year Plan, and to double the total economic output or per capita income by 2035'.[132] In order to double China's per capita income in the period 2022-35, the country would have to achieve a compound annual growth rate of around 5 per cent, and it is this figure that was speculated to be the growth rate that Beijing would aim for. A primary mover behind setting any such floor would be the growing issue of unemployment in China, which, coupled with small investor anger over real estate losses, could prove to be a fiery cocktail for the CCP.

The fact remains that the pandemic-related lockdowns have had a severe impact on China's employment situation. In February 2021, China introduced a new way to dress up this fact by declaring that 200 million of its citizens were now 'flexibly employed'.[133] Beginning August 2021, lottery

---

[130] 'China's Economy Grows 8.1% in 2021, Slows in Second Half.' *Economic Times*, 17 January 2022, https://economictimes.indiatimes.com/news/international/business/chinas-economy-grows-8-1-in-2021-slows-in-second-half/articleshow/88942559.cms.

[131] Hancock, Tom, and Enda Curren. 'Investors Know China's Economy Is Slowing Down. But They Don't Know How Bad It Is.' *Print*, 24 October 2021, theprint.in/world/investors-know-chinas-economy-is-slowing-down-but-they-dont-know-how-bad-it-is/755846.

[132] 'Xi Says Economy Can Double as China Lays Out Ambitious Plans.' *Bloomberg*, 3 November 2020, www.bloomberg.com/news/articles/2020-11-03/china-s-xi-says-economy-can-double-in-size-by-2035.

[133] 'China Records 200 Million Flexible Workers – People's Daily Online.' *People*, 2022, en.people.cn/n3/2022/0211/c90000-9956524.html.

sales, which are inversely related to the unemployment rate, also began to decline sharply, providing further evidence of a worsening unemployment situation in the country, contrary to official figures.[134] A weakening labour market obviously impinges on consumer sentiment, and even in the first half of 2021 when the economy was supposedly recovering, weakness in consumer sentiment remained palpable and retail sales for the most part remained below 2019 levels. Indeed, post the COVID-19 shock, it is difficult to see Chinese consumers shedding their traditional saving instincts – given the uncertain economic climate, the continued lack of a proper social security net, adverse demographics and above all, the slump in the real estate sector, where most of their savings are parked. Simply put, the country cannot bank upon consumer spending to serve as a bulwark for its transformation to higher-end industries. Indeed, in the short run, there seems to be little hope for success of China's 'dual circulation policy', announced by Jinping in May 2020, as per which China would depend mainly on 'the domestic cycle of production, distribution, and consumption – for its development, supported by innovation and upgrades in the economy'.[135]

The first quarter of 2022 would see China's real estate sector falling into an ever deeper crisis, with negative surprises in the form of even supposedly sound developers announcing their inability to service debt.[136, 137] In January

---

[134] 'China's Lottery Sales Paint a Bleaker Picture of Unemployment.' *Bloomberg*, 8 November 2021, www.bloomberg.com/news/articles/ 2021-11-08/china-s-lottery-sales-paint-a-bleaker-picture-of-unemployment.

[135] Yao, Kevin. 'What We Know about China's "Dual Circulation" Economic Strategy.' *Reuters*, 16 September 2020, https://www.reuters.com/article/china-economy-transformation-explainer-idUSKBN2600B5.

[136] 'China's Latest Default Warning Takes Shock Factor to Extreme.' *Bloomberg*, 20 February 2022, www.bloomberg.com/news/articles/2022-02-20/china-s-latest-default-warning-takes-shock-factor-to-new-extreme.

[137] Horta, Sofia. 'Crisis in China's Property Industry Deepens with No

2022, Chinese stock markets had a major fall, leading to $1.2 trillion in investor wealth getting wiped out as international investors dumped shares across the board.[138] In any case, fourth-quarter growth in 2021 had fallen to just 4 per cent.[139] With bad news spreading, Beijing seemed to set in motion the much anticipated stimulus led by PBOC's liquidity easing measures. The PBOC, which had already cut benchmark borrowing rates and the RRR in December 2021, would do so again in January 2022. It would also start pumping policy loans into the economy. However, a lot of the credit was being channelled towards SOEs, which were being prepared to absorb stranded assets in the private sector besides preparing them to boost exports.[140] To supplement this, it had been reported back in December 2021 itself that fiscal measures would be in the offing.[141]

End in Sight.' *Bloomberg*, 18 February 2022, www.bloomberg.com/news/articles/2022-02-18/crisis-in-china-s-property-industry-deepens-with-no-end-in-sight. Accessed 28 February 2022.

[138] 'China's $1.2 Trillion Stock Selloff Triggers Media, Fund Support.' *Bloomberg*, 28 January 2022, www.bloomberg.com/news/articles/2022-01-28/china-s-1-2-trillion-rout-spurs-state-media-mutual-fund-rescue?cmpid=BBD012822_CAS&utm_medium=email&utm_source=newsletter&utm_term=220128&utm_campaign=closeasia.

[139] 'China's Economy Grows 8.1% in 2021, Slows in Second Half.' *Economic Times*, 17 January 2022, https://economictimes.indiatimes.com/news/international/business/chinas-economy-grows-8-1-in-2021-slows-in-second-half/articleshow/88942559.cms.

[140] 'PBOC Pumps in More Liquidity, Spurring Gains in Chinese Stocks.' *Bloomberg*, 15 February 2022, www.bloomberg.com/news/articles/2022-02-15/pboc-pumps-in-more-liquidity-to-shore-up-economic-growth?cmpid=BBD021522_CAS&utm_medium=email&utm_source=newsletter&utm_term=220215&utm_campaign=closeasia.

[141] Hancock, Tom. 'China Seen Adding Fiscal Stimulus after Setting 2022 Targets.' *Bloomberg*, 12 December 2021, www.bloomberg.com/news/articles/2021-12-12/china-seen-adding-fiscal-stimulus-soon-after-setting-priorities.

However, how successful infrastructure-augmenting fiscal stimulus measures implemented via local governments will be remains to be seen. Falling land prices have constrained the ability of LGFVs to undertake massive new investments.[142] And transfers from the central government to local governments were more in the nature of offsets for tax cuts being given by the latter.[143] Moreover, Beijing's decision in January 2022 to allow LGFVs to obtain debt repayment rescheduling from commercial banks only sought to underline the precarious state of their balance sheets.[144] Indeed, their dubious debt position and the simple fact that China did not have that many 'shovel-ready' projects any more meant that local governments were not really in a position to deliver stimulus, and this was reflected in LGFV borrowing falling below expectations.[145] Compounding the inability of debt-addled LGFVs to boost investment sufficiently would be the continuing power shortages that crimp the output of stimulus-supporting, commodity-intensive industries. The loan advances to SOEs in a bid to boost exports may also not yield the desired results as the world reopens and demand shifts towards services. What is more, China's stimulus is coming at a time when the Fed

---

[142] 'China Local Land Sales Fall Just as Beijing Calls for Spending.' *Bloomberg*, 12 January 2022, www.bloomberg.com/news/articles/2022-01-12/china-local-land-sales-fall-just-as-beijing-calls-for-spending.

[143] Houses and Holes. 'China Fights Losing Stimulus Battle as Property Dies.' *MacroBusiness*, 22 February 2022, https://www.macrobusiness.com.au/2022/02/china-fights-losing-stimulus-battle-as-property-dies.

[144] 'China Allows LGFVs in Guizhou to Negotiate Debt Extension.' *Bloomberg*, 27 January 2022, www.bloomberg.com/news/articles/2022-01-27/china-allows-lgfvs-in-poor-province-to-negotiate-debt-extensions?srnd=fixed-income.

[145] 'China's Local Government Bond Sales Fall Short of Expectations.' *Bloomberg*, 27 January 2022, www.bloomberg.com/news/articles/2022-01-27/china-s-local-government-bond-sales-fall-short-of-expectations?srnd=fixed-income.

Reserve is all set to tighten, and this is likely to impact demand for Chinese products adversely.[146]

With domestic consumer demand unable to sustain the restructuring of its economy towards more productive sectors, export bounce not likely to persist in 2022, and fiscal stimulus unlikely to deliver impressive results, Chinese planners may well be hard put to put a floor to growth in the next few years. There is simply no alternative prong that can offset the demise of the property monster. So, the only thing staving off a Minsky moment sometime in the future would be the PBOC's accommodative stance. And though the PBOC has vowed to stay accommodative till growth potential is reached, it is aware that room for further monetary easing will become increasingly limited given that the Fed will deliver several rate increases through the course of 2022.[147] In fact, the possibility of severe portfolio outflows from China in a manner reminiscent of what happened in 2015 is very much on the cards given foreign investor anger over bond and tech stock losses. It is therefore not surprising that China has sought to lean against capital inflows since the beginning of the pandemic precisely because of their fickle nature. [148, 149] Be that as it may, some $527 billion in 'hot money' had flowed into China between March 2020

---

[146] 'China Warns of Export Woes Due to Less Stimulus Overseas.' *Bloomberg*, 25 January 2022, www.bloomberg.com/news/articles/2022-01-25/china-warns-of-export-woes-due-to-less-stimulus-overseas.

[147] 'PBOC Chief Vows Supportive Policy as Growth Returns to Potential.' *Bloomberg*, 16 February 2022, www.bloomberg.com/news/articles/2022-02-16/pboc-s-yi-vows-supportive-policy-as-growth-returns-to-potential.

[148] Horta, and Curran, 'China's Epic Battle with Capital Flows Is More Intense than Ever.' *Bloomberg*, 6 April 2021, www.bloomberg.com/news/articles/2021-04-06/china-s-epic-battle-with-capital-flows-is-more-intense-than-ever.

[149] 'China Forex Regulator Aims to Defuse Risk of External Shocks.' *Reuters*, 21 January 2022, https://www.reuters.com/markets/currencies/china-forex-regulator-aims-defuse-risk-external-shocks-2022-01-21/.

and June 2021, and a lot of that seems to be set to leave the country, especially at a time when the Fed will raise interest rates.[150] Joining foreign investors would be domestic players who would look to circumvent stringent capital controls via the use of new digital assets. China's decision to proscribe cryptocurrencies in September 2021 should be seen in this light.[151]

Given that China's current account surplus has passed its pandemic-era peak and capital outflows will rise in 2022, the RMB will enter a period of growing downward pressure. A weaker RMB would beget further capital outflows and it remains to be seen whether China will be able to avoid a Minsky moment and a hard landing. Given China's debt load, the central bank may not be able to raise rates in time, even if the currency shows chronic weakness against the dollar. In any case, a weaker RMB and a fall in growth would mean that China would not cross the US in nominal GDP terms any time soon either. Neither would the RMB rival the dollar as a reserve currency in the near future. In fact, if Washington has its way, it will never allow this to happen. With that in mind, we now turn to the story of how the key geo-economic relationship that underpinned the neoliberal era – that is, the US–China coupling – has now unravelled and is giving way to intense strategic competition.

---

150 Hong, Shen, et al. 'China's Nightmare Evergrande Scenario Is An Uncontrolled Crash.' *Economic Times*, 17 September 2021, https://www.economictimes.indiatimes.com/markets/stocks/news/chinas-nightmare-evergrande-scenario-is-an-uncontrolled-crash/articleshow/86289301.cms.

151 'China Declares All Crypto-Currency Transactions Illegal.' *BBC News*, 24 September 2021, https://www.bbc.com/news/technology-58678907.

SEVEN

ON 24 JANUARY 1980, THE US CONGRESS PASSED A TRADE agreement which conferred a 'Most Favoured Nation' (MFN) status upon the People's Republic of China.[1] This was particularly significant as it meant that Chinese exports to America would from then on be exempt from the high tariff rates stipulated by the Smoot–Hawley Act of June 1930, a concession usually reserved for America's 'friends' in the trading sphere.[2] As negotiated, Beijing reciprocated by granting an MFN status to the US as well. These developments, which came just a year after the formal normalization of diplomatic ties, marked the high point of a decade-long US–China rapprochement, which began with the so-called 'ping-pong' diplomacy of 1971.[3] It was engendered by a mutual need to balance the Soviet Union that had achieved nuclear parity with the US, and had been testing China's northern borders since the 1969 Ussuri River clashes.

By the late 1970s, China, now led by Deng Xiaoping, who was once a pariah in Mao's Cultural Revolution, had turned to the US for a technology and trade relationship that would help reinvigorate its economy and restore the

---

[1] Wang, Dong. 'U.S.–China Trade, 1971–2012: Insights into the U.S.–China Relationship.' *Asia–Pacific Journal*, Volume 11, Issue 24, Number 4, 16 June 2013, https://apjjf.org/2013/11/24/Dong-Wang/3958/article.html.

[2] Ibid.

[3] Devoss, David A. 'Ping-Pong Diplomacy.' *Smithsonian Magazine*, April 2002, http://www.smithsonianmag.com/history/ping-pong-diplomacy-60307544/?no-ist.

confidence of the populace in the communist governance model. Since 1978, China, under Deng, had begun a programme of economic reforms called 'Socialism with Chinese Characteristics' that included the liberalization of trade and investment norms. Beginning in 1980, foreign investment was permitted in four special economic zones (SEZs) on the country's eastern seaboard, with three being in the province of Guangdong and one in Fujian.[4] These SEZs were meant to position China as a new location for the global processing trade, that had begun in the 1970s, when American companies started moving consumer goods production overseas to destinations that had abundant cheap labour. Speaking to journalists in 1980, Deng gave the following rationale for establishing these zones:

> Technology, science and even advanced production management, which is also a kind of science, will be useful in any society or country. We intend to acquire technology, science and management skills to serve our socialist production.[5]

It was another matter that American companies weren't really looking to share advanced technology with low-cost offshore destinations that were meant to service the country's rising overconsumption. This is precisely why US enterprises were allowed to operate in China only through joint ventures with domestic companies or government organizations. The idea was that the foreign partner would bring technology and expertise, and the domestic partner would, in exchange, smoothen out the system, as it were. Chinese complaints about inadequate technology-sharing by

---

[4] Crane, Bret, et al. 'China's Special Economic Zones: An Analysis of Policy to Reduce Regional Disparities.' *Regional Studies, Regional Science*, Volume 5, Issue 1, 2018, https://doi.org/10.1080/21681376.2018.1430612.

[5] Deng Xiaoping's archived interview. 'Answers to the Italian Journalist Oriana Fallaci.' *CPC Encyclopaedia*, 21 and 23 August 1980, http://cpcchina.chinadaily.com.cn/fastfacts/2010-10/18/content_11425373.htm.

the US were, however, a common feature throughout the 1980s.

Nonetheless, the country's trade with the US increased sevenfold, from $1 billion in 1978 to $7 billion in 1985.[6] By the mid-1980s, many more coastal SEZs would crop up, and since increased US economic interaction with China served as a bellwether for the latter's emergence on the world trading scene, overall Chinese trade increased almost threefold – from $20.6 billion to $60.2 billion during 1978–85, mainly in the direction of Europe and East Asia.[7] Wherever the US went, Western Europe and East Asia seemed to follow. In fact, though American investment was very important, the top two investors in China during this period were Hong Kong and Macau, with the US trailing in third place. China's export-oriented processing trade saw it receiving capital from East Asian Chinese, who were now keen to tap into the newest low-cost destination for final processing in the region.

As the Cold War heightened under the Reagan administration through the 1980s, China's attraction as a location for offshoring labour-intensive, high-volume production increased. Moreover, it freed up US workers for employment in lucrative primary sectors and military industries. This is reflected in the fact that textiles and clothing accounted for more than 40 per cent of the total value of Chinese exports to the US by the second half of the 1980s. It rose from being America's 28th most important trade partner in 1980 to being the 10th in 1990.[8] Cold War balancing and thicker trade ties contributed to the Reagan administration relaxing controls on the export of advanced technology to China by putting such exports under category 'V' in 1983 – a level of control reserved for America's allies.

---

[6] Crane, 'China's Special Economic Zones: An Analysis of Policy to Reduce Regional Disparities.'

[7] Ibid.

[8] Ibid.

This paved the way for more such transfers of technology. In the 1980s, on five occasions, China would notch up annual GDP growth rates exceeding 10 per cent.[9] The Chinese miracle was under way.

THE CHINA PRICE

The tragic events of 4 June 1989, when Chinese tanks rolled down Tiananmen Square to suppress the protests led by students and workers, did serve as a speed bump in its relationship with the US. In the wake of the incident, the US imposed sanctions on China, which led to a decline in bilateral trade volumes in 1990 – a first in two decades. The economic conditions, which served as the background for the Tiananmen Square protests, also served to temporarily weaken the power of Deng and his reformers. The path of reform that had boosted growth to double-digit levels had also led to a credit glut and a housing boom, which had sent inflation soaring to 18.5 per cent in 1988.[10] Tens of millions of workers flooded into the cities, with students marching with them in solidarity. Socialist hardliners within the CPC held hasty reforms responsible for the upheaval.

---

[9] 'GDP Growth (Annual %) – China.' Based on World Bank national accounts data and OECD national accounts data files from 1961 to 2019, *World Bank*, 2019, https://data.worldbank.org/indicator/NY.GDP.MKTP.KD.ZG?end=1990&locations=CN&start=1980.

[10] Li, Yunqi. 'China's Inflation: Causes, Effects, and Solutions.' *Asian Survey*, 7 July 1989, pp. 655–68, https://www.jstor.org/stable/2644672?seq=1#metadata_info_tab_contents. See also: Reuters. 'Inflation Hits Peak in China.' *New York Times*, 29 November 1988, https://www.nytimes.com/1988/11/29/business/inflation-hits-peak-in-china.html; Keidel, Albert. 'China's Economic Fluctuations and Their Implications for Its Rural Economy.' *Carnegie Endowment*, 2007, https://carnegieendowment.org/files/keidel_report_final.pdf; Kojima, Ryota, et al. 'Inflation Dynamics in China.' *Bank of Japan*, July 2005, https://www.boj.or.jp/en/research/wps_rev/wps_2005/data/wp05e09.pdf.

Deng chose to step down from his official position and retire from public life after 1989. But in 1992, he conducted his famous 'Southern Tour' of SEZs in southern China, in which he extolled the virtues of continuing on the path of reform.[11] While the audience was national, the settings he chose to make his point were precisely those places on China's eastern seaboard that had gained the most from liberalization and trade. Deng now chose to use them to highlight what was possible by declaring that 'some areas must get rich before others'.[12] The idea being that the country's coastal provinces would become prosperous first, via liberalization and export processing trade, in order to provide the resources and demand for pulling up the rest of the country. It is believed that the Southern Tour played a vital role in ensuring China continued down the path of economic reform and trade integration.

From around 1993, inward FDI into China started climbing rapidly – most of it unsurprisingly directed towards those very coastal provinces that had already proven their mettle in the processing trade, with light manufactures and textiles. But this time, a chunk of the FDI was headed into mechanical components and electronics industries. Once again, though, the US investment was important – majority of the inward investment actually came from China's East Asian export-oriented predecessors that were themselves looking for a cheaper location. Taiwan and Japan began to greatly increase their investments into the country as a final processing centre for assembling and shipping goods to the West. Japan, and to a lesser extent Taiwan, would supply intermediates and components that would be put together

---

[11] Chen, Zhuang. 'The Symbolism of Xi Jinping's Trip South.' *BBC News*, 10 December 2012, https://www.bbc.com/news/world-asia-china-20662947.

[12] Tong, Bao. 'How Deng Xiaoping Helped Create a Corrupt China.' *New York Times*, 3 June 2015, https://www.nytimes.com/2015/06/04/opinion/bao-tong-how-deng-xiaoping-helped-create-a-corrupt-china.html.

by the Chinese for final export to the US. And this supply chain relationship would be reflected in bilateral trade balances, with the country beginning to run a significant trade surplus vis-à-vis the US, while experiencing a trade deficit with respect to Japan and Taiwan. In the years ahead, state-enforced worker discipline, abundant migrant labour, excellent infrastructure, export subsidies, cheap credit, tariff exemptions for intermediate imports, plus a scant regard for environmental externalities, all contributed towards the emergence of the dreaded 'China Price'. Godless China was truly a godsend for Western capitalism.

NOT SO CHEAP AFTER ALL

Unfortunately, this very 'China Price' turned out to be not so cheap for the country after all. It is now believed that Chinese workers have been paid below their productivity for most of the miracle years, with a sharp increase in wages being seen only recently. And this wouldn't be particularly surprising, since those tens of millions of workers, who migrated to coastal industrial zones to enable this miracle, wouldn't have had much bargaining power with their employers anyway. Not only would the constant inflow of unskilled and semi-skilled migrants have put downward pressure on wages, the overall system managing rural–urban migration in China was (and still is) loaded against migrant workers.

The hukou system of land registration practised in China, wherein a person gets residential and other state facilities only in the place where they are registered – usually their place of birth – basically discriminates against migrant workers by denying them the right to public services in the urban areas, where they actually dwell.[13] This system also governs the

[13] Dollar, David. 'Sino Shift.' *Finance and Development*, Volume 51, Number 2, June 2014, https://www.imf.org/external/pubs/ft/fandd/2014/06/dollar.htm.

right to buy property in a particular area, and in 2012, only 35.4 per cent of the population had urban hukou, whereas 52.6 per cent of the population actually lived in urban areas by that year.[14] Migrant workers in urban areas continue to live in either the construction sites where they work or in dormitories provided by sweatshops. Obviously, given the state of affairs, migrant workers with no real local foothold as it were, have been at a disadvantage vis-à-vis their employers in terms of wage bargaining, especially during the period when migrant ranks were swelling rapidly. Census figures released in 2020 showed that 45.4 per cent of the population had urban hukou, while the percentage of those living in urban areas had increased to 63.9 per cent.[15] These figures indicate that the so-called hukou reforms initiated in 2014 with the aim of narrowing the difference between the urban population percentage and the urban hukou percentage to 15 per cent from the 17.2 per cent figure in 2012 had failed. The difference had instead increased to 18.5 per cent with the floating population between rural and urban areas at 376 million as compared to 232.1 million in 2012.[16]

Over the years, local governments in China have also appropriated land in coastal areas and elsewhere by paying farmers less than prevailing market prices. This is in contrast to Japan, where, despite the existence of land expropriation laws, market-based compensation was the norm, which served to boost farmer income. Indeed, one of the other reasons for the 'China Price' was that the sites for industrial production came rather cheap. Meanwhile, households also got a lesser share of the profits from increased production

---

[14] Chan, Kam. 'What the 2020 Chinese Census Tells Us About Progress in Hukou Reform.' *Jamestown*, 30 July 2021, https://jamestown.org/program/what-the-2020-chinese-census-tells-us-about-progress-in-hukou-reform.

[15] Ibid.

[16] Ibid.

than their counterparts in other East Asian countries during their industrialization phase because Chinese SOEs, till very recently, distributed a very low quantum of dividends. Instead, almost all after-tax earnings were retained by SOEs for reinvestment. The sum total of below-productivity compensation, dispossession of land without adequate compensation and an underwhelming share in industrial profits has contributed to keeping the share of household income in national income less than what it could have been.

At the same time, the lack of any social security and the hukou system contributed to increasing precautionary motivations for saving among Chinese households. Also, in the late 1990s, at least 21 million workers were let go by SOEs, and this may have further aggravated the tendency to save in the 2000s.[17] While many of the laid-off workers ultimately died in penury, their sons did manage to find jobs as China was growing at a blistering pace, led by investment, during that period. Overall, though, the chief reason for a high savings rate in China, as it was in Japan and other East Asian tigers, was this: a repressed financial system. Beijing also practised financial repression like its neighbours, which led to a lack of choice in terms of financial investments for households, with bank deposits being the only safe place to hold their savings. With these deposits providing depressed returns for their savings, households looked to save as much as they could to increase the quantum of their future interest earnings. After all, the idea was to 'tax' households via low deposit rates for their savings to finance rapid industrialization.

China's peculiar features have served to create a situation wherein, during its high-growth phase, it has experienced savings and investment rates that are appreciably higher than

---

[17] Lin, Karen Jingrong, et al. 'State-owned Enterprises in China: A Review of 40 Years of Research and Practice.' *China Journal of Accounting Research*, Volume 13, Issue 1, March 2020, pp. 31–55, https://doi.org/10.1016/j.cjar.2019.12.001.

those of any of its East Asian neighbours. In other words, it managed to squeeze its consumers far more than any of its neighbours in the quest for rapid growth through capital deepening. Topping this bias towards savings and investment was the massive amount of FDI that was allowed into the country for processing trade in which China's value-added component in export was as low as 20 per cent, with most of the value captured overseas. And while that FDI was enjoying high rates of return on Chinese soil, the country's own foreign exchange reserves were progressively earning lesser and lesser interest, thanks to the accommodative foreign policies followed by the Fed in the US. Foreigners were clearly gaining more from the Chinese miracle than one would think.

THE SHIFT

With the onset of the GFC in 2008, China knew it had to change course. The export-processing model could no longer work to power growth, with wage demands rising across the board, even as Western markets entered a period of chronic weakness. It was clear that China would have to climb the value chain, and climb it fast. While its growth had become the envy of the world, the country now had an economy with insufficient domestic consumption demand and overexposure to dollar-denominated assets that were increasingly yielding less and less as the Fed took its policy rate to the ZLB and engaged in QE. Beijing had to somehow exit the dollar trap while increasing domestic consumption.

Obviously, RMB internationalization leading to reserve status would serve both objectives. It would allow China to spread its foreign exchange risk overseas and the tendency of a reserve currency to appreciate would increase the purchasing power of the country's populace. Cheap imports can also generate jobs after all, by allowing the modern retail sector to expand with lower costs. Being able to transact in the country's currency would also lower costs for China's finance and insurance sectors.

Indeed, RMB internationalization would help in the nation's financial development, which was a prerequisite for it to be able to sustain and grow consumption, even as it drew down on investment into overcapacity and unproductive sectors. By providing its citizens with new avenues for storing value, China could get them to consume more by reducing the precautionary motive to save. Even its stimulus measures that boosted the real estate sector definitely seemed to be aimed at generating a wealth effect that could aid consumption. Over time, the yuan's ascent to reserve currency status would help China draw seigniorage from across the world, absorb real production value from others by merely circulating its own debt, besides enjoying vastly increased macroeconomic flexibility. This would be particularly useful if the country's surpluses in goods and services trade turned into a structural deficit, owing to the draw down in savings. In short, China wanted its own hegemony bonus.

And what better time to achieve this than right after the GFC, when America's own hegemony seemed to be in jeopardy? It was also a time when China had already become the top trading nation, the world's largest creditor, had a huge stock of savings and was generally seen as having passed the GFC test with flying colours on account of its stimulus programme. It is not surprising, therefore, that the country made its first bid for securing SDR status for the RMB back in 2010 itself, merely a year after it set up offshore currency trading centres. This early bid to get the currency out of the 'internationalization gate', as it were, perhaps also betrayed a fear that China's buoyancy may not last for too long – just as Japan's fortunes had reversed rather quickly in the 1980s. Essentially, with this bid, China sought to leverage its independent heft on to the world stage, to chart a new path for the yuan, while it could. Accounting for a greater share of both world output and world trade, the China of the early

2010s was in a structurally superior position, as compared to the Japan of the 1990s, which is when the latter made a belated attempt to internationalize the yen.

China's structural heft, however, did not prove to be enough, and its 2010 attempt to secure SDR was thwarted by the US. That, and the subsequent 'Pivot to Asia', announced by the Obama administration in 2012, was taken by Beijing as confirmation that America would seek to calibrate, or even thwart, China's geo-economic rise, much the way it had done to Japan in the 1980s. The country, of course, countered this with the unveiling of what became the Belt and Road Initiative in 2013 – designed as it was to facilitate RMB internationalization even as some capital controls remained in place. This was important because it is generally believed that for a currency to become widely used in international transactions, it must become fully convertible on the capital account. China, however, could not do that then, and that is why the BRI's role in actively boosting RMB use was so significant, even as the country moved to steadily liberalize capital controls.

For a while, things looked hunky-dory for the RMB as it weathered the 2013 taper tantrum rather well, and the PBOC's foreign exchange reserves peaked in June 2014. The international media at the time was awash with news about how the RMB was breaking new ground as an international currency. Unfortunately, the very path that had made China structurally important in the global economy and a net exporter of capital for a while would get in the way of the RMB's rise to reserve currency status. By the end of 2014, the long shadow of the country's post-GFC stimulus would catch up with the RMB as investors sought to flee a debt-addled economy, thereby putting immense pressure on the currency. The sharp stock market declines that followed also put to rest any notion that China had been able to create liquid and deep capital markets, another feature considered necessary for the RMB's ascent. As we noted before, throughout 2015 and 2016, the PBOC would struggle to keep the currency's value against the dollar stable, as it burnt through a trillion dollars' worth of foreign exchange reserves and reinstituted strict capital controls.[18]

So severe were the outflows that the RMB's inclusion in the IMF's SDR basket in October 2016 would by itself do very little to stem the tide. The China of 2016 was not perceived in the same light as the China of 2010. By that time, its debt-fuelled economy had clearly decelerated and fears of debt-deflation were growing by the day. Naturally, RMB, which was seen as weak and lacking capital convertibility, was unlikely to find favour as a reserve currency. Thus, it was not surprising that its internationalization was essentially stalled during 2015–17, with its share in international payments declining from 2.79 per cent in October 2015 to 1.61 per cent at the beginning of 2018.[19]

Though the currency regained some of its strength vis-à-vis the dollar in late 2017 and early 2018, Trump's trade war would put paid to any hopes of a secular strengthening. Despite the US president labelling China as a chronic currency manipulator, the PBOC let the yuan slide in order to offset the impact of Trump's tariffs. By August 2019, the RMB breached the 'psychological' mark of seven to a dollar, as the trade war kept escalating with new tariffs being brought into play. With the onset of the pandemic, the safe haven effect initially pushed the RMB into further weakness with respect to the dollar as investors rushed to take safety in dollar-denominated assets. However, from around May 2020, this impulse had weakened as they began a search for yield subsequent to the Fed's balance sheet expansion.

---

[18] See chapter six.

[19] Economist Intelligence Unit. 'Renminbi Internationalisation and the BRI Rebuilding Momentum.' *HSBC*, 10 April 2018, https://www.business.hsbc.com/china-growth/renminbi-internationalisation-and-the-bri-rebuilding-momentum.

China seemed like an attractive prospect, given that it had reopened its economy before any other country, and its stimulus measures promised to boost corporate profitability in certain sectors. Unsurprisingly, the RMB has strengthened against the dollar since then and was once again below the seven to a dollar mark at the time of writing. Regardless, given Beijing's ever-tightening capital controls, a broad internationalization of the currency is no longer on the cards in the foreseeable future.

As of July 2021, only around 2.44 per cent of allocated global central bank reserves were held in the form of RMB, a mere smidge in comparison to the 59.53 per cent of such holdings in the US dollar.[20] As a global payments currency too, the RMB had faltered, with its share being only 2.19 per cent in July 2021.[21] Even though the US accounted for a lesser share of global trade than China, the dollar continued to be used for 39.38 per cent of the international payments at the end of July 2021.[22] As of July 2021, the dollar was the leader in the trade finance market too, with a share of 87.76 per cent as opposed to the RMB's 1.73 per cent.[23]

KEY CURRENCY AREA

Now, though the RMB has not made much headway in terms of internationalization on a global scale since 2009, it has nonetheless registered gains in being used as a trade settlement currency in China's near abroad. This is especially

---

[20] Calculated from: 'Access to Macroeconomic and Financial Data.' *International Monetary Fund*, last updated on 30 June 2021, https://data.imf.org/?sk=E6A5F467-C14B-4AA8-9F6D-5A09EC4E62A4.

[21] 'RMB Tracker: Monthly Reporting and Statistics on Renminbi (RMB) Progress Towards Becoming An International Currency.' *SWIFT*, last updated on 19 August 2021, https://www.swift.com/swift-resource/251231/download.

[22] Ibid.

[23] Ibid.

true in East and Southeast Asia, which can be considered a single trading region. Given China's economic weight, its dominant share in intra-regional trade and its position as the single-largest trading partner for all countries in the region, this is not surprising. Deep trade ties with China have understandably created incentives for RMB-based transactions in countries of the region. Moreover, China has also allowed pools of RMB liquidity, which have built up in the hands of many of its regional trading partners (due to their acceptance of payments in the currency for exports, alongside their trade surpluses with China) to be invested in RMB-denominated bonds with better yields than US treasury bills or European sovereign bonds. In general, the country has successfully leveraged the current conditions of 'freer trade', which emerged in the region post-GFC. This is reflected in the sheer number of bilateral and multilateral free trade agreements (FTAs) either concluded or under negotiations, in which Beijing actively promoted the RMB.

As such, FTAs have been a key driver of regional integration, even as other policy initiatives have remained moribund, with firms across the region opting to use these agreements. And because they have helped China promote the RMB, even though it hasn't progressively liberalized its capital account since the 2015–16 capital outflow incident detailed in the last chapter (in fact, since then it has instituted stricter capital controls), it is not surprising that the country has been working towards the harmonization of the region's various FTAs into a single plurilateral arrangement. In fact, research suggests that such an arrangement will create more incentives for transactions in national currencies, which is likely to aid even greater RMB use given China's regional position and how actively it is promoting its currency. Accordingly, the country now seems more focused on a deeper 'regionalization' of the RMB in Asia itself, rather than a broad internationalization. This would be in keeping with the so-called 'new' theories of currency internationalization, which posit that a currency is most likely to find favour in its neighbourhood before breaking out on a truly global level. After all, the first direct trading mechanisms for local currencies against the RMB (that is, without the need for an intermediate step involving conversion into the US dollar) were introduced in seven countries on China's periphery, and Hong Kong was the first RMB offshore trading centre.

Paradoxically, Trump's disruptive protectionism provided Beijing with somewhat of an opening to pursue such a strategy (that is, of deeper regional integration to support the RMB) by energizing the prospects for the Regional Comprehensive Economic Partnership, which seeks to create a mega free trade area in the Asia–Pacific, sans the US. Until November 2019, RCEP negotiations were being conducted by the Association of Southeast Asian Nations (ASEAN) and its existing free trade partners – Japan, China, Australia, New Zealand, South Korea and India (which opted out that month). The RCEP first got a fillip in early 2017, when Trump's abrupt pull-out led to the collapse of the rival Trans-Pacific Partnership (TPP), which had excluded China. The TPP's demise increased Beijing's leverage with the seven potential RCEP members, including Japan, South Korea and Vietnam, which had all also been a part of TPP talks. The Trump administration's subsequent moves to remove unilateral trade concessions, while imposing tariffs on potential RCEP members, only served to increase their urgency to conclude talks that had dragged on for years and missed many milestones in the process.

The hastening of RCEP negotiations – which had started in 2018 – was seen as a move on Asia's part to send a message to Trump about his protectionist policies. It was quite in keeping with a 2018 World Bank study that had suggested that emerging countries should deepen trade ties between themselves to mitigate the impact of US protectionism. Some ASEAN members, such as Malaysia, were particularly keen to further consolidate the regionalization of manufacturing value chains that had begun with Japanese offshoring of labour-intensive segments after *endaka fukyo*. These had then grown through South Korea's own climb up the value chain, and now revolved around China's rise as a manufacturing powerhouse of unprecedented scale. Indeed, a very significant proportion of trade between the so-called ASEAN Plus Three, with the 'Plus Three' being China, South Korea and Japan, was intra-industry trade of a vertical nature, involving the movement of parts and components within the same production chain to a final processing site for export to other regions. The participants of this regionalized 'Confederacy of the Value Chain' all have their relative strengths in various intermediate segments of a product chain – although China is the dominant site for final processing and then export to other parts of the world. For many products, China imports intermediates, even though it has fully developed domestic supply chains for the same, thereby showing the sheer quantum of final processing that takes place on its soil for certain categories of goods.

Even in the pre-pandemic era, both multinationals in China as well as Chinese companies themselves had begun offshoring relatively simple labour-intensive manufacturing, as well as the labour-intensive segments of more complex products, to neighbours with cheaper labour, such as Vietnam and Thailand. Such offshoring from China accelerated with the beginning of the US–China trade war, as companies sought to escape Trump's tariffs with a 'China Plus One' strategy. This strategy, first developed by Japanese MNCs, has seen companies maintaining their existing base within China for servicing the domestic market, while directing future investments towards the creation of production lines and supply chains in another country for non-Chinese markets. In the wake of the trade war, Vietnam in particular, owing to its geographical proximity to China, its skilled but cheap labour and decent industrial parks, emerged as a major beneficiary.

For this Confederacy of the Value Chain, a harmonization of regulations and standardization of market practices, via the RCEP, above and beyond what existing FTAs had already achieved, may have seemed sensible in the face of US protectionism and the decline in regional trade that set in from the beginning of the US–China trade war. After all, research shows that regional FTAs brought into force since the GFC had prevented the collapse of the region's trading prospects by lowering costs. However, whatever standardization the RCEP leads to would benefit China disproportionately – since many of its own standards with respect to intellectual property, environmental protection and employment security are most likely to be adopted, given its weight within the formulation. This, in turn, would lead to even greater regional integration on China's terms, which could be used to heighten RMB use.

In this context, it should be noted that the RCEP is the perfect foil to the BRI, in that it is an omnibus regional free trade framework suited to Beijing's interests that will mostly ride the digitally enabled trade and investment infrastructure being created via the BRI. In fact, China's commerce ministry has alluded to this synergy quite a few times in the past. Some think tanks and academics from ASEAN countries echo these sentiments. For instance, Joseph Matthews, a senior professor at the BELTEI International University in Phnom Penh, Cambodia, had this to say to *Xinhua* in June 2020 about the complementarity between the RCEP and BRI: 'Without effective communication and connectivity, the RCEP cannot flourish and economic potential cannot be utilized by partner countries.'[24] He added, 'The BRI involvement in infrastructure development and enhancing

---

[24] Pengfei, Mao, and Nguon Sovan. 'Spotlight: RCEP Agreement Could Be New Booster for Regional Development, Say Officials, Scholars.' *Xinhua*, 16 July 2020, http://www.xinhuanet.com/english/2020-07/16/c_139217953.htm.

the logistic capability of the region is a prerequisite for any further progress in the bloc.'[25]

Indeed, for most ASEAN states, participation in the RCEP is a natural corollary to becoming a part of a BRI-orchestrated supply chain and logistics architecture. This will in turn leverage 'Fourth Industrial Revolution' technologies, such as artificial intelligence (AI) and 5G networks conforming to Chinese standards of performance and transparency. And China would obviously seek to advance RMB-based loans and direct RMB-denominated investments by its companies towards those countries that are keen to situate elements of this architecture. Thus, the RCEP and BRI represent the twin prongs of a China-oriented regional integration push designed to foster the greater use of the RMB.

Beijing has, however, been somewhat canny about this prospect, by casting greater regional integration as something that would lead to the higher use of other national currencies in the region as well. Indeed, as we have seen in chapter three, several Asian countries would like to reduce their dependence on the dollar (although this is easier said than done) in order to insulate themselves from future risk-off episodes. In particular, China has sought to appease Japan, with the PBOC increasing its holdings of yen reserves since 2016. What is more, the Chiang Mai Initiative for Multilateralization (CMIM), which has built up a liquidity pool of $240 billion to aid member countries during a potential dollar liquidity squeeze, decided in May 2019 to add both yen and yuan holdings to the pool. This was a signal to member states to be more open about letting their banks and businesses increase exposure to these currencies, since greater emergency liquidity denominated in both was likely to be available. As an official statement from the CMIM on the move reveals:

---

[25] Ibid.

> Increased mutual agreements on initiatives relating to the promotion of local currency usage and a greater role for local currencies as reserve currency, local currency contributions to the CMIM may be one enhancement option.[26]

From China's perspective, heightened RMB use in the region would lead to the central banks of other RCEP members making efforts to stabilize their currencies, vis-à-vis the RMB. This would lead to greater co-movement of regional currencies, thereby reducing currency risk for those looking to lend and borrow in RMB. Greater RMB borrowings in regional countries could induce central banks to hold even more reserves in the currency in order to serve as lenders of last resort; thereby leading to even more co-movements. Over time, regional currencies could likely co-move more with the RMB than the dollar, thus leading to the emergence of a so-called RMB zone, or 'key currency area', where it would be the dominant currency.

Such a zone would exhibit what is called 'portfolio bias', wherein countries within a currency zone tend to have most of their foreign investments denominated in the dominant currency. This would allow the issuer of the dominant currency to finance very large trade deficits, as has been the case with the US for four decades now. This also helps the US keep the interest expense on its debt low. Naturally, this would all be rather useful for a future Chinese economy that seeks to depend more on internal consumption and has a huge public debt overhang.

Indeed, a key currency view of global imbalances is one explanation for why there has been no great fall in the value of the dollar, despite America running such large deficits. It's because these are offset by capital flows to the US from other countries within the zone. On the other hand, the dollar

---

[26] 'Joint Statement of the 22nd ASEAN+3 Finance Ministers' and Central Bank Governors' Meeting.' *ASEAN+3 Macroeconomic Research Office*, 2 May 2019, https://www.amro-asia.org/joint-statement-of-the-22nd-asean3-finance-ministers-and-central-bank-governors-meeting.

zone as a whole does not run a deficit anywhere near that scale with respect to other key currency areas, such as the Eurozone. Thus, it is the international financial position of the dollar zone as a whole which props up the value of the currency, rather than the individual financial position of the US.

At the time of writing, however, there was no conclusive evidence that an RMB zone has already taken shape, despite some studies to the contrary. Also, its potential size is now likely to be significantly smaller than what it could have been, if at all. After all, on 4 November 2019, during the RCEP convention held on the sidelines of the 35th ASEAN summit in Bangkok, India pulled out of the proposed pact, with Prime Minister Narendra Modi stating:

> Today, when we look around we see during seven years of RCEP negotiations, many things, including the global economic and trade scenarios have changed. We cannot overlook these changes. The present form of the RCEP Agreement does not fully reflect the basic spirit and the agreed guiding principles of RCEP. It also does not address satisfactorily India's outstanding issues and concerns. In such a situation, it is not possible for India to join RCEP Agreement.[27]

It was always a bit fanciful for India to think that it could have secured its interests in an RCEP framework whose core agenda is driven by a network of East and Southeast Asian producer economies, now led by China. The fact of the matter remains that despite India having FTAs with ASEAN, Japan and South Korea, it has not managed to become a member of the Confederacy of the Value Chain. Rather, these FTAs have led to a ballooning of India's trade deficit with members of this grouping and scant integration with

---

[27] Web Desk. 'India to Stay Out of RCEP in Its Present Form.' *Week*, 4 November 2019, https://www.theweek.in/news/world/2019/11/04/india-to-stay-out-of-rcep-in-its-present-form.html.

their value chains. No doubt, geography has played a role in this. One only has to observe the distance between China's Pearl River delta (a major manufacturing area) and Vietnam's Hanoi to understand why the latter's industrial parks have been so sought after by Chinese firms and non-Chinese MNCs looking to escape Trump-era tariffs. But equally important has been the fact that India's transaction costs continue to be higher, given its weaker infrastructure, among other things. Now, though India might be a little distant to be readily integrated into the confederacy's value chain(s), it is the closest major market to the same. This matters at a time when the intensity of trade in goods is on the decline the world over. For China, India's inclusion into the RCEP would have been a prize that besides enlarging its zone of influence would have also served as a tool to further expand the same, given the subcontinent's position in South Asia and its ties with West Asia.

Due to India's relative lack of manufacturing competitiveness vis-à-vis China in certain sectors, and its role as a nearby sink for the confederacy's exports, all its members were enthusiastic supporters of the de facto India–China FTA that the RCEP was going to be, with an early reduction of tariffs by New Delhi. India's market would have provided some compensation for even the worst-case scenario – of members decoupling from the US. Conversely, New Delhi's proposal to use 2019 as a base year for tariff reductions (as opposed to 2014, when tariffs for various goods were lower) did not receive much support within the group. Also, with the US–China trade war leading to a pile-up of industrial inventories across suppliers in the confederacy, India's bid to put in place a tariff auto-trigger mechanism for blunting possible import surges from China did not find too many takers either.

Truth be told, the confederacy was never going to agree easily to a 'two-speed RCEP', which gave these types of concessions to India – at the risk of the latter opting out. In fact, RCEP's lax rules of origin would have ensured the mass arrival of certain tariff non-exempted items to India's shores via ASEAN anyway. After all, the ASEAN–India FTA (AIFTA) is nowadays being used by Chinese exporters to circumvent Indian tariffs through re-export from ASEAN ports, while claiming significant value addition. Unsurprisingly, rules of origin were yet another sticking point in the negotiations for New Delhi.

Whatever mobile electronics manufacturing India has managed to attract from the confederacy in recent times has been chiefly on account of the anti-China tariffs it has in place, along with the lure of its own domestic market. India's acceptance of RCEP membership would have meant that it had to give up the one instrument that had worked for it. Alongside India, Australia and New Zealand were also slated to be among the net goods importers within the RCEP. But even they would have benefitted from the RCEP to the detriment of India, on account of their prowess in industrial agriculture, which could have decimated India's small-scale farms and dairies – already under pressure from other FTAs, such as the one with Sri Lanka.

At the same time, India's low-cost services sector, which enjoys a comparative advantage as compared to its counterparts in the confederacy member states, would not have got the much-desired market access that 'Act East' has been working for. It is interesting to note that even as global trade intensity in manufactured goods has been falling, trade intensity in services has been on the rise, with countries such as India poised to benefit. As such, confederacy members have been ring-fencing their services sectors with non-tariff barriers. China, in particular, imposes the greatest range of so-called technical barriers to trade against India's services exports. Hardly surprising, given Beijing's emphasis on rebalancing its economy towards consumption-supported services.

Indeed, China wants its economic rebalance to be crafted on its own terms, which is why it has sought to impose its own standards of e-commerce and data localization on the

RCEP. This too was not acceptable to India. In this matter, however, other RCEP participants were sympathetic to New Delhi. Besides the fact that India would have been a major outlet for manufacturing exports, the non-Chinese part of the confederacy also wanted India in the RCEP to counterbalance Beijing's influence.

However, with India out of the picture that option was no longer available. And without the Indian market to serve as a cushion, whatever message the confederacy was going to send to Trump, via the RCEP, stood undeniably dampened. As the Thai ambassador to India, prior to the November 2019 RCEP summit, had mused, 'An RCEP without India is not worth it and India's part of the future. The people who [talk of] leaving India out and so on, it's just posturing.'[28] He added, 'Maybe we get goods but you have to give India services... And some of India's issues that they have been facing – like rules of origin, domestic regulation in services – these issues have to be addressed.'[29]

But those issues weren't addressed, and the RCEP's overall prospects remain unclear. The onset of the pandemic saw all expectations of an early conclusion to negotiations – sans India, of course – being washed away, and it was only in August 2020 that the 15 remaining countries resumed negotiations via teleconferencing. And then, finally, on 15 November 2020, the 15 remaining members of the RCEP signed the pact via a video conference.[30]

---

[28] Laskar, Rezaul H. 'RCEP Deals Incomplete without India: Thai Envoy.' *Hindustan Times*, 2 August 2019, https://www.hindustantimes.com/india-news/rcep-deals-incomplete-without-india-thai-envoy/story-oxYyxXHDTv9wzN6llcViTN.html.

[29] Ibid.

[30] Ng, Charmaine. '15 Countries, Including Singapore, Sign RCEP, the World's Largest Trade Pact.' *Straits Times*, 15 November 2020, https://www.straitstimes.com/singapore/politics/15-countries-including-singapore-sign-rcep-the-worlds-largest-trade-pact.

Be that as it may, the fact remains that once India dropped out of the picture, the RCEP does not have the same allure it did for the likes of Japan and Australia. Rather, in the post-pandemic scenario, the two countries are seeking to work closely with India to reduce their dependence on Chinese supply chains, and have begun discussions on a Supply Chain Resilience Initiative (SCRI) involving the latter.[31] Supportive of such trilaterals, the US has itself initiated an 'Economic Prosperity Network' that aims to create an alliance of 'trusted partners', engendering industrial supply chains that do not depend on China.[32] For this purpose, America has already initiated a dialogue with India, Australia, Japan, South Korea and Vietnam. Obviously, RCEP membership will have an impact on ties with Washington, as various members of the Confederacy of the Value Chain have found out since the US–China trade war began.[33]

Trump's tariffs had led to China losing some $35 billion worth of exports between March 2018 and October 2019.[34] This in turn had a knock-on effect across the confederacy because of the vertically integrated nature of their intra-

---

[31] Dhal Samanta, Pranab. 'India–Japan–Australia Supply Chain in the Works to Counter China.' *Economic Times*, 19 August 2020, https://economictimes.indiatimes.com/news/economy/foreign-trade/india-japan-australia-supply-chain-in-the-works-to-counter-china/articleshow/77624852.cms?utm_source=contentofinterest&utm_medium=text&utm_campaign=cppst.

[32] Pamuk, Humeyra, and Andrea Shalal. 'Trump Administration Pushing to Rip Global Supply Chains from China: Officials.' *Reuters*, 4 May 2020, https://www.reuters.com/article/us-health-coronavirus-usa-china-idUSKBN22G0BZ.

[33] Takahashi, Toru. 'Subtle Threat to ASEAN: US Indifference to Indonesia and Thailand.' *Nikkei Asia*, 11 August 2021, https://asia.nikkei.com/Politics/International-relations/Biden-s-Asia-policy/Subtle-threat-to-ASEAN-US-indifference-to-Indonesia-and-Thailand.

[34] Farge, Emma. 'Trump Tariffs Cost China $35 Billion, Hurt Both Economies: U.N.' *Reuters*, 5 November 2009, https://www.reuters.com/article/us-usa-trade-china-un-idUSKBN1XF267.

industry trade, with China's suppliers seeing their exports suffer, thereby contributing to a decline in the region's trade. What is more, given the problems with China's rebalancing act and the fact that its domestic consumer cannot replace the American consumer any time soon (not least for the reasons discussed earlier in this chapter), betting solely on Beijing's strategy in the absence of India's 'buy-in' doesn't seem like a great idea any more.

In fact, the continuing exodus of foreign manufacturers from China – first, as a result of the trade war, and now due to the COVID-19 shock – is only serving to exacerbate the dominance of the country's home-grown firms in their domestic market through the acquisition of new capacities, which MNCs have exited.[35] Also, China's attempts to substitute imports of high-technology components will only serve to dampen such exports by advanced confederacy members, such as Japan and South Korea.

On the other hand, the opportunity for the lesser developed confederacy members lies in capturing the workshop activities that are leaving China in sizeable quantities for the first time in years. Despite the country's labour-cost advantage having eroded considerably since 2008, it had till recently proved remarkably successful in holding on to competitiveness in a number of industries.[36] Although the domestic market may

---

[35] Ghosh, Prince. 'The Exodus of Chinese Manufacturing: Shutting Down "The World's Factory."' *Forbes*, 18 September 2020, https://www.forbes.com/sites/princeghosh/2020/09/18/the-exodus-of-chinese-manufacturing-shutting-down-the-worlds-factory/#43ba55c0c2f2.

[36] 'Back in 2000, Chinese manufacturing labor costs averaged only 46 cents per hour – 53 times lower than the $25 per hour average in the US. Since then, Chinese manufacturing labor costs have been rising by 15.6% per year on average – faster than gains in productivity of 10.4% per year. In the US, meanwhile, manufacturing labor costs have increased 2.7% per year, while productivity growth has averaged 1.8%.' Taken from Colotla, Ian, et al. 'China's Next Leap in Manufacturing.' *Boston Consulting Group*, 13 December 2013, https://www.bcg.com/publications/2018/china-next-leap-in-manufacturing.

continue to be served by local firms, the COVID-19-related supply chain disruptions were so severe that transnational firms realized that dependency on any one geography, that is, China, could no longer be considered a prudent choice. On top of that, this particular geography seemed increasingly fraught with geopolitical risk as well. The imperative of building resilience in the face of both geographical as well as geopolitical risks meant that MNCs could no longer simply move to a neighbouring ASEAN country in 'China Plus One' mode and call it a day. The possibility that the said ASEAN country may become part of a China-dominated economic bloc could not be discounted. Unsurprisingly, a wider range of countries beyond ASEAN, including India, have become recipients of China Plus One–type investments as multinationals scramble to de-risk supply chains. In such an environment, prudence dictates that ASEAN members looking to capture offshoring from China be on the right side of America – as Vietnam has been finding out.

Angered by instances of Vietnam being used as a transhipment hub by Chinese firms looking to circumvent US tariffs, Washington imposed punitive taxes on the country in 2018[37] and threatened to do so again in 2019. This threat came in light of a surge in Vietnam's exports to the US since the beginning of the trade war. This surge saw America's trade deficit with Vietnam reaching $55.8 billion by the end of October 2019, an increase of over 41 per cent from a year ago.[38] In June 2019, Trump had labelled Vietnam as 'almost the single worst abuser of everybody' followed by US Trade Representative Robert Lighthizer telling a Senate

[37] Shira, Dezan, et al., 'Impact of U.S. Steel Tariffs on Vietnam.' *Vietnam Briefing News*, 28 May 2018, https://www.vietnam-briefing.com/news/impact-of-u-s-steel-tariffs-on-vietnam.html.

[38] United States Department of Commerce. 'Trade in Goods with Vietnam.' *Census Bureau*, https://www.census.gov/foreign-trade/balance/c5520.html.

Committee the next month that the country must move to reduce the deficit and open its market to American exports.

Generally speaking, any further escalation in US tariffs during the pandemic era would be particularly worrisome, for Vietnam is one of the few confederacy members that has a trade deficit with China. And it would see this deficit increase as a result of Chinese companies merely relocating the final processing to its soil, while exporting semi-finished and intermediate goods to their Vietnamese partners or subsidies. At the same time, serious tariffs may lead to the country's end-production processes getting shut out of the US market, which in turn could increase Vietnam's overall current account deficit as well, leading to possible balance of payments problems in the future.

Naturally, Hanoi has been scrambling to appease Washington in recent years. In order to curb the practice of Chinese goods getting re-exported from its soil by simply being relabelled as 'Made in Vietnam', the country's Ministry of Industry and Trade decided in June 2019 to impose anti-dumping tariffs on certain items from China. This move essentially pulled in the opposite direction from what the RCEP is supposed to engender with its 'regional cumulation' provision dovetailed to facilitate such exports. Clearly, not everybody is ready to jump head first into a China-led economic bloc – one without India – especially when it might lead to getting disconnected from the US market itself.

Beyond newly industrializing countries such as Vietnam, it is perhaps the Japanese who are most disappointed with India's exit. Like Vietnam, Japan too was hoping to benefit from being able to re-export Chinese manufactures to India that were still subject to New Delhi's tariff lines using the RCEP's lax rules. Indeed, reports suggest that Japan did not support India on the issues delineated above during RCEP negotiations. Moreover, given that the yen is fully convertible on the capital account, while the yuan isn't likely to be any time soon, Tokyo may have also felt that if the RCEP did indeed lead to the greater use of regional currencies, the yen probably stood to benefit more than the yuan. But without India in the picture, the RCEP may not hold the same level of utility for Japan, despite Tokyo's ratification of the treaty in June 2021. Replying to a question with respect to his country's accession to the RCEP, Hideki Makihara, Japan's deputy minister for economy, trade and industry, had said on 29 November 2019: 'We aren't thinking about that at all yet. All we are thinking of is negotiations including India.'[39]

A week later, visiting Japanese ministers would be firmly told by Narendra Modi that India had no interest in joining the RCEP. Taken together with Makihara's reply, it remains to be seen how much utility Japan gains via RCEP since its main exports to China such as machinery are exempt from tariffs anyway. Moreover, since the onset of the pandemic, Japan has been actively encouraging its manufacturing firms to leave Chinese soil. To this end, in April 2020, Tokyo announced a $2 billion package as a part of its pandemic stimulus to aid Japanese manufacturing firms to exit China and return to home soil.[40] Tokyo also earmarked another $200 million to assist Japanese firms in leaving China for a third-country destination. Incidentally, India was included in the list of relocation destinations eligible for subsidy support by Tokyo in September 2020.[41]

---

[39] Reynolds, Isabel. 'Japan Won't Sign RCEP if India Doesn't Join.' *Economic Times*, 29 November 2019, https://economictimes.indiatimes.com/news/economy/foreign-trade/japan-wont-sign-rcep-if-india-doesnt-join/articleshow/72287757.cms.

[40] Tajitsu, Naomi, et al. 'Japan Wants Manufacturing Back from China, But Breaking up Supply Chains is Hard to Do.' *Reuters*, 9 June 2020, https://in.reuters.com/article/us-health-coronavirus-japan-production-a/japan-wants-manufacturing-back-from-china-but-breaking-up-supply-chains-is-hard-to-do-idINKBN23F2ZO.

[41] Gakuto, Takako. 'Japan Adds India and Bangladesh to "China Exit" Subsidy Destinations.' *Nikkei Asia*, 4 September 2020, https://asia.nikkei.

Now, even as the RCEP's future usefulness to Japan remains uncertain, Tokyo and Washington have already moved to conclude a limited FTA of their own in 2019, which was a further signal that the confederacy members were amenable to shallow trade deals with the US to keep its ire at bay.[42] Even though the trade deal didn't address Japan's main concern – automotive tariffs – it was nevertheless accepted, given that it would help stave off pressure from the US on the nearly $70 billion deficit the latter has with the former.[43] The deal was clearly designed to be a 'win' for Washington, since Japan committed to slashing tariffs on $7 billion worth of American agricultural produce in return for some concessions on capital goods.

It was also in keeping with the US desire to increase agricultural, energy and defence exports to its allies and 'strategic partners' across the world, and amongst the confederacy, in particular. Indeed, America's global export 'basket' in the future may increasingly resemble that of Russia more than it may care to admit – and this helps partly explain continued US–Russia tensions, since they are competing for many of the same markets. In any case, during the Trump era, America had been saying that its trade friction with the rest of the world could essentially be divided into two prongs: China and automotive. Japan, on its part, probably hopes that this deal would bring the US more in sync with the Comprehensive Trans-Pacific Partnership (CPTPP), which was brought into force on 30 December 2018, and is essentially the old TPP minus the US.

---

com/Economy/Japan-adds-India-and-Bangladesh-to-China-exit-subsidy-destinations.

[42] Trump, Donald, and Shinzo Abe. 'Joint Statement of the United States and Japan.' *Office of the United States Trade Representative*, issued on 25 September 2019, https://ustr.gov/countries-regions/japan-korea-apec/japan/us-japan-trade-agreement-negotiations.

[43] United States Department of Commerce. 'Trade in Goods with Japan.' *Census Bureau*, https://www.census.gov/foreign-trade/balance/c5880.html.

As a matter of fact, key provisions of the CPTPP have already been included in the new US–Mexico–Canada trade agreement, and the US had in 2018 even expressed a willingness to consider joining the pact. What is more, American corporations have started encouraging confederacy members, such as Thailand, to join the CPTPP. Such calls are likely to find support from Japan, which may now be more focused on expanding the partnership, given that the RCEP is no longer that lucrative and the US may be open to joining the CPTPP sometime in the future.

And Tokyo certainly seems to be doing its bit to entice America. The agricultural tariff reductions extended as part of the US–Japan bilateral deal grants American farmers the same level of access as that granted to their competitors from CPTPP member states – New Zealand, Australia and Canada. And joining Japan in giving such confidence-building measures (CBMs) to the US is Vietnam, which in December 2019 stated that it was looking to bring down tariffs on a variety of American agricultural products to the same levels it imposed on other CPTPP members. This was in addition to overall Vietnamese pledges to import more US coal, natural gas and farm products to reduce the trade deficit. In July 2021, the US agreed to drop its threat to impose punitive tariffs on Vietnam with the latter pledging to abjure any deliberate currency devaluations to gain a competitive edge.[44] The US Department of Treasury agreed to drop the label of 'currency manipulator' for Vietnam, that it had accorded to the latter in December 2020, despite maintaining that the country continued to technically qualify for that appellation as per the criterion under a 2015 US law for the same.[45]

Washington would also be mighty pleased with even greater imports of American military hardware by Vietnam, an emerging defence partner, and Japan, a treaty ally, as

[44] Shira, 'Impact of U.S. Steel Tariffs on Vietnam.'

[45] Ibid.

well as other confederacy members wary of Chinese expansionism. Burgeoning US defence sales in the region will also strengthen the case being made against the use of Chinese 5G networks by its allies on grounds of maintaining interoperability and secrecy. On this matter, countries such as Vietnam would not require much prodding, since they are in any case very concerned about Beijing's ability to compromise their military networks through the deployment of cutting-edge civilian network technologies. Which is why Vietnam's national telecom company, Viettel, has painstakingly developed its own 5G wireless technology, and Hanoi is not likely to allow Huawei's 5G on its soil.

An RCEP without India is not going to be enough for China to outweigh the wariness that many of its neighbours feel towards its rising military power, which, in the wake of the pandemic, seems to have become a key facet of regional assertion. Au contraire, national security considerations are going to emerge as a major barrier to Beijing's efforts to spread its home-grown standards, and the associated software and network systems, in its vicinity – especially with the US providing encouragement for the same. For instance, Singapore, a long-standing American ally within ASEAN, has opted for European suppliers instead of Huawei to build the majority of its 5G network. So important are national security concerns becoming with respect to questions related to trade in the digital age that in August 2019 Japan decided to withhold the export of three key electronic components to South Korea, on the grounds that it would compromise the former's security. As such, both countries have been involved in a political dispute since early 2019, which has seen them withdrawing from a key bilateral intelligence-sharing pact. Obviously, a Japan–South Korea split does not augur well for attempts to expand the CPTPP, but then neither does it bode well for the sustainability of RCEP.[46]

---

[46] 'Japan Tells South Korea It Will Skip Trilateral Summit over Labor

Thus, as we can see, India's withdrawal from the partnership has led to the RCEP's diminution, with the very real possibility that existing tensions within the confederacy will lead to a truncated bloc at some point since countries may now have to choose sides between Washington and Beijing. Accordingly, China's hopes of carving out a key currency area in Asia by using the RCEP also stand diminished. Instead, the rival TPP effort, now reincarnated as the CPTPP, seemed to be gaining ground at the time of writing. The latter, in its scope, seems complementary to the Indo-Pacific security architecture envisaged by the US and sought to be energized via the maritime 'Quad' formulation, which includes, besides itself, India, Japan and Australia. The United Kingdom, which formally began talks to join the CPTPP in June 2021, expressed the hope that it could persuade the US to join as well.[47] And Australian trade minister Dan Tehan expressed the view in July 2021, that the Biden's administration's move to orchestrate a digital trade pact for all Indo-Pacific economies could be a step towards the US formally joining the CPTPP.[48] Although, some observers believe that it is unlikely that the US will join the CPTPP in the short run.[49] Be that as it may, any potential diminution of the RCEP will militate against China's attempt to create an Asia-wide

Row.' *Kyodo News*, 13 October 2020, https://english.kyodonews.net/news/2020/10/1e353a3c37e7-japan-tells-s-korea-it-will-skip-trilateral-summit-over-labor-row.html.

[47] Payne, Sebastian. 'UK Aims to Conclude Pacific Trade Group Talks by End of 2022.' *Financial Times*, 28 August 2021, https://www.ft.com/content/c0e5f8da-c327-4439-9a30-b1fa3832d56b.

[48] Bloomberg. 'Biden's Digital Trade Deal Could See US Rejoin Asia-Pacific Pact Trump Ditched.' *South China Morning Post*, 23 July 2021, https://www.scmp.com/economy/china-economy/article/3142176/joe-bidens-digital-trade-deal-could-see-us-rejoin-asia.

[49] Lee, Yen. 'Kamala Harris Is Set to Visit Southeast Asia as U.S.-China Tensions Rise. Here's What to Expect.' *CNBC*, 20 August 2021, https://www.cnbc.com/2021/08/20/vp-kamala-harris-to-visit-singapore-vietnam-amid-us-china-tensions.html.

digital zone of influence, in which its technological standards will hold sway. Taken together with the global US pushback against its ambitions, China may have to be content with its own market, plus that of a clutch of allies as outlets for its high-technology sectors.

THE HUAWEI AFFAIR: A NEW COLD WAR

The US has, however, been making it difficult for China to create high-technology products for even its own market. After all, America is also a part of the Confederacy of the Value Chain, on account of its specialization in critical components, such as semiconductors and proprietary software. It also has control over a lot of the intellectual property underpinning the production of high-technology items, which allows it to define standards across the board. And it has been using this very dominance to increase costs for China's ascent up the value chain.

A case in point would be Washington's graded war against China's Huawei, the world's largest telecommunications equipment vendor and leading 5G vendor, that began under Trump and continues under Biden. The US began its sanctions assault on Huawei and several of its subsidiaries and affiliates by putting them on the US Commerce Department's so-called 'Entity List' in May 2019, which meant that American firms could no longer conduct any sort of business with them without receiving a specific licence.[50] Fuelling the acrimony between the US and China, the White House went one step further in May 2020 to 'strategically target Huawei's acquisition of semiconductors that are the direct product of certain US software and technology' regardless of

[50] Press Trust of India. 'US Blacklists Huawei, Places It on Entity List.' *Economic Times*, 16 May 2019, https://economictimes.indiatimes.com/news/international/business/us-blacklists-huawei-places-it-on-entity-list/articleshow/69353632.cms.

where they were being produced.[51] This further constricted Huawei's sourcing of custom-made semiconductors by ensuring that its own designs could not be produced by any foundry using US-origin software or technology. And in August 2020, the Commerce Department made it clear that any use of US software or fabrication equipment to produce semiconductors for Huawei was proscribed, regardless of whose design it was, unless a licence had been obtained. The Biden presidency amended export licences for sales to Huawei in a way that made them even more restrictive in March 2021.[52] In June 2021, Biden would also sign an executive order expanding the scope of Trump-era prohibitions on US investments into Chinese companies that are suppliers to the Chinese military and are involved in the sale of surveillance equipment.[53] Naturally, Huawei featured prominently in the list of targeted firms.

While China may be the largest producer of scientific papers and has probably surpassed the US in overall R&D investment, it continues to lag behind America in key technologies such as semiconductors.[54] Semiconductor

---

51 'U.S.–China Tensions Rise as Trump Administration Moves to Cut Huawei off From Global Chip Suppliers.' *CNBC*, 15 May 2020, https://www.cnbc.com/2020/05/15/us-china-tensions-rise-as-trump-administration-moves-to-cut-huawei-off-from-global-chip-suppliers.html.

52 Freifeld, Karen. 'Biden Administration Adds New Limits on Huawei's Suppliers.' *Reuters*, 12 March 2021, https://www.reuters.com/article/us-usa-huawei-tech-idUSKBN2B3336.

53 United States, Executive Office of the President [Joseph R. Biden Jr]. 'Executive order 14032: Establishing a Federal Earthquake Risk Management Standard.' 3 June 2021, https://www.whitehouse.gov/briefing-room/presidential-actions/2021/06/03/executive-order-on-addressing-the-threat-from-securities-investments-that-finance-certain-companies-of-the-peoples-republic-of-china.

54 Mervis, Jeffery. 'NSF Rolls out Huge Makeover of Science Statistics.' *Science*, 15 January 2020, https://www.sciencemag.org/news/2020/01/nsf-rolls-out-huge-makeover-science-statistics.

chips are a major vulnerability for China's electronics and telecom industry, given that only 16 per cent of the chips used are manufactured at home. The global semiconductor shortage that began in 2020 as a result of pandemic-related supply disruptions coupled with prior stockpiling by the likes of Huawei has only served to further underline this weakness.[55] In order to reduce this obvious shortcoming, Beijing has announced a target of meeting 70 per cent of its requirements for semiconductor chips from domestic sources as a part of 'Made in China 2025'. That is, however, easier said than done because even the advanced manufacturing processes needed to produce reliable and modern chips is subject to US control. From Synopsys, Inc. and Cadence Design Systems, Inc., which lead the market for software used to design semiconductors, to companies such as Lam Research Corp. and Applied Materials, which manufacture chipmaking equipment, the US footprint is literally end-to-end in the semiconductor space.

And then there is America's geopolitical heft. In November 2019, a Dutch manufacturer of extreme ultraviolet (EUV) lithography machines withheld supplies to China's biggest contract computer chipmaker, Semiconductor Manufacturing International Corp. (SMIC), pending a renewal or extension of a licence for the same from the Dutch government. Though the Netherlands denied it, it was well understood that US pressure won the day. In October 2020, Washington stepped up pressure on SMIC by restricting its access to accessories and raw materials by making licensing mandatory for any US firm looking to supply these items to it.[56]

---

[55] The heightened demand for electronic items both for medical and recreational purposes has also been a factor in this. See: AFP. 'The Chips Are down: Why There's a Semiconductor Shortage.' *Times of India*, 1 August 2021, https://timesofindia.indiatimes.com/business/international-business/the-chips-are-down-why-theres-a-semiconductor-shortage/articleshow/84938991.cms.

[56] Pham, Sherisse. 'The United States Is Taking Aim at China's

Even many high-end chips currently being built in Chinese foundries are subject to US sanctions, as Huawei-owned fabless semiconductor company HiSilicon found out in May 2019. HiSilicon, touted as Huawei's answer to US sanctions, designs system on chips (SoCs) that have a CPU at their core developed by ARM, a UK-based company.[57] Now after Huawei's entity listing, ARM had to suspend links with HiSilicon since its proprietary designs contained US inputs. The company instructed employees to halt 'all active contracts, support entitlements, and any pending engagements' with Huawei and its subsidiaries to comply with US restrictions, and a company memo acknowledged that its designs contained 'US-origin technology'.[58]

Earlier, in October 2018, a $5.65 billion plant by Chinese company Fujian Jinhua Integrated Circuit Co. Ltd to build dynamic random access memory chips was essentially ruined when its Western partners suspended collaboration owing to US pressure, even before the plant had started production. So, even though China may have made great strides in recent years in developing key technologies and equipment for 5G communications, and produced technology services firms that have been able to innovate at a global scale, the fact remains that the US has a lead when it comes to the core technologies and subsystems that underpin this success. Even in the case of an arena such as machine learning, Chinese companies continue to depend on open-source platforms

---

Biggest Chipmaker.' *CNN*, 5 October 2020, https://edition.cnn.com/2020/10/05/tech/smic-us-sanctions-hnk-intl/index.html.

[57] A system on a chip (SoC), also referred to simply as 'chip', is an integrated circuit that integrates either all or almost all components of what is considered to be a computer. These components typically include a central processing unit (CPU), memory, input/output ports and secondary storage – all available on a microchip no larger than a coin.

[58] Lee, Dave. 'Huawei: ARM Memo Tells Staff to Stop Working with China's Tech Giant.' *BBC News*, 22 May 2019, https://www.bbc.com/news/technology-48363772.

built by the likes of Google and Microsoft. In general, the US is ahead of China in terms of AI theory development, which underpins all AI-based applications.

Influence of the US over the supply chain for high-technology items was so great that Huawei's much smaller rival ZTE was brought to its knees when it was put on the Entity List and had to come around to the terms imposed by Washington, which included coughing up a $1 billion fine for violating US sanctions on Iran and North Korea. Huawei, however, managed to weather the May 2019 entity listing better than ZTE. In the six months following the blacklisting, Huawei's smartphone business registered some 24 per cent growth, with the company also claiming it had signed 65 commercial contracts to build 5G networks, with about half of these being in European countries. The head of Huawei's 5G business claimed in November 2019: 'The entity listing has had no impact on Huawei's 5G equipment whatsoever.'[59] And: 'The performance and specification of the products with our own components will only be better.'[60]

Apparently, Huawei had diversified its supplier base enough such that it had managed to supply 3,00,000 5G base stations since its blacklisting – accounting for around 75 per cent of such units supplied in the course of 2019. Huawei also introduced the 'Mate 30' smartphone in November 2019, which was completely 'de-Americanized' as far as its hardware components were concerned. These developments

---

[59] Busvine, Douglas. 'Despite Political Headwinds, Huawei Wins 5G Customers in Europe.' *Reuters*, 15 October 2019, https://www.reuters.com/article/us-huawei-tech-europe/despite-political-headwinds-huawei-wins-5g-customers-in-europe-idUSKBN1WU2GI#:~:text=%E2%80%9CNO%20IMPACT%E2%80%9D&text=But%2C%20said%20Yang%2C%20Huawei%20had,even%20without%20U.S.%2Dsourced%20components.&text=%E2%80%9CThe%20entity%20listing%20has%20had,whatsoever%2C%E2%80%9D%20Yang%20told% 20Reuters.

[60] Ibid.

seemed to be in keeping with Huawei founder and CEO Ren Zhengfei's comments in the immediate wake of the May 2019 blacklisting, when he stated, 'The US is helping us in a great way by giving us these difficulties. Under external pressure, we have become more united than ever. If we aren't allowed to use US components, we are very confident in our ability to use components made in China and other countries.'[61]

Indeed, the Chinese seem to be using the trade war to galvanize themselves to pursue the Made in China 2025 goals more aggressively. Self-sufficiency has understandably emerged as a popular theme, with even Alibaba founder Jack Ma saying in 2018, 'If we do not master the core technologies, we will be building roofs on other people's walls and planting vegetables in other people's yards.'[62]

While the drive to attain technology independence is an admirable goal, the reality is that substituting high-end US imports will be a rather time-consuming and expensive proposition, as China will have to reinvent the wheel in many cases. The country is being projected to spend $29 billion alone on the semiconductor substitution effort alone, which will also focus on developing chips tailored to AI applications. In this domain, HiSilicon and others have even been claiming some early successes through the development of chips using open-source architecture, such as UC Berkley's RISC-V rather than ARM designs. But questions about the quality, performance and reliability of these domestic developments will persist in the eyes of foreign observers. After all, a similar endeavour by China in the late 1990s and early 2000s ended

---

[61] Kynge, James. 'Ren Zhengfei's Interview with the *Financial Times*.' *Huawei*, 24 June 2019, https://www.huawei.com/it/facts/voices-of-huawei/ren-zhengfeis-interview-with-the-financial-times.

[62] Kynge, James, Yuan Yang, and Sue-Lin Wong. 'Huawei: Still Fighting for Survival Despite Trump Truce.' *Financial Times*, 3 July 2019, https://www.ft.com/content/a6db14d8-9993-11e9-9573-ee5cbb98ed36.

in abysmal failure, despite billions of dollars being sunk in the cause.

While, Huawei may have registered appreciable growth in 2019, almost all of it came from domestic sales, with the company cornering a greater share of the Chinese market at the cost of domestic rivals. Huawei had also been quietly using legal workarounds since the entity listing to stockpile chips from some US companies.[63] However, such stockpiled chips don't last forever, and even local copies of the same produced in Chinese foundries have a limited shelf life in technological terms.

And when it came to its 5G smartphones, Huawei was in any case betting on HiSilicon-designed SoCs of the Kirin family that had been especially created for such phones. These specialized chips, however, need to be made using leading chipmaker Taiwan Semiconductor Manufacturing Company's (TSMC) cutting-edge 5 nanometre (nm) node technology in order to give Huawei 5G smartphones the edge they need over their rivals.

But America's 15 May 2020 edict, declaring that no foundry using its technology or software can process any new orders from Huawei after 15 May 2020 without a licence and must ship all prior orders by 14 September 2020, put paid to this dream.[64] It ensured that TSMC immediately stopped

---

[63] These American companies have continued selling to Huawei by citing rules that limit the US government's ability to restrict exports since de minimis provisions exempt certain products, if companies can show that 75 per cent of the work being done to create it occurs outside the US. Many American tech companies have operations outside the US that help them argue their products are exempt. Chipmakers run design bureaus around the world to support 24-hour development cycles, and many have outsourced manufacturing to Asian contractors.

[64] Kundaliya, Dev. 'TSMC Confirms Plan to Stop Supplying Chips to Huawei in Two Months.' *Computing*, 17 July 2020, https://www.computing.co.uk/news/4017925/tsmc-confirms-plan-stop-supplying-chips-huawei-months.

taking new orders from Huawei and committed to stopping all supplies to the Chinese firm by 14 September 2020. This was a devastating blow to the production prospects of Huawei's 5G phones, not to mention their competitiveness, since TSMC is the world's only chipmaker capable of producing 5 nm chips. As an aside, the best that SMIC can do currently is 14 nm node chips and, in any case, it too uses proprietary American technology. As a result, Huawei has been forced to backtrack on its handset offerings. In early August 2020, a Huawei executive admitted that the company was running out of chipsets for its phones on account of US sanctions and would have to give up on the Kirin line of SoCs altogether, because it probably wouldn't be able to get them fabricated to specifications.[65]

For a while, Huawei looked for workarounds and settled on sourcing inferior chips for its 5G phones from Taiwan's chip developer MediaTek, which too used TSMC facilities for fabricating such designs. The chip designs belonged to MediaTek, and therefore even if they were being fabricated by TSMC, this did not technically violate American sanctions. But this loophole too would be closed on 17 August 2020 by the US Commerce Department when it made it clear that no chip built using American proprietary inputs irrespective of its designer could be sold to Huawei without first obtaining a licence for the same.[66] This can be considered the veritable death knell for Huawei's 5G smartphone ambitions for the foreseeable future. In July 2021, Huawei had to launch its

[65] 'Huawei Running out of Phone Chips.' *Taipei Times*, 10 August 2020, https://www.taipeitimes.com/News/biz/archives/2020/08/10/2003741396.

[66] 'Commerce Department Further Restricts Huawei Access to U.S. Technology and Adds Another 38 Affiliates to the Entity List.' US Department of Commerce, 17 August 2020, https://www.commerce.gov/news/press-releases/2020/08/commerce-department-further-restricts-huawei-access-us-technology-and.

latest smartphone models with 4G rather than 5G, citing US restrictions as the reason.[67]

Alongside hardware, the lack of credible software replacements for US-origin products, even at the consumer end, also remains a major lacuna in China's efforts to chart an independent path. Huawei's Android smartphones are, for example, highly dependent on US cybersecurity software. What is more, the company's efforts till date to develop a domestic alternative to the Android operating system have yielded a far less stable and secure alternative. Now, even if Huawei were somehow able to plug these gaps, the fact remains that post-blacklisting, it still can't offer Google Play Store or other Google apps, which greatly diminishes its appeal to non-Chinese users. What is more, Washington has expanded its Entity List to even include Chinese apps such as WeChat and ByteDance's TikTok, both of which have immense appeal outside China. Cognizant of the US ability to circumscribe Huawei on the software side as well, Zhengfei commented in November 2019 that 'it may take two or three years for Huawei to recover from the blacklisting'. China's dependence on US-origin software, such as operating systems, of course, extends far beyond Huawei's smartphones.

Thus, America's sanctions war on 'rising' Chinese tech companies is clearly designed to diminish their international competitiveness in critical emerging sectors, such as 5G communications and AI. This is supplemented by US diplomatic outreach across its military alliances, urging partners to follow suit in abjuring Chinese high-technology systems. Indeed, Washington's strategy during the course of the trade war is to prevent any kind of Chinese 'lock in'

---

67 Browne, Ryan. 'Huawei Launches New Smartphones Without 5G as U.S. Sanctions, Chip Shortage Bite.' *CNBC*, 29 July 2021, https://www.cnbc.com/2021/07/29/huawei-p50-smartphone-launched-without-5g-as-chip-shortage-bites.html.

on a significant scale internationally, as far as the industries of the future are concerned. American lobbying has already seen RCEP signatories such as Australia and New Zealand proscribe Huawei. Washington also put significant pressure on London to follow suit, with the UK National Security Council having already recommended the same. But while the UK kept resisting such pressure throughout 2019, in July 2020 it too decided to officially shut its doors to Huawei.[68] France, it seems, will keep Huawei out by imposing restrictions that will lead to the gradual phasing out of the company's equipment from its domestic networks.[69] And though Germany has resisted US pressure to ban the Chinese tech giant outright, it has nevertheless raised the bar for participation in domestic 5G networks with respect to governance so high that the company is effectively excluded anyway. Rounding this off has been Belgium's decision to keep Huawei out of the heart of the EU as it were.[70] By January 2021, 26 out of 27 EU members had joined America's 'Clean Networks' programme, first announced in August 2020, which essentially requires a trusted network to be devoid of Chinese mobile carriers, apps, app stores, cloud storage and undersea cables – basically the entire digital stack that might be purported to be under Beijing's influence.[71]

---

[68] White, Chris. 'Britain Bans a Chinese Tech Giant From Building Out 5G Technology.' *Daily Signal*, 14 July 2020, https://www.dailysignal.com/2020/07/14/britain-bans-a-chinese-tech-giant-from-building-out-5g-technology/.

[69] Mathieu Rosemain, Gwénaëlle. 'Exclusive: French Limits on Huawei 5G Equipment Amount to de Facto Ban by 2028.' *Reuters*, 22 July 2020, https://www.reuters.com/article/us-france-huawei-5g-security-exclusive-idUSKCN24N26R.

[70] Mukherjee, Supantha, and Gwénaëlle Mathieu Rosemain. 'Huawei Ousted from Heart of EU as Nokia Wins Belgian 5G Contracts.' *Reuters*, 9 October 2020, https://in.reuters.com/article/us-orange-nokia-security-5g/huawei-ousted-from-heart-of-eu-as-nokia-wins-belgian-5g-contracts-idINKBN26U0YY.

[71] Keith Krach, Under. 'Under Secretary Keith Krach Remarks on U.S.–

Overall, China's situation has become unenviable. On the one hand, US tariff impositions are eroding its international price competitiveness in a range of old industries – and on the other, the tech sanctions are designed to prevent it from attaining scale in new industries beyond its borders. Though China accounted for 21 per cent of global value-added output from R&D-intensive industries in 2018 (America's share was 38 per cent), it is still some distance away from turning into an economy driven purely by advanced sectors.[72] According to one estimate, the country is still some 35.75 years away from reaching a stage when the value added from advanced sectors will account for 30 per cent of its GDP.[73]

Realizing that it doesn't have a particularly strong hand, Beijing has been making reconciliatory noises since early 2019 about removing restrictions on the operations of foreign firms in its market, respecting intellectual property and giving up the policy of forcing foreign companies to transfer technology in lieu of market access. For instance, in March 2019, the National People's Congress somewhat hurriedly approved a new law governing foreign investment

---

Eswatini Clean Network Declaration.' *United States Department of State*, 15 January 2021, https://2017-2021.state.gov/under-secretary-keith-krach-remarks-on-u-s-eswatini-clean-network-declaration.

[72] National Science Board. *Science and Engineering Indicators 2020: The State of U.S. Science and Engineering*. National Science Foundation, https://ncses.nsf.gov/pubs/nsb20201/https://ncses.nsf.gov/pubs/nsb20201/assets/nsb20201.pdf.

[73] '"There is still some distance from the goal of 30 per cent of GDP," said Zhang, who estimated that only when value added output reaches 30 per cent will it become the "new" engine of China's economic growth. "At this growth rate, it will take 35.75 years [to reach that goal], which obviously does not meet the demands for high-speed growth and high quality [output] in the Chinese economy."' Taken from Lee, Amanda. 'China Will Need More than 35 Years to Upgrade to Hi-Tech Manufacturing Industry, Study Finds.' *South China Morning Post*, 19 July 2019, https://www.scmp.com/economy/china-economy/article/3019316/china-will-need-more-35-years-upgrade-hi-tech-manufacturing.

that ostensibly sought to address US concerns – although its wording was dismissed as vague by foreign observers. In October 2019, Chinese Premier Li Keqiang further chose to highlight the role played by FDI in China's growth: 'Foreign capital plays a unique and important role in China's economic development. To promote high-quality development and modernization, we must always attach great importance to the use of foreign capital.'[74]

And in November 2019, China explicitly stated that it was 'aiming to reduce frequent IP violations by 2022' and 'planned to make it easier for victims of transgressions to receive compensation'. With these measures, Beijing had obviously been looking to placate major US firms as much as Washington, in order to encourage the former to lobby with the latter to ease tensions. Not that US business bodies need much motivation in this respect, given that estimates suggest that there are some $700 billion worth of US industrial assets in China, generating around $500 billion in domestic sales per year.[75]

The fact that China produces only a small fraction of its semiconductor requirements also means that its imports are of a huge magnitude, given the total amount of electronic items produced in the country. In 2018 alone it spent $260 billion on chip import, which far exceeded the $162 billion that it spent on buying crude oil from abroad. Taken together with China's other key component imports, it is not surprising that many US companies do not view the trade war too favourably. Instead, they argue that sales to China fund their R&D efforts, which allows them to stay ahead in the game.

[74] 'China to Further Utilize Foreign Investment.' *State Council*, People's Republic of China, 7 November 2019, http://english.www.gov.cn/policies/latestreleases/201911/07/content_WS5dc3de08c6d0bcf8c4c16b5e.html.

[75] Rabouin, Dion. 'The Tech War between the U.S. and China Escalates.' *Axios*, 21 September 2020, https://www.axios.com/tech-war-china-us-tiktok-feb7ab13-bd86-4cc4-bc87-c547c3962951.html

Post Huawei's entity listing, Qualcomm in particular had been lobbying for a licence to supply to Huawei, with its argument being that foreign rivals, such as Samsung and MediaTek, were unnecessarily gaining at its expense.

US consumers too have been feeling the brunt of Trump-era tariffs as a part of the higher costs passed on to them by importers. Though some of the tariff shock has been absorbed by importers themselves, it has not provided enough of a cushion to insulate consumers altogether. So, while tariff proponents may claim that it is the Chinese who are bearing the entire brunt of the tariff increases, even as the US administration collects more revenue, the fact remains that consumers have also been impacted by the trade war.

Indeed, these considerations played a role in making the US amenable to an 'interim' truce in the trade war, which became the so-called Phase I deal announced in December 2019, signed in January 2020.[76] An earlier attempt to wrap up this deal in May 2019 had failed, but this time it seemed to have resulted in an 86-page negotiated agreement. In essence, the US agreed to cancel a 15 per cent tariff that was scheduled to be imposed on 15 December 2019 on $160 billion worth of Chinese goods in the so-called List 4B and halve the existing 15 per cent tariff on $120 billion on List 4A goods. It also agreed to maintain a 25 per cent tariff on the $250 billion worth of List 1, 2 and 3 goods. In return, China agreed not to impose higher tariffs on US cars and other goods, 'to purchase more US goods and services including agricultural goods, to tighten legal protection of intellectual property rights, to promise not to force transfer

---

[76] 'Economic and Trade Agreement between the Government of the United States of America and the Government of the People's Republic of China.' *Office of the United States Trade Representative*, signed on 15 January 2020, https://ustr.gov/sites/default/files/files/agreements/phase%20one%20agreement/Economic_And_Trade_Agreement_Between_The_United_States_And_China_Text.pdf.

of technology through joint ventures, to open market access especially for financial services, and to deal with US complaints about currency manipulation'.[77]

However, this much-touted Phase I deal turned out to be a bit of a damp squib, with China buying less than 60 per cent of the US goods and services it had committed to import under the agreement during the course of 2020.[78] Meanwhile, the underlying reasons for the trade war – namely, the battle for technological and currency supremacy – are now becoming front and centre. Just as it did with Japan in the 1980s, America is quite clearly looking to thwart a modern-day Pax Sinica that will shrink its geopolitical space. Beyond the economic implications of China's desire to be proficient in emerging areas such as AI and 5G, lies the military dimension of these dual-use technologies. And though military developments can lead to commercial products entering the marketplace, the reverse is also true. This sentiment was echoed by United States Trade Representative Robert Lighthizer, who, during a US Senate Appropriations Committee hearing in July 2018, had this to say in reply to a question on whether the trade fight with China was 'stupid':

> Look, if your conclusion is China is taking over all our technology and the future of our children is a stupid fight, then you are right, we should capitulate. My view is that's how we got where we are. I don't think it's a stupid fight.[79]

---

[77] Tran, Hung. '"Phase One" Agreement: Whither the US–China Trade War?' *Atlantic Council*, 16 December 2019, https://www.atlanticcouncil.org/blogs/new-atlanticist/phase-one-agreement-wither-the-us-china-trade-war.

[78] Lobosco, Katie. 'Biden Has Left Trump's China Tariffs in Place. Here's Why.' *CNN*, 24 March 2021, https://www.cnn.com/2021/03/24/politics/china-tariffs-biden-policy/index.html.

[79] Restuccia, Andrew, and Megan Cassella. '"Ideological soulmates": How a China Skeptic Sold Trump on a Trade War.' *Politico*, 26 December 2018, https://www.politico.com/story/2018/12/26/trump-lighthizer-china-trade-war-1075221.

Simply put, AI and next-generation networks such as 5G are general purpose technologies that will simultaneously transform everyday life and the methods by which firms conduct business. They'll be as fundamental to civilization in the near future as electricity and the internet are today. Naturally, they will also shape warfare in the twenty-first century. And the ultimate guarantor of currency dominance is military dominance, something that both America and China believe flows from technological dominance. As Benoît Cœuré, member of the executive board of the ECB, speaking at the Council on Foreign Relations, New York City, observed on 15 February 2019:

> I will venture very warily into what is certainly not central bankers' territory. But empirical evidence supports the view that the US dollar benefits from a substantial security premium. Nations that depend on the US security umbrella hold a disproportionate share of their foreign reserves in dollars.[80]

So, even as final touches were being put on the trade deal in December 2019, the US was mulling over an increase in threshold limits for what can be defined as 'US origin', in order to close the loopholes Huawei had been using to source products from American firms.[81] Moreover, American legislature was also putting in place laws that effectively shut Huawei and other Chinese telecom makers out from the US market for good on national security grounds.[82] This

---

[80] Cœuré, Benoît. 'The Euro's Global Role in a Changing World: A Monetary Policy Perspective.' Speech delivered at the Council on Foreign Relations, New York City, 15 February 2019, https://www.ecb.europa.eu/press/key/date/2019/html/ecb.sp190215~15c89d887b.en.html.

[81] Fried, Ina. 'Huawei Gets a Win on U.S. Export Waivers.' *Axios*, 21 November 2019, https://www.axios.com/huawei-trade-with-united-states-0d9ce941-6c37-41d4-85cc-fd8bf5134da8.html.

[82] For example: Section 889 of the National Defense Authorization Act prohibits Huawei and others from selling certain gears in the US: 'Text

was in addition to the US adding Chinese facial recognition technology firms and institutes involved in supercomputing research to its Entity List.

Perhaps realizing that a decoupling on the tech side, to a greater or lesser extent, was inevitable, back in December 2019, Beijing ordered government offices and public institutions to 'rip and replace' up to 30 million pieces of foreign hardware – and the attendant software – with products from domestic vendors, within three years. China has also created an 'Unreliable Entity List' as a rejoinder to America's proscribing tactics, and there is every likelihood that an increasing number of American firms will be targeted in the future. These developments suggest that a 'digital iron curtain' has become a real possibility, wherein the internet as we know it will splinter into two camps, with differing standards and systems and limited interoperability between themselves. While the splinternet would be an expensive proposition for all parties, it would be especially limiting for Beijing's ambitions, since it may reduce China's competitiveness in advanced sectors for a long time to come. As Zhengfei himself observed in June 2019: 'China cannot succeed if it is

---

– H.R.5515 – 115th Congress (2017–2018): John S. McCain National Defense Authorization Act for Fiscal Year 2019.' *Congress.gov*, 13 August 2018, https://www.congress.gov/bill/115th-congress/house-bill/5515/text.

A bill in Congress, H.R. 4459, would establish funds to help smaller carriers replace their current Huawei gear with equipment not alleged to pose a national security risk: 'H.R.4459 – 117th Congress (2021–2022): SIMSA.' *Congress.gov*, 16 July 2021, https://www.congress.gov/bill/117th-congress/house-bill/4459.

President Trump signed an executive order in May declaring a national emergency and prohibiting US companies from using telecom services that are solely owned, controlled or directed by a foreign adversary: Higgins, Tucker. 'Trump Declares National Emergency over Threats against US Technology amid Campaign against Huawei.' *CNBC*, 15 May 2019, https://www.cnbc.com/2019/05/15/trump-signs-executive-order-declaring-national-emergency-over-threats-against-us-technology.html.

entirely dependent on indigenous innovation. It will waste a lot of time on indigenous innovation.'[83]

But if push comes to shove, that is what China will do, and in fact is already doing. Zhang Chi, chairman of Xin Ding Capital, put it thus during an August 2020 fundraiser for Chinese chipmaker Haigon Information Technology: 'China must promote domestic replacement to avoid being strangled, even as its current technology lags by far.'[84] As mentioned earlier, China's 'self-reliance' push is making it even less of a market for Japan, South Korea and other advanced economies. Coupled with their security concerns about the country, it is easy to see why the US-led world order is not going to evaporate overnight. A large part of the blame for this lies with China itself, naturally. Its increasingly revanchist foreign policy, backed by rising military power, has, to put it mildly, not instilled confidence in the neighbourhood. And, as detailed before, the pull of the Chinese market is not going to prove to be enough to tide over these concerns.

At the moment, Beijing has only managed to seemingly get Russia on its side, to an extent owing to the latter's own competition with the US. This has even translated into Russia dumping American treasury securities for Chinese ones.[85] Dollar holdings of the Central Bank of Russia declined from 30 per cent of total foreign exchange reserves in 2018 to 9.7 per cent in 2019, while the share of RMB-

---

[83] Holland, Tom. 'China's Wrong, the US Can Kill off Huawei. But Here's Why It Won't.' *South China Morning Post*, 27 May 2019, https://www.scmp.com/economy/china-economy/article/2188281/us-china-trade-war-was-supposed-save-american-industry-it.

[84] Shen, Samuel, and Josh Horwitz. 'In U.S.–China Tech War, Investors Bet on China's Localisation Push.' *Reuters*, 20 August 2020, https://www.reuters.com/article/us-china-market-tech-idUSKCN25G0PU.

[85] Tan, Weizhen. 'The Yuan Won't Unseat the Dollar Soon – but It Could Grow in Prominence if China Dominates in Tech and Trade.' *CNBC*, 1 September 2020, https://www.cnbc.com/2020/09/02/outlook-for-china-yuan-and-the-us-dollar-amid-tech-war-trade.html.

denominated assets rose from 2 per cent to 14 per cent in the same period.[86] In fact, it is these Russian purchases that helped the yuan clock the 2 per cent mark in global reserves holdings share. This Sino-Russian 'financial alliance' also led to the share of the dollar in trade settlements between them to fall below the 50 per cent mark in the first quarter of 2020. Payments in bilateral currencies are of course being facilitated via China's Cross-Border Interbank Payments System (CIPS) and Russia's System for Transfer of Financial Messages, which are national alternatives to SWIFT.

Apart from strategic alliances, China is also trying to provide more avenues for international investors to purchase RMB-denominated assets, by having managed to get its stock and bond markets included in global indices such as MSCI for stocks and Bloomberg Barclays for bonds. Meanwhile, the PBOC has also rolled out the world's most advanced central bank digital currency (CBDC) project known as Digital Currency Electronic Payment (DC/EP) which has already seen pilot programmes in four major Chinese cities. The DC/EP is a cash-like liability of the PBOC and it is being made available to the general public as well as foreign visitors through account-based interfaces. While it is initially meant for domestic retail use, China may try to deploy it for RMB-invoiced trade with foreign parties, thereby using it as another vector for internationalizing the yuan.

Be that as it may, the RMB still accounts for only a small fraction of global foreign exchange reserve holdings, and China continues to need the dollar for a range of international transactions, not least because its firms continue to borrow heavily in dollars and BRI counterparties wish to be advanced loans in the US's currency. As long as that is the case, China will remain subject to the financial channel of the exchange rate (see chapter three for details) and be worried about dollar liquidity from time to time which, in turn, means

---

[86] Ibid.

that it would continue to hold a large 'war chest' of dollars. Indeed, that is precisely what happened in the wake of the COVID-19 shock, which was initially another global risk-off episode that saw a huge amount of dollar liquidity rush back to the safe haven of the US. Subsequently, however, matters eased with the Fed's operationalization of various dollar-local currency swap lines with EME central banks (although not with the PBOC) and the onset of QE from March 2020. Since then, as the US–China bilateral relationship has worsened, threats to seize the PBOC's holdings of US debt and to cut off China from the dollar system altogether have emanated from Washington.[87] This has naturally unnerved the Chinese, whose attempts to internationalize the RMB are now being driven by a serious desire to cut dollar dependency. But China remains on the horns of a dilemma. As long as it keeps in place capital controls, the RMB will not be seen favourably by global investors, and as long as it is not seen favourably by global investors the country won't be able to remove capital controls because of liquidity worries. As such, the PBOC's drawdown of dollar holdings can only be gradual, subject to a variety of factors, such as progress made in RMB internationalization, the attractiveness of euro- and yen-denominated government debt and the vagaries of the US–China bilateral economic relationship in terms of trade and capital flows.

Now, even as China will find it difficult to decouple from the dollar, America will not be able to cut dependence on Chinese supply chains overnight either. While the rhetoric has been one of 'reindustrializing' America, there are actually many types of industries that simply will not return to the US, even if huge subsidies are offered. As the makers of

---

[87] Shen, Samuel, et al. 'In China, Fears of Financial Iron Curtain as U.S. Tensions Rise.' *Reuters*, 13 August 2020, https://in.reuters.com/article/us-usa-china-decoupling-analysis/in-china-fears-of-financial-iron-curtain-as-u-s-tensions-rise-idINKCN2590NJ.

'Cap America' who had offshored to China put it, '[It is] very difficult if not impossible to bring back to America because most of the major cloth mills have already relocated to other countries, sewing machine manufacturers followed them, and most of the technicians who service the machines have retired.'[88]

Post the pandemic, advanced economies will nevertheless look to create highly automated domestic lines for essential items – such as masks, for instance. An early example of this would be the Japanese company Iris Ohyama, which started mask production in the country, having availed of Tokyo's subsidy to relocate from China's Suzhou and Dalian.[89] Notably, Iris Ohyama also has plans to start manufacturing in the US, France and South Korea. Many of these new 'resilience-oriented' production lines will operate on the old 'just in case' manufacturing principle, which had been totally supplanted by 'just in time' manufacturing concepts, before the pandemic foregrounded the need for greater resilience even at the cost of some inefficiency-related losses. For example, the *Atlantic* reported the following in a March 2020 article titled 'The Modern Supply Chain Is Snapping':

> The Institute for Supply Management, which conducts monthly economic surveys, found that nearly 75 percent of the companies it contacted in late February and early March reported some kind of supply-chain disruption due to the coronavirus. And 44 percent of the companies didn't have a plan to deal with this kind of disruption.[90]

---

[88] Holland, 'China's Wrong, the US Can Kill Off Huawei. But Here's Why It Won't.'

[89] Akiyama, Hiroyuki. 'Japan Companies Line up for "China Exit" Subsidies to Come Home.' *Nikkei Asia*, 9 September 2020, https://asia.nikkei.com/Economy/Japan-companies-line-up-for-China-exit-subsidies-to-come-home.

[90] O'Leary, Lizzie. 'The Modern Supply Chain Is Snapping.' *Atlantic,* 19 March 2020, https://www.theatlantic.com/ideas/archive/2020/03/supply-chains-and-coronavirus/608329.

So, it would be reasonable to expect that large reserves of both essential raw materials and finished products will be maintained by manufacturers of essential items to cater to unanticipated events. In a related move, the US and Europe are now striving to remove their dependence on China for critical materials such as rare earths too. Beyond essential medical items and critical materials, the pandemic-era global semiconductor shortage means that America is also determined to revive its market share in global semiconductor manufacturing, which has fallen from 24 to 12 per cent over 2000–20.[91] Though the US still dominates the industry through intellectual property, the centre of gravity of the actual foundry business has shifted to East Asia and revolves around the likes of TSMC. As such, in May 2020, TSMC announced that it was going to start building a $12 billion foundry the next year in Arizona, whose main output would be the cutting-edge 5 nm chips, with the facility expected to be operational by 2024.[92] By October 2021, it was being reported that TSMC was well into building this facility which aims to churn out 20,000 wafers every month.[93] With a view to consolidating such investments, on 8 June 2021, the US Senate passed the US Innovation and Competition Act of 2021, which authorized, among other spending on advanced research into emerging technologies, $52.4 billion in federal investments for the domestic semiconductor research, design, and manufacturing provisions as enshrined

---

[91] Ioannou, Lori. 'A Brewing U.S.–China Tech Cold War Rattles the Semiconductor Industry.' *CNBC*, 18 September 2020, https://www.cnbc.com/2020/09/18/a-brewing-us-china-tech-cold-war-rattles-the-semiconductor-industry.html.

[92] Ibid.

[93] Schoolov, Katie. 'Inside TSMC, the Taiwanese Chipmaking Giant That's Building a New Plant in Phoenix.' *CNBC*, 16 October 2021, https://www.cnbc.com/2021/10/16/tsmc-taiwanese-chipmaker-ramping-production-to-end-chip-shortage.html.

in the CHIPS for America Act, passed by the US Congress earlier in 2021.[94]

At the end of the day, America is basically looking to direct where the production lines leaving China end up so as to maximize its own interests. While there will be some reshoring as we saw above, the US will use its policy power to help countries that can not only be 'trusted' on the intellectual property front but also offer contra access opportunities. Mexico, for example, fits the bill, because its supply chains are already integrated with US industries, and can export manufacturing services and specialized components for final processing lines there. America is, in a sense, looking to break up the massive trade deficit it has with China into smaller deficits with a larger number of players by making them more amenable to US exports as well.

However, both the US and Japan know that China's big advantage in the Fourth Industrial Revolution continues to be its ability to produce contemporary network equipment at scale. This in turn means that the country today has the greatest capacity to create dense internet-of-things-based networks. The denser a network the greater its value. Neither America nor Japan can match this on their own. In fact, they are acutely aware that they need a player that has the potential to reach the concentrated manufacturing scale of China in this domain. Such a player, of course, can only be India, which already manufactures more mobile phones than any other country barring China. What is more, it is also a global hub for MNCs conducting network technology R&D. These attributes have not been missed by either the US or Japan. In a report submitted to the US Congress in October 2020, America's National Security Commission on Artificial

[94] Geske, Dawn. '$52B Chip Bill Passes Senate in "Competition to Win" against China.' *International Business Times*, 9 June 2021, https://www.ibtimes.com/52b-chip-bill-passes-senate-competition-win-against-china-3221600.

Intelligence recommended that it enter into a formal AI cooperation agreement with India (as well as other Quad members) in order to win the global technology competition, and preserve open and free societies. Meanwhile, India and Japan finalized a pact to cooperate on 5G and AI during the same month as well.[95] Clearly, all eyes are on India to see if it can overcome its challenges and deliver on its potential. Given this setting, we now turn to the state of the Indian economy and the path that lies ahead.

---

[95] 'India, Japan Finalise Pact for Cooperation in 5G Tech, AI and Critical Information Infra.' *Times of India*, 7 October 2020, http://timesofindia.indiatimes.com/articleshow/78533793.cms?utm_source=contentofinterest&utm_medium=text&utm_campaign=cppst https://timesofindia.indiatimes.com/india/india-japan-finalise-pact-for-cooperation-in-5g-tech-ai-and-critical-information-infra/articleshow/78533793.cms.

EIGHT

ON A SCORCHING DAY IN MAY, TWENTY EXHAUSTED INDIVIDUALS decided to rest on the railway tracks near the village of Satana in the Indian state of Maharashtra. It was the year 2020, and they had walked 36 kilometres from the factory in Jalna (also in Maharashtra) that had let them go due to the nationwide COVID-19 lockdown declared on 23 March 2020. With the lockdown in place, which included the suspension of passenger train services, the group felt that the railway tracks were safe enough to lie on. Tragically, they were anything but, because even though passenger trains that could have otherwise taken them to their native place in the state of Madhya Pradesh were not running during the lockdown, the goods trains were. Sixteen of the 20 were mowed down, while the remaining four barely managed to escape. The incident laid bare the breadth of the human tragedy that the pandemic-related lockdown had engendered. Survivor Sajjansingh Dhurve recollected the incident:

> We were exhausted and sat on the track to drink water. Some of us chatted before dozing off. The train arrived soon after and ran over most of my mates. Four of us heard their cries and woke up, and barely managed to jump aside.[1]

---

[1] Akhef, Mohammad. 'Maharashtra: 16 Die as Train Runs over Tired Migrants Sleeping on Tracks.' *Times of India*, 9 May 2020, https://timesofindia.indiatimes.com/india/16-die-as-train-runs-over-tired-migrants-sleeping-on-tracks/articleshow/75636960.cms.

Dhurve and his compatriots were part of at least 10.6 million Indian migrant workers, who, finding themselves unemployed in an instant due to the hastily declared 'stay in place' lockdown, chose to make their way home by whatever means possible, including walking hundreds of kilometres, in the peak of summer.[2]

Later, in September 2020, while answering a parliamentary question related to the number of migrants who may have perished in the process of trying to reach their homes, the government would say that it did not have specific figures for the same.[3] However, it did disclose at the time, albeit provisionally, that there had been some 81,385 accidents on Indian roads during March–June 2020 that had resulted in 29,415 fatalities.[4] When that figure is placed alongside the number of those who died of thirst, hunger and exhaustion, the quantum of desperate journeying migrants who did not actually make their way back home in April–May 2020 is not likely to be insignificant. In any case, those 10.6 million homesick migrants were only a fraction of an estimated 121 million who lost their jobs in the wake of the March 2020 lockdown.[5] While the lockdown was necessary to avoid the virus from ripping through India and to buy time for the healthcare sector to prepare, it is undeniable that the preventive measure itself precipitated a colossal human tragedy, in the form of the migrant exodus across India's urban landscape.

---

[2] Ministry of Road Transport and Highways, Government of India. 'Death of Migrant Workers in Road Accidents.' *Lok Sabha, Parliament of India*, 22 September 2020, http://164.100.24.220/loksabhaquestions/annex/174/AU2044.pdf.

[3] Ibid.

[4] Ibid.

[5] Vyas, Mahesh. 'Job Losses in White and Blue Collar Workers.' *Centre for Monitoring Indian Economy*, 14 September 2020, https://www.cmie.com/kommon/bin/sr.php?kall=warticle&dt=2020-09-14%20 21:47:53&msec=416.

The impact on the Indian economy was also quick and severe, with demand collapsing for several sectors during the lockdown. As an initial mitigative measure, New Delhi had announced a $22.5 billion stimulus package (called the Pradhan Mantri Garib Kalyan Package [PMGKP]) on 26 March 2020[6] that included in its ambit free rations for some 800 million citizens for a period of three months, some meagre transfers ranging from ₹1,000–1,500 ($13–20) for some 230 million citizens, insurance for health workers and a ₹20 increase in the wages for the Mahatma Gandhi National Rural Employment Guarantee Act (MREGA) work programmes. But this was obviously a pittance compared to the demand destruction taking place. With both Indian industry and states clamouring for stimulus measures to save India's economy, the Modi government would unveil a ₹20 lakh crore (just over $280 billion) second stimulus measure called 'Atmanirbhar Bharat Package' (later called 'Atmanirbhar Bharat Package 1.0' or simply ABP 1.0 since more similarly titled packages would be launched) on 12 May 2020.[7] While seemingly substantial, this package flattered to deceive. The package included in its ambit various liquidity support measures taken by the Reserve Bank of India (RBI) as well as government loan moratoriums and credit guarantees, with actual stimulus spending by New Delhi being only a small fraction of the total package.

On the face of it, the total size of the package was equivalent to 10 per cent of India's nominal GDP, but the immediate fiscal spending component in it amounted to a mere 1 per

---

[6] Choudhury, Saheli Roy. 'India Announces $22.5 Billion Stimulus Package to Help Those Affected by the Lockdown.' *CNBC*, 26 March 2020, https://www.cnbc.com/2020/03/26/coronavirus-india-needs-a-support-package-larger-than-20-billion-dollars.html.

[7] 'Aatma Nirbhar Bharat Package – Progress So Far.' *Press Information Bureau, Ministry of Finance, Government of India*, 1 October 2020, https://pib.gov.in/PressReleasePage.aspx?PRID=1660691.

cent of the same.[8,9,10] The ABP 1.0, which included the earlier PMGKP allocation, did not see any kind of direct transfers to micro, small and medium enterprises (MSMEs) struggling to stay afloat during the lockdown.[11] What the MSME sector instead got was the promise of emergency liquidity support from banks with loans guaranteed by the government. Meanwhile, the government had announced that they would take care of employer and employee PF contributions for firms with less than 100 employees, but businesses said that this relief measure was of little help considering how they were struggling to sustain basic operations.[12,13] At the time, ABP 1.0 was less than half of what India's emerging economy

---

[8] Choudhury. 'India Announces $22.5 Billion Stimulus Package to Help Those Affected by the Lockdown.'

[9] Merwin, Radhika. 'Why the ₹20-Lakh Crore Stimulus Adds up to Just ₹2-Lakh Crore Direct Impact.' *BusinessLine*, 19 May 2020, https://www.thehindubusinessline.com/portfolio/news-analysis/why-the-20-lakh-crore-stimulus-adds-up-to-just-2-lakh-crore-direct-impact/article31620474.ece. Accessed 10 August 2021.

[10] PTI. 'Total Fiscal Impact of "Rs 20L Cr Package" to Be Rs 1.50 Lakh Cr: Report.' *Economic Times*, 17 May 2020, https://economictimes.indiatimes.com/news/economy/finance/total-fiscal-impact-of-rs-20l-cr-package-to-be-rs-1-50-lakh-cr-report/articleshow/75789230.cms. Accessed 10 August 2021.

[11] PTI. 'Rs 20 Lakh Crore Economic Stimulus Package Includes Rs 8 Lakh Crore Liquidity Measures by RBI: FM.' *Deccan Herald*, 17 May 2020, https://www.deccanherald.com/business/economy-business/rs-20-lakh-crore-economic-stimulus-package-includes-rs-8-lakh-crore-liquidity-measures-by-rbi-fm-838626.html.

[12] Punj, Shweta. 'Further Delay in Stimulus for MSMEs Can Jeopardise India's Growth Story.' *India Today*, 5 May 2020, https://www.indiatoday.in/business/story/delay-in-stimulus-for-msmes-can-jeapordise-india-s-growth-story-1674457-2020-05-05.

[13] India's labour participation rate is down from 45–46 per cent before demonetization in 2016 to about 36 per cent now. According to a labour ministry report (2015–16), the ratio of blue-collar to white-collar workers is 78:22, with blue-collar workers employed largely in machine operations, transportation, production, equipment cleaning, etc.

peers had spent as a proportion of their GDP on average, to mitigate the impact of the pandemic.[14] The government seemed to be exercising fiscal prudence at a time when revenue collection was dwindling due to the lockdown, as evidenced by the steep fall in GST collections during April–May 2020.[15]

In fact, it would turn out that government spending under 'defence and public administration' actually declined by 10 per cent during the April–June quarter of financial year (FY) 2020–21.[16] Clearly, the government was rejigging its outlay wherever it could rather than give flat out stimulus. Nevertheless, overall public expenditure did rise by 16 per cent during April–June 2020. But this did not provide enough of a cushion to dampen the effect of the lockdown on India's GDP, which contracted by 24.4 per cent on a year-on-year basis during the first quarter of 2020.[17,18] Barring

---

[14] FE Bureau. 'Stimulus of Barely 2% of GDP Offset by Spending Rejig.' *Financial Express*, 13 November 2020, https://www.financialexpress.com/economy/stimulus-of-barely-2-of-gdp-offset-by-spending-rejig/2127652/.

[15] Jayaswal, Rajeev. 'GST Revenue Fell 56% in April–May.' *Hindustan Times*, 16 June 2020, https://www.hindustantimes.com/india-news/gst-revenue-fell-56-in-april-may/story-E9dDKDTxL1BLcM1nWdMcAM.html.

[16] Kumar, Nirbhay. 'Defence, Public Admin GVA Shrank 10% in Q1 despite China Border Threat.' *Business Today*, 31 August 2020, https://www.businesstoday.in/latest/economy-politics/story/defence-public-admin-gva-shrank-10-percent-in-q1-despite-china-border-clash-271650-2020-08-31.

[17] 'India's Economy Contracts by 23.9%, Worst in Decades.' *Hindustan Times*, 31 August 2020, https://www.hindustantimes.com/india-news/india-s-gdp-growth-rises-falls-by-23-9-per-cent-in-april-june-quarter/story-Yj1GGTR7fuHAQ6QNL0jpBL.html.

[18] This has been subsequently revised downwards to 23.8 per cent. 'India's GDP Growth Slows to 5.4% in Q3, Estimated to Rise 8.9% in FY22.' *Business Standard*, 22 February 2022, https://www.business-standard.com/article/economy-policy/india-s-gdp-grows-5-4-in-q3-estimated-to-rise-8-9-in-fy22-122022801077_1.html.

Peru and Macau, no other economy would contract by the same percentage during the same period. Indeed, India was easily the worst affected major economy during the first quarter of FY 2020–21 on account of national lockdowns, and various international entities at the time predicted double-digit contraction in India's GDP for that period.[19] With hardly any direct income support being provided, in June 2020 it was reported that 30 per cent of India's urban population was likely to drawdown its lifetime savings by the end of the month since it was becoming increasingly difficult to meet essential consumption.[20] The damage to household balance sheets was becoming rather palpable.

Assessing that India could ill-afford a prolonged lockdown, New Delhi began lifting lockdown measures in phases from June 2020 onwards, even though daily COVID-19 cases were on the rise at the time. By August 2020, economic activity had resumed sufficiently for many of the estimated 121 million who had become unemployed virtually overnight to regain their jobs.[21] This was reflected in the decline in the unemployment rate, which fell below 7 per cent by September 2020 from over 20 per cent in April 2020.[22] The migrant crisis had once again revealed the critical role that short-term 'out of state' workers play in the Indian economy, and businesses were clamouring for their return. Whether it be the loading of salt at Kandla port for export or the construction of luxury

---

[19] The financial year stretches from April 2020 to March 2021.

[20] Rao, Ganesh, Praveen Ravi and Vishnu Padmanabhan. '139 Million People across Indian Cities Likely to Run out of Savings by Month-End.' *Mint*, 16 June 2020, https://www.livemint.com/news/india/139-million-people-across-indian-cities-likely-to-run-out-of-savings-by-month-end-11592205172025.html.

[21] Vyas. 'Job Losses in White and Blue Collar Workers.'

[22] 'Unemployment Rate Falls to 6.67% in September from 8.35% in August: CMIE.' *Business Today*, 5 October 2020, https://www.businesstoday.in/current/economy-politics/unemployment-rate-falls-to-667-in-september-from-835-in-august-cmie/story/417890.html.

condos in Hyderabad, migrant workers, quite simply, were indispensable. Indeed, governments of the southern Indian states, some of whom have enacted 'sons of soil' legislations that reserve jobs for locals, seemed to fall over each other in their bid to woo migrant labourers from states such as Bihar back to their erstwhile sites of work once lockdown restrictions began to be lifted. But, while most migrants may have returned by September 2020, many had not. This was partly reflected in the fact that India's labour force participation rate (LFPR) declined subsequent to the COVID-19-induced lockdowns, with many either unwilling or unable (on account of business closures) to return to their sites of previous employment.[23] Indeed, the headline unemployment rate falling below 7 per cent in September 2020 was not as comforting as one might have thought it to be, since it had been accompanied by a decline in the number of people actively looking for work.[24] This, combined with the estimated loss of nearly 6 million white-collar jobs during the 2020 lockdowns, meant that no broad-based recovery in demand was happening during that period.[25]

It was true that pent-up demand for some manufacturing sectors had nevertheless built up. For instance, automobile output witnessed year-on-year growth for the first time in

---

[23] At 40.7 per cent, India's Labour Participation Rate was considerably lower than the 42 per cent or more registered before the lockdown. See: Vyas, Mahesh. 'Impact of Lockdown on Labour in India.' *Indian Journal of Labour Economics*, Volume 63, Number 1, 2020, pp. 73-77, https://link.springer.com/article/10.1007/s41027-020-00259-w.

[24] Nanda, Prashant. 'Unemployment Rate Falls in September, but It's Deceptive, Says CMIE.' *Mint*, 2 October 2020, https://www.livemint.com/news/india/unemployment-rate-falls-in-september-but-it-s-deceptive-says-cmie-11601625253329.html.

[25] Nanda, Prashant. '6 Million White-Collar Workers Lost Their Jobs during the Lockdown.' *Mint*, 17 September 2020, https://www.livemint.com/news/india/almost-6-million-white-collar-workers-lost-jobs-between-may-august-2020-cmie-11600358442931.html.

months in September 2020, as the pendulum swung towards a desire for personal mobility once again, given the restrictions on public transport, not to mention the perceived risk. This helped push the September 2020 purchaser's manufacturing index (PMI) to expansionary territory.[26] However, not all sectors were showing growth in capacity utilization. And unsurprisingly, contact-intensive services continued to register negative growth on a year-on-year basis. Despite the removal of lockdown restrictions, economic conditions remained quite weak, as evidenced by various high-frequency indicators (HFIs), with a report from India's central bank speaking of significant retrenchment in the economy.[27]

To shore up flagging aggregate demand there were wide-ranging calls for fresh fiscal stimulus from various quarters including the IMF.[28] In fact, the IMF was echoing an earlier call made by it in July 2020 for greater stimulus by New Delhi, observing that India had the fiscal space to provide more 'above the line' support.[29] But the cumulative deficit had crossed its annual budgeted target within the first four months of FY 2020–21.[30] And the central government had

---

[26] Nahata, Pallavi. 'India's Manufacturing PMI Surges To The Highest In Over Eight Years.' *BloombergQuint*, 1 October 2020, https://www.bloombergquint.com/economy-finance/manufacturing-pmi-surges-to-the-highest-in-over-eight-years.

[27] 'High Frequency Indicators Point to Retrenchment in Economic Activity: RBI Report.' *BusinessLine*, 25 August 2020, https://www.thehindubusinessline.com/economy/high-frequency-indicators-point-to-retrenchment-in-economic-activity-rbi-report/article32437197.ece.

[28] ANI. 'IMF: India Needs More Stimulus to Battle Covid Impact.' *Times of India*, 11 September 2020, https://timesofindia.indiatimes.com/business/india-business/india-needs-more-stimulus-to-battle-covid-impact-imf/articleshow/78053276.cms.

[29] Kelkar, Nachiket. 'IMF Sees Scope for More Monetary and Fiscal Stimulus in India.' *Week*, 29 July 2020, https://www.theweek.in/news/biz-tech/2020/07/29/imf-sees-scope-for-more-monetary-and-fiscal-stimulus-in-india.html.

[30] Swamy, Manasi. 'Central Government spending curtailed.' *CMIE*, 3 October

already borrowed more than half of its record borrowing target of ₹12 lakh crore for FY 2020–21 by September 2020 itself.[31] The government was also apparently waiting for the economy to open up more before it gave a stimulus package so that the money would actually be spent.[32]

By October 2020, though, a combination of pent-up and festival demand would lead to heightened spending, which in turn would further boost GST collections that had already returned to growth on a year-on-year basis by September 2020.[33] With GST collections on the rise, the economy mostly reopen, and a comfortable external balance marked by 'search for yield' foreign portfolio inflows, New Delhi once again seemed to be warming up to the idea of fresh stimulus to aid recovery. To begin with, New Delhi announced a small interim stimulus on 12 October 2020 called ABP 2.0, amounting to about 0.1 per cent of GDP that consisted of payment of cash vouchers in lieu of leave travel concession (LTC) and a special festival cash advance to government employees.[34] However, this

---

2010, https://www.cmie.com/kommon/bin/sr.php?kall=warticle&dt=2020-10-03%2022:23:09&msec=516.

31 Special Correspondent. 'Government Retains ₹12-Lakh-Crore Borrowing Plan.' *The Hindu*, 30 September 2020, https://www.thehindu.com/business/Economy/govt-retains-12-lakh-cr-borrowing-plan/article32735916.ece.

32 PTI. 'Government May Look at Second Stimulus Once Covid Infections Ebb: Expenditure Secy.' *Times of India*, 25 August 2020, https://timesofindia.indiatimes.com/business/india-business/government-may-look-at-second-stimulus-once-covid-infections-ebb-expenditure-secy/articleshow/77742728.cms.

33 Jayaswal, Rajeev. 'September's GST Revenue Best of This Fiscal as Business Activity Picks up.' *Hindustan Times*, 1 October 2020, https://www.hindustantimes.com/business-news/september-s-gst-revenue-best-of-this-fiscal-as-business-activity-picks-up/story-esloAJGR9cKe95wxbunxpI.html.

34 PTI. 'India Inc. Welcomes Govt Stimulus to Boost Demand.' *Economic Times*, 12 October 2020, https://economictimes.indiatimes.com/news/economy/policy/india-inc-welcomes-govt-stimulus-to-boost-demand/articleshow/78624414.cms.

was hardly going to move the demand needle.[35] Notably, there was no announcement on direct income support for either private households or firms, although it was well understood that it was the one thing that could rekindle economic activity. Sample this statement from the IMF's chief economist, Gita Gopinath, in October 2020:

> What we are seeing around [the] world is that these direct support measures—which put income in the hands of low-income houscholds or into SMEs—seem to have a much bigger impact in terms of bringing back a faster recovery.[36]

Stimulus advocates also feared that whatever recovery was happening in the economy could stall once the pent-up demand petered out and firms had rebuilt inventories. Seemingly cognizant of the situation, government functionaries started making noises about a fresh stimulus package to aid the economy's recovery.[37,38] This fresh package, dubbed ABP 3.0, would be announced on 15 November

---

[35] Das, Koustav. 'Explained: Why Latest Stimulus Lacks Firepower to Boost Festive Season Demand.' *India Today*, 16 October 2020, https://www.indiatoday.in/business/story/festive-season-stimulus-lacks-firepower-to-boost-demand-economy-moodys-1732121-2020-10-16.

[36] Warrier, Panchami. 'IMF's Gita Gopinath Says India Has Scope For More Fiscal Stimulus Despite Constraints.' *BloombergQuint*, 15 October 2020, https://www.bloombergquint.com/economy-finance/imfs-gita-gopinath-says-india-has-scope-for-more-fiscal-stimulus-despite-constraints.

[37] ANI. 'India Stimulus Package: Government Working on Another Stimulus Package, Says Finance Secretary.' *Times of India*, 2 November 2020, https://timesofindia.indiatimes.com/business/india-business/government-working-on-another-stimulus-package-finance-secretary/articleshow/78991878.cms.

[38] 'Finance Minister to Announce Next Stimulus Package Soon: DEA Secretary Tarun Bajaj.' *Times of India*, 3 November 2020, https://timesofindia.indiatimes.com/business/india-business/finance-minister-to-announce-next-stimulus-package-soon-dea-secretary-tarun-bajaj/articleshow/79021766.cms.

2020. But yet again, ABP 3.0 would be made up in the main of old capital expenditure schemes and an extension of the credit guarantee schemes given in ABP 1.0, with insubstantial direct income support. Altogether, this third package would take the total budgetary impact of COVID-19 related stimulus spending to about 2 per cent of GDP, still shy of the average 2.5 per cent that had been spent by other emerging economies by then.[39] It was observed that even this spending was being offset by drawdowns under other heads and it was feared that the government would not actually end up exceeding its budget estimates for total expenditure in FY 2020–21.[40]

Perhaps the government was taking comfort in the fact that the removal of the lockdown conditions had seen a greater-than-anticipated revival of economic activity in the country. India's GDP contracted by 7.3 per cent in the second quarter of FY 2020–21, a figure that was lower than even what a first-ever RBI 'Nowcast', which is basically a short-term prediction based on HFIs available more frequently than official statistics obtained after a couple of months, had predicted.[41,42] Indications were that the Indian economy would return to growth on a year-on-year basis in the third quarter of FY 2020–21 itself, a full three months earlier than

---

[39] FE Bureau. 'Stimulus of Barely 2% of GDP Offset by Spending Rejig.' *Financial Express*, 13 November 2020, https://www.financialexpress.com/economy/stimulus-of-barely-2-of-gdp-offset-by-spending-rejig/2127652/.

[40] Ibid.

[41] 'India's GDP Grows 1.6% in Fourth Quarter, Contracts 7.3% in FY21.' *Business Standard*, 31 May 2021, https://www.business-standard.com/article/economy-policy/india-s-gdp-growth-slows-to-1-6-in-fourth-quarter-contracts-7-3-in-fy21-121053101001_1.html.

[42] Soni, Mallika. 'India in Historic Recession, RBI 'Nowcast' Shows.' *Hindustan Times*, 12 November 2020, https://www.hindustantimes.com/business-news/india-in-historic-recession-rbi-nowcast-shows/story-FWFuI0qxhkUJgkHjWhR7dL.html.

expected. As such, by early 2021, various global agencies too began to revise upwards their growth outlook for the Indian economy during FY 2020–21.[43] While after the first-quarter figures most had estimated the Indian economy would contract by around 10 per cent during the financial year, international estimates now put that figure in the 6–7 per cent range. These better-than-earlier estimates for the severity of the COVID-19 shock were accompanied with projections of a sharp rebound in growth for FY 2021–22. The Indian government itself projected that India's economy could shrink by 7.7 per cent due to the COVID-19 shock in FY 2020–21, and believed that it could rebound by 11 per cent in the next financial year.[44] The RBI made similar estimates, with its forecast for FY 2020–21 being a 7.5 per cent contraction and a growth rate of 10.3 per cent in FY 2021–22.[45] These official estimates for FY 2020–21 at least seemed on the mark, with the economy registering a positive year-on-year GDP growth of 0.5 per cent during the third quarter of that period.[46]

By January 2021, the number of COVID-19 cases were dwindling and the mood had apparently brightened enough for Modi to say at Davos that 'the country has saved humanity from a big disaster by containing corona effectively' during

[43] For example: PTI. 'Moody's Ups GDP Growth Forecast to 13.7% in FY22.' *Times of India*, 26 February 2021, https://timesofindia.indiatimes.com/business/india-business/moodys-ups-gdp-growth-forecast-to-13-7-in-fy22/articleshow/81221253.cms.

[44] *Economic Survey 2020–21: Volume 2,* Ministry of Finance, Government of India, https://www.indiabudget.gov.in/economicsurvey/doc/echapter_vol2.pdf.

[45] 'RBI Revises Real GDP Growth Projection For 2020–21 To -7.5%.' *NDTV Profit*, 4 December 2020, https://www.ndtv.com/business/7-5-real-gdp-growth-projected-for-2020-21-says-rbi-2334040.

[46] 'India's GDP Grows 8.4% in Second Quarter of FY22 vs 7.4% Contraction Last Year.' *Times of India*, 30 November 2021, https://timesofindia.indiatimes.com/business/india-business/indias-gdp-grows-8-4-in-second-quarter-of-fy22/articleshow/88006507.cms.

a late January address to the World Economic Forum.[47] His finance minister, N. Sitharaman, in turn attributed the brightening mood to having 'spent, spent, spent', since the actual fiscal deficit for FY 2020–21 was projected to reach 9.3 per cent of GDP instead of the budgeted 3.5 per cent.[48] However, this widening of the fiscal deficit was led more by a shortfall in tax revenues than a rise in expenditure. Moreover, the contraction in nominal GDP, which turned out to be greater than what had been projected in the advanced estimates, had also contributed significantly to it. Be that as it may, above-the-line measures in support of poor households continued to represent only a fraction of the heightened spending. This was not surprising since ABP 2.0 and 3.0 did not focus on direct transfers. Even the much-touted increase in capital expenditure as reflected by the revised estimates would turn out to be lower when the actual figures came out in May 2021. As feared, there was a gap between what was being projected and what was actually spent.

Back in March 2021, with cases at their lowest levels, a mood of triumphalism seemed to be setting in at New Delhi. What with India exporting millions of vaccines under its 'Vaccine Maitri' programme and the health minister declaring that India was in the 'end-game of the pandemic'.[49] It certainly seemed as if the government felt that India had left COVID-19 behind for good and it could re-embark on a path of fiscal consolidation. This was reflected in the budget

---

47 'PM's Address at the World Economic Forum's Davos Dialogue.' Prime Minister's Office, 28 January 2021, www.pmindia.gov.in/en/news_updates/pms-address-at-the-world-economic-forums-davos-dialogue.

48 '"We Have Spent, We Have Spent, We Have Spent": Finance Minister On Budget.' *NDTV*, 1 February 2021, https://www.ndtv.com/india-news/nirmala-sitharaman-on-budget-2021-we-have-spent-we-have-spent-we-have-spent-2361283. Accessed 10 August 2021.

49 'Covid-19: How India Failed to Prevent a Deadly Second Wave.' *BBC News*, 18 April 2021, https://www.bbc.com/news/world-asia-india-56771766.

estimates for total expenditure in FY 2021–22 which were just a little bit over what had been spent in FY 2020–21, with revenue spending actually projected to decline from a year ago.[50] Clearly, stimulus measures were being dialled back.

And then the tragic second wave struck India in April 2021. The second wave, caused primarily by the so-called Delta variant,[51] proved devastating for India in terms of the sheer number of fatalities it inflicted on the population. Modi resisted declaring a nationwide lockdown and instead left it to the states to do the same, while urging them to use lockdowns only as a 'last resort'.[52] More importantly, the government was also compelled to extend the stimulus measures it had been thinking of withdrawing.[53] Nevertheless, the decision to not impose another severe lockdown despite the mounting fatality figures and the continuation of stimulus measures contributed to the economic impact of the second wave being far more muted than the first. As it turned out, India's economy managed to grow by 20.1 per cent on a year-on-year basis during the first quarter of FY 2021–22.[54]

---

[50] Pattanayak, Banikinkar. 'Chunky Spend: Capex to See Sharp Hike Again in FY23.' *Financial Express*, 10 December 2021, https://www.financialexpress.com/economy/capex-to-see-sharp-hike-again-in-fy23/2385762/.

[51] Dutt, Anonna. 'Delta Caused 82% Covid Cases in 3 Months: Data.' *Hindustan Times*, 31 July 2021, https://www.hindustantimes.com/india-news/delta-caused-82-covid-cases-in-3-months-data-101627670776015.html.

[52] 'Use Lockdowns Only as Last Resort: PM to States.' *Hindustan Times*, 20 April 2021, https://www.hindustantimes.com/india-news/use-lockdowns-only-as-last-resort-pm-to-states-101618945213238.html.

[53] 'Govt Unveils ₹6.28 Lakh Cr Stimulus Post Second COVID Wave.' *The Hindu*, 29 June 2021, https://www.thehindu.com/business/Economy/nirmala-sitharaman-unveils-new-covid-recovery-package-expands-credit-relief/article35020572.ece.

[54] Magazine, Aanchal. 'Q1 Growth Rate 20.1%, Real GDP Still below Pre-Covid Level.' *Indian Express*, 31 August 2021, https://indianexpress.com/article/business/economy/india-q1-april-june-gdp-live-updates-gross-domestic-product-data-7479976/.

This was, however, lower than what would have happened had there been no second wave at all. And despite this 'world beating' growth, the fact that the economy had contracted by 24.4 per cent in the same quarter a year earlier meant that India's GDP still remained some 9.2 per cent lower than what it was during the first quarter of FY 2019–20, that is, two years prior.[55]

In the second quarter of FY 2021–22, the economy would post a real GDP growth rate of 8.4 per cent on a year-on-year basis.[56] This was broadly in line with median estimates made by private economists and the RBI based on HFIs suggesting that growth would be in the 7–9 per cent range for this period.[57,58] Though GDP for the second quarter of FY 2021–22 exceeded India's output for the corresponding period in FY 2019–20, the Indian economy was still a shade under the level it had attained by the end of September 2019, that is, at the half-yearly mark.[59]

Stepping beyond headline GDP growth figures, if one were to look at the various components of aggregate demand,

---

[55] Ibid.

[56] 'India GDP Highlights: India's GDP Expands 8.4% in July–September Quarter; Economists See Some Challenges Ahead.' *Financial Express*, 30 November 2021, https://www.financialexpress.com/economy/india-gdp-live-q2-india-economic-growth-report-card-lockdown-goods-services-agriculture-manufacturing-core-sector/2379048/.

[57] Suneja, Kirtika. 'GDP Boosted by Base Effect and Vaccination, Economists Peg Q2 Growth at 6.5–9.9%.' *Economic Times*, 20 December 2021, https://economictimes.indiatimes.com/news/economy/indicators/gdp-boosted-by-base-effect-and-vaccination-economists-peg-q2-growth-at-6-5-9-9/articleshow/87616639.cms.

[58] 'Indian Economy Likely to Grow 7.7% in Jul–Sep Led by Multi-Speed Recovery: ICRA.' *Mint*, 21 October 2021, https://www.livemint.com/economy/indian-economy-to-grow-7-7-in-jul-sep-led-by-multi-speed-recovery-icra-11634805495616.html.

[59] 'Q2 GDP Growth at 8.4%, Government Sees Double-Digit Rise in FY22.' *Times of India*, 1 December 2021, https://timesofindia.indiatimes.com/business/india-business/q2-gdp-growth-at-8-4-government-sees-double-digit-rise-in-fy22/articleshow/88017212.cms.

the all-important measure of private final consumption expenditure (which is the single largest component of GDP on the expenditure side in India) remained significantly below pre-pandemic levels even after the second quarter of FY 2021–22.[60] Although, with half of India's eligible population vaccinated and active cases at their lowest in months, personal mobility had improved considerably by late 2021.[61] This was also reflected by a rise in various 'alternative' high-frequency indicators, such as footwear sales, city billboard usage, product and services advertisements, travel-related searches, and demand for smartphones, which serve as proxies for gauging consumer mobility and confidence.[62] According to the Confederation of All India Traders, Diwali 2021 apparently recorded the highest annual sales ever for that particular festive season.[63]

While these trends seem encouraging, it is suspected that Diwali spending was driven by well-off households and a result of some pent-up demand.[64] Indeed, while items of

---

[60] 'Press Note on Estimates of Gross Domestic Product for the Second Quarter (July–September) 2021–2022.' *Ministry of Statistics and Programme Implementation*, Government of India, 30 November 2021, http://mospi.nic.in/sites/default/files/press_release/PRESS_NOTE-Q2_2021-22N.pdf.

[61] PTI. 'Half of India's Adult Population Fully Vaccinated: PM Says Important to Keep up Momentum.' *The Hindu*, 6 December 2021, https://www.thehindu.com/news/national/half-of-indias-adult-population-fully-vaccinated-pm-says-important-to-keep-up-momentum/article37861334.ece.

[62] Menon, Shailesh. 'How Strong Is the Economic Recovery? Economists Go the Extra Mile to Find Out.' *Economic Times*, 6 November 2021, https://economictimes.indiatimes.com/news/economy/indicators/how-strong-is-the-economic-recovery-economists-go-the-extra-mile-to-find-out/articleshow/87559167.cms.

[63] Abrar, Peerzada. 'Diwali Festive Sale Crosses Rs 1.25 Trn, Breaks All Records in 10 Yrs: CAIT.' *Business Standard*, 5 November 2021, https://www.business-standard.com/article/companies/diwali-festive-sale-crosses-rs-1-25-trn-breaks-all-records-in-10-yrs-cait-121110500886_1.html.

[64] Kaul, Vivek. 'India's Economic Recovery, a Glass Half Full?' *Mint*, 31 October 2021, https://www.livemint.com/economy/the-economic-glass-is-half-full-11635699012548.html.

conspicuous consumption such as Hackett jackets and Versace bags were flying off the shelves, items demanded by those aspiring to enter the middle class were not.[65] For instance, two-wheeler sales, which can be considered reflective of discretionary spending by lower-income households, were at decadal lows in 2021, if the year 2020 is kept aside.[66] Consumer confidence levels continued to be in pessimistic territory at the end of 2021, though improving over time.[67,68] The lower middle class and the poor were, as of late 2021, curbing discretionary spending by either avoiding purchases altogether or trading down by buying cheaper items. Anecdotal evidence gathered from specific market areas such as Delhi's Ramphal Chowk suggested that consumers were hesitating to buy staple kitchen appliances such as mixers, grinders and electric kettles, with interviewed sellers stating that sales were still a fraction of pre-pandemic levels.[69]

The COVID-19 shock had divided the working population into two unequal parts: those who could work from the safety of their homes sitting in front of a laptop and 'ordering in' and those who were basically out of work, having been part of a set-up where they spent most of their time outdoors and queued in front of ration shops on weekends. The first set was arguably better off since the pandemic than before, having been able to save up

---

[65] Singh, Karan Deep. 'Weak Recovery Leaves India's Middle Class Anxious and Frugal.' *New York Times*, 30 November 2021, https://www.nytimes.com/2021/11/30/business/india-economy-gdp.html.

[66] Kaul. 'India's Economic Recovery, a Glass Half Full?' *Mint*.

[67] Misra, Jagadish. 'What the Consumer Gloom Means for the Indian Economy.' *Mint*, 12 December 2021, https://www.livemint.com/economy/what-the-consumer-gloom-means-for-the-indian-economy-11639331253452.html.

[68] Sharma, Yogima. 'Consumer Sentiment Still below Pre-Covid Levels: CMIE.' *Economic Times*, 16 December 2021, https://economictimes.indiatimes.com/news/economy/indicators/consumer-sentiment-still-below-pre-covid-levels/articleshow/88317492.cms.

[69] Singh. 'Weak Recovery Leaves India's Middle Class Anxious and Frugal.'

on travelling expenses during the lockdowns, assuming of course that they survived the virus itself or weren't divested of a major part of their savings as medical expenses. A lot of the consumption being witnessed now is essentially delayed consumption by the 'classes'. The very different impact of the pandemic on different wealth classes can also be gauged from the fact that consumption by gated communities in India's cities is expected to grow two and a half times by 2026.[70] Meanwhile, government final consumption expenditure was still over 5 per cent below pre-pandemic levels by the end of the second quarter of FY 2021–22.[71]

In any case, the one bright spot for aggregate demand was export growth, with India's merchandise exports having staged a smart turnaround during the course of calendar year 2021 on the back of double-digit growth for the eight consecutive months staring from January. Merchandise exports was one of the 19 HFIs out of a total of 22 usually tracked by the central government and analysts that had crossed their corresponding pre-pandemic levels in October 2021.[72] As such, the Department of Economic Affairs (DEA) said in its monthly review for November 2021 that 'by end of the first half itself of the financial year, the country was ready with the macro and micro growth drivers to kick start its investment cycle'.[73] The DEA's review also mentioned a note

---

[70] Mukherjee, Writankar. 'Consumption in Gated Communities in India Poised to Grow 2.5 Times to Touch $500 Billion in Five Years: Report.' *Economic Times*, 20 December 2021, https://economictimes.indiatimes.com/news/economy/indicators/consumption-in-gated-communities-in-india-poised-to-grow-2-5-times-to-touch-500-billion-in-five-years-report/articleshow/87619005.cms.

[71] 'Press Note on Estimates of Gross Domestic Product for the Second Quarter (July–September) 2021–2022.'

[72] 'Monthly Economic Review (November 2021).' *Department of Economic Affairs, Government of India*, https://dea.gov.in/sites/default/files/November%202021_0.pdf.

[73] Ibid.

by US brokerage house Jeffries, which believed that India's economy was on the cusp of a cyclical upturn similar to the one observed during 2003–10.[74] Jeffries's assessment was in turn based on an analysis of six specific factors including 'a spike in housing demand, higher corporate profitability, more corporate deleveraging, a fall in bank NPAs, low interest rates and a rebound in corporate capex'.[75] Other observers have also made similar arguments in that a confluence of positive factors such as improving bank balance sheets, heightened infrastructure spending, etc., portended a revival in India's investment cycle.[76,77,78] To be sure, business optimism in corporate India was at a near eight-year high, as gauged by an index in November 2021, and top-listed firms had registered record profits during the second quarter of FY 2021–22.[79,80]

---

[74] Ibid.

[75] 'India's Economy Could Repeat 2003–10 Growth. 6 Key Factors Explained.' *Mint*, 18 October 2021, https://www.livemint.com/economy/jefferies-sees-these-6-key-factors-to-help-indian-economy-repeat-2003-10-growth-its-key-stock-picks-11634523831160.html.

[76] 'Highest Capex in a Decade Will Be Strong Tailwinds for Infra, Manufacturing.' *Economic Times*, 10 September 2021, https://economictimes.indiatimes.com/markets/stocks/news/highest-capex-in-a-decade-will-be-strong-tailwinds-for-infra-manufacturing/articleshow/86091023.cms.

[77] Chakravarty, Manas. 'India Is on the Cusp of an Upswing in the Business Cycle.' *MoneyControl*, 2 November 2021, https://www.moneycontrol.com/news/opinion/india-is-on-the-cusp-of-an-upswing-in-the-business-cycle-7658351.html. Accessed 20 December 2021.

[78] Mahanta, Vinod. 'Tell-Tale Signs of India's Economic Recovery Are Now Visible: McKinsey's Rajat Dhawan.' *Economic Times*, 20 December 2021, https://economictimes.indiatimes.com/news/economy/indicators/tell-tale-signs-of-indias-economic-recovery-are-now-visible-mckinseys-rajat-dhawan/articleshow/88246801.cms.

[79] J.C., Anand. 'Business Optimism in India at Near 8-Year High: Report.' *Economic Times*, 28 November 2021, https://economictimes.indiatimes.com/news/economy/indicators/business-optimism-in-india-at-near-8-year-high-report/articleshow/87959405.cms.

[80] Kant, Krishna. 'India Inc. Earnings Hit Record Rs 2.4 Trillion in September Quarter.' *Business Standard*, 15 November 2021, https://www.

About 44 per cent of global business leaders said in a Deloitte survey that they were planning either 'additional or first-time investments in India', with nearly two-thirds of the first-time investments slated to be made within two years from the time of the survey which was fielded in April 2021.[81] Even the RBI seems to believe that India's investment cycle could see an upswing during FY 2022–23.[82]

Be that as it may, gross fixed capital formation (GFCF), which can be considered a stand-in for private investment, was still down over 8 per cent in absolute terms at the half-yearly mark of FY 2021–22 as compared to the same point during FY 2019–20.[83] As of end 2021, India was yet to shake off the downturn in the investment cycle that had begun in 2013.[84]

Ultimately, any significant uptick in investment (which had been tepid for years even before the COVID-19 shock) may initially require a broader recovery in consumption, which was yet to return to pre-pandemic levels in October 2021, as we saw earlier. That no broad-based recovery in demand was happening in the Indian economy even by the

---

business-standard.com/article/companies/india-inc-earnings-hit-record-rs-2-4-trillion-in-september-quarter-121111500046_1.html.

[81] Dave, Sachin. 'Global Businesses Confident about Investing in India, 44% Business Planning Investments: Deloitte.' *Economic Times*, 14 September 2021, https://economictimes.indiatimes.com/news/economy/indicators/global-businesses-confident-about-investing-in-india-44-business-planning-investments-deloitte/articleshow/86191263.cms.

[82] PTI. 'Economic Recovery Taking Hold; Private Investment Should Resume: RBI Governor Shaktikanta Das.' *Times of India*, 16 November 2021, https://timesofindia.indiatimes.com/business/india-business/economic-recovery-taking-hold-private-investment-should-resume-rbi-governor-shaktikanta-das/articleshow/87739011.cms.

[83] 'Press Note on Estimates of Gross Domestic Product for the Second Quarter (July–September) 2021–2022.'

[84] PTI, 'Economic Recovery Taking Hold; Private Investment Should Resume: RBI Governor Shaktikanta Das.'

end of 2021 was accepted even by the RBI. Shaktikanta Das, the RBI governor, admitted in a speech in November 2021:

> Contact-intensive services are still to regain the lost capacity despite rapid improvement in the recent period. The Q1:2021–22 data on GDP revealed that there still exists significant gap in both private consumption and investment, relative to their pre-pandemic levels in 2019–20. So, while the economy is picking up pace, it is yet to cover a lot of ground before it gets broad-based and entrenched. This points to the need for sustained impetus so that growth could return to, or better still, exceed the pre-pandemic trend.[85]

With private investment and consumption still below pre-pandemic levels in nominal terms even after the second quarter of FY 2021–22, this 'sustained impetus', at least for the immediate future, will have to come from the government. In October 2021, Sitharaman stated to a news agency:

> They [fiscal stimulus measures] will continue. The emphasis on building health infrastructure will continue, and so will government spending on capital expenditure and infrastructure.[86]

Seemingly in line with this thinking, New Delhi extended the free ration scheme called Pradhan Mantri Garib Kalyan Anna Yojana (PMGKAY) for another four months in November 2021, having first extended it in the wake of the second wave.[87] Reports also suggested that India was

---

[85] 'Contours of Economic Recovery.' *Reserve Bank of India*, 16 November 2021, https://rbidocs.rbi.org.in/rdocs/Speeches/PDFs/GOVERNORSPEECH2EE1CEB500744BA5BE26984369CE2000.PDF.

[86] FE Bureau. 'More Stimulus to Come If Needed, Says FM Nirmala Sitharaman.' *Financial Express*, 18 October 2021, https://www.financialexpress.com/economy/more-stimulus-to-come-if-needed-says-fm-nirmala-sitharaman/2351949/.

[87] IANS. 'Centre Extends Pradhan Mantri Garib Kalyan Anna Yojana till March 2022.' *Business Standard*, 25 November 2021, https://www.business-

planning to introduce a highly subsidized cooked food scheme for the poor and enhance transfers to farmers under the existing scheme called PM-KISAN.[88] Perhaps, the government had realized that direct support measures would be very important if the recovery GDP growth rate was to be in double digits, as the government had been projecting throughout 2021. This was especially relevant given the uncertainty surrounding the Omicron variant which was far more transmissible than previous strains. In line with Sitharaman's promise, New Delhi must do more to help India's state governments increase healthcare capacity and vaccination coverage (including potential booster doses) as that would serve as a hedge against the Omicron-generated third wave or any subsequent outbreaks. It would also in no way be prejudicial to boosting consumer sentiment. After all, the stimulus package announced after the second wave initially consisted of relief measures that would have led to an extra outgo of around ₹48,900 crore, a fraction of the headline value of the package.[89] Of course, since then, New Delhi has had to increase spending on account of taking over the fiscal burden of vaccination onto itself from the states and the PMGKAY extensions. In any case, despite any enhanced spending, projections from late 2021 suggested that the government would be comfortably below its fiscal deficit target for FY 2022–23 on account of buoyant revenue collections even if disinvestment proceeds were

---

standard.com/article/current-affairs/centre-extends-pradhan-mantri-garib-kalyan-anna-yojana-till-march-2022-121112401453_1.html.

[88] Sahu, Prasanta. 'Budget FY23 to Fall Short on Reforms.' *Financial Express*, 12 December 2021, https://www.financialexpress.com/economy/budget-fy22-to-be-low-on-reforms/2387171/.

[89] Roychoudhury, Arup. 'FinMin Frets over Extra Expenditure as Budget Preparations Begin.' *MoneyControl*, 19 October 2021, https://www.moneycontrol.com/news/business/economy/finmin-frets-over-extra-expenditure-as-budget-preparations-begin-7600551.html. Accessed 20 December 2021.

below estimates.[90] According to two government sources quoted in a November 2021 report by Reuters, India would apparently use this revenue buoyancy to finance welfare schemes rather than 'trying to beat its fiscal deficit target or lower borrowing'.[91]

The fact remains that the 2020 lockdown led to the destruction of very many lives and livelihoods. Unemployment continued to hover around the 7 per cent mark by end-2021.[92] The manufacturing sector, which regained the pre-pandemic level of output at the end of the second quarter of FY 2021–22, had not managed to make up for payroll losses. Contact-intensive service sectors were still at around 80 per cent of pre-pandemic levels.[93] To be sure, many who had lost their jobs in these sectors had found some sort of employment in the countryside. This could be surmised by the increase in demand for MNREGA jobs.[94] Agriculture had remained buoyant throughout the pandemic and rural demand was a source of succour for a while. However, the landless in the countryside had been very badly hit, with even nominal wages having stagnated and the additional market pressure from returnees quickly gobbling up MNREGA works.[95] In

---

[90] 'Centre's Fiscal Deficit May Be Better at 6.6% in FY22: Fitch.' *Mint*, 22 November 2021, https://www.livemint.com/economy/centres-fiscal-deficit-may-be-better-at-6-6-in-fy22-fitch-11637594142247.html.

[91] Ahmed, Aftab. 'India to Use Revenue Surge to Fund Welfare Drives, Not Beat Fiscal Deficit Target: Sources.' *Reuters*, 5 November 2021, https://www.reuters.com/world/india/india-use-revenue-surge-fund-welfare-drives-not-beat-fiscal-deficit-target-2021-11-05/.

[92] 'Unemployment Rate in India.' *CMIE*, https://unemploymentinindia.cmie.com/.

[93] 'Press Note on Estimates of Gross Domestic Product for the Second Quarter (July–September) 2021–2022.'

[94] PTI. 'Covid-19: Demand for MGNREGA Work Rises as Urban Unemployment Grows.' *India Today*, 18 May 2021, https://www.indiatoday.in/business/story/covid-19-demand-for-mgnrega-work-rises-as-urban-unemployment-grows-1804066-2021-05-18.

[95] Bera, Sayantan. 'Poverty and Hunger Stalk India's Countryside.' *Mint*,

fact, India's post-COVID-19 shock unemployment figures mask a lot of disguised unemployment, with those having lost their urban jobs just about getting by in the countryside.

According to a Pew Research report released in March 2021, some 75 million Indians may have fallen back into extreme poverty (that is, earning less than $1.90 a day) due to the impact of the COVID-19 recessionary shock.[96] This was six times more than what the World Bank had estimated back in May 2020.[97] The report also estimated that India's middle class may have shrunk by a third. In January 2021, the World Bank estimated that there could be an additional 150 million worldwide poor, with some 60 per cent of that number in South Asia.[98] It also believed that middle-income countries such as India and Nigeria had been significantly affected by the pandemic.[99] According to the CMIE, at least 97 per cent of Indian households have suffered a loss in real income.[100] These numbers are indicative of the dent the

---

12 December 2021, https://www.livemint.com/news/india/the-rural-recovery-is-still-far-from-sight-11639325067930.html.

[96] Kochhar, Rakesh. 'In the Pandemic, India's Middle Class Shrinks and Poverty Spreads While China Sees Smaller Changes.' Pew Research Center, 18 March 2021, https://www.pewresearch.org/fact-tank/2021/03/18/in-the-pandemic-indias-middle-class-shrinks-and-poverty-spreads-while-china-sees-smaller-changes/.

[97] Kumar, Ankit. 'Covid-19 Could Push 12 Million Indians into Extreme Poverty: World Bank.' *India Today*, 7 May 2020, https://www.indiatoday.in/india/story/covid-19-could-push-12-million-indians-into-extreme-poverty-world-bank-1675173-2020-05-07.

[98] Lakner, Christoph. 'Updated Estimates of the Impact of COVID-19 on Global Poverty: Looking Back at 2020 and the Outlook for 2021.' *World Bank*, 11 January 2021, https://blogs.worldbank.org/opendata/updated-estimates-impact-covid-19-global-poverty-looking-back-2020-and-outlook-2021.

[99] 'Overview.' *World Bank*, 14 October 2021, https://www.worldbank.org/en/topic/poverty/overview. Accessed 10 August 2021.

[100] 'Explained: How Lower Demand Impacts India's Covid-Hit Economy.' *India Today*, 18 May 2021, https://www.indiatoday.in/

pandemic has probably made in the gains accrued due to 273 million Indians having moved out of multidimensional poverty between 2005–06 and 2015–16, according to data released by the United Nations Development Programme (UNDP) and the Oxford Poverty and Human Development Initiative (OPHI).[101] Beyond the dismalness of the figures, there has been a palpable rise in the number of homeless persons on the streets of major cities such as Delhi.[102]

The immense economic pain the pandemic has wrought upon the Indian economy makes it clear that both households and small firms will require continued direct support for a few years, although the weight of enhanced spending will have to shift towards productivity enhancement. Thus, the first major choice the Indian government is facing is whether to continue support measures and enhanced spending or to dial back in the name of fiscal prudence as soon as some buoyancy is noted. Moving on from the issue of boosting the 'recovery' GDP growth rate during FY 2021–22, solid fiscal support will be a key ingredient for enhancing India's growth potential, especially with the concerns around Omicron and possible future 'variants of concern' looming on the horizon. To be sure, the size of the recovery growth rate, as we shall see, is important for determining the nature of India's future growth path. But beyond the issue of growth figures for FY 2021–22 lies the issue of sustaining India's ability to grow at a fair clip in the years ahead.

---

business/story/explained-how-lower-demand-impacts-india-s-covid-hit-economy-1804054-2021-05-18.

[101] 'India Lifted Record 273 Million out of Poverty in 10 Years, Says UN Report.' *Business Standard*, 17 July 2020, https://www.business-standard.com/article/current-affairs/at-273-mn-india-recorded-largest-reduction-in-poverty-over-10-years-un-120071700468_1.html.

[102] Agarwal, Priyani. 'Home Is Where Art Was: Delhi Flyovers' Makeover Undone.' *Times of India*, 26 July 2021, http://timesofindia.indiatimes.com/articleshow/84739334.cms.

THE ISSUE OF ENHANCING POTENTIAL GROWTH

Contemporary research posits that every recession leads to a decline in potential output, which is defined as the maximum sustainable productive capacity of an economy over time.[103] It is basically an estimated measure of the maximum amount of goods and services an economy can produce in any given situation without giving rise to inflationary pressures. Potential output typically stands lowered in the wake of a recession on account of firms going out of business, attendant job losses and declining labour force participation. So, there is not just a loss of output, but a loss of the factors of production itself. Along with this, there could be losses in total factor productivity, which means that added stimulus is needed not just to boost flagging demand in order to make use of spare capacity, but also to prevent a significant attrition of India's economic capabilities.

Because of the lowered level of sustainable productive capacity, any growth recovery in the economy also happens along a lower trend path.[104] This means that there are permanent output losses in the wake of any economic recession. This is in contrast to expectations of a so-called V-shaped recovery as predicted by business cycle theory wherein added demand support, whether in the form of monetary or fiscal stimulus, simply helps close the 'output gap' which is the difference between actual and potential output. Subsequent to the output gap being closed, business cycle theory assumes that the economy 'returns' to its old growth trajectory. Unfortunately, studies have shown that

---

[103] Powell, Tyler, et al. 'What Is Potential GDP, and Why Is It so Controversial Right Now?' *Brookings*, 22 February 2021, https://www.brookings.edu/blog/up-front/2021/02/22/what-is-potential-gdp-and-why-is-it-so-controversial-right-now/.

[104] Cerra, Valerie, and Sweta C. Saxena. 'The Economic Scars of Crises and Recessions.' *IMF Blog*, 14 March 2019, https://blogs.imf.org/2018/03/21/the-economic-scars-of-crises-and-recessions/.

every recessionary shock instead pushes the economy on to a lower growth trajectory, with both demand and supply in the economy getting impaired. The impairment in output potential is referred to as 'scarring'.

Moreover, scarring can be very large depending on the severity and type of recession. In India's case, the COVID-19 shock is expected to have caused a permanent economic loss of around 11 per cent of GDP, according to one estimate.[105] Which is precisely why it is important to ensure that the recovery growth rate is as high as possible to minimize the depth of scarring. Limiting scarring and boosting sentiment are the key ingredients for setting up a virtuous investment cycle. Indeed, the investment rate is often a casualty of deep recessions, and this in turn directly impinges on future growth rates.

Any permanent economic loss will therefore have an impact on India's ability to grow in the medium term, and estimates about the potential extent of the same have also emerged since the COVID-19 shock of 2020. In October 2021, Alfred Schipke, the IMF's mission chief for India, stated that:

> We think the impact [of the pandemic] is coming from the capital accumulation channel. Investment took a big hit, that means capital stock is somewhat lower than it would have been otherwise. Then of course there is some damage to the labour market. So, we have reduced potential growth [of India] by 25 basis points to 6%.[106]

This estimate was actually an improvement on those made in the wake of the lockdowns and the massive contraction that

[105] Haq, Zia. 'The "Missing Middle" in India's Economic Recovery.' *Hindustan Times*, 10 March 2021, www.hindustantimes.com/business/missing-middle-in-india-s-economic-recovery-101615347987440.html.

[106] Mishra, Asit. 'IMF Slashes India's Potential GDP Forecast by 25 Bps to 6%.' *Mint*, 18 October 2021, https://www.livemint.com/economy/imf-reduces-india-s-potential-growth-forecast-by-25-bps-to-6-11634565370951.html.

took place subsequently. For instance, about a year earlier, in November 2020, Oxford Economics had observed:

> We forecast India's growth equilibrium to worsen substantially over the medium term, with potential growth averaging just 4.5 per cent over 2020–2025 in our latest baseline, as opposed to our pre-virus forecast of 6.5 per cent. But, given the low likelihood of such a comprehensive response, we project India's GDP per capita to be 12 per cent below our pre-virus baseline even in 2025, implying the largest amount of scarring among major economies globally.[107]

The IMF's more optimistic projections were probably a result of India's economy weathering the second wave better than anticipated. Other projections continued to emphasize the impact of scarring on the Indian economy. This is from Nomura in October 2021:

> In our base case, India's business cycle peaks in H1 2022 and then momentum starts to moderate in H2, reflecting cyclical factors and the impact of the scarring effects, which we believe have lowered the potential growth rate.[108]

Even the RBI's Das admitted in January 2021 that India had been scarred by the pandemic.[109] Major ratings agency Fitch,

---

[107] PTI. 'Oxford Economics Revises Downwards India Growth Forecast; Pegs at Average 4.5 Pc for 2020–25.' *Financial Express*, 19 November 2020, https://www.financialexpress.com/economy/oxford-economics-revises-downwards-india-growth-forecast-pegs-at-average-4-5-pc-for-2020-25/2132170/.

[108] PTI. 'Growth Cycle Not Durable, Will Peak in First-Half of 2022: Nomura.' *Economic Times*, 15 January 2022, https://economictimes.indiatimes.com/news/economy/indicators/growth-cycle-not-durable-will-peak-in-first-half-of-2022-nomura/articleshow/88208810.cms.

[109] 'We've Been Scarred by Covid Pandemic, Task Ahead Is to Restore Growth: RBI Governor.' *Times of India*, 11 January 2021, https://timesofindia.indiatimes.com/business/india-business/weve-been-scarred-by-covid-pandemic-task-ahead-is-to-restore-growth-rbi-governor/articleshow/80215813.cms.

which has been giving more optimistic projections for India's growth path, nevertheless, stated in January 2021:

> The growth will be supported by the expectation of the rollout of an effective vaccine, but we expect the level of GDP to remain well below its pre-pandemic path even after the health crisis has passed.[110]

Now, the prevention or limitation of permanent losses cannot be accomplished with simple monetary stimulus designed to close the output gap or forbearance and loan guarantee programmes. At a time when firm balance sheets are already under stress, greater lending is probably going to end up making them even worse. In the initial phase of such a recessionary shock, it is rather direct income support that is called for, and this can only be done by the fiscal authority, that is, the government. After all, central banks can lend but they cannot spend. Repairing balance sheets or closing the output gap even with a lowered potential output path might be difficult unless support is provided.

It is precisely to prevent major permanent output losses that advanced economies resorted to enormous fiscal stimulus despite high levels of pre-existing debt by nationalizing salaries through direct income support to firms. The multiplier effect of such transfer payments is not high, so the agenda initially is to try and preserve as much as possible. Obviously, they judged that the need to protect the economic capabilities of the country was more important than a higher debt-to-GDP ratio and the risk of fiscal dominance. Moreover, a countercyclical fiscal expansion may result in a lower rather than a higher government debt-to-GDP ratio

---

[110] PTI. 'India's Medium-Term Growth to Slow to around 6.5% after Initial Rebound: Fitch.' *Times of India*, 14 January 2021, https://timesofindia.indiatimes.com/business/india-business/indias-medium-term-growth-to-slow-to-around-6-5-after-initial-rebound-fitch/articleshow/80269559.cms.

further down the road. This sentiment was well captured by Isabel Schnabel, member of the Executive Board of the ECB, in a speech delivered on 11 September 2020:

> The current pandemic crisis is a case in point. Fiscal expansion is indispensable at the current juncture to sustain demand and mitigate the long-term costs of the crisis. Monetary policy can complement these efforts. But by itself, it may not be sufficient to stabilise the economy. This is all the more true if different sectors, or regions, of the economy are affected in different ways.
>
> In such times, it would be wrong to constrain fiscal policies today to protect monetary dominance tomorrow. Quite on the contrary, using fiscal and structural policies more actively in the current environment may foster central bank independence.[111]

To reiterate, the possibility of deep losses that scar the economy is why there are few takers for a wave of creative destruction that will permanently depress output. As has been seen in the case of Europe's austerity embracing countries, it takes years to recoup even old output levels with the economy's ability to grow severely impaired. In the case of major powers, what is at stake is also the country's geoeconomic position on which hinges its overall future.

And it is not only countries which seem to have fiscal space that decided to give a major fiscal rescue package early on in the crisis. Brazil, despite its fiscal space being more limited than India and constrained by fiscal spending rules, chose to provide much greater direct income support to households and firms. India limited direct transfers to just ₹500 per account besides offering free rations in the initial

---

[111] 'The Shadow of Fiscal Dominance: Misconceptions, Perceptions and Perspectives.' *European Central Bank*, 11 September 2020, https://www.ecb.europa.eu/press/key/date/2020/html/ecb.sp200911~ea32bd8bb3.en.html.

period. But the post-COVID-19 shock situation calls for some more direct support to households and small firms to keep balance sheets afloat. More direct transfers to the MSME sector, which contributes around 30 per cent of India's GDP and employs around 50 per cent of industrial workers, should certainly be considered. Such direct transfers are best given early on during a crisis because that is the best way to prevent a deleterious effect on firm and household balance sheets and stave off a significant decline in both aggregate supply and demand.

Indeed, for India, the issue is not merely one of preserving potential growth, but of enhancing it. Growth, quite simply put, is essential to India's poverty reduction goals and now assumes ever greater importance given the recessionary impact of the pandemic. In this context, beyond the initial transfer payments to protect households and firms (which as mentioned earlier may have to be continued for a while longer), the direction of spending has to be such that it not only boosts demand but enhances the productive capacity of the economy. An IMF study which looked at the experience with fiscal stabilization during the past three decades in a broad sample of 85 advanced, emerging-market and developing economies came up with this 'loud and clear' message, according to Xavier Debrun, deputy chief of the Fiscal Policy and Surveillance Division in the Fiscal Affairs Department:

> [G]overnments can use fiscal policy to smooth fluctuations in economic activity, and this can lead to higher medium-term growth.[112]

---

[112] Lakner, Christoph, et al. 'Updated Estimates of the Impact of COVID-19 on Global Poverty: Looking Back at 2020 and the Outlook for 2021.' *World Bank*, 11 January 2021, https://blogs.worldbank.org/opendata/updated-estimates-impact-covid-19-global-poverty-looking-back-2020-and-outlook-2021.

Infrastructure is an obvious candidate for directed spending to boost potential growth. Indeed, even the Modi government is apparently eyeing low-gestation-period infrastructure projects as a target for stimulus spending and has set up the National Infrastructure Pipeline for this purpose. The multiplier effect of capital spending in India has been estimated to be as high as 3.0, which means that every rupee spent on infrastructure will result in the value of output rising by three times that number.

Infrastructure projects will also be the key to reducing transaction costs and help the Indian economy tie in with the global restructuring of supply chains that is underway. To take full advantage of that restructuring, public expenditure will also have to be directed towards creating home-grown capabilities that will underpin manufacturing prowess in the fourth industrial revolution. India cannot afford to retain its traditional approach of being a follower in techno-industrial waves. General purpose technologies (GPTs) such as AI and 5G may diffuse even less readily than developments from previous industrial revolutions, with intellectual property being ever so zealously guarded.

So, besides income support, the government will have to also support varied productivity and growth-enhancing measures besides directing funds towards deep R&D in emerging GPTs. These will also play a role in subduing supply-side inflationary pressures that continue to crop up intermittently. Naturally, fiscal policy will be asked to do a lot at a rather difficult time. It will also have to do so for some time to come. As the government's own Economic Survey for FY 2020–21 observed:

> For India, in the current scenario, when private consumption, which contributes to 54 per cent of GDP is contracting, and investment, which contributes to around 29 per cent is uncertain, the relevance of counter-cyclical fiscal policies is paramount. In fact, as Krugman prescribed, a sustained, productive program of permanent stimulus directed towards

> public investment, in both physical and human capital, is the need of the hour.[113]

And without sustained spending by the treasury, India's fiscal numbers might end up looking uglier. It is better that fiscal support is given to shore up household and small firm balance sheets rather than a situation of low growth and high debt arising down the road. As the IMF itself put it in July 2020:

> This is an unusual emergency. We do believe that India, despite its limited fiscal space, could maybe provide above the line support. It's possible they are retaining some policy power for later down the line. We do see scope for further fiscal support as well as we still think there could be potential for monetary policy support as long as inflation continues to fall.[114]

As we shall see, the RBI, as the government's official debt manager, can help the central government find some fiscal space in this era, with methods that cannot be deemed to be 'monetization' any more. A play for growth has to be made instead of worrying excessively about debt. Heightened spending now is not so much of a choice as a necessity. Naturally, India will face choices about its overall macroeconomic regime, especially with respect to the 'mix' of fiscal and monetary policies. But before we turn to those choices, let us first look at the macroeconomic regime it has been operating under in recent times and briefly trace the evolution of fiscal–monetary relations in India since the era of liberalization began.

---

[113] 'Does Growth Lead to Debt Sustainability? Yes, But Not Vice-Versa!' *Economic Survey 2020–21*, Ministry of Finance, Government of India, https://www.indiabudget.gov.in/economicsurvey/doc/echapter_vol2.pdf.

[114] Kelkar, Nachiket. 'IMF Sees Scope for More Monetary and Fiscal Stimulus in India.' *Week*, 29 July 2020, https://www.theweek.in/news/biz-tech/2020/07/29/imf-sees-scope-for-more-monetary-and-fiscal-stimulus-in-india.html.

STATE OF PLAY

In early July 2018, Urjit Patel, the then governor of the RBI, voiced his concerns about the spillover effects of the Fed's QT on emerging markets, in an opinion piece titled 'Emerging Markets Face a Dollar Double-Whammy'[115] published in the *Financial Times*. Patel feared that the Fed's ongoing roll-off (reduction of Fed holdings of the US government securities) was not taking into account the rapid expansion of the US Treasury debt issue that followed Trump's tax cuts. With the Fed no longer reinvesting in new US treasury debt, an immense amount of dollar liquidity was getting sucked out of emerging economy bond markets as it rushed towards US government debt markets experiencing rising yields.[116] This was leading not just to a fall in the price of emerging market bonds but was also putting currencies such as the rupee under considerable depreciation pressure, in a manner reminiscent of the Taper Tantrum of 2013. Indeed, Patel believed that absent a course correction by the Fed in the form of a reduction in the pace of its roll-off, many emerging economies (EMEs) were faced with the prospect of a 'sudden stop', thereby endangering not just overall global growth but America's own so-called economic recovery as well.

India was, of course, not an exception to this trend, with its foreign liabilities having grown seven-fold over 2008–18.[117]

---

[115] Patel, U. 'Emerging Markets Face a Dollar Double-Whammy.' *Financial Times*, 3 June 2018, https://www.ft.com/content/e193381a-64c1-11e8-bdd1-cc0534df682c.

[116] What this means is, say there is a major buyer, X, for US Government bonds. Suddenly, X pulls out of the market, just as many more bonds were coming into the market. Obviously, initially the price of those bonds would fall, leading to the issuer offering better yields for the bonds (that is, better interest rates). Those rising interest rates, however, become sufficiently attractive for capital parked elsewhere in the world in riskier assets (also, see chapter three).

[117] 'India External Debt: % of GDP, 1970–2022.' *CEIC Data*, https://www.ceicdata.com/en/indicator/india/external-debt--of-nominal-gdp. Accessed 23 January 2022.

Moreover, the country's foreign assets were also somewhat lower than its foreign liabilities.[118] It is not for nothing that Patel was so concerned about a possible repeat of the Taper Tantrum. Naturally this sort of concern got reflected in the RBI's decision to raise the key policy rate just a few days after Patel's article was published. On 6 June 2018, the RBI's Monetary Policy Committee (MPC) – which holds the responsibility of fixing the key policy (interest) rate for the Indian economy – would take a decision by unanimous vote to increase the repurchase agreement (REPO), which is the key policy rate, under the liquidity adjustment facility of the RBI by 25 basis points or 0.25 per cent.[119] In its Second Bi-monthly Monetary Policy Statement, 2018–19, which announced this decision, the MPC seemingly echoed the sentiments expressed by Patel in his article a few days ago:

> In most EMEs, however, bond yields have risen on reduced foreign appetite for their debt due to growing dollar shortage in the global market and on prospects of higher interest rates in AEs. In currency markets, the US dollar touched its highest level in May since December 2017… EME currencies have, by and large, depreciated against the US dollar.[120]

---

[118] The ratio of India's international financial assets to international financial liabilities increased to 70.9 per cent in March 2021 from 65.6 per cent a year ago.

[119] 'Second Bi-monthly Monetary Policy Statement, 2018–19 Resolution of the Monetary Policy Committee (MPC) Reserve Bank of India.' *Reserve Bank of India*, 6 June 2018, https://rbidocs.rbi.org.in/rdocs/PressRelease/PDFs/PR3190CD624DC4A2BD4F20AF3F8C8CAD81A513.PDF. Note: Like many other EME central banks, the RBI sought to achieve this objective by varying the key policy rate in a 'corridor' between a discount rate called the marginal standing facility (MSF) by the RBI and the reverse repo rate. This decision since 2016 has been taken by the MPC which is quite similar to the Fed's FOMC. However, since the pandemic, this corridor system has almost transitioned to a de-facto 'floor' system, which is how most AE central banks operate today.

[120] 'Minutes of the Monetary Policy Committee Meeting June 4–6, 2018.'

This particular rate hike served to illustrate just how much influence the spillovers of US monetary policy were having on India's own domestic monetary policy decision-making.

Now, since September 2016, as a result of a May 2016 amendment in the RBI Act of 1934, the RBI had adopted an explicit inflation-targeting framework in pursuit of its stance that the 'primary objective of the monetary policy is to maintain price stability while keeping in mind the objective of growth'.[121] Specifically, till 31 March 2021, the RBI's monetary policy was to be driven by the:

> [O]bjective of achieving the medium-term target for consumer price index (CPI) inflation of 4 per cent within a band of +/- 2 per cent, while supporting growth.[122]

Though the CPI (including food and fuel prices) or retail inflation for April 2018 at 4.6 per cent was within the prescribed band, the RBI was worried about an 'upside risk' to inflation on account of rising crude prices, and any major exchange-rate depreciation would have served to amplify the effects of the same. Explaining its decision to raise interest rates, the MPC would state:

> A major upside risk to the baseline inflation path in the April resolution has materialised, viz., 12 per cent increase in the price of Indian crude basket, which was sharper, earlier than expected and seems to be durable. Crude oil prices have been volatile recently and this imparts considerable uncertainty to the inflation outlook – both on the upside and the downside. Several other risks remain. First, global financial market developments have emerged as another

---

Reserve Bank of India, 20 June 2018, https://rbidocs.rbi.org.in/rdocs/PressRelease/PDFs/PR3320556E3589C58C4978B8E24686472796DD.PDF.

[121] 'Report on Currency and Finance.' *Reserve Bank of India*, 26 February 2021, https://m.rbi.org.in/scripts/PublicationsView.aspx?id=20342.

[122] 'Overview – Monetary Policy.' *Reserve Bank of India*, https://www.rbi.org.in/scripts/FS_Overview.aspx?fn=2752. Accessed 15 January 2022.

> important source of uncertainty. Second, the significant rise in households' inflation expectations as gathered in the May 2018 round of the Reserve Bank's survey could feed into wages and input costs in the coming months… Against the above backdrop, the MPC decided to increase the policy repo rate by 25 basis points and keep the stance neutral.[123]

With foreign portfolio investors having already withdrawn $6.7 billion on a net basis from India's capital markets between April 2018 and June 2019, the RBI had clearly chosen to act against any further exchange rate declines by raising the policy interest rate and making portfolio investments in India more attractive. This decision was incidentally supported by some analysts and even seen as long overdue, as reflected in the following view from an economist at the National Institute of Public Finance and Policy (NIPFP) shared with *Bloomberg*:

> Given the international conditions – rising oil prices, the Fed's rate policy, and the fact that other emerging markets have already begun raising rates – RBI should have probably raised rates earlier.[124]

Interestingly, the RBI believed that its rate hike was 'neutral' in so much as its effect on output was concerned since in its view 'domestic economic activity has exhibited sustained revival in recent quarters and the output gap has almost closed'.[125] India's central government, however, did not see

---

[123] 'Second Bi-monthly Monetary Policy Statement, 2018–19 Resolution of the Monetary Policy Committee (MPC) Reserve Bank of India.'

[124] Nag, Anirban. 'RBI Joins Peers with Rate Hike to Counter US Fed Policy, Stronger Dollar.' *Business Standard*, 7 June 2018, https://www.business-standard.com/article/finance/rbi-joins-peers-with-rate-hike-to-counter-us-fed-policy-stronger-dollar-118060700123_1.html.

[125] 'Core Inflation Is Rising, in Sign of Robust Growth.' *Mint*, 13 July 2018, https://www.livemint.com/Money/TguoVy4MFtSBxaDoXe4qWL/Core-inflation-is-rising-in-sign-of-robust-growth.html.

things that way and wanted a reduction of interest rates to boost the economy heading into an election year, as it were. Moreover, an election year also meant that there would be greater-than-usual fiscal spending and thereby greater borrowing. Naturally, an accommodative stance from the RBI in the form of lower interest rates was also desirable from that point of view for the treasury. Based on empirical studies, it is believed that in India, monetary policy actions influence output with a lag of two to three quarters while inflation feels their effects after three to four quarters, and the impact on either persists for eight to twelve quarters.[126] Thus, with elections scheduled for May 2019, a rate hike in June 2018 wasn't a very auspicious development for the government. The RBI had asserted its operational independence.

SUBSERVIENT NO MORE

Since the era of liberalization beginning in the 1990s, the RBI has been progressively freeing itself of fiscal dominance in order to conduct monetary policy in an environment of global capital flows that looked unfavourably upon inflationary tendencies. Thus, the RBI's journey towards operational independence, as was the case with its counterparts in other emerging economies, was supported by the high tide of globalization when it seemed that all countries would have to hereon conform to an open multilateral investment and trading system with governments remaining at arms length from their increasingly market-driven economies. The so-called 'end of history' moment.

However, it must be said that the RBI's movement towards operational independence was rather gradual and

---

[126] 'Monetary Transmission in India: Why Is It Important and Why Hasn't It Worked Well?' *Reserve Bank of India,* 16 November 2017, https://rbidocs.rbi.org.in/rdocs/Speeches/PDFs/DGVVAS34AEAD82174B44EA854710B1103E0988.PDF.

has unfolded over a period of over two decades. Through the 1990s, the government would give up on the practise of setting administered interest rates, while also moving towards financing its deficits via direct market-based borrowing. In April 1997, following the exchange of letters and agreements with the government, the RBI would secure the discontinuation of automatic debt monetization that used to be done through the issuance of ad-hoc hills. Following this would be the Fiscal Responsibility and Budget Management Act of 2003 (FRBM 2003), which prohibited the RBI from participating in primary issuances of all government securities, just like is the case with the Fed or the BoJ. The FRBM 2003 also introduced fiscal rules related to how much the government could deficit finance in a year.[127,128]

Slowly, but surely, Indian macroeconomic policy-making seemed to be shifting towards monetary dominance, wherein the central bank pursues a price stability mandate, whereas the fiscal authority seeks to consolidate its finances in a way that it becomes sustainable over time. The onset of the GFC, however, meant that fiscal consolidation had to be paused by the Indian government and concomitantly the progress towards monetary dominance also slowed down commensurately. The Taper Tantrum, accompanied by a bout of double-digit inflation, brought renewed focus on the need to tame price rise and 'anchor' inflationary expectations. And that is precisely what Raghuram Rajan, appointed to the post

---

[127] 'Role of State in Developing Debt Markets.' *Reserve Bank of India*, 18 September 2012, https://rbidocs.rbi.org.in/rdocs/Speeches/PDFs/RSDAP210912F.pdf.

[128] A fiscal rule imposes a long-lasting constraint on fiscal policy through numerical limits on budgetary aggregates. Fiscal rules typically aim at correcting distorted incentives and containing pressures to overspend, particularly in good times, so as to ensure fiscal responsibility and debt sustainability. The rules accompanying the FRBM 2003 also required the government to reduce the fiscal deficit (FD) to 3 per cent of GDP, and eliminate the revenue deficit by 31 March 2008.

of RBI governor in September 2013, sought to do. Dubbed an 'inflation hawk' by the press, Rajan, who firmly believed that price stability was a prerequisite for long-term growth, oversaw the release of the Urjit Patel Committee Report in January 2014 which made a case for moving the RBI to a flexible inflation-targeting (FIT) mandate:

> While inflation is clearly a monetary phenomenon in the medium run, several nonmonetary factors – both domestic and external; supply side and demand side – can lead to significant deviations from the target in the short run, which may also impact the medium-term path through persistence and unanchored inflation expectations. It is necessary, therefore, that the adoption of flexible inflation targeting is based on reasonably clear identification of the pre-conditions.[129]

With the arrival of the Modi regime in May 2014, there was once again a move to consolidate the government's finances. After all, India wanted to shed the tag of being a 'fragile five' country (see chapter three) and New Delhi conveyed to the RBI its desire to maintain a more passive fiscal stance with stricter adherence to FRBM 2003.

The turn towards a monetary-led macroeconomic framework ultimately manifested itself in the adoption of the FIT mandate for the RBI in 2016, as mentioned above. It is called 'flexible' since it allows inflation to be within a band rather than fixate at a point.[130] This is also supposed

---

[129] 'Chapter II: Revisiting the Choice of Nominal Anchor for India's Monetary Policy.' *Reserve Bank of India*, 21 January 2014, https://m.rbi.org.in/scripts/PublicationReportDetails.aspx?UrlPage=&ID=746.

[130] As such, FIT, according to the RBI's Deputy Governor Michael Debabrata Patra is achieved by five specific features: (a) a dual mandate – 'price stability, keeping in mind the objective of growth'; (b) an inflation target defined in averages rather than as a point; (c) achievement of the target over a period of time rather than continuously; (d) a reasonably wide tolerance band around the target to accommodate measurement

to give the RBI more leeway in supporting growth while nevertheless implementing its primary mandate of price stability. To be sure, price stability has always been considered a part of the RBI's mandate, deriving from the preamble to the RBI Act itself:

> To regulate the issue of Bank notes and keeping of reserves with a view to securing monetary stability in India and generally, to operate the currency and credit system of the country to its advantage.[131]

As C. Rangarajan, a former RBI governor, stated in a 1998 speech, the above mandate has come to be interpreted as:

> In a broad sense, the objectives of monetary policy can be no different from the overall objectives of economic policy. The broad objectives of monetary policy in India have been: (a) to maintain a reasonable degree of price stability; and (b) to help accelerate the rate of economic growth. The emphasis as between the two objectives has changed from year to year, depending upon the prevailing conditions.[132] Be that as it may, since the adoption of FIT, the RBI has been quite aware of its growing operational independence as evidenced by this observation from the June 2018 resolution of MPC, which announced the rate hike: It is important that public

---

issues, forecast errors, supply shocks and, as vividly demonstrated recently, black swan events like the pandemic; and (e) failure being defined as three consecutive quarters of deviation of inflation from the tolerance band, rather than every deviation from the target. Taken from 'Monetary Policy: Trial by Pandemic.' *Reserve Bank of India*, 16 September 2021, https://rbidocs.rbi.org.in/rdocs/Speeches/PDFs/SPDG160921296148EC2A734FD9AC696E7EB73C266D.PDF.

[131] 'Organization and Functions.' *Reserve Bank of India*, https://www.rbi.org.in/commonperson/English/Scripts/Organisation.aspx. Accessed 15 January 2021.

[132] 'Role of Monetary Policy in Attaining Growth with Stability: The Indian Experience.' *Reserve Bank of India*, 2 April 2007, https://rbidocs.rbi.org.in/rdocs/Speeches/PDFs/76578.pdf.

> finances do not crowd out private sector investment activity at this crucial juncture. Adherence to budgetary targets by the Centre and the States – which appears to be the case thus far – will also ease upside risks to the inflation outlook considerably.[133]

BAD LOANS, BAD BLOOD

But this June 2018 assertion of operational independence was not good news for struggling firms in the country whose debt-service costs were set to rise. Neither was it the best news for India's public-sector-dominated banking system that was beset with a massive non-performing asset (NPA) problem which could now get worse because more borrowers would struggle to service debt. Moreover, India's NPA-ridden banking system was known to transmit interest rate changes in an asymmetric manner.[134] Rate hikes by the RBI were getting readily passed on to loan customers while reductions were not, at least not commensurately.[135] The government therefore feared that the RBI's hike would impair credit growth at a time when it was still just recovering.

Perhaps more than the rate hikes, the government saw the RBI's 'excessive' supervision of the banking sector as

---

[133] 'Second Bi-monthly Monetary Policy Statement, 2018–19 Resolution of the Monetary Policy Committee (MPC) Reserve Bank of India.'
See also: 'Interest Rate Pass-Through from the Weighted Average Call Rate to the Primary Commercial Paper Market in India Using Daily Data: An Empirical Analysis.' Centre for Advanced Financial Research and Learning, 13 December 2018, https://www.cafral.org.in/sfControl/content/Speech/ 1312018112113AMArunKumarKaustavSarkar.pdf.

[134] Das, Sonali. 'Monetary Policy in India: Transmission to Bank Interest Rates.' International Monetary Fund, June 2015, https://www.imf.org/external/pubs/ft/wp/2015/wp15129.pdf.

[135] 'Operating Procedure of Monetary Policy.' *Reserve Bank of India*, 2 April 2007, https://rbidocs.rbi.org.in/rdocs/Publications/PDFs/ 04CH_260220210E9EE1D12DFE4F21A019BAB56F218DCC.PDF.

a key reason behind relatively tepid credit growth. Since the GFC, central banks around the world had come to see financial stability as being the key to price stability. They were constantly 'pushing' against global financial cycles from building up excessive risks in the system. The RBI was no exception and naturally wanted to maintain tight oversight with respect to the Indian banking sector, which dominated the financial landscape in India. In a country known for so-called policy loans, it was obviously a matter of time before this emerged as a source of major friction.

To be sure, the government had itself brought in what was a landmark legislation for India at the time in the form of the Insolvency and Banking Code (IBC) in 2017. It had also moved to recapitalize public-sector banks. While welcoming the IBC and making it the lynchpin of its strategy to clean up NPAs in the banking system, the RBI had also introduced a revised prompt corrective action (PCA) framework on 13 April 2017 which was implemented with respect to the bank financials as on 31 March 2017.[136] The PCA framework first introduced by the RBI in 2002 typically places curbs on lending, branch network expansion and dividend distribution for banks that were placed under it with a view to repairing the balance sheets of the same. The RBI's 'revised' PCA framework tightened the criteria whereby a bank under it could resume normal lending operations again. With 11 PSU banks being sequestered under PCA, who together had previously accounted for 19 per cent of all lending, the government was obviously eager for the RBI to relax the criteria that led to a bank being sequestered under PCA. Especially so that they could keep lending as usual in support of the economic engine ahead of a general election the next year. But the RBI wanted these banks to be slowly nursed

---

[136] Acharya, Viral V. 'Prompt Corrective Action: An Essential Element of Financial Stability Framework.' *Bank for International Settlements,* 12 October 2018, https://www.bis.org/review/r181012k.pdf.

back to health. Given what was at stake, the RBI's revised PCA led to a major disagreement between the government and the RBI. The RBI too wanted the NPL problem to be addressed as soon as possible in a bid to get rid of extend and pretend in the Indian financial sector – a key learning from Japan. But as soon as possible was never going to be quick enough for the government in this arena.

The RBI also wanted the IBC to be used aggressively and introduced new rules forcing lenders to declare a delinquent borrower even if payments were overdue by a day. That was apparently aimed at easing mounting bad loans, particularly from the power sector. Unsurprisingly, this became a major sticking point between the treasury and the RBI.

Patel also refused to acquiesce to New Delhi's demands that the RBI part with a greater share of its accumulated earnings than it would have agreed to in the normal scheme of things. The RBI's remittances to the government are governed under Section 47 of the RBI Act, 1934, which states:

> After making provisions for bad and doubtful debts, depreciation in assets, contribution to staff and superannuation funds and for all matters for which provisions are to be made by or under the Act or that are usually provided by bankers, the balance of the profits of the Bank is required to be paid to the central government.[137]

Unfortunately for Patel, his assessment of how much 'provisioning' was to be done was not the same as what New Delhi deemed fit. Eager to be able to spend more without heightened borrowing from the market, the government had been eyeing a greater dividend from the RBI for FY 2018–19. It had even removed Nachiket Mor, an MPC member

---

[137] 'Transfer of Excess Funds from RBI to Government.' *Press Information Bureau, Ministry of Finance, Government of India*, 12 February 2019, https://pib.gov.in/Pressreleaseshare.aspx?PRID=1564081.

who had been vociferously opposed to a higher-dividend payout by the central bank.[138]

A Patel-helmed RBI also publicly dissented with the government's move to bring in a separate payments regulator, something that the RBI felt should remain within its remit.[139] With the list of policy disagreements piling up, Patel decide to file his papers on 10 December 2018.[140] This announcement came just four days before the RBI's next board meeting on 14 December 2018, which had promised to be yet another stormy affair.

But much more than traditional wrangling about interest rates, it was the dissonance on bank supervision and bad-loan resolution via the aggressive use of the IBC framework that ultimately led to Patel's departure. This has been hinted at in Patel's 2020 book *Overdraft: Saving the Indian Saver* which has the following passage:

> Instead of buttressing and future-proofing the gains thus far, an atmosphere to go easy on the pedal ensued. A case of our old failing of a premature pronouncement of victory, perhaps? Until then, for the most part, the finance minister and I were on the same page, with frequent conversations on enhancing the landmark legislation's operational efficiency.[141]

---

138 'Urjit Patel Resignation: These Six Things Drove Urjit Patel and Government Apart.' *Economic Times*, 10 December 2018, https://economictimes.indiatimes.com/news/economy/policy/these-six-things-drove-urjit-patel-and-government-apart/articleshow/67027013.cms.

139 Ibid.

140 Bloomberg. 'RBI Governor Urjit Patel Resigns as Rift with Govt Widens.' *Mint*, 10 December 2018, https://www.livemint.com/Politics/Q3ekh4jLcesHGlC5TmHqkJ/Patel-resigns-as-rift-with-government-over-capital-reserves.html.

141 Rangan, M.C. 'What Led to Urjit Patel's Premature Exit from the RBI? Inside His Tell-All Book.' *Economic Times*, 26 July 2020, https://economictimes.indiatimes.com/news/economy/policy/what-led-to-urjit-patels-premature-exit-from-the-rbi-inside-his-tell-all-book/articleshow/77147679.cms.

THE TWIN SHOCKS

And thus, Patel became the second single-term RBI governor to depart within a span of three years due to a not-so-smooth relationship with India's central government. Nobody said that upholding operational independence was going to be easy, forget about trying to be an activist central bank. Indeed, Patel probably turned out to be a step ahead in this matter than even his predecessor, Raghuram Rajan, who too had left the bank, since he reportedly felt that his political bosses were not exactly behind him.[142] Perhaps Rajan's being lukewarm to the Modi government's currency reform idea or demonetization, as it came to be called, played a major role in their not renewing his contract once his tenure as governor expired.

In his memoir *I Do What I Do*, Rajan had this to say about his exchanges with the government on the issue of demonetization:

> I was asked by the government in February 2016 for my views on demonetization, which I gave orally. Although there might be long-term benefits, I felt the likely short term economic costs would outweigh them, and felt there were potentially better alternatives to achieve the main goals. I made these views known in no uncertain terms. I was then asked to prepare a note, which the RBI put together and handed to the government. It outlined the potential costs and benefits of demonetization, as well as alternatives that could achieve similar aims. If the government, on weighing the pros and cons, still decided to go ahead with demonetization, the note outlined the preparation that would be needed, and the time that preparation would take. The RBI flagged what would happen if preparation was inadequate.

---

[142] Jain, Rupam, et al. 'Inside the "Constant Quibbling" and Drama That Led to India's Central Bank Chief's Departure.' *Insider*, 19 June 2016, https://www.businessinsider.com/r-indian-central-bank-chief-felt-undermined-in-weeks-before-quitting-sources-2016-6.

> The government then set up a committee to consider the issues. The deputy governor in charge of currency attended these meetings. At no point during my term was the RBI asked to make a decision on demonetization.[143]

In his 8 November 2016 speech announcing demonetization, Modi had dubbed the move as a fight against corruption, black money, fake notes and terrorism.[144] Unfortunately, as is now well-documented, demonetization did not do much in any of these departments. For one, as the RBI revealed in its Annual Report for 2016–17 released in August 2017:

> Subject to future corrections based on verification process when completed, the estimated value of SBNs (specified bank notes) received as on June 30, 2017, is ₹15.28 trillion.[145]

Given that the total value of demonetized currency was approximately ₹15.41 lakh crore, this meant that the overwhelming majority of the demonetized Specified Bank Notes (SBNs) (some 99 per cent) had returned to the system by June 2017 itself. Commenting on the development in September 2017, Rajan observed that 'the fact that 99% has been deposited certainly does suggest that aim [of curbing black money] has not been met'.[146] With its verification process complete, the RBI's annual report for 2017–18

---

143 Rajan, Raghuram G. *I Do What I Do*. Noida: HarperCollins, 2017.

144 'Full Text: PM Modi's 2016 Demonetisation Speech That Shocked India.' *Business Standard*, 8 November 2017, https://www.business-standard.com/article/economy-policy/full-text-pm-modi-s-2016-demonetisation-speech-that-shocked-india-117110800188_1.html.

145 'Annual Report 2016–17.' *Reserve Bank of India,* 30 August 2017, https://rbidocs.rbi.org.in/rdocs/AnnualReport/PDFs/RBIAR201617_FE1DA2F97D61249B1B21C4EA66250841F.PDF.

146 'Raghuram Rajan Breaks Silence, Says Neither He nor RBI under Him Wanted Demonetisation.' *Hindustan Times*, 3 September 2017, https://www.hindustantimes.com/india-news/raghuram-rajan-breaks-silence-says-he-wasn-t-on-board-for-demonetisation/story-6rXr8VWBpFd4w37NySulEN.html.

confirmed that 99.3 per cent of the demonetized SBNs had found their way back into the banking system with a total face value of '₹15,310.73 trillion'.[147] This indicates that only around ₹10,720 crore of the demonetized currency (that is, the RBI's liabilities) had been nullified.[148] Others, while making a distinction between overall black wealth and black money held in the form of untaxed currency notes, suggested that the move would never have been effective in any case since only 1 per cent of the former is held in the form of the latter.[149] In any case, ₹10,720 crore was in all likelihood a mere fraction of even that 1 per cent.

The much-higher-than-expected return of demonetized currency also dashed the government's hopes of a seigniorage windfall for the RBI that would have resulted in greater remittances to it. In December 2016, the State Bank of India (SBI) had estimated that SBNs amounting to a face value of ₹2.5 lakh crore may not return to the system.[150] Based on such calculations, a view had emerged that demonetization would lead to a substantial lowering of the liabilities of the RBI, which in turn would open up the possibility of greater surplus transfer to the sovereign. Instead, with far more demonetized currency than anticipated returning to the

---

147 'Annual Report 2017–18.' *Reserve Bank of India*, 24 August 2018, https://rbidocs.rbi.org.in/rdocs/AnnualReport/PDFs/0ANREPORT201718077745EC9A874DB38C991F580ED14242.PDF.

148 'Demonetised Notes: 99.30% of Demonetised Money Back in the System, Says RBI Report.' *Economic Times*, 30 August 2018, https://economictimes.indiatimes.com/news/economy/finance/after-almost-two-years-of-counting-rbi-says-99-3-of-demonetised-notes-returned/articleshow/65589904.cms.

149 Kumar, Arun. 'Black Money Perpetuates Poverty.' *BusinessLine*, 23 January 2018, https://www.thehindubusinessline.com/opinion/black-money-perpetuates-poverty/article10048551.ece.

150 PTI. 'Rs 2.5 Lakh Crore Won't Come Back into Banking System: SBI.' *Economic Times*, 2 December 2016, https://economictimes.indiatimes.com/industry/banking/finance/rs-2-5-lakh-crore-wont-come-back-into-banking-system-sbi/articleshow/55756927.cms.

system, the whole exercise actually resulted in a net loss of seigniorage to the RBI. In October 2019, the SBI itself said in a research report that:

> In the current case, there is a seigniorage loss, as the face value of Rs 15.28 lakh crore (15.28 trillion) of Rs 17.10 lakh crore (17.1 trillion) has been printed. The net transfer of profits to the Union Government, as a result, have fallen drastically during this year by 53.5 per cent.[151]

Now, whatever impact demonetization had on the practice of taking bribes was also limited to the immediate, with such activities likely resuming once the economy was resupplied with new high-denomination notes. It would be a brave assertion indeed if one were to claim that corruption in general had reduced in India on account of demonetization or anything else. India's consistently low scores in the Corruption Perception Index brought out by Transparency International in recent times would suggest otherwise. India's rank actually fell from 80 to 86 in 2021 as compared to the previous year.[152] Now, while there were optimistic claims that the problem of fake Indian currency notes or FICN had been 'solved' by demonetization on account of a substantive drop in seizures in the immediate wake of the move, such seizures have nevertheless risen steadily since.[153]

---

151 PTI. 'Demonetisation Hit RBI's Seigniorage, Increased Printing Cost: SBI Research.' *Business Standard*, 31 August 2017, https://www.business-standard.com/article/economy-policy/demonetisation-hit-rbi-s-seigniorage-increased-printing-cost-sbi-research-117083100484_1.html.

152 PTI. 'India Falls to 86th Rank in Corruption Perception Index 2020.' *Economic Times*, 28 May 2021, https://economictimes.indiatimes.com/news/economy/indicators/indias-rank-slips-to-86th-in-corruption-perception-index-2020/articleshow/80512814.cms.

153 Tripathi, Rahul. 'Fifth Anniversary of Demonetisation: 2020 Witnessed 190% Jump in Fake Currency Seizure.' *Economic Times*, 9 November 2021, https://economictimes.indiatimes.com/news/india/fifth-anniversary-of-demonetisation-2020-witnessed-190-jump-in-fake-currency-seizure/articleshow/87595655.cms.

Compounded by the delays in reflating the economy due to a need to print new notes, recalibrate machines, etc., demonetization essentially became a Volcker shock for India's unorganized sector where cash transactions dominated both borrowing and settlements. And the unorganized sector accounted for around 50 per cent of India's GDP and employed about 80 per cent of the workforce at the time.[154,155] The impact on the agricultural sector could be seen from a precipitous decline in two-wheeler sales in the wake of demonetization. The deleterious impact on the real estate sector, which was both cash-dependent as well as afflicted by a surfeit of unorganized players, was another example. Post-demonetization, the total number of developers in the top nine Indian cities had fallen by over 50 per cent by 2017–18.[156] Naturally, the impact was also felt on upstream industries such as cement and steel.[157] Retail sales showed a similar trajectory with CAIT claiming sales of consumer durables and appliances dropping by 40 per cent in the first four months of 2017. Textiles was another severely affected sector with mass layoffs. In general, MSMEs, which

---

[154] 'MSME Sector Added Jobs after Demonetisation: Government Data.' *ET Now News,* 21 November 2019, https://www.timesnownews.com/business-economy/economy/article/msme-sector-added-jobs-after-demonetisation-government-data/518149.

[155] Arun, M.G. 'How Demonetisation Took Its Worst Toll on Unorganised Sector Employing 80 per cent of India's Workforce.' *India Today*, 21 July 2017, https://www.indiatoday.in/magazine/up-front/story/20170731-demonetisation-jobs-lost-unorganised-sector-jobless-growth-india-economy-1025552-2017-07-21.

[156] Tiwary, Divya. 'Demonetization 3rd Anniversary: Sectors That Suffered the Most.' *CNBC TV18*, 8 November 2019, https://www.cnbctv18.com/finance/demonetization-3rd-anniversary-sectors-that-suffered-the-most-4665231.htm.

[157] Singhal, Rajrishi. 'How Demonetisation Impacted the Indian Economy.' *Mint*, 30 August 2018, https://www.livemint.com/Politics/uCSwolE7ugfGfuv2O0wWbN/How-demonetisation-impacted-the-Indian-economy.html.

contributed about 30 per cent of India's GDP, with a majority of them being unregistered (aka 'unorganized') were adversely affected by demonetization and the GST regime that came soon afterwards.[158] Close to 50,000 MSMEs shut shop in the year 2017–18 alone in Tamil Nadu, one of India's most industrialized states.[159] And though the central government pointed towards statistics that show that the MSME share in exports had remained stable post-demonetization, the RBI talked about reverse import substitution taking place on account of disrupted supply chains:

> During 2017–18, there was a surge in imports, especially in the category of non-oil non-gold items, which broke out of the traditional co-movement with export behaviour but coincided with a period of sluggish manufacturing activity. This has given rise to concerns that disruptions in the production/supply chain during post-demonetisation have forced domestic demand to spill over into imports in order to overcome domestic supply constraints. This phenomenon of reverse import substitution could reduce GDP in India through leakages of domestic demand into external markets.[160]

Velusamy, a weaver from the town of Tirupur in Tamil Nadu, had this to say about the immediate aftermath of demonetization:

---

158 Kumar, Ashok. 'Small Industries in Ruins after Demonetisation, GST.' *The Hindu*, 6 November 2017, https://www.thehindu.com/news/cities/Delhi/small-industries-in-ruins-after-demonetisation-gst/article19989094.ece.

159 Kandavel, Sangeetha. 'What Revival? Close to 50,000 MSMEs Shut up Shop in Tamil Nadu in Past Year.' *The Hindu*, 8 June 2018, https://www.thehindu.com/news/national/tamil-nadu/what-revival-close-to-50000-units-shut-shop-in-past-year/article24107824.ece.

160 Kapoor, Ravi Shanker. 'DeMo: Success or Failure?' *Sunday Guardian Live*, 10 November 2018, https://www.sundayguardianlive.com/opinion/demo-success-failure.

> I used to weave for mass weavers for a fixed coolie [wages]. After demonetisation, I did not get any work. My coolie for the completed work was reduced all of a sudden. This activity pushed us into steep debt.[161]

Several other such anecdotal stories would emerge about the impact of demonetization in subsequent years.[162] Indeed, job losses were the other legacy of demonetization. According to a CMIE estimate, 1.5 million jobs were lost during the first four months of 2017, that is, right after demonetization.[163] Subsequent research posited that employment opportunities had reduced sufficiently for almost 15 million workers to leave the workforce in the three months following demonetization.[164] A later analysis by researchers at Bengaluru-based Azim Premji University suggested that 5 million lost their jobs between 2016 and 2018.[165]

Now, as we observed earlier, all recessionary shocks lead to permanent losses. And demonetization was definitely a recessionary shock for India's informal sector. Various entities

---

[161] A., Neelambaran. 'Disaster of Demonetisation: Tamil Nadu Industries Struggle to Regain Shape.' *NewsClick*, 13 April 2019, https://www.newsclick.in/disaster-demonetisation-tamil-nadu-industries-struggle-regain-shape.

[162] Borgohain, Ananya. 'All Evidence Suggest Unorganised Sector, SMEs Worst Hit by Demonetisation: Arun Kumar.' *Economic Times*, 7 November 2017, https://economictimes.indiatimes.com/small-biz/sme-sector/all-evidence-suggest-unorganised-sector-smes-worst-hit-by-demonetisation-arun-kumar/articleshow/61542781.cms.

[163] Arun, 'How Demonetisation Took Its Worst Toll on Unorganised Sector Employing 80 per cent of India's Workforce.'

[164] Lahiri, Amartya. 'Deposits after Demonetisation Rose by Rs 6 Trillion and yet Bank Credit Fell, Study Shows.' *ThePrint*, 5 March 2020, https://theprint.in/opinion/deposits-after-demonetisation-rose-by-rs-6-trillion-and-yet-bank-credit-fell-study-shows/375880/.

[165] '5 Million Men Lost Their Jobs after Demonetisation, Says SWI 2019 Report.' *Business Standard*, 17 April 2019, https://www.business-standard.com/article/economy-policy/5-million-men-lost-their-jobs-after-demonetisation-says-swi-2019-report-119041700386_1.html.

suggest that demonetization cost India 1–2 per cent of its extant GDP.[166,167] Unfortunately, demonetization will go down in history as yet another example of why destabilizing shocks to the economy must be avoided. And the treasury should certainly not engage in de facto monetary policy of this variety. Central banks across the world have stopped targeting monetary aggregates precisely because of their outsized and unpredictable effects.[168] Instead, as we have seen, they basically implement monetary policy by targeting a short-term nominal interest rate alongside yield curve management.

Back in 2017, while still buffeted by the shock of demonetization, India's economy, especially the informal sector, ended up being subject to another shock, in the form of the rollout of a rather imperfect goods and services tax (GST). In principle, the GST is a sound idea designed as it is to create a single market out of India's segmented state markets.[169] However, it is at its most efficient when a single GST rate is applied across various goods and services.

That, however, was not to be. India instead got a multi-speed GST with no less than five different rates being

---

[166] ANI. 'Demonetisation Came at a Huge Cost for Indian Economy, Says Raghuram Rajan.' *Business Standard*, 7 September 2017, https://www.business-standard.com/article/economy-policy/demonetisation-came-at-a-huge-cost-for-indian-economy-says-raghuram-rajan-117090701569_1.html.

[167] 'Demonetization Impact: Demonetisation Hit Growth by 2 Percentage Points: US Study.' *Economic Times*, 19 December 2018, https://economictimes.indiatimes.com/news/economy/policy/demonetisation-hit-growth-by-2-percentage-points-us-study/articleshow/67154320.cms.

[168] This current in central banking flows from an analysis done by the economist Poole in the 1970s which revealed that central bank policy insulates output and prices from the effects of large and unpredictable disturbances to the money–demand relationship by setting a target for i rather than M.

[169] Since then, there have been changes in the GST regime. GST has also brought into focus Centre–state financial relations.

applied across a range of goods and services. What was more, a whole bunch of commodities were kept outside the purview of GST altogether – petroleum products (crude oil, natural gas, petrol, diesel and aviation turbine fuel), electricity, alcohol for human consumption, and real estate were kept outside the ambit of the GST regime. As a result, what ensued was that a number of businesses found that the rate at which they could pass on taxes was lower than the rates that they paid on key inputs and this obviously dented profitability. What is worse, due to glitches in the GST portal, the process for claiming input credits on taxes already paid became as cumbersome as ever. Naturally, the unorganized sector, which in any case was going to take a hit from the introduction of GST, was the worst affected. The competitiveness of this sector relied to a great extent on its being able to escape taxes and regulatory compliance burdens. With GST becoming mandatory, their entire cost structure 'shifted' up even as demand had already been weakened by demonetization.

These twin shocks unsurprisingly created an aggregate demand problem in India with a deep impact on employment in the unorganized sector. While the formal sector grew at the cost of the unorganized sector, ultimately the overall hit led to demand weakness for all firms. This was compounded by the RBI's twin rate hikes in 2018. And it is not surprising that the effects became palpable by mid-2019 which is when monetary policy tightening would have been expected to show its greatest effect.

Be that as it may, after months of denial, New Delhi finally began to admit that there was a slowdown in the economy.[170] The CEO of the NITI Aayog even attributed this slowdown

[170] 'Slowdown Not Recession Says Nirmala Sitharaman: Is Modi Govt Still in Denial on Economy?' *ThePrint*, 28 November 2019, https://theprint.in/talk-point/slowdown-not-recession-says-nirmala-sitharaman-is-modi-govt-still-in-denial-on-economy/327676/.

to 'too much of reforms' having being undertaken by the Modi government.[171] As such, even before the COVID-19 shock, there was active debate within India as to whether a fiscal push should be given to close the output gap as it were. The government would act in the manner of providing a corporate tax cut in a bid to boost investment, and the RBI would finally deliver a rate cut in 2019. However, the government's supply-side measure of a corporate tax cut did little to boost growth by itself and India's GDP grew by a mere 4.0 per cent during FY 2019–20.[172] So, it was an Indian economy already in slowdown, beset by demand weakness due to policy shocks and weak credit growth, that braced itself for what was to come in early 2020: the COVID-19 shock.

AN UNCONVENTIONAL EMBRACE

The RBI's response to this unprecedented economic and health emergency was more decisive than what the treasury managed. India's central bank immediately took down interest rates to unprecedently low levels albeit with plenty of distance remaining between them and the Zero Lower Bound (ZLB). The RBI brought down the key policy rate – the repo rate – through cuts on 27 March 2020 and 22 May 2020 respectively by a cumulative 115 basis points to 4 per cent.[173] Alongside, it also reduced the fixed

---

[171] 'Too Much of Reforms Led to Slowdown: NITI Aayog CEO.' *The Hindu*, 3 August 2019, https://www.thehindu.com/business/too-much-of-reforms-has-led-to-slowdown-niti-aayog-ceo/article28802882.ece.

[172] PTI. 'India's GDP growth rate for 2019-20 revised downwards to 4% from 4.2%.' *Business Standard*, 29 January 2021, https://www.business-standard.com/article/economy-policy/india-s-gdp-growth-rate-for-2019-20-revised-downwards-to-4-from-4-2-121012902037_1.html#:~:text=The%20government%20on%20Friday%20revised,sectors%20like%20manufacturing%20and%20construction.

[173] 'REPO Rate: Current Repo Rate, Reverse Repo Rate 2022, RBI Announcements.' BankBazaar, https://www.bankbazaar.com/home-loan/repo-rate.html. Accessed 4 February 2022.

rate reverse repo by 155 basis points in a phased manner during the same period, that is, March–May 2020. This was particularly important because with the sheer amount of liquidity being poured into the banking system by the RBI through open market operations (OMOs) and a cut in reserve requirements, the effective policy rate driving the 'evolution of money market rates and even longer-term interest rates' was now the fixed rate reverse repo, which was playing the same role for the RBI that the IOER did for the Fed once QE was started: absorbing excess reserves held by commercial banks.[174]

Pledging its balance sheet to mitigate the crisis along with the forward guidance that it would do 'whatever it takes' to keep conditions accommodative for a recovery, the RBI would pour even more liquidity through the introduction of several emergency lending measures, including those targeted at specific sectors of the economy, which could be termed as unconventional measures.[175, 176, 177] The RBI had instituted similar unconventional measures in the wake of the GFC as well, such as allowing banks to provide on-tap lending

---

[174] Patra, Michael Debabrata. 'RBI's Pandemic Response: Stepping out of Oblivion.' *Reserve Bank of India*, 28 January 2022, https://rbidocs.rbi.org.in/rdocs/Speeches/PDFs/TAPER2022IMC73A0D5F8677C4BD68ED3B2641240B967.PDF.

[175] Patra, Michael Debabrata. 'Monetary Policy: Trial by Pandemic.' Bank for International Settlements, 16 September 2021, https://www.bis.org/review/r210921c.pdf.

[176] RBI infused massive amounts of liquidity cumulating to 8.7 per cent of GDP. See: Patra, 'Monetary Policy: Trial by Pandemic.'

[177] Forward guidance has become an essential part of the RBI's unconventional toolkit, with the monetary policy committee reiterating in every statement 'that the policy stance would remain accommodative, including with explicit time-contingent and state-contingent guidance'. See: Patra, 'RBI's Pandemic Response: Stepping out of Oblivion.' *Reserve Bank of India*, 28 January 2022, https://rbidocs.rbi.org.in/rdocs/Speeches/PDFs/TAPER2022IMC73A0D5F8677C4BD68ED3B2641240B967.PDF.

to NBFCs.[178] Specifically, the RBI sought to lower long-term interest rates directly via its long-term repo operations (LTRO) and targeted LTRO (TLTRO) measures. TLTROs, besides increasing liquidity, also sought to influence the direction of that liquidity. However, this time around, the RBI also ventured into large-scale local-currency bond purchases in response to the exigency.[179]

In doing so, it joined a host of other EME central banks that too had ventured into large-scale local currency bond purchases as a global crisis mitigation measure for the first time.[180] Like the RBI, many of these EMEs had used unconventional measures shy of QE-style policies to provide liquidity during the GFC and the 2013 Taper Tantrum. With the COVID-19 shock, though, they all decided to expand the unconventional policy toolkit as it were, in a so-called 'dealer or buyer of last resort' mode.[181] Basically, EME central banks stepped in with major government bond purchases to prevent market dislocations due to panic flight from their country's sovereign debt markets. These interventions turned out to be broadly successful in reassuring investors, as reflected by a fall in local currency bond yields subsequent to large-scale asset purchase announcements by EME central banks, and insignificant movements in exchange rates.[182] At the time, the agenda behind EME central bank bond purchases was seen as being more limited than that of AE central banks whose own bond purchases were clearly aimed at providing monetary

---

[178] Mohan, Rakesh, and Partha Ray. 'Indian Monetary Policy in the Time of Inflation Targeting and Demonetisation.' Brookings India Working Papers, 4 May 2018, https://www.brookings.edu/wp-content/uploads/2018/06/Final-Monetary-Policy.pdf.

[179] Arslan, Yavuz, et al. 'Central Bank Bond Purchases in Emerging Market Economies.' BIS Working Papers, 2 June 2020, https://www.bis.org/publ/bisbull20.pdf.

[180] Ibid.

[181] Ibid.

[182] Ibid.

stimulus and credit support to firms in addition to preserving smooth market functioning.

The RBI's initial purchases too were done with a view 'to ensure that all market segments remain liquid and stable, function normally with adequate turnover'.[183] After the initial bout of purchases aimed at preventing domestic bond markets from freezing up, the RBI, however, continued its government bond buying, albeit at a slower pace. These purchases from June 2020 onward clearly served to facilitate the central government's record borrowing programme by keeping market conditions orderly and yields manageable. As Das would outline in his December 2020 speech:

> The Reserve Bank's role as the debt manager and the banker to the government was tested to the hilt in 2020, marked by the highest ever level of market borrowing. Our policies have resulted in the lowest weighted average cost of borrowing in 16 years and the highest weighted average maturity of the stock of public debt on record. The weighted borrowing cost for the centre stands at a new low of 5.82 per cent as on December 1 even with additional borrowings for state governments as against 6.88 per cent during the corresponding period of last year. The government borrowings programme – both centre and the states – has progressed smoothly so far in the year and I would like to reiterate what I said in October – the importance of cooperative solutions for orderly market movements. We need to be competitive and not combative.[184]

Altogether, the RBI injected some ₹3.13 lakh crore (over $40 billion) of liquidity during FY 2020–21 via government bond purchases.[185] And it is certainly true that

---

[183] Ibid.

[184] 'Governor's Statement.' *Reserve Bank of India*, 4 December 2020, https://www.rbi.org.in/Scripts/BS_PressReleaseDisplay.aspx?prid=50746.

[185] 'Governor's Statement.' *Reserve Bank of India*, 7 April 2021, https://rbidocs.rbi.org.in/rdocs/PressRelease/PDFs/PR37GSE79E078854F140D7972F9A50A4B86193.PDF.

the unprecedented borrowing programmes of both central and state governments of around ₹22.0 lakh crore would not have been possible 'at record low costs with elongated maturity during 2020–21' without the RBI's unconventional interventions. So, like its counterparts in the West, the RBI was able to find fiscal space for the treasury via measures that indirectly reduce the costs of raising and servicing public debt. The RBI's interest rate cuts and public asset purchase programmes were both instrumental in this respect. While the policy rate cuts brought down the entire interest rate structure (akin to a stack of books becoming lower in height, when the bottom volume is removed), its purchase of long-term government bonds reduced term risk premia (similar to the gap between each book in the stack being compressed). Now, this 'flattening of the yield curve' obviously also helped lower borrowing rates for the private sector. As Das said in December 2020:

> The measures taken by the Reserve Bank over the year gone by have also resulted in a significant moderation in the structure of interest rates across the spectrum, narrowing of risk spreads, and a record issuance of corporate bonds.[186]

Indeed, flattening the yield curve was an essential part of the RBI's efforts to lend credibility to its forward guidance of keeping conditions accommodative for as long as needed. Back in 2007 itself, the RBI had brought out a paper where it called the yield curve a public good while outlining the importance of maintaining its sanctity:

> [T]he fact that the yield curve acts as a public good enjoins upon all participants, in particular the regulators, the responsibility of ensuring that it is free from any undesirable and manipulative influence, as this would lead to a loss in its informational value and result in market inefficiency

[186] 'Governor's Statement.' *Reserve Bank of India*, 4 December 2020, https://www.rbi.org.in/Scripts/BS_PressReleaseDisplay.aspx?prid=50746.

> brought about by incorrect pricing of other financial instrument.[187]

Das has been echoing this sentiment since the pandemic and ensuring an 'orderly evolution of the yield curve' has been a major goal of RBI policy in the wake of the pandemic.[188] The RBI was in effect 'QE-ing' even before reaching the ZLB/ELB.

But, as happens with QE-type policies, their productivity diminishes over time, and by February 2021, the RBI found that 'Given the strong inter-connectedness of financial markets across borders and progressive integration into the global financial cycle, there was an upsurge of investor unease in India.' This led to a significant upsurge in G-SEC yields by 10 March 2021. And thus, the RBI:

> Taking note of the market's discomfort and in consonance with our commitment to ensure ample liquidity and orderly market conditions, the Reserve Bank scaled up its open market operations (OMOs) in February and conducted five special OMOs (operation twists) in February and March; increased the amount for the operation twist (OT) auction on March 4, 2021 from ₹10,000 crore to ₹15,000 crore; and adopted an innovative asymmetrical special OMO (purchase of ₹20,000 crore and sale of ₹15,000 crore) on March 10, 2021 to reinforce the compression of term premia as well as to inject liquidity which drew a favourable market response.[189]

This sort of RBI intervention was hardly unanticipated by analysts. Back in June 2020 itself, a report from ICICI

---

[187] 'Government Securities Market.' *Reserve Bank of India*, https://rbidocs.rbi.org.in/rdocs/Publications/PDFs/77576.pdf.

[188] Chakraborty, Chiranjivi. 'Negative Yields Come to India, as RBI Tries to Put a Leash on Short Sellers.' *Economic Times*, 19 March 2021, https://economictimes.indiatimes.com/markets/bonds/negative-yields-come-to-india-as-rbi-tries-to-put-a-leash-on-short-sellers/articleshow/81589359.cms.

[189] 'Governor's Statement.' *Reserve Bank of India*, 7 April 2021.

Securities predicted that India's central bank may adopt a form of 'soft yield curve control' wherein 'strong, sporadic interventions around specific thresholds, which may not be in keeping with any specific script that had been anticipated in the wake of the pandemic', would be made to keep 'cap' sell-offs in bonds.[190] Beginning FY 2021–22, the RBI became more explicit about its key role in preserving the orderly pricing of financial assets. Referring to the success with its interventions in February–March 2021, Das stated in April 2021:

> For the year 2021–22, drawing on this experience, we have decided to put in place what is termed as a secondary market G-SEC acquisition programme or G-SAP 1.0, to give it a distinct character. Under the programme, the RBI will commit upfront to a specific amount of open market purchases of government securities with a view to enabling a stable and orderly evolution of the yield curve amidst comfortable liquidity conditions.[191]

G-SAP 1.0 would be followed by G-SAP 2.0 and 3.0, with the RBI pumping in some ₹2.2 lakh crore (just under $29 billion) before ending these explicit QE rounds in September 2021.[192,193] Thus, in recent times, the RBI has basically mimicked the unconventional measures adopted by AE central banks since the GFC.

---

[190] Bloomberg. 'RBI's "Soft Yield-Curve Control": Here's How This Innovative Tool with Tame Bond Yield Spikes.' *Financial Express*, 16 June 2020, https://www.financialexpress.com/market/rbis-soft-yield-curve-control-heres-how-this-innovative-tool-with-tame-bond-yield-spikes/1992970/.

[191] 'Governor's Statement.' *Reserve Bank of India*, 7 April 2021.

[192] Patra, 'RBI's Pandemic Response: Stepping out of Oblivion.'

[193] Das, Saikat. 'RBI Offers Comfort to Bond Market Unnerved by G-SAP Withdrawal.' *Economic Times*, 9 October 2021, https://economictimes.indiatimes.com/markets/bonds/gsaps-scrapped-for-now-bond-traders-fret/articleshow/86870647.cms.

It can be argued that a major reason behind the RBI's ability to mimic the behaviour of AE central banks subsequent to the COVID-19 shock was the credibility conferred by the prior adoption of the FIT framework.[194,195] The credibility of FIT in India naturally derives from its attendant track record leading up to the pandemic. As laid out by the RBI's Das in April 2021:

> From the time after the Monetary Policy Committee (MPC) was constituted in September 2016, average CPI inflation for the period October 2016 to February 2020 – prior to the onset of the COVID-19 pandemic – was 3.8 per cent, down from the average of 7.3 per cent during January 2012 to September 2016. Our research suggests that trend inflation has moderated during the flexible inflation targeting period to around 4 per cent in recent times. The experience during the COVID-19 period has testified to the flexibility of the framework to respond to sharp growth-inflation trade-offs and extreme supply-side shocks over the course of the business cycle.[196]

The RBI certainly seems to believe that the performance of FIT provided it with a measure of credibility required to engage in balance-sheet policies without sparking a major negative reaction from the markets, firms or households. In its February 2021 Report on Currency and Finance, India's central bank had this to say:

> [I]nflation expectations, especially those of professional forecasters, have become better anchored in India and inflation outcomes have become more stable, with lower volatility

---

[194] Eichengreen, Barry. 'Inflation Targeting in India: An Interim Assessment.' VOX, CEPR Policy Portal, 12 October 2020, https://voxeu.org/article/inflation-targeting-india-interim-assessment.

[195] Benigno, Gianluca. 'Credible Emerging Market Central Banks Could Embrace Quantitative.' VOX, CEPR Policy Portal, 29 June 2020, https://voxeu.org/article/credible-emerging-market-central-banks-could-embrace-quantitative-easing-fight-covid-19.

[196] 'Governor's Statement.' *Reserve Bank of India*, 7 April 2021.

> in the exchange rate and short-term interest rates. This has enhanced the ability of the RBI to respond to an exceptional shock like COVID-19 that is not of the authorities' own making. This led up to the view that inflation targeting and its institutional arrangements had a payoff in terms of policy credibility and room for manoeuvre.[197]

Prior to the COVID-19 shock, there had been talk of modifying FIT to include a core inflation target in addition to a CPI target or even moving to targeting only core inflation.[198,199] However, RBI research posits that India is not yet ready for core inflation targeting. Instead, given the critical role of food inflations in keeping inflationary expectations 'anchored', it is important for the time being to persist with a CPI target:

> Contrary to conventional wisdom, it was found that food inflation can un-anchor expectations, spillover into core inflation and hence warranted an appropriate monetary policy response rather than benign 'looking through'. This result reinforced the choice of headline inflation as the appropriate inflation metric for India.[200]

And since:

> the success of FIT lies in providing certainty to people about the course of future inflation by minimising its fluctuations.

---

[197] 'Chapter I: Flexible Inflation Targeting (FIT) in India.' Report on Currency and Finance, *Reserve Bank of India*, 26 February 2021, https://m.rbi.org.in/scripts/PublicationsView.aspx?id=20342.

[198] Sikarwar, Deepshikha. 'RBI Should Target Core Inflation at 3 Per Cent: Pronab Sen.' *Economic Times*, 20 April 2022, https://economictimes.indiatimes.com/news/economy/indicators/rbi-should-target-core-inflation-at-3-per-cent-pronab-sen/articleshow/73309202.cms.

[199] 'View: About Time RBI Shifts to Explicit Core Inflation Targeting.' *Economic Times*, 7 December 2018, https://economictimes.indiatimes.com/markets/stocks/news/view-its-high-time-rbi-shifts-to-explicit-core-inflation-targeting/articleshow/66976635.cms.

[200] 'Chapter I: Flexible Inflation Targeting (FIT) in India.' Reserve Bank of India.

> This is the crux of price stability. It is measured by the second moment about the mean, i.e., inflation volatility, measured by its standard deviation, declined to 1.4 during October 2016–March 2020 from 2.4 in 2012–16.[201]

Unsurprisingly, the RBI strongly batted for an extension of the FIT framework and this view was reciprocated by the treasury, which, on 31 March 2021, decided to retain 'the inflation target at 4 per cent with the lower and upper tolerance levels of 2 per cent and 6 per cent, respectively, for the next five years (April 2021–March 2026)'.[202] The government's decision to extend FIT alongside its supply-side measures to temper inflation has been hailed by the RBI as shining examples of the fiscal-monetary coordination approach being exhibited by macroeconomic policymaking in India. From the RBI's Patra in January 2022, to wit:

> A shining example of monetary fiscal coordination, which was placed on record by the statement of April 7, 2021 was the maintenance of status quo in the monetary policy framework by the government, entrenching a regime in which the inflation target is set by the government and the RBI is mandated to achieve the target. Yet another instance that the statements of June 4, August 6, October 8 and December 8, 2021 underscore is the set of strong supply side interventions by the government that broke the back of then stubborn food inflation and brought headline inflation back into the tolerance band.[203]

Fiscal-monetary coordination, also known globally as a 'stronger together' approach, was critical to FIT's pre-pandemic record as well.[204] From the RBI's 2021 Report on Currency and Finance:

---

[201] Ibid.

[202] 'Governor's Statement.' *Reserve Bank of India*, 7 April 2021.

[203] Patra, 'RBI's Pandemic Response: Stepping out of Oblivion.'

[204] Bartsch, Elga. 'Stronger Together? The Policy Mix Strikes Back.' VOX, CEPR Policy Portal, 15 December 2020, https://voxeu.org/article/stronger-together-policy-mix-strikes-back.

> A combination of successive record harvests, improvements in supply management and moderate increases in MSPs contributed to disinflation under FIT. This underscores the need for close coordination between the central bank and supply management authorities to achieve.[205]

The RBI has of course done more than its fair share for 'stronger together', as we saw above, by acting as a monetary backstop to the government in the wake of the COVID-19 shock.[206] To the extent that it even 'owned accusations' of being 'behind the curve' on inflation by stating that this approach had served the economy rather well.[207] Till February 2022, the RBI seemed sanguine about its choice of not joining other AEs and EMEs in a tightening cycle. After all, household inflation expectations had also moderated by early 2022.[208] But these were based on surveys taken prior to the conflict in Ukraine, which is of course having an inflationary impact around the world. Amid accusations that it was basically in the throes of fiscal dominance, the first signs of a change in the RBI's approach came in March 2022, when Patra told an audience that both inflation and growth projections for the year were to be revised.[209,210] With the

---

[205] 'Chapter I: Flexible Inflation Targeting (FIT) in India.' Report on Currency and Finance, *Reserve Bank of India*, 26 February 2021.

[206] Patra, 'RBI's Pandemic Response: Stepping out of Oblivion.'

[207] 'RBI's behind the Curve Approach Has Served Us Well: Dy Guv Patra.' *Mint*, 28 January 2022, https://www.livemint.com/industry/banking/rbis-behind-the-curve-approach-has-served-us-well-dy-guv-patra-11643357606126.html.

[208] 'Households' Inflation Expectations Survey.' *Reserve Bank of India*, 10 February 2022, https://rbidocs.rbi.org.in/rdocs/Publications/PDFs/IESHJAN202202B31D06C2E048BBBAFC4289BCC36A1E.PDF.

[209] Keshavdev, V. 'RBI More Concerned About Govt Borrowing, Not Inflation: Subhash Garg.' *Fortune India*, 9 March 2022, https://www.fortuneindia.com/macro/rbi-more-concerned-about-govt-borrowing-not-inflation-subhash-garg/107381.

[210] 'India May Relook Inflation, Growth Projections, Says RBI Deputy Governor Michael Patra.' *Economic Times*, 12 March 2022, https://

April 2022 meeting, the MPC overtly changed its stance, stating:[211]

> The MPC is of the view that since the February meeting, the ratcheting up of geopolitical tensions, generalised hardening of global commodity prices, the likelihood of prolonged supply chain disruptions, dislocations in trade and capital flows, divergent monetary policy responses and volatility in global financial markets are imparting sizeable upside risks to the inflation trajectory and downside risks to domestic growth.
>
> Given the evolving risks and uncertainties, the MPC has decided to keep the policy repo rate unchanged at 4 per cent. The MPC also decided to remain accommodative while focusing on withdrawal of accommodation to ensure that inflation remains within the target going forward, while supporting growth.

And in the post-MPC press conference, Das admitted that inflation had been put before growth in the 'sequence of priorities'.[212] It seems that the Indian economy's revival from lockdown lows has given the RBI the confidence to focus on its primary mandate, that is, inflation control. As Das revealed in April 2022:

> According to the second advance estimates released by the National Statistical Office (NSO) on February 28, 2022, real GDP rose by 8.9 per cent in 2021–22. Private consumption

---

economictimes.indiatimes.com/news/economy/indicators/india-may-relook-inflation-growth-projections-says-rbi-deputy-governor-michael-patra/articleshow/90164512.cms; Patra, Michael Debabrata. 'Taper 2022: Touchdown in Turbulence.' *Reserve Bank of India*, 11 March 2022.

[211] 'Monetary Policy Statement, 2022–23.' *Reserve Bank of India*, 8 April 2022, https://rbidocs.rbi.org.in/rdocs/PressRelease/PDFs/PR3863D6040CE9CF4DE0AC9F6AF94F522C03.PDF.

[212] 'Edited Transcript of Reserve Bank of India's Monetary Policy Press.' *Reserve Bank of India*, 8 April 2022, https://rbidocs.rbi.org.in/rdocs/Speeches/PDFs/EDITED11042022A563E6EF0F7843CFB99D2B10C4C32FD9.PDF.

> and fixed investment – key drivers of domestic demand – however, remain subdued, with these two components being only 1.2 per cent and 2.6 per cent respectively, above their pre-pandemic levels. On the supply side, contact-intensive services still trail the 2019–20 level. Nevertheless, the Indian economy is steadily reviving from its pandemic induced contraction.[213]

At the time of writing, there were worries whether it was already too late, with the CPI in March 2022 touching almost 7 per cent.[214] But it is unlikely that a generalized inflationary episode similar to the one witnessed over 2011–13 that led up to the Taper Tantrum would take place.[215] For one, aggregate demand is in a far weaker state in 2022 than it was back in 2013. The labour market is also quite weak. While real wages in the countryside strengthened by 7.4 per cent during the period 2009–13, no such spiral is likely today.[216] Moreover, inflation expectations are much better anchored in 2022 than they were back in 2011–13. Indeed, it has been observed that the RBI's signalling has become more effective, with smaller changes in interest rates now needed to signal the central bank's intent.[217] The pass through via the exchange rate is also lower today than it used to be back in 2011.[218] And though

---

[213] 'Governor's Statement.' *Reserve Bank of India*, 8 April 2022, https://rbidocs.rbi.org.in/rdocs/PressRelease/PDFs/PR15GOVERNOR5AA91FD102FB403291B57E2BEDD74D54.PDF.

[214] Karunakar, Rahul. 'RBI May Be Forced To Hike Rates Sooner As March Inflation Spikes To 6.95%.' *NDTV*, 12 April 2022, https://www.ndtv.com/business/rbi-may-be-forced-to-hike-rates-sooner-as-march-inflation-spikes-to-6-95-2882035.

[215] Patra, 'Taper 2022: Touchdown in Turbulence.'

[216] Ibid.

[217] 'Chapter I: Flexible Inflation Targeting (FIT) in India.' Report on Currency and Finance, *Reserve Bank of India*, 26 February 2021.

[218] 'Chapter 5: Open Economy Flexible Information Targeting.' Report on Currency and Finance, *Reserve Bank of India*, 26 February 2021, https://rbidocs.rbi.org.in/rdocs/Publications/PDFs/05CH_26022021B17C0FA103E642788C21FC1C4F8BD242.PDF.

the RBI did not increase the repo rate in the April 2022 MPC meeting, its liquidity management operations had in effect already tightened monetary conditions, as we shall see in a bit. On 5 May 2022, it would go even further and hike the repo rate by 40 basis points, citing inflationary pressures on account of geopolitical tensions.[219] With America and Europe entering what will initially be a stiff, tightening cycle, and the Chinese economy precariously poised, it is likely that global growth will see a sharp fall in 2022, with its attendant impact on crude and commodity prices thereby bringing relief to a major 'upside risk' to inflation. The RBI will probably not have to go very far to restrain inflationary pressures.

Be that as it may, it is of paramount importance that India's fiscal and monetary authorities do not pull in different directions going forward. Just as the RBI acted as a backstop for the government, it is important that the latter reciprocate the favour as it were, and provide headroom to the RBI with its own policies. 'Stronger together' always carries the risk of fiscal dominance, and therefore it is important that the monetary authority is seen to be retaining instrument independence if inflationary expectations are to remain anchored to the RBI's inflation target. This means that extreme 'crisis options' such as helicopter money where monetary policy becomes completely subservient to the fiscal authority are best avoided. Even on its merits, helicopter money does not bring much to the table by way of an upside, while the downside risks are significant.

---

[219] PTI. 'Inflationary Pressures Likely To Continue Going Forward on Geopolitical Tension.' Times of India, 4 May 2022, https://timesofindia.indiatimes.com/business/india-business/inflationary-pressures-likely-to-continue-going-forward-on-geopolitical-tensions-rbi/articleshow/91315068.cms.

HELICOPTER MONEY OR GOOD OLD QE?[220]

When the COVID-19 induced lockdowns first happened there was talk the world over of using helicopter money, given the massive demand on fiscal policy to prevent a major contraction. In India, those in favour of a bigger stimulus began calling upon the Reserve Bank of India (RBI) to monetize any deficit spending that cannot be covered through market borrowings by invoking the escape clause in the Fiscal Responsibility and Budget Management (FRBM) Act.[221] While New Delhi did use the escape clause to suspend deficit targets for the year, to their credit the RBI and the government eschewed any move towards overt or permanent monetization and opted for QE-style policies instead.[222] In particular, there were suggestions that

[220] For a more general version of the argument made in this section, see: Borio, Claudio, and Anna Zabai. 'Unconventional Monetary Policies: A Re-appraisal.' BIS Working Papers, July 2016, https://www.bis.org/publ/work570.pdf.

[221] Noronha, Gaurav. 'Government Can Use the Escape Clause in the FRBM Act to Monetise the Deficit: Usha Thorat.' *Economic Times*, 16 May 2020, https://economictimes.indiatimes.com/news/economy/finance/government-can-use-the-escape-clause-in-the-frbm-act-to-monetise-the-deficit-usha-thorat/articleshow/75767170.cms.

[222] According to the IMF, India activated the escape clause in February 2020 before the pandemic, which allowed a temporary deviation of deficit not exceeding ½ percentage points of GDP a year, and raised the FY 2019–20 and FY 20–21 deficit to ½ percentage points of GDP above the previous estimate to 3.8 and 3.5 per cent of GDP, respectively. With the significant economic fallout from the pandemic, the government suspended the fiscal rule through FY 20–21 in order to provide fiscal support, and announced that the FRBM Act will be amended to reflect the authorities' revised fiscal path. See: Davoodi H.R., P. Elger, A. Fotiou, D. Garcia-Macia, X. Han, A. Lagerborg, W.R. Lam, and P. Medas. 'Fiscal Rules and Fiscal Councils: Recent Trends and Performance during the COVID-19 Pandemic.' *IMF*, 27 January 2022, pp.16, https://www.imf.org/-/media/Files/Publications/WP/2022/English/wpiea2022011-print-pdf.ashx.

India resort to 'helicopter money', typically understood to be a 'permanent' monetization of deficit spending achieved through the creation of non-interest-bearing liabilities by the central bank.[223] It is therefore worthwhile to examine whether helicopter money will really be worth it in a future crisis where the government has apparently little room for fiscal manoeuvre.

In such a scenario, a so-called 'helicopter drop' could take the form of the RBI directly funding transfers by the government to MSMEs and the unemployed. Since, the RBI has to give a 'permanent character' to the monetization, it could do so by either buying a zero-coupon (non-interest-bearing) perpetual bond from the government or by simply crediting the latter's account with it and registering a negative liability on its own balance sheet. The emphasis is on 'permanent' since the idea is to perpetually rid the government of any liabilities arising from its expenditure. Moreover, the permanent monetization is also meant to convey to the private sector that it need not fear future tax increments to offset the same. The 'inflation-tax' on the private sector will be projected by proponents to be limited, since in depressed conditions additional spending is likely to be taken up more by output growth than price rise. So, is helicopter money a 'free lunch' for India, given the circumstances? The answer unfortunately is no, as we shall see.

Any helicopter drop will lead to a commensurate increase in commercial bank reserves, and it is unlikely that banks will be willing to hold a sizeable increase without being paid interest on it. This increase in bank reserves would occur even if the helicopter drop was done in the form of cash payments because the populace as a whole already holds

---

[223] 'RBI Should Implement "Helicopter Money" to Counter Economic Crisis: Telangana CM.' *Mint*, 11 April 2020, https://www.livemint.com/news/india/rbi-should-implement-helicopter-money-to-counter-economic-crisis-telangana-cm-11586633899851.html.

most of the currency it desires and anything more will end up being deposited in bank accounts. Now, in 'normal' times, banks hold reserves (a certain level of balances in their deposit accounts with the RBI) to meet the RBI's reserve requirements as well as to insure against the uncertainty related to fund flows. In 'good times', they economize on their reserve holdings. The RBI takes advantage of this behaviour by supplying banks with just enough reserves to meet their demand and channels a 'corridor' for the RBI's 'operating target', which is the rate at which banks advance unsecured overnight loans to each other and is aimed at being as close to the repo rate, which is the policy rate, as possible. The 'floor' of that corridor traditionally has been the reverse repo rate, which is the rate at which the RBI voluntarily absorbs excess liquidity. Meanwhile, the ceiling is the marginal standing facility (MSF), which is the rate at which the RBI lends to commercial banks which are suddenly short of liquidity. Both the reverse repo rate and the MSF are for short-term borrowing (lending) operations.

In depressed economic circumstances, banks may hold sizeable excess reserves which they typically agree to lend to the RBI at the reverse repo rate or whatever rate is being offered for their reserves by the RBI. If the system becomes sloshed with excess reserves, the RBI's operating target rate, which is called the weighted average call rate (WACR), will start closing in on the reverse repo rate, as happened in the wake of demonetization and with the onset of the pandemic as well when the RBI poured liquidity into the system. With the system full of reserves, the RBI typically changes the way it pursues the operating target, by setting it equal to the reverse repo rate (or any other specified absorption rate). In a system sloshed with reserves, commercial banks would be indifferent between holding the same and lending it to other banks at the reverse repo rate.

During such times, it is the reverse repo rate (or whichever deposit rate is being used) which becomes the de facto policy rate serving as the benchmark for all other interest rates in the economy. The corridor system of managing liquidity thus turns into a so-called 'floor'-based system, as is the case with the Fed and other AE central banks. According to the RBI's 2021 Report on Currency and Finance:

> After the COVID-19 pandemic, the Reserve Bank once again asymmetrically widened the corridor during March–April 2020, operating a de facto floor system as various conventional and unconventional measures flooded liquidity into the system and kept financial conditions ultra-easy to counter the pandemic.[224]

Now, as long as the interest rate at which the RBI is absorbing excess liquidity is positive, the helicopter drop would not be a cost-less monetization from the perspective of the consolidated government, that is, the treasury and the central bank together. In that sense, it would be no different from a purchase of marketable government securities by the RBI, since on the consolidated balance sheet, any government (i.e. treasury)-issued liabilities (marketable securities) held as assets by the RBI will cancel out, while the commercial bank reserves thus created stay on as liabilities. Of course, with a helicopter drop, the treasury's own debt will not rise. But the interest paid on the excess reserves by the RBI would reduce its profits and thereby whatever it can remit to the fiscal authority. So, the only way in which a helicopter drop can lead to a permanent (that is, for all time) 'cost-less' monetization is if the RBI sets the reverse repo rate or whatever deposit rate it is using to absorb excess reserves to zero and keeps it there indefinitely, which is akin to giving up on monetary policy altogether, and basically a recipe for

---

[224] Mitra, Arghya Kusum, et al. 'Operating Procedure of Monetary Policy.' Report on Currency and Finance, *Reserve Bank of India*, 26 February 2021, https://rbidocs.rbi.org.in/rdocs/Publications/PDFs/04CH_260220210E9EE1D12DFE4F21A019BAB56F218DCC.PDF.

hyperinflationary disaster. It is also meaningless when talking about India, given that the interest rates are unlikely to hit the ZLB or ELB anytime soon.

The RBI can always force commercial banks to hold the increase in reserves as part of an extended reserve requirement and thereby not pay any interest on them. But this would be akin to a tax on commercial banks (and therefore not costless for society) and at variance with the RBI's endeavour to make banks 'on-lend' to various distressed parties during depressed times. India is no stranger to this kind of financial repression for the purpose of deficit financing. Till 1997, the RBI used to automatically monetize the treasury's deficits by purchasing 91-day ad-hoc bills from the latter, and banks were forced to hold the resulting reserves through high reserve requirements. However, as we noted earlier, the phasing out of that practice alongside the adoption of fiscal rules as enshrined in the FRBM act, which also stopped the RBI from purchasing government debt directly, marked India's move away from fiscal dominance and towards monetary dominance, culminating in the adoption of FIT in 2016.

A helicopter drop would be a complete reversal of this trend and would end up denting the credibility of the RBI with the concomitant implications for price stability. Thus, if the need for seigniorage support is deemed inevitable, it is best done though large-scale government bond purchases via the secondary market with a measure of yield curve control. Full impact seigniorage should be avoided. The RBI's pandemic response has shown that the Indian G-SEC market is already deep enough for QE-style policies which when deployed will not unhinge expectations or lead to runaway credit expansion by banks.[225] It also has wide acceptability in

---

[225] Also, unlike a large helicopter drop done by registering a negative liability on the RBI's balance sheet, mere marketable government bond purchases will not send the RBI's equity into negative territory, necessitating recapitalization at some point with fiscal resources.

the market given that the RBI managed to pull off soft-yield curve control cooperatively. In fact, once it became clear that New Delhi intended to borrow an even greater sum during FY 2022–23 than the record borrowing of FY 2020–21, there have been calls on the RBI to actually remove a significant portion of the bond supply by the market in order to keep things orderly.[226] The withdrawal of various extraordinary liquidity measures by the RBI which has been underway and the use of India's Forex reserves to stem any downward pressure on the rupee due to the Fed taper will actually open up space for the RBI to further increase G-SEC holdings.

After all, the RBI is likely to continue with an ample reserves framework for some time even though Das did say in April 2022 that the central bank had decided to fully restore the 'liquidity management framework instituted in February 2020', which is of course a corridor-based system.[227] By 'ample' the RBI means 'a level of liquidity that would keep the system in surplus even after meeting the requirements of all financial market segments and the productive sectors of the economy'.[228] Like the Fed found out, it is not so easy to 'move out' of an expanded balance sheet.[229] And there is no need to per se. A floor-based system is arguably more suitable for this era of uncertainty that necessitates unconventional responses. According to recent research, an expanded balance sheet can improve monetary transmission and boost the supply of stable short-term assets to the market, besides enhancing a central bank's ability to pour liquidity during an exigency.[230] Incidentally, the RBI has on occasion said

[226] 'RBI Faces Pressure to Stem Yield Shock amid Avalanche of Bond Supply.' *Mint*, 5 April 2022, https://www.livemint.com/economy/rbi-faces-pressure-to-stem-yield-shock-amid-avalanche-of-bond-supply-11649136300602.html.

[227] 'Governor's Statement.' *Reserve Bank of India*, 8 April 2022.

[228] 'Governor's Statement.' *Reserve Bank of India*, 7 April 2021.

[229] See chapter one for details.

[230] Bernanke, Ben. 'Should the Fed Keep Its Balance Sheet Large?'

that monetary transmission has improved as a result of ample liquidity conditions.[231]

Interestingly, in April 2022, the RBI revealed:

> It may be noted that the interest rate for around 80 per cent of the total liquidity absorbed under the LAF during Q4: 2021–22 has firmed up close to the policy repo rate due to the rebalancing of liquidity through VRRR auctions.[232]

Since the onset of the pandemic, the RBI has been using VRRRs or variable reverse repos which are longer-duration reverse repo operations to absorb liquidity. What Das's statement reveals is that monetary tightening has been underway for a while in India since the RBI has been pushing up the WACR closer to the repo rate even while it kept the latter unchanged. As explained earlier, due to the huge liquidity surplus, the de facto policy rate had become the reverse repo rate which had been set at some 65 basis points below the repo rate since May 2020. But with the VRRRs, the RBI has obviously pushed the de facto benchmark rate for the economy above that. Indeed, these efforts actually paved the way for the creation of a new floor that Das announced in the same address:

> The amendment to Section 17 of the RBI Act in 2018 empowered the Reserve Bank to introduce the Standing Deposit Facility (SDF). By removing the binding collateral constraint on the central bank, the SDF strengthens the operating framework of monetary policy. Accordingly, it has now been decided to introduce the SDF as the floor of the LAF corridor. This would provide symmetry to the

---

Brookings, 2 September 2016, https://www.brookings.edu/blog/ben-bernanke/2016/09/02/should-the-fed-keep-its-balance-sheet-large/.

[231] Shukla, Saloni. 'High Liquidity to Push Borrowing Costs Lower: RBI.' *Economic Times*, 6 August 2020, https://economictimes.indiatimes.com/markets/stocks/news/high-liquidity-to-push-borrowing-costs-lower-rbi/articleshow/77390847.cms.

[232] 'Governor's Statement.' *Reserve Bank of India*, 8 April 2022.

> operating framework of monetary policy by introducing a standing absorption facility at the bottom of the LAF corridor, similar to the standing injection tool at the upper end of the corridor, namely the marginal standing facility (MSF). Thus, at both ends of the LAF corridor, there will be standing facilities – one to absorb and the other to inject liquidity. Accordingly, access to SDF and MSF will be at the discretion of banks, unlike repo/reverse repo, OMO and CRR which are available at the discretion of the Reserve Bank.[233]

The MPC meeting of April 2022 set the SDF at 3.75 per cent, that is, 25 basis points below what was then the repo rate. Being a 'standing facility', that is, one that will be used at the discretion of commercial banks, SDF is essentially analogous to the IOER that was introduced by the Fed in 2008. Without further significant VRRRs, the WACR will close in on the SDF and the de facto policy/benchmark rate for the economy will be the SDF, which was increased to 4.15 per cent in May 2022.[234] But the fact that like IOER, the SDF will not be a hard floor with the RBI retaining the old reverse repo rate in its toolkit is another indication that excess liquidity conditions will not be removed by the RBI anytime soon.

With the era of balance-sheet policies firmly underway at the RBI, it is important that the government live up to its role as a backstop for the monetary authority. This would give further confidence to the RBI to deploy balance-sheet expansion techniques up to their efficient scale, without being daunted by the possibility of facing losses. While the issue of how much capital the RBI should hold has been formalized through the acceptance of recommendations of the Bimal Jalan committee, the government would do well to

---

[233] 'Governor's Statement.' *Reserve Bank of India*, 8 April 2022.

[234] *Reserve Bank of India*, https://www.rbi.org.in/Scripts/BS_PressReleaseDisplay.aspx?prid= 53652.

legally guarantee automatic fiscal support to the RBI in the event that the latter's capital heads into negative territory.[235] This will add another layer of credibility to India's 'stronger together' approach, making the country future-ready for any new exigency.

FISCAL STRATEGY

Ultimately, for 'stronger together' to work, the fiscal authority must also dovetail its spending practices to the twin aims of growth and price stability. It is only with growth that India's public debt levels will remain stable, and it is also only with growth that India's supply-side potential output levels will increase and this would serve to check inflationary tendencies. On the other hand, it is only with price stability that affirmative decisions on sizeable longer-term investments will be made by the private sector that will sustain growth over time. To reconcile these twin objectives, government spending must be aimed at increasing productivity and reducing market friction and crowding in private investment. Fortunately, it is indeed possible to adopt a direction of spending that simultaneously aids the cause of both growth as well as price stability, with infrastructure spending being a leading example. For instance, it has been observed that 'improvements in road network, tele-density, market penetration and irrigation facilities helped reduce multi-stage mark-ups over the food supply chain in India'.[236] Obviously, these measures are in no way detrimental to the cause of growth either, as noted earlier. In that context, the

---

[235] 'RBI Dividend News: RBI Approves Dividend of Rs 57,000 Crore to Government.' *Times of India*, 14 August 2020, https://timesofindia.indiatimes.com/business/india-business/rbi-approves-dividend-of-rs-57000-crore-to-government/articleshow/77544022.cms.

[236] 'Supply Chain Dynamics and Food Inflation in India.' *Reserve Bank of India*, 11 October 2019, https://www.rbi.org.in/scripts/BS_ViewBulletin.aspx?Id=18527.

recent decision to boost infra spending for FY 2022–23 by 35.4 per cent in the budget is a step in the right direction.[237]

Besides the direction of spending, rules with respect to the overall fiscal sustainability regime must also be strengthened with the addition of an independent fiscal council at the earliest, which incidentally was a key recommendation of the FRBM review committee report released in 2017.[238] Specifically, the report called for a fiscal council that

> will serve both an ex-ante role – providing independent forecasts on key macro variables like real and nominal GDP growth, tax buoyancy, commodity prices – as well as an ex-post monitoring role, and also serve as the institution to advise on triggering the escape clause and also specify a path of return.

And that:

> International experience suggests that fiscal councils can improve fiscal outcomes and forecast accuracy, often materially, especially when they are (a) independent; (b) command a strong media profile; (c) tasked with monitoring fiscal rules; and (iv) involved in forecast assessment.

An independent fiscal council may go a long way in making fiscal spending truly countercyclical in India and will add that crucial layer of credibility to the fiscal management regime which will give even greater leeway during exigencies. It will thus play a role akin to what a strong FiT regime will do

---

[237] Nahata, Pallavi. 'Budget 2022: Government's Capex Hiked by 35.4% for FY23.' *BloombergQuint*, 1 February 2022, https://www.bloombergquint.com/business/budget-2022-governments-capex-hiked-by-354-for-fy23; Incidentally, India's effective capital expenditure outlay for 2022–23, which includes grants in aids for capital assets, is actually lower than the budget estimate for 2021–22. It is only higher than the revised (latest) estimate.

[238] FRBM Review Committee, 'Responsible Growth: A Debt and Fiscal Framework For 21st Century India.' Department of Economic Affairs, Government of India, https://dea.gov.in/sites/default/files/Volume%201%20FRBM%20Review%20Committee%20Report.pdf.

on the monetary side. However, specifying debt ceilings for general government debt in an amended FRBM Act can be avoided for the time being given the current context.

While the direction of spending is ever so important, the revenue side of the equation must also be managed properly to generate the desired growth-cum-price stability regime. To begin with, India's GST regime has to be revitalized at the earliest as the government has been apparently planning to do by 'pruning tax exemptions, removing anomalies from taxing raw materials and intermediates higher than finished products (that is, inverted duty structure), and reducing the number of GST slabs'.[239] As noted by Vijay Kelkar, who headed the task force that recommended the introduction of GST in India, the removal of exemptions and the reduction of the number of GST slabs will go a long way in increasing the competitiveness of Indian industry and alleviating cost-push inflation, all the while increasing revenue collections by lowering incentives for evasion.[240] Administratively, it is vital that the current mandatory requirement for GST participants to file returns in multiple states (that is, wherever they operate) and face as many audits (besides that from central tax authorities) be done away with. This incredibly cumbersome requirement has actually increased compliance costs besides making the government's GST-promoting chant of 'one nation, one tax' ring hollow.

These structural changes are pending even as New Delhi will end by June 2022 the compensation it provides to states for the revenue shortfall incurred by them by moving to the GST framework. As such, many states are worried about the hit to their finances and this has reportedly made them

---

239 Seth, Gireesh. 'Coming Soon, a Structural Revamp of GST.' *Mint*, 15 February 2022, https://www.livemint.com/economy/revamp-of-gst-likely-in-phases-hike-in-textile-rates-on-cards-11644949326500.html.

240 Renavikar, Vijay. 'How India Can Reinvent the Goods and Services Tax.' *Mint*, 2 November 2021, https://www.livemint.com/politics/policy/indian-gst-2-o-time-for-bold-changes-11635868831715.html.

amenable to a move by the GST council to do away with the current 5 per cent slab and move many items to a new 8 per cent slab.[241] The inflationary implications of such a move are obvious and not exactly desirable in the current environment. Indeed, India's central government may want to look at extending compensation for a while longer (even if it is through additional borrowing) to stave off such a move to allow consumption to recover a bit more. This might even help in nudging states that have currently not followed the centre in reducing taxes on fuel to do so.[242]

On the regulatory side of things, the government should defer to the RBI's conservative approach to managing the financial health of the commercial banking sector, which is still at the core of finance in India. There should be no repeat of the contest seen over the 'revised' PCA framework that was described earlier. The RBI on its part must not drop the ball either as it may have done with the IL&FS issue, when it failed to sequester what was a systemically important financial institution. In any case, the recent move to set up a PCA framework for NBFCs is a welcome step.[243] The RBI will naturally also have to step up its game for the fintech era.[244] India's ability to evolve suitable regulatory and

---

[241] PTI. 'GST Council May Do Away with 5% Rate; Move Items to 3% and 8% Slabs.' *Economic Times*, 1 May 2022, https://economictimes.indiatimes.com/news/economy/policy/gst-council-may-do-away-with-5-rate-move-items-to-3-8-slabs/articleshow/90890399.cms.

[242] Chaturvedi, Rakesh Mohan. 'PM Modi Calls on States Again To Bring Down VAT on Fuel.' *Economic Times*, 28 April 2022, https://economictimes.indiatimes.com/news/india/pm-modi-calls-on-states-again-to-bring-down-vat-on-fuel/articleshow/91137262.cms.

[243] 'PCA Framework for NBFCs.' *Reserve Bank of India*, 14 December 2021, https://www.rbi.org.in/Scripts/BS_PressReleaseDisplay.aspx?prid= 52717.

[244] Nayak, Gayatri. 'RBI Gearing up to Fintech Challenge, Asks Banks to Be Vigilant Too.' *Economic Times*, 2 November 2021, https://economictimes.indiatimes.com/industry/banking/finance/banking/rbi-gearing-up-to-fintech-challenge-asks-banks-to-be-vigilant-too/articleshow/87491262.cms.

cybersecurity practices for the fintech sector in particular and digital lending in general will be an important element for enhancing both financial stability and growth in general.[245]

Some recent steps taken by the government such as giving deposit insurance up to ₹5 lakh will strengthen the RBI's hand and reduce the probability of old-style bank runs.[246] An aggressive approach to removing existing NPAs in the system should remain in place as that is a very important ingredient in kick-starting the investment cycle in India. In that light, the recent operationalization of two asset reconstruction companies or bad banks was welcome news.[247] Less encouraging was the news to the effect that lenders had failed to transfer their bad assets to the newly formed ARCs by the deadline of 31 March 2022.[248] Moves to make the IBC mechanism more effective by reducing the time taken to achieve resolution are the need of the hour as well.[249] Overall, the NPA situation in the Indian banking

---

245 J, Anand. 'Third Wave of Venture Finance: Revenue-Based Lending Takes Root in India's Lush Digital Economy.' *Economic Times*, 20 March 2022, https://economictimes.indiatimes.com/prime/fintech-and-bfsi/third-wave-of-venture-finance-revenue-based-lending-takes-root-in-indias-lush-digital-economy-/primearticleshow/90186455.cms.

246 'Bank Deposit Insurance Cover Upped to Rs 5 Lakh, Refund in 90 Days: Goyal.' *Business Standard*, 12 December 2021, https://www.business-standard.com/article/economy-policy/bank-deposit-insurance-cover-increased-to-rs-5-lakh-piyush-goyal-121121200340_1.html.

247 Singh, Ritu. 'India's Bad Bank Gets RBI Nod; Banks Set to Transfer Rs 50,000 Crore of NPAs by March 31.' *CNBC TV18*, 28 January 2022, https://www.cnbctv18.com/finance/indias-bad-bank-gets-rbi-nod-banks-set-to-transfer-rs-50000-crore-of-npas-by-march-31-12282752.htm.

248 Ghosh, Shayan. 'Lenders Miss Deadline to Transfer Assets to Bad Bank.' *Mint*, 6 April 2022, https://www.livemint.com/industry/banking/procedural-delays-led-to-missing-march-deadline-on-bad-bank-asset-transfer-11649245936426.html.

249 Prasad, Gireesh. 'Bankruptcy Resolution Shifting to Fast Track.' *Mint*, 20 February 2022, https://www.livemint.com/politics/policy/centre-readies-fresh-round-of-ibc-tweaks-11645383818919.html.

sector was showing signs of improvement as of early 2022.[250] The improving NPA situation has unsurprisingly been mirrored by better credit growth.[251,252]

Despite the NPA situation not being as worrisome as it was in 2018, the RBI nevertheless stated in November 2021 that it still believes that banks would need recapitalization once extraordinary monetary and fiscal support unwinds.[253] New Delhi, however, is reluctant to infuse more tranches of capital into PSU banks (having already pumped in ₹3.06 lakh crore since FY 2017–18) and reports suggest that it is more in favour of privatizing banks than providing fiscal support.[254,255] Looking to privatize some banks is per se not a bad idea at this juncture. After all, the overwhelming majority of banks in the

---

[250] Purswani, Nitin. 'India's Huge Pile of Toxic Loans Has Declined, but Don't Celebrate Just Yet.' *Economic Times*, 1 April 2022, https://economictimes.indiatimes.com/opinion/et-commentary/indias-huge-pile-of-toxic-loans-is-declining-but-dont-celebrate-just-yet/articleshow/90576699.cms.

[251] Misra, Jagadish. 'What Rising Loan Disbursals Mean for the Economy.' *Mint*, 28 February 2022, https://www.livemint.com/industry/banking/how-does-credit-disbursal-boost-the-economy-11646069355669.html.

[252] According to the RBI: 'Money supply (M3) and bank credit by commercial banks rose (y-o-y) by 8.7 per cent and 9.6 per cent, respectively, as on March 25, 2022.' See: 'Monetary Policy Statement, 2022–23.' *Reserve Bank of India*, 8 April 2022, https://rbidocs.rbi.org.in/rdocs/PressRelease/PDFs/PR3863D6040CE9CF4DE0AC9F6AF94F522C03.PDF.

[253] Ghosh, Shayan. 'Banks Need to Raise More Capital to Deal withStress, Says RBI.' *Mint*, 28 December 2021, https://www.livemint.com/industry/banking/banks-need-more-capital-to-deal-with-stress-and-credit-demand-says-rbi-11640690241411.html.

[254] Narayan, Subhash. 'Privatization of Govt Banks May Have to Wait a Little Longer.' *Mint*, 22 March 2022, https://www.livemint.com/news/india/privatization-of-psbs-likely-by-sep-20-cap-on-foreign-holdings-to-go-11647974281902.html.

[255] Verma, Sunny. 'Explained: Why Has Moody's Upgraded India's Sovereign Rating Outlook?' *Indian Express*, 6 October 2021, https://indianexpress.com/article/explained/india-moodys-ratings-outlook-stable-explained-7555130/.

RBI's PCA framework were government-owned, suggesting a systemic tendency towards low-quality politicized lending. At the same time, privatization should not become a thinly disguised move towards a 'main bank system' à la Japan or even China where industrial conglomerates end up having their own banks delivering policy loans to group companies, often to acquire public assets. As such, the Modi government has outlined a plan to raise some ₹6 lakh crore ($81.9 billion) by leasing out state-owned infrastructure assets over 2022–24 to fund new capital expenditure without further widening the budget deficit.[256] The monetization or privatization of public assets should be seen less as a fiscal sustenance measure and more as a means of financing specific national capabilities that build resilience and boost growth. As always, it is what fiscal space is used for that matters than the creation of fiscal space itself.

In fact, the direction of government spending is important for reassuring ratings agencies who keep a hawk eye on India's overall debt levels. However, it is sometimes the case that the strongest case may fail to convince them and a downgrade may be in the offing. So, then, the question arises: should India be scared of a ratings downgrade?

In May 2020, then Chief Economic Adviser Krishnamurthy Subramanian had 'defended' India's muted stimulus measures in the wake of the pandemic due to fears of ratings downgrades on account of a slippage in fiscal consolidation targets.[257] It had also been reported that India would keep its stimulus for FY 2020–21 limited to around

---

[256] Singh, Siddhartha. 'Modi Govt Plans To Raise Rs 6 Lakh Cr from Infra Assets Sale in Four Years.' *ThePrint*, 23 August 2021, https://theprint.in/economy/modi-govt-plans-to-raise-rs-6-lakh-cr-from-infra-assets-sale-in-four-years/720659.

[257] Bhattacharya, Nikita. 'Is India's Sovereign Ratings Downgrade Risk Higher than Peers?' *Mint*, 11 May 2020, https://www.livemint.com/news/india/is-india-s-sovereign-ratings-downgrade-risk-higher-than-peers-11589174603453.html.

$60 billion in order to appease global ratings agencies.[258] Remarkably, the net stimulus given by New Delhi during FY 2020–21 was actually quite close to that number. While Sitharaman may have said in February 2021 that the government wasn't 'worried about rating agencies as the higher borrowing number is in order to stimulate growth, followed by an articulated path of fiscal consolidation', the fact is that New Delhi continues to deal carefully with global ratings agencies.[259] This might be especially so because New Delhi has been actually looking to get an upgrade to India's sovereign rating.[260]

Be that as it may, ratings agencies have repeatedly flagged India's high general government debt levels as being higher than what India's similarly rated peers have. In fact, in the wake of the pandemic, India did see a downgrade from Moody's, with its sovereign ratings being sent to the lowest investment grade, one step away from junk status.[261] The other global ratings agencies of 'consequence', that is, Fitch and S&P, too had voiced their concern about India's debt

---

[258] Reuters. 'India Set to Cap Stimulus Package at $60 Billion to Protect Credit Rating.' *Times of India*, 1 May 2020, https://timesofindia.indiatimes.com/business/india-business/india-set-to-cap-stimulus-package-at-60-billion-to-protect-credit-rating-report/articleshow/75496690.cms.

[259] Jha, Somesh. 'Not Worried about Rating Agencies, Says Nirmala Sitharaman.' *BloombergQuint*, 25 February 2021, https://www.bloombergquint.com/economy-finance/not-worried-about-rating-agencies-says-nirmala-sitharaman.

[260] 'India's Ratings Don't Reflect Economy's Fundamentals: CEA.' *The Hindu*, 29 January 2021, https://www.thehindu.com/business/Economy/indias-ratings-dont-reflect-economys-fundamentals-cea/article33699155.ece.

[261] 'India's Credit Rating Cut Puts It One Step Away from Junk.' *Economic Times*, 2 June 2020, https://economictimes.indiatimes.com/markets/stocks/news/indias-credit-rating-cut-puts-it-one-step-away-from-junk/articleshow/76151725.cms.

sustainability in the wake of the pandemic.[262] Since then, India has seen Moody's upgrade the outlook for its ratings (which has not changed since the downgrade) from negative to stable.[263] And Fitch and S&P have also reaffirmed India's lowest-investment-grade ratings.[264,265]

As such, ratings agencies are not too convinced about India's medium-term consolidation plans. And as we can see, India's sovereign ratings lie just above junk levels. So, the question arises: How worried should India be of a hypothetical ratings cut to junk status in the near future for whatever reason? Well, as things stand today, a ratings cut would not 'automatically' lead to any major portfolio outflows since India is not part of any global bond index.[266] There will be some pressure on G-SEC yields, but, as we have seen before, the RBI is capable of preventing market dislocations. Naturally, the RBI's debt-management-related liquidity interventions would put further pressure on the rupee but the consequences of that too would be manageable given India's large forex reserves, numerous swap agreements, sizeable forward assets, very low levels of foreign-currency-

---

[262] Bhat, Swati. 'UPDATE 1: Fitch Warns India against Further Deterioration in Fiscal Outlook.' Reuters, 28 April 2020, https://www.reuters.com/article/india-ratings-fitch-idUSL3N2CG2NE.

[263] Akash, Podishetti. 'Moody's Affirms India's Sovereign Rating, Upgrades Outlook to Stable.' *Mint*, 5 October 2021, https://www.livemint.com/economy/moodys-changes-india-s-rating-outlook-to-stable-from-negative-11633439553314.html.

[264] 'Fitch Affirms India at "BBB-"; Outlook Negative.' *Fitch Ratings*, 16 November 2021, https://www.fitchratings.com/research/sovereigns/fitch-affirms-india-at-bbb-outlook-negative-16-11-2021.

[265] Mishra, Asit. 'S&P Retains Its Lowest Rating for India with Stable Outlook.' *Mint*, 13 July 2021, https://www.livemint.com/economy/sp-retains-india-s-lowest-investment-grade-sovereign-rating-11626186109135.html.

[266] Sircar, Subhadip. 'This Is What Is at Risk If India's Sovereign Rating Is Cut to Junk.' *ThePrint*, 4 June 2020, https://theprint.in/economy/this-is-what-is-at-risk-if-indias-sovereign-rating-is-cut-to-junk/435402/.

denominated government debt, and the fact that most of India's sovereign debt is in any case owed to domestic players.

This also means that India is currently adequately prepared to deal with any capital outflow pressure arising out of the Fed's 2022 taper.[267] As of end-March 2022, India's forex reserves stood at $607 billion, enough to provide cover for 12 months' worth of imports, as compared to end-March 2013 when they were adequate for only six months' worth of imports.[268,269] Short-term external debt on a 'residual maturity basis' was equal to only 40.3 per cent of India's Forex reserves in end-March 2022, down from 59 per cent in end-March 2013. The short-term external-debt-to-GDP ratio was 8.6 per cent in end-September 2021 as compared to 9.4 per cent in end-March 2013.[270] In any case, India's ratio of overall external debt to GDP is currently lower than that of most EMEs.[271]

In fact, India's external strength is noted by ratings agencies as an important factor behind India's ratings being investment-grade despite having higher government debt levels than similarly rated peers. As Fitch stated in November 2021:

> Risks associated with India's high public debt are partly offset by the country's ability to finance its deficits domestically, which is a strength relative to most 'BBB' peers. Foreign currency government debt comprises only 6% of total debt

---

[267] Bhalla, Aakriti. 'Taper Minus Tantrum: Indian Economy More Resilient Today; Well Placed to Absorb US Fed Tightening Shock.' *Financial Express*, 7 February 2022, https://www.financialexpress.com/economy/taper-minus-tantrum-indian-economy-more-resilient-today-well-placed-to-absorb-us-fed-tightening-shock/2427666/.

[268] Nayak, Gayatri. 'India's Forex Reserves Enough to Cover Just a Year's Imports.' *Economic Times*, 16 April 2022, https://economictimes.indiatimes.com/news/economy/finance/import-cover-of-forex-reserves-shrinks-30-percent-in-fy22/articleshow/90859445.cms.

[269] Patra, 'Taper 2022: Touchdown in Turbulence.'

[270] Ibid.

[271] Ibid.

(BBB median: 33%) and only 2% of government securities are held by non-residents.[272]

Incidentally, a 2016 World Bank study found statistically significant effects of downgrades on mostly foreign-currency-denominated debt.[273]

For the past few years, however, New Delhi has been trying to get India included in various global bond indices in the name of the government being able to borrow cheaply from non-residents, thereby leaving more room for the private sector to borrow domestically. However, large gross portfolio borrowings from abroad even in rupees can end up constraining monetary policy given their fickle nature. As Das stated in February 2022, while replying to a question about India's inclusion:

> Last year, we… introduced FAR, the fully accessible route, whereby certain bonds where, you know, there is no limit with regard to how much of FDI and investment from outside will come in. Bond inclusion, you are right. It works both ways to have a greater flow of resources into the country, but when the index becomes adverse then that could be sudden outflows. And the strongest point of our debt profile is that it is largely more than 90 per cent denominated in the Indian rupee in domestic currency. Exposure to foreign exchange in our domestic borrowing, that is, the government borrowing, is not more than five to six per cent. So, inclusion in the domestic bond market, as top rates it can operate both ways, to that extent. So that is precisely the reason why RBI and the government are taking a very calibrated approach on this issue.[274]

---

[272] 'Fitch Affirms India at "BBB-"; Outlook Negative.' *Fitch Ratings*.

[273] 'Analysis: How Do Credit Downgrades Affect Short-Term Government Borrowing?' World Bank Group, 17 August 2016, https://www.worldbank.org/en/news/feature/2016/08/17/analysis-how-do-credit-downgrades-affect-short-term-government-borrowing.

[274] 'Edited Transcript of Reserve Bank of India's Monetary Policy Press.' *Reserve Bank of India*, 10 February 2022, https://rbidocs.rbi.org.in/

So, the inclusion in bond indices is a double-edged sword. While it could in theory lead to lower yields and even provide some support to the rupee, it may also make India's external sector more vulnerable through the build-up of what are ultimately unstable inflows. This matter was flagged by Urjit Patel back in 2020 who saw FAR and the push for index inclusion as an unnecessary and risky invitation to 'bond tourists'.[275] Any substantial build-up of foreign debt due to bond index inclusion could put India one adverse event away from a balance of payments episode. Like a sudden ratings downgrade to junk status, for instance. Or a sanctions freeze on reserves. All the fortification in the world will not matter if there is a sudden freeze on India's reserves, as was done to Russia by the West in March 2022 due to the conflict in Ukraine.[276] Though Russia has $585 billion in reserves of which $284 billion had been frozen it had to technically default on a part of its sovereign debt denominated in dollars that came due in April 2022 by offering to pay in roubles.[277] So difficult had it become for Moscow to get its hands on dollars for repayment. It finally avoided an outright default on this debt by dipping into dollar reserves that were kept outside the jurisdiction of the US and its allies.[278] This of

rdocs/Content/PDFs/MPCT1502202219AC6ABEFAF34A5BAD8FA9B21C44B254.PDF.

[275] Bloomberg. 'India Should Keep Public Finances Healthy: Former RBI Chief Urjit Patel.' *Economic Times*, 6 April 2020, https://economictimes.indiatimes.com/news/economy/policy/india-should-keep-public-finances-healthy-former-rbi-chief-urjit-patel/articleshow/75005368.cms.

[276] Hersher, Monica, and Joe Murphy. 'Graphic: Russia Stored Large Amounts of Money with Many Countries. Hundreds of Billions of It Are Now Frozen.' *NBC News*, 18 March 2022, https://www.nbcnews.com/data-graphics/russian-bank-foreign-reserve-billions-frozen-sanctions-n1292153.

[277] Faulconbridge, Guy. 'Russia May Be in Default, Moody's Says.' *Reuters*, 15 April 2022, https://www.reuters.com/world/europe/moodys-says-russia-may-be-default-dollar-bonds-2022-04-15.

[278] King, Ben. 'Russia Beats Final Deadline to Avoid Debt Default.' *BBC News*, 3 May 2022, https://www.bbc.com/news/business-61313296.

course means that in these unstable times the case for Indian government borrowing in dollar-denominated offshore bonds is even weaker than it was back in 2019 when the government first mulled this move before backing out.[279] As Raghuram Rajan noted in a recent article titled 'Economic Weapons of Mass Destruction':

> A widespread fear of indiscriminate sanctions would lead to more defensive behavior. Following the action taken against Russia's central bank, China, India, and many other countries will worry that their own foreign-exchange holdings (of advanced-economy debt) may prove unusable if a few countries decide to freeze their assets. With few other assets possessing the liquidity of dollar or euro reserves, countries will start limiting activities that necessitate reserve holdings, such as cross-border corporate borrowing.[280]

Even if cross-border corporate borrowing isn't being curtailed at the moment, the government would do well to at least keep itself away from borrowing in dollars through offshore bonds. To be sure, foreign-currency-denominated borrowings by New Delhi increased in the wake of the pandemic, these were in the form of long-term loans from multilateral agencies. As such, the government expects its external debt to grow by almost ₹40,000 crore in the course of FY 2022–23.[281]

The government and the RBI would do better to deepen the onshore G-SEC market, and the recent step to throw

---

[279] Kaul, Vivek. 'Debt Fears over India's Decision to Borrow from Abroad.' *BBC News*, 17 July 2019, https://www.bbc.com/news/world-asia-india-48960315.

[280] Rajan, Raghuram. 'Economic Weapons of Mass Destruction.' *Project Syndicate*, 17 March 2022, https://www.project-syndicate.org/commentary/economic-wmds-and-the-risk-of-deglobalization-by-raghuram-rajan-2022-03.

[281] Government of India. 'Debt Position of the Government of India.' Union Budget, 31 March 2022, https://www.indiabudget.gov.in/doc/rec/annex9.pdf.

open that market to domestic retail investors is a positive development. There has been a favourable response to this move with several retail investors even moving funds from fixed deposits to Indian G-SECs.[282] In recent times, Indian households have been gradually diversifying away from physical assets to financial ones to store savings, and it is not surprising that safe assets such as G-SECs are finding favour with them.[283] To further encourage and consolidate this move towards financial savings, the government and the RBI must obviously do all they can to maintain financial stability. Indeed, macroprudential regulation assumes great importance at a time when sectors such as real estate are seeing an upswing, even as the government has allowed foreign debt flows into real estate investment trusts (REITs).[284] Foreign inflows clearly have the potential to amplify any new domestic asset bubbles, and the RBI's move to tighten regulation for NBFCs which are among the heaviest overseas borrowers is the right decision.[285]

Despite RBI Deputy Governor T. Rabi Sankar stating in an October 2021 speech that 'India is on the cusp of

---

[282] Das, Saikat. 'RBI's Retail Direct a Hit with Investors as GSecs Trump FDs.' *Economic Times*, 21 March 2022, https://economictimes.indiatimes.com/industry/banking/finance/banking/rbis-retail-direct-a-hit-with-investors-as-gsecs-trump-fds/articleshow/90341194.cms.

[283] 'Household Savings at Record High in FY21: Where People Are Putting Their Money.' *Times of India*, 4 February 2022, https://timesofindia.indiatimes.com/business/india-business/household-savings-at-record-high-in-fy21-where-people-are-putting-their-money/articleshow/89340885.cms.

[284] 'Real Estate on the High Rise Again.' *Economic Times*, 14 March 2022, https://economictimes.indiatimes.com/opinion/et-editorial/real-estate-on-the-high-rise-again/articleshow/90209592.cms.

[285] Shukla, Piyush. 'Timeline: How RBI Cut the Arbitrage of NBFCs and Moved to Bank-like Regulations.' *MoneyControl*, 25 April 2022, https://www.moneycontrol.com/news/business/banks/timeline-how-rbi-cut-the-arbitrage-of-nbfcs-and-moved-to-bank-like-regulations-8407561.html.

some fundamental shifts in this space' with respect to capital account management, the time for full capital account convertibility is not yet here.[286] In that same speech, Sankar himself highlighted the importance of capital controls which can prove more effective than macroprudential regulations in certain situations:

> Capital flow measures are effective insofar as they lead to safer external liability structures, by reducing dependence on foreign borrowing and could be particularly effective during sudden-stop episodes. They work essentially by avoiding risky flows or containing short-term debt or controlling currency exposure of domestic borrowers. Especially for economies where capital flows are relatively large, or the exposure of banking systems is significant, these measures could be more effective than macro prudential tools.[287]

Today, even the IMF acknowledges that unfettered flows of capital result in greater instability for limited gain and are thereby more agreeable to the use of capital controls.[288] At the time of writing, FDI (which is considered stable) dominates India's net capital flows and is on its own sufficient to finance the current account deficit.[289] Foreign portfolio investments in equity are a distant second to FDI, with debt flows being

---

[286] 'Capital Account Convertibility: India on the Cusp of Fundamental Shifts, Says RBI Dy Guv.' *BusinessLine*, 14 October 2021, https://www.thehindubusinessline.com/money-and-banking/capital-account-convertiblity-india-on-the-cusp-of-fundamental-shifts-says-rbi-dy-guv/article36999586.ece.

[287] Reserve Bank of India. https://rbidocs.rbi.org.in/rdocs/Speeches/PDFs/FEDAI1410202197 69D899E5C74D20A60553DE6D38B6FE.PDF

[288] Korinek, Anton, et al. 'The IMF's Updated View on Capital Controls: Welcome Fixes But Major Rethinking is Still Needed.' *Brookings*, 18 April 2022, https://www.brookings.edu/blog/up-front/2022/04/18/the-imfs-updated-view-on-capital-controls-welcome-fixes-but-major-rethinking-is-still-needed/

[289] Patra, 'Taper 2022: Touchdown in Turbulence.'

even smaller. This is exactly the 'hierarchy' of inflows that is desirable from a stability perspective. New Delhi would do well to preserve it.

Capital controls can of course be rendered meaningless if cryptocurrencies go unfettered. The RBI has already made its position clear that 'Private cryptocurrency is a big threat to macroeconomic stability and financial stability' and wants an outright ban on their use.[290,291] For the time being, however, the Modi government has chosen instead to tax cryptocurrencies, a move that was interpreted by some as a step towards legitimization.[292] Although Sitharaman clarified in February 2022 that the government had neither legitimized nor banned cryptocurrencies, with a decision on the same being subject to consultations that were underway.[293] Whether by opting for an outright ban like China or very heavy regulation, India must ensure that greater demand by households for financial assets doesn't end up in any significant exposure to cryptocurrencies.

Now, keeping capital controls in place would mean that the prospects for 'internationalizing' the rupee would

---

290 'Edited Transcript of Reserve Bank of India's Monetary Policy Press.' *Reserve Bank of India*, 10 February 2022, https://rbidocs.rbi.org.in/rdocs/Content/PDFs/MPCT1502202219AC6 ABEFAF34A5BAD8FA9B21C44B254.PDF.

291 Mahanta, Vinod. 'RBI's Crypto Ban Talks Give the Shivers to Small Investors.' *Economic Times*, 16 February 2022, https://economictimes.indiatimes.com/tech/technology/rbis-crypto-ban-talks-give-the-shivers-to-small-investors/articleshow/89604356.cms.

292 'Crypto Tax in India Explained: How Much You May Have to Pay, Tips to Prepare.' *India Today*, 22 February 2022, https://www.indiatoday.in/business/story/crypto-tax-india-income-tax-returns-itr-rules-explained-1916340-2022-02-22.

293 PTI. 'Govt Has Sovereign Right to Tax Cryptocurrency; Decision on Banning or Not Banning to Come Later: FM.' *Times of India*, 11 February 2022, https://timesofindia.indiatimes.com/business/india-business/govt-has-sovereign-right-to-tax-cryptocurrency-decision-on-banning-or-not-banning-to-come-later-fm/articleshow/89497207.cms.

be dampened as well. But it is probably not yet time for the rupee's coming-out party. Having said that, India must promote greater use of the rupee in invoicing and settlements, as this will reduce the FCER effect (see chapter three) and help Indian exports become more responsive to exchange-rate depreciations. A central bank digital currency or 'digital rupee', which is on the anvil at the RBI, would be a natural fit for this purpose.[294] The digital rupee would also make alternative payment arrangements, such as the proposed rupee-rouble trading system, that are not controlled by the US much more viable. [295]

THE LAST WINDOW

While the recipe on the capital side is more readily implementable, India has much greater work to do on the current account side of things. A major reason why India is better placed to deal with any 'risk off' or sudden stop scenario today is because its current account deficit is at a far more manageable level than it was back in 2013, that is, during the Taper Tantrum. As the RBI's Patra put it in a March 2022 speech:

> The current account deficit is expected to remain within 2.5 per cent of GDP, having averaged 1.1 per cent of GDP during 2014–21. By contrast, Taper 2013 had been preceded by the current account deficit averaging 3.7 per cent during 2009–13, with a peak of 6.8 per cent in the third quarter of

---

[294] Nahar, Pawan. 'CBDC Coming This Year; Revenue Possibility in VDAs: FM.' *Economic Times*, 8 March 2022, https://economictimes.indiatimes.com/markets/cryptocurrency/cbdc-coming-this-year-revenue-possibility-in-vdas-fm/articleshow/90075555.cms.

[295] Reuters. 'India May Set Up Rupee Trade Accounts with Russia to Soften Sanctions Blow.' *Economic Times*, 26 February 2022, https://economictimes.indiatimes.com/industry/banking/finance/banking/india-may-set-up-rupee-trade-accounts-with-russia-to-soften-sanctions-blow/articleshow/89840625.cms.

> 2012–13. The improvement in the current account in the recent period and going forward draws strength from robust export performance, both goods and services, with targets set at US$ 450 billion and US$ 300 billion, respectively, for 2022–23.[296]

Despite improved export performance, the fact remains that India continues to suffer from a chronic deficit in the goods trade, which in turn points towards a need to boost manufacturing competitiveness. For instance, according to one industry insider, India's electronics-producing sector suffers from a 'disability' of around 8–11 per cent as compared to foreign competitors.[297] A major contributor to this disability are India's relatively high logistics costs, which account for 13–14 per cent of GDP, as compared to 8–10 per cent in AEs. Naturally, infrastructure outcomes that focus on reducing the share of logistics in India's GDP to the government's target of 8 per cent will have to be implemented sans delay.[298] For that to happen, New Delhi must greatly improve inter-ministerial coordination.[299]

Keeping India's trade deficit in check will require increasing both its export competitiveness as well as substituting imports where sustainably possible. Like the East Asian industrializers, India should not see import substitution

---

[296] Patra, 'Taper 2022: Touchdown in Turbulence.'

[297] 'Cover Story: Chasing Manufacturing Excellence.' *Manufacturing Today*, 16 August 2021, https://www.manufacturingtodayindia.com/people/11342-cover-story-chasing-manufacturing-excellence.

[298] Shettigar, Jagadish, and Pooja Misra. 'Why India is in a Hurry to Fix Logistics Bottlenecks.' *Mint*, 15 November 2021, https://www.livemint.com/politics/news/how-an-efficient-logistics-could-aid-the-economy-11636997795357.html.

[299] Dash, Dipak K. 'Dire Need to "Remove Frictions" among Ministries, Departments for Gatishakti Impetus: Highway Secy.' *Times of India*, 1 March 2022, https://timesofindia.indiatimes.com/india/dire-need-to-remove-frictions-among-ministries-departments-for-gatishakti-impetus-highways-secy/articleshow/89906373.cms.

and export promotion in silos either. Both approaches are necessary for attaining the requisite scale and supply-chain depth that underpins competitiveness. Comparative advantage in any case is created, not revealed. India's own pharmaceutical industry is an example of sequential import substitution and export promotion. This sector initially grew by creating generic versions of expensive imported drugs and then graduated to a very high degree of export intensity once India embraced TRIPS. Today, India's pharmaceutical sector needs a new round of import substitution to remove its heavy dependence on China for active pharmaceutical ingredients (APIs) given the tremendous disruptive risks involved.

As such, API is one of 14 sectors where the Modi government has introduced production-linked incentive (PLI) schemes for boosting local output. Apparently, local manufacturing of at least 35 out of 53 APIs for which India is acutely dependent on imports was already underway by end-March 2022.[300] It is interesting that after years of talking about a sector-neutral industrial policy, the Modi government finally decided to bite the bullet and is now actively seeking to remove disabilities and build scale by offering output-target-linked subsidies.

Initially launched in March 2020 for three sectors, namely mobile manufacturing and specified electronic components, critical key starting materials/drug intermediaries and APIs, and manufacturing of medical devices, the PLI scheme was expanded by April 2021 to include a further 10 sectors. These were automobiles and auto components, pharmaceutical drugs, specialty steel, telecom and networking products,

---

[300] PTI. 'Local Manufacturing of 35 APIs Started After PLI Scheme: Mandaviya.' *Economic Times*, 29 March 2022, https://economictimes.indiatimes.com/industry/healthcare/biotech/pharmaceuticals/local-manufacturing-of-35-apis-started-after-pli-scheme-mandaviya/articleshow/90519863.cms.

electronic/technology products, white goods (ACs and LEDs), food products, textile products (MMF segment and technical textiles), high-efficiency solar PV modules, and advanced chemistry cell (ACC) battery. The total projected outlay for all 13 sectors together was ₹1.97 lakh crore to be made available over a five-year period starting from FY 2021–22. A small PLI scheme was approved in September 2021 for drone and drone components as well. And after years of dithering, India finally bit the bullet by unveiling a ₹76,000 crore 'India Semiconductor Mission' that seeks to develop a 'semiconductor and display manufacturing ecosystem' in India.[301] At the moment, India does not have a single commercial fab on its soil, even as its demand for semiconductors is expected to touch $80 billion by 2025.[302] As such, the lack of domestic semiconductor fabrication capability is a core strategic vulnerability for India that needs to be addressed at the earliest.

In February 2022, ratings agency ICRA said that the PLI scheme would attract new manufacturing capital expenditure to the tune of approximately ₹4 lakh crore over the next five years.[303] The World Bank's 'Global Economic Prospects' also believes that India's growth will be boosted by this scheme. BNP Paribas has estimated that the PLI scheme may add 1.7 per cent to India's GDP by 2027 by 'generating $150 billion in new sales'. Given its obvious focus on the electronics value

---

[301] 'India Semiconductor Mission.' *Press Information Bureau, Ministry of Electronics & IT, Government of India*, 23 March 2022, https://pib.gov.in/PressReleasePage.aspx?PRID=1808676.

[302] Doval, Pankaj. '"Chip demand may hit $110 billion by "30".' *Times of India*, 29 April 2022,http://timesofindia.indiatimes.com/articleshow/91165793.cms?utm_source=contentofinterest&utm_medium=text&utm_campaign=cppst.

[303] Press Trust of India. 'PLI scheme to unlock India's manufacturing capacity: Icra.' *Economic Times*, 18 February 2022, https://economictimes.indiatimes.com/small-biz/sme-sector/pli-scheme-to-unlock-indias-manufacturing-capacity-icra/articleshow/89655309.cms.

chain, the government intends to increase exports from this sector to $300 billion by 2025.[304]

However, even as the PLI scheme kicks off, with output apparently already rising from some of the targeted sectors, India's imports from China have also increased, despite the border standoff in the same period. This is hardly surprising since Indian industry is majorly dependent on China for parts and components. That, however, is a clear indication that the PLI schemes need to add layers that are focused on growing the supply chain for final processed goods through support for MSMEs. Naturally, there will also have to be a concomitant focus on securing supplies of critical materials including rare earths.

A strong, resilient and deep domestic supply chain will greatly increase India's attractiveness for those looking to diversify away from China. While there will be some reshoring in the AEs, as we have noted earlier in this book, there will be much greater restocking. If this move away from just-in-time concepts of inventory management have to not become cost-prohibitive, the West will require a new deflationary force in the form of the Indian worker. Even as the old globalization retreats, a new window of opportunity has opened up. But it is probably the last such window for India's manufacturing growth, and will require a concerted effort, ticking the right boxes on both the industrial and institutional side of things.

On the institutional side, India has begun correctly by negotiating two important but somewhat limited free trade agreements (FTAs) with the UAE and Australia. The CEPA with UAE in particular has a 'permanent safeguard

---

[304] Press Trust of India. 'India poised to grow electronics manufacturing to $300 billion in 3-4 years: Minister.' *MoneyControl*, 3 November 2021, https://www.moneycontrol.com/news/business/economy/india-poised-to-grow-electronics-manufacturing-to-300-billion-in-3-4-years-minister-7671541.html.

mechanism that can be resorted to in a situation of a sudden surge in imports, along with strict rules of origin that will prevent products from other countries slipping into the CEPA trade route'.[305] If implemented properly, this would become a good template for further such agreements, most notably with the EU. Indeed, India's deepest alignment going forward will probably be with the EU which agreed to set up a Technology Council with India in April 2022, something that it only has had with the US till date.

Even as this window is taken, issues related to environmental sustainability will get increasingly foregrounded. Especially in light of India's commitment to transition to a net-zero economy by the year 2070. While climate change will obviously make headlines, equally important will be the need to manage the energy–food–water nexus as India embarks on a new wave of industrial urbanization. But that is perhaps a story or book for another day.

[305] Khan, Shariq, and Neha Dewan. 'Industry Calls India-UAE CEPA Pact Game Changer, but Warns of Bottlenecks Ahead.' *Economic Times*, 22 February 2022, https://economictimes.indiatimes.com/small-biz/trade/exports/.

CONCLUSION

AS RUSSIAN FORCES TURN UKRAINIAN CITIES TO RUBBLE, LITTLE doubt remains that we live in a grave new normal shaped as much by the pandemic as a struggle for a new world order. The post-GFC great power competition chronicled in this book has now acquired a distinctive hard edge to it, with the attendant consequences for smaller countries caught in the middle. Gone is the old neoliberal credo that sought to spread a West-centric globalism prescribing free trade and financial integration.

Rather than temper territorial temptations, trade and financial integration are being weaponized and used as new domains of escalation during the course of conflict or even for coercion in situations short of war. Indeed, as global military competition intensifies, barriers to technology commerce will only rise further building on the trends covered in this book such as Trump's trade war with China. As such, the West's unprecedented sanctions on Russia are clearly aimed at engineering a financial crisis in that country and will remain in place beyond the conflict in Ukraine itself. Russia too chose to attack Ukraine at a time when pandemic-induced supply-side inflationary pressures are rife globally, calculating that a crippling embargo on critical energy exports was unlikely, especially given European dependence on the same.

Whether economics is an extension of war or vice versa is now moot. In the current contest between major powers to create exclusive spheres of influence, conventional conflicts may indeed occur (Ukraine being a tragic example) but they will be limited in time and space on account of nuclear deterrence. The nuclear balance will make this global struggle more diffuse and prolonged in nature than the convulsions of the two world wars. Instead, the use of proxies (whether state or non-state), cyberwarfare and of course engineered financial crises will be the weapons of choice.

Be that as it may, America's 'sanctionomics' too has its pitfalls. The freezing of Russian foreign exchange reserves in a bid to crash the ruble alongside the removal of several Russian banks from SWIFT will crystallize long-standing fears in other capitals about suddenly being disconnected from the global financial system due to Washington's diktats. Sanctionomics will likely provide further impetus to create more robust versions of the non-dollar financial and payments architecture that are still at a nascent stage as analyzed earlier. US financial unilateralism will be taken note of in all capitals whose central banks hold a large chunk of their foreign exchange reserves in the form of US government securities (g-secs) and the level of dollar holdings going forward will be ever more contingent on a country's overall economic relationship with the US.

For the time being, however, the dollar will continue to reign supreme. As we have seen in the course of this book, neither the euro nor the yuan are in a position to challenge dollar hegemony given the economic trajectories of their issuers. The burst of inflation that has accompanied the pandemic is certainly eroding the attractiveness of safe US g-secs what with their yields being deeply negative in real terms. But then so are the yields of European g-secs with the Eurozone experiencing its worst inflation in decades as well. And China's unbalanced and debt-addled economy can hardly be seen as more of a safe haven than America's. Rather, Beijing's fears related to capital flight as the Fed tightens monetary policy has meant that Chinese capital controls have become more stringent and that by itself militates against the idea of internationalizing the yuan. Ironically, Japanese g-sec yields are relatively attractive compared to US or European yields today, since even the pandemic has failed to ignite significant inflation in the land of the Rising Sun. But once the Fed and the ECB quell inflationary tendencies, very likely via a technical recession, that relative attractiveness will wane.

The threat from privately issued forms of money that depend on distributed ledger technologies to the dollar is also vastly overblown. Cryptocurrencies are highly volatile, lack any underlying assets to back them and can manage only low transaction throughputs. It is no wonder that their use as a means of payments is highly limited. So-called Stablecoins that are cryptocurrencies benchmarked to some sovereign currency or widely traded commodity may have a better future if regulated but are currently used mostly to facilitate trade in other digital assets. However, governments and central banks will ensure that they have the 'Stablestcoin' in the form of new Central Bank Digital Currencies (CBDCs) that will pay no interest but bear no risk either being issued by central banks. Besides taxing certain cryptocurrencies to oblivion or even banning them outright, monetary authorities worldwide will coordinate efforts to bring digital money to heal. After all, a central bank's ability to conduct monetary policy is contingent upon the inability of other agents to offset the same by changing the size or mix of their own liabilities. This means that there should be no privately issued securities in circulation that substitute perfectly for the constituents of the monetary base, i.e., currency plus commercial bank reserves. The US will also deal with CBDCs issued by China or the Eurozone with a commercial bank-intermediated non-interest bearing CBDC of its own, i.e., a 'digital dollar'. For the foreseeable future, the greatest enemy of the US dollar therefore is the US government's tendency to overuse its incumbency.

In the near-term, America will continue to use that systemic incumbency to push forward its global aims. Russia's aggression against Ukraine is helping consolidate America's position vis-à-vis the Franco-German alliance in Europe, with the latter having to support the American position on Russia even to the detriment of their own economic interests. In the Indo-Pacific theatre, too, America's alliance structure is providing geopolitical teeth in the form of the AUKUS (Australia-UK-US) military configuration that has a distinct nuclear edge to it and is aimed at threatening China's all important Eastern seaboard. The US strategy could well be to ultimately negotiate a so-called G-2, with it leading the more powerful side in a bipolar world.

Such a G-2 world, however, will not be in India's interest whose future lies in multipolarity. It is not surprising therefore that even the Modi government has found its Nehruvian instincts and chosen to not abandon Russia despite the latter's actions in Ukraine. Of course, India's position as the key geopolitical and geoeconomic 'Swing State' in the world allows it the luxury of pursuing strategic autonomy. The challenge for India going forward would be to sharpen its democratic mojo rather than succumb to authoritarian temptations. India needs more democracy, not less. The current trend of social disharmony, engendered by the extant political class will have to be checked if India has to take its rightful place in the new world order.

ACKNOWLEDGEMENTS

WRITING THE ACKNOWLEDGEMENTS FOR A BOOK THAT HAS taken over six years and two-and-a-half drafts is, in fact, quite easy. One merely has to remember those who have been tolerant of such a tortuous process!

My father, Sukumar Jha – the individual who literally taught me how to spell. Without his unfailing support, I would not be writing anything at all.

Poulomi Chatterjee, my long-suffering editor, whose encouragement and kindness to an errant author will not be forgotten.

Swarnima Narayan, who graciously took over from Poulomi to see this book off to press.

Manidipa and Nilanjan Roy, who may not have wished for a crazy son-in-law in the first place, but have adjusted admirably to the new normal by now.

Sarajit, my brother, whose championing of neoliberal ideas at the breakfast table gave me early exposure to the sort of debates I would need to address later in my life. Vinu, his wife, for continuing to condone such (loud) debates whenever my brother and I are in the same room. Saksham and Meenakshi, who never gave up asking, 'Is Kaku's book ever going to be done?'

The anonymous readers whose suggestions helped refine the manuscript.

Jyotsna Raman for painstakingly editing the book, and Shyama Warner and Shreya Chakravertty for their patient proofreading.

Mukundan Alexander, my research assistant, along with interns Aditya Padinjat and Aditi Warrier, who helped this book cross the finish line.

And, finally, Devapriya Roy – love, life and lender of last resort.